HOME FIRES BURNING

The Great War Diaries
of Georgina Lee

HOME FIRES
BURNING

GAVIN ROYNON

FOREWORD BY HEW STRACHAN

PUBLISHING

First published in the United Kingdom in 2006 by
Sutton Publishing Limited · Phoenix Mill
Thrupp · Stroud · Gloucestershire · GL5 2BU

© Edited by Gavin Roynon, 2006

Gavin Roynon has asserted the moral right to be identified as the editor of this work.

British Library Cataloguing in Publication Data
A catalogue record for this book is available from the British Library.

ISBN 0-7509-4386-6

For Patsy
La Meilleure Epouse

Typeset in Goudy 10.5/13pt
Typesetting and origination by
Sutton Publishing Limited
Printed and bound in England by
J.H. Haynes & Co. Ltd, Sparkford

CONTENTS

BOOK I: JULY 30 – AUGUST 29, 1914   1

Dread in all our hearts – Stock Exchange closed – Belgium's appeal to the King – 'we are in for it at last' – weeping women at Paddington – Army and Navy Stores under siege – hunting down German spies – no standing room in St Paul's – sewing bed-jackets and pyjamas for the wounded – why Churchill raved like a lunatic – desperate need for recruits – *vive le général French!* – German goods disappear from shops – no toys at Hamley's – a walk on Wimbledon Common – Asquith backs Kitchener's appeal – 'mutiny' of Irish Guards – destruction of Louvain.

BOOK II: AUGUST 30 – OCTOBER 7, 1914   27

Paris prepares for siege – heroism of Captain Grenfell – Welsh distrust of 'fighting for the English' – telegram from Viceroy of India – 'send a copy to the Kaiser!' – recruitment meeting in the 'worst' county – Dolgelly's blank record – Smuts brings South Africa into the War – Allied victory on the Marne – Rheims Cathedral – an act of vengeance? – lingering death of Georgina's father-in-law – *Aboukir*, *Hogue* and *Cressy* torpedoed – the Mayor of Brussels arrested – a widow at eighteen.

BOOK III: OCTOBER 9 – DECEMBER 10, 1914   45

Fall of Antwerp – DORA and the Lights of London – Captain Williams and HMS *Hawke* – fire at Glaslyn – a narrow squeak for Grandpa – an extraordinary sight at Aldershot – the German POW camp at Frimley – an unpopular resignation at the Ritz – Prince Louis of Battenberg steps down – Turkey declares war – special wedding licence needed – Charles joins the Veterans Corps – fall of Tsingtao – why Captain Müller of the *Emden* was given back his sword – death of Georgina's father at Glaslyn – two Kings meet at Ypres.

FOREWORD

In some respects the author of these diaries is not Georgina Lee, but her infant son, Harry, who was nine months old when the First World War broke out. It was to Harry that she addressed what she wrote, and it was thanks to Harry, however unconscious he was of the fact at the time, that they became such a truly outstanding chronicle of the conflict. Maternal love gives her entries the warmth and humanity which engage the reader's emotions. However, at the same time her determination that, when Harry grew up, he should be able to comprehend the context in which his family's doings were set, ensures domesticity is cloaked in a wider story. Georgina Lee spent the years between 1914 and 1919 entirely in Britain, and yet she gives today's reader – like Harry, when he was old enough to read his mother's journal – a sustained and self-contained account of a global war.

Much of this narrative was clearly pieced together from newspapers. The original diaries include her cuttings, and when in Blair Atholl she expressed her frustration at not being able to get the latest London editions. Thus her commentary often reflects the current journalistic vogue. On 21 May 1915, with Asquith's Liberal Government in disarray, she condemned Winston Churchill's impetuosity for Britain's naval disasters; six months later, without a flicker of irony or apparent self-awareness, she described the former First Sea Lord as 'one of the ablest men England has ever had'. These internal contradictions confirm that, however polished and well informed her descriptions, she resisted the temptation to revisit them, so leaving inconsistencies in place and ensuring that the account she has bequeathed us is firsthand.

Its quality, its immediacy and its depth of knowledge rebut any suggestion that those who spent the war at home were the dupes of propaganda. Her thirst for information demanded the truth: 'no good', she wrote on 20 March 1915, 'is gained by keeping the country in a fool's paradise'. From the first she was not buoyed by any false expectations that the war would be short or easy. She embraced the injunction of the Secretary of State for War, Lord Kitchener, that the war would last at least three years, and, almost four years later, as the news of the German offensives of March 1918 percolated back to London, her anxiety left her scarcely able to eat. However, Georgina Lee suffered less directly from the war than most women of her age. She had married late in life; her son was – obviously enough – too young to serve, but, as importantly, her husband was too old. Not one of her close relatives was killed, her most immediate experience of bereavement being the death of a young captain in the Gordon Highlanders in 1917.

Until then that officer, Eugene Crombie, had kept her in touch with the realities of the Western Front. So too had her brother-in-law, 'Uncle Guy' of the Buffs. It was Guy

Lee who told her that the retreat from Mons was a rout and that Saxon soldiers attempting to surrender were shot out of hand. Other correspondents reported with chilling exactness the level of casualties, the nature of wounds inflicted by shellfire, and the quagmire of the trenches. For too long scholars of the First World War allowed themselves to be persuaded by the war novelists of the late 1920s that those at home were swept up by a tide of patriotic rhetoric which opened a gulf in understanding between them and those at the Front. Recent writing has set out to show the opposite – to emphasise how most soldiers longed to return to civilian life, to home and hearth, and that those at home were desperate for information that would help them comprehend the true nature of the fighting. Georgina Lee's diaries corroborate such interpretations.

Nor was she as exempt from direct attack herself as received wisdom might allow. Her husband's work as a solicitor kept her in London, worried by the increasing threats of air raids but determined not to have her life dominated by them. Rationality told her that the chances of being hit were small; concern for her son did not permit her to be quite so cavalier. Her household grew. Nationally, domestic service declined in the war as men were called up and women moved to the better-paid munitions industries. But by 1917 the Lees employed twice as many servants as they had in 1914, and nannie, cook and the maids were increasingly opposed to staying in the metropolis. The Smuts Committee, which reported in 1917 on the German raids on London and recommended the creation of an independent air force in response, highlighted the effects of bombing on the morale of the working class in the East End of London. Here class and geography intersected: the East End was closer to Germany and contained the docks and other obvious industrial targets. In the West End, where Georgina lived, class and geography diverged. But the comparative infrequency of bombing did not prevent social stereotypes from asserting themselves.

Georgina herself contributed to the war effort in conformity with her comparative affluence and with an energy and commitment facilitated by Harry's much-loved nannie. The role of charitable work in the war effort is only just beginning to find its historians, and it is still too early to assess its overall scale. Many of Georgina Lee's endeavours were devoted to those who were indirect victims of the war, the poor and underprivileged of Britain, as she knitted clothes for the children of soldiers and helped at the Ragged School Union. But Georgina spoke fluent French, her artist father having taken his family to live in Boulogne. As a result she worked particularly with the Belgian refugees who arrived in Britain in the autumn of 1914. Her commitment to hospital visiting, and to preparing hospital clothes and packing bandages, found its focus in the Belgian Red Cross. Her identification with the invaded territories of Belgium and northern France explains her own unswerving commitment to the war and her determination to see it through to victory. Empathy with people whose lives had been shattered by foreign occupation – whether they stayed or fled – fed her own patriotism. Attending a thanksgiving service in Bristol Cathedral nine days after the Armistice was signed, she felt 'a sudden emotion' choke her throat. The flags of the Allies 'are the emblems of so much glory, such heroism and devotion, exultation and final triumph after the agony of four and a quarter years'. Not the least of the achievements of these diaries, their fluency and fullness, is that those feelings bridge the divide of the years.

Hew Strachan
Chichele Professor of History of War
University of Oxford

ACKNOWLEDGEMENTS

I t was due to a fortuitous, but most fruitful, conversation at an authors' lunch that I first met Ann de La Grange Sury and learnt of the existence of her grandmother's diaries. From the start I was intrigued by Georgina Lee's original idea of addressing her war diary to her infant son Harry, as though she was putting a message in a bottle and casting it upon the waters, for him to find one day. Where did she find the iron resolve that enabled her to keep up her diary right through the war and beyond, until Armistice Day 1919? As she often wrote at great length – there are eleven volumes – I was compelled sometimes to leave out more of the contents of the diaries than I would have wished.

I am grateful to Ann – who is Harry's daughter – for entrusting me with this valuable primary source. She has written a detailed biographical note about Georgina Lee and her family, which is printed as an appendix. Ann has also taken a great deal of trouble to construct the Davis and Lee family trees, which will help those readers who are baffled by the diarist's numerous relations. She has also provided several photographs from her family archives.

Much research has been necessary at the Imperial War Museum: a most enjoyable pursuit, in view of the positive attitude of the team in the Reading Room, who are a model of courtesy and always helpful. In particular, my warm thanks are again due to Roderick Suddaby, Director of the Department of Documents for his helpful advice on editing principles to follow when dealing with those terrible twins, exclusion and inclusion. I am also grateful to Alan Wakefield for helping me to track down some striking photographs of Home Front scenes, from the extensive Imperial War Museum photo-archives. Sir Martin Gilbert kindly gave his permission to reprint his map of German Air Raids over London, 1914–1918, from his *Routledge Atlas of the First World War*. I am grateful to David Walker and Hazel Cook for enabling me to reprint a detailed contemporary map of Chelsea, which belongs to the Kensington Town Library.

My friend and former colleague Patrick Wilson has again read sections of the diaries, pointed out certain errors and given me some very useful advice. Dr Hugh Cecil kindly helped me with the structure of the book and Malcolm Brown steered me in the right direction when I was drifting towards rocks and shoals in my introduction. Dr Edwin Robertson gave me a vivid first-hand account of his experience as a schoolboy of the Silvertown ammunition dump explosion at West Ham on 19 January 1917. Jon Nuttall, Head of Administration and Curator of the Royal Hospital, Chelsea, provided exact details of the casualties and damage to the buildings in Light Horse Court caused by the Zeppelin raid on 16 February 1918. See plate section.

Dominiek Dendooven has dealt with various queries involving the King of the Belgians and the Belgian Army, and Annick Vandenbilcke provided useful information from the Documentation Centre at Ypres, about the Belgian refugees. Every effort has been made to trace the copyright owner of Louis Raemaeker's cartoons, but so far without success.

Constructing a new book requires input from many different people and so good teamwork is the essence of a first-class publishing house. It has again been a rewarding experience to work with the team at Sutton, whom I cannot commend too highly. In particular I should like to thank Nick Reynolds for his overall supervision and sound advice, also Jonathan Falconer and Julia Fenn for their willing and positive support. I am again very grateful to Clare Jackson for her flexible approach and meticulous attention to detail as project editor and to Bow Watkinson, whose professional scanning skills are second to none.

My wife Patsy devoted much time to reading through the entire text and pinpointed various inconsistencies and ambiguities which I had not noticed. My daughter Tessa also did some helpful proof-reading. Penelope Hatfield, the archivist at Eton College, kindly clarified some confusion about the Dunsmure family. Eric Harrison and Anthony Quick gave me useful information about the Haig Brown family.

Finally, I am again indebted to Janet Easterling, who has presented the text of this book in a highly professional way for the publishers. She has tolerated numerous last-minute amendments and extra footnotes and has still kept to a tight deadline. Without her invaluable contribution, this book might never have seen the light of day.

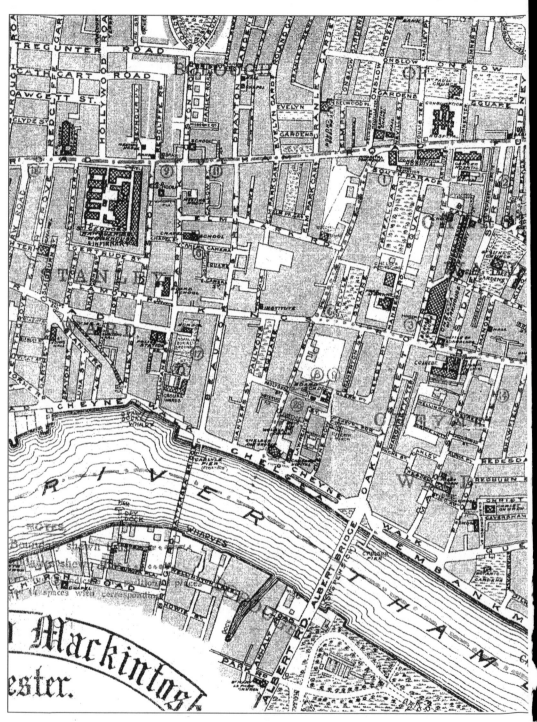

The Borough of Chelsea in 1902. The Lee family lived here throughout the Great War. Many streets and buildings in this area were bombed. Georgina Lee describes in her diary the devastation and the

reactions of Londoners to the frequent air raids. (*Royal Borough of Kensington and Chelsea Libraries and Arts Services*)

NOT SO REMOTE FROM
THE CONFLICT

In one sense, Georgina Lee was fortunate. She benefited from a broad, liberal education and belonged to that social stratum which enjoyed a comfortable Edwardian lifestyle in the – for some – halcyon days before 1914. On the other hand, she married late. Her firstborn and ultimately only child, Harry, was less than a year old when war broke out. Her dilemma was to know whether this precious son would be safe in London. She decided he would not – and packed him off with Nannie to her father's house, Glaslyn, on the River Wye in Radnorshire.

Georgina then experiences all the pangs of conscience of a mother who has distanced herself from her precious baby. 'What's new?' I hear some harassed young mothers of today asking. But Great Britain is at war, the Germans are sweeping through Belgium and invasion may be imminent. Georgina Lee decides to alleviate her conscience by addressing her diary to baby Harry. She wants him to be familiar one day with the grim events in Europe, but at present 'You are too small to understand'.

She opens her diary on 30 July 1914, five days before Asquith officially declared war, and launches into the highly personal style which is to be her hallmark. Her warm affection for her son shines throughout – and somehow by 'speaking' to him through her diary, she gains some solace for the lengthy periods when she is not with him. Single-minded devotion to Harry lends a striking coherence and unity to the whole and impels her to continue writing her diary for over five years until the first anniversary of the Armistice.

What then is the character of this remarkable lady, who is so committed to her infant son, that she creates a complete war diary for him? She emerges as a warmhearted and compassionate wife and mother, a popular figure with a wide circle of friends, who is more at ease than her husband with all sorts and conditions of men. She is intensely loyal, but sometimes confides her worries about him to her diary. Although they only have the one precious child, both she and Charles have many siblings and belong to large families, whose welfare is never out of her mind for long. Judging by the frequent letters she receives from her brothers and brothers-in-law, she is the hub of the extended family.

There are very few other published sets of Home Front diaries which chronicle the entire war from start to finish. Georgina keeps going throughout and does not limit herself to family concerns. She gives an informed account of the progress of the war at home and abroad and its effect on her life and that of her friends. If it is still claimed that British civilians, unlike those in Belgium and France, were remote from the real conflict, the *Georgina Lee Diaries* challenge that concept. They provide valuable evidence to the contrary, adding substantially to our understanding of how Londoners reacted to wartime conditions.

At the start, the reader is brought face to face with the panic-stricken days of late July and early August 1914. Even before Great Britain enters the war, Georgina Lee describes the closing of the Stock Exchange and the Bank of England, Paddington paralysed by a rail strike, 'Church Full' notices outside St Paul's, a moratorium on the paying of bills, and chaotic scenes at large department stores. Hoarding of food is rife in London. Among the worst culprits are customers at Harrods, where the store is forced to stop selling goods over the counter. On the east coast an invasion is expected in Harwich any day, trenches are being dug and nobody may leave the town after 6 pm.

In London, an ever-mounting phobia assumes that individuals with Germanic-sounding names are spies. Even the First Sea Lord, Prince Louis of Battenberg, whose connection with the Royal Navy goes back more than forty years, has to stand down. Georgina does not subscribe to this until the gas-bomb scare in 1915. As she had spent her formative years in France and had studied in Germany for two years, she has a European awareness and displays a special sympathy for German-born individuals with British spouses, who are now placed in quasi-POW camps.

In 1915, Georgina witnesses the great women's march on 17 July. Led by Mrs Pankhurst, 50,000 women processed through London, petitioning for women to be allowed to work in the munitions factories. Georgina watches Lloyd George with an approving eye, as he addresses the demonstration and displays his skills as an orator: 'Without women victory will tarry and the victory which tarries means a victory whose footprints are footprints of blood'. The wind of change for women was blowing strongly. Less than three years later, in June 1918, women over the age of 30 were granted the right to vote, provided they were householders or wives of householders.

Georgina becomes involved with several groups helping the war effort, but her greatest challenge comes with her appointment in March 1916 as superintendent of the Belgian Surgical Depot in Kensington. During the last week of June 1916, she responds to a special appeal to provide thousands of shell dressings within three or four days. There is frantic activity when it is realised that a major British offensive is about to be launched: 'Shell dressings! Words horribly suggestive of the gaping wounds caused by splinters of shell. I worked and worked, never looking up . . . How devastating to be making preparations for the appalling bloodshed we know is to begin in a few days.'

Georgina's prediction was right. Almost 20,000 British soldiers were killed on the first day of the Battle of the Somme. Such grim statistics were not released to the public until much later. But Paddington, where Georgina saw the hospital trains arrive from the ports, told its own story. The platforms were covered with stretchers and a porter told Charles Lee that, on one day alone, 4,000 wounded had arrived there. The same was true of Charing Cross and Victoria. To see the injured arrive from a few miles across the Channel, maimed and battle-scarred, brought the grim reality of the war very close.

Georgina is appalled by the news of the sinking of the *Lusitania* and shocked beyond measure by the drowning of Kitchener, the executions of Edith Cavell and of Captain Fryatt, and the torpedoing of hospital ships. But she does not yield to doom and gloom.

She witnesses the emotional departure scenes at Victoria and does her best to cheer up those for whom every farewell to son or husband may be their last.

So much attention has been afforded to the Blitz in 1940, that the extent of damage to life and limb from the air in the First World War is often forgotten. One thousand four hundred and thirteen people were killed and 3,408 injured as a result of air-raids.* Of these casualties, more than half were Londoners. East coast towns such as Southend, Margate, Harwich, Ramsgate, Folkestone and Dover were also frequent targets. The motive for these attacks was to render city life intolerable and to destroy morale. Georgina Lee's diaries show that the Germans succeeded in neither respect.

Initially, Zeppelins had a certain novelty value. A dozen airships cross the coast on an early September night in 1916 and Georgina – rushing outside their Kensington house to see a Zeppelin – reveals her irritation when she is dragged back inside for safety's sake by her husband and fails to see it. Aeroplane raids presented a greater threat and one of the worst was the first daylight raid on London on 13 June 1917. Seventy-two bombs fell within a radius of a mile from Liverpool Street station, 162 people were killed and 432 injured. These raids continued unremittingly until May 1918, and the Lee family experienced most of them.

Towards the end of 1917, the outlook remained bleak as Georgina began the tenth volume of her diary. The Eastern Front had collapsed and Lenin had withdrawn Russia from the war. 'Yet another book and the war seems farther from its end than it did three years ago. We have entered a very critical, fierce stage and once again Germany's position is better, for the time being, than our own.'

Thousands of German troops are transferred from East to West and the great German offensive, so long expected, begins in March 1918. News comes to Georgina via a Grenadier officer that the Germans have exploited a thick fog and are effectively breaking through the Fifth Army. Unbelievably, after the sacrifice of all those lives, the British Army is back on the line of the Somme. Not since the Mons crisis in the early weeks of the war has she felt so worried. Happily, after a few agonising days, the German advance appears to be faltering. 'Thank God!' she writes with disarming honesty, 'I feel inclined to be on my knees all day – so unlike me!'

Nonetheless she heads her diary entry for March 31 **Easter Sunday in the Great Crisis**. Her husband, Charles, tells her that every available man is off to France. This leaves scarcely a man to mount guard at Buckingham Palace! But Foch is now in supreme command and gradually the tide turns. The Germans are pushed back and in the autumn the proud Habsburg Empire, rent by internal conflict, collapses. Georgina records joyfully how the German government, now isolated, her citizens starving, is forced to bid for an armistice, to avoid revolution.

Far better now for readers to dig into the diary itself and get to the heart of the matter. They will trace the wonderful exhilaration when news of the Armistice comes through. Georgina goes out into the streets of London on 11 November 1918, with her 5-year-old son. She gives an eyewitness account of the elated crowds, the flag-waving,

---

*   Joseph Morris, *The German Air Raids on Great Britain, 1914–1918*, Preface, p. v.

the celebrations and the pandemonium. Yet, for so many, the exhilaration is bitter-sweet:

> *Florence Younghusband [one of Georgina's friends] was on the top of a bus when the guns were fired. In front of her were two soldiers, one with his face horribly scarred. He looked straight ahead and remained stonily silent; the other just bowed his head in his hand and burst out crying. The omnibus conductress dropped into the vacant seat by Florence, leant her head on her shoulder and cried too. 'I lost my man two months ago, I can't be happy today,' she murmured.*

> *Gavin Roynon*

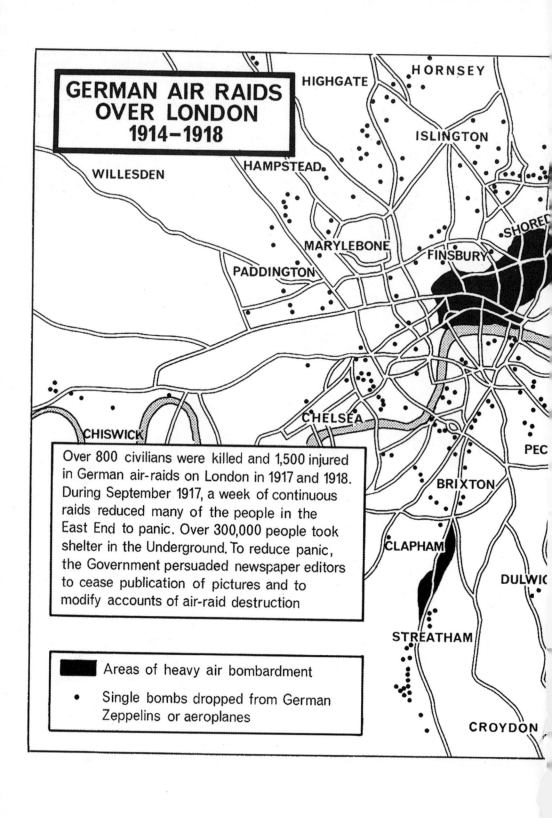

GERMAN AIR RAIDS OVER LONDON 1914–1918

HIGHGATE

HORNSEY

ISLINGTON

WILLESDEN

HAMPSTEAD

SHORE

MARYLEBONE

FINSBURY

PADDINGTON

CHISWICK

CHELSEA

PEC

Over 800 civilians were killed and 1,500 injured in German air-raids on London in 1917 and 1918. During September 1917, a week of continuous raids reduced many of the people in the East End to panic. Over 300,000 people took shelter in the Underground. To reduce panic, the Government persuaded newspaper editors to cease publication of pictures and to modify accounts of air-raid destruction

BRIXTON

CLAPHAM

DULWIC

STREATHAM

Areas of heavy air bombardment

• Single bombs dropped from German Zeppelins or aeroplanes

CROYDON

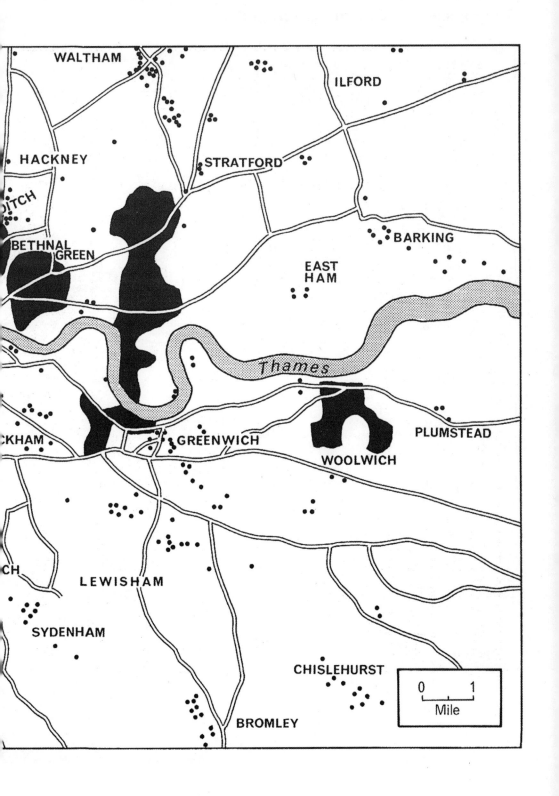

WALTHAM

ITCH

HACKNEY

ILFORD

STRATFORD

BETHNAL
GREEN

BARKING

EAST
HAM

Thames

PLUMSTEAD

CKHAM

GREENWICH

WOOLWICH

CH

LEWISHAM

SYDENHAM

CHISLEHURST

0   1

Mile

BROMLEY

The Families of LEE and ROMER-LEE

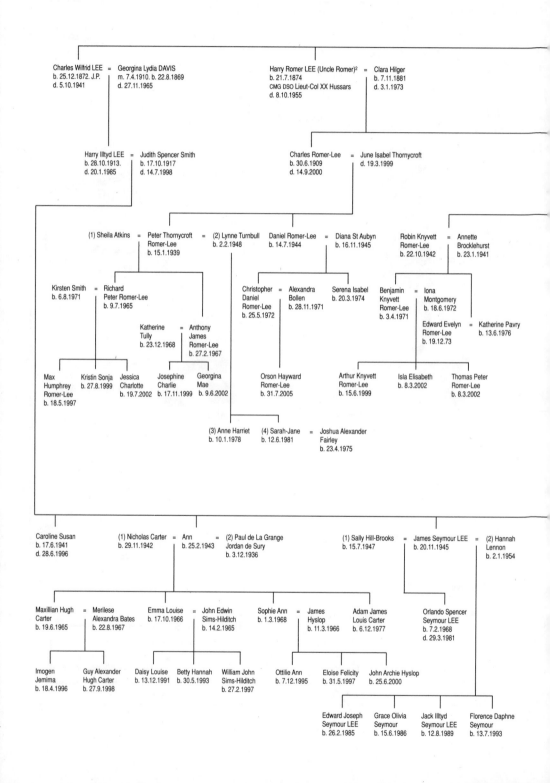

Charles Wilfrid LEE = Georgina Lydia DAVIS
b. 25.12.1872. J.P. m. 7.4.1910. b. 22.8.1869
d. 5.10.1941 d. 27.11.1965

Harry Romer LEE (Uncle Romer)[2] = Clara Hilger
b. 21.7.1874 b. 7.11.1881
CMG DSO Lieut-Col XX Hussars d. 3.1.1973
d. 8.10.1955

Harry Illtyd LEE = Judith Spencer Smith
b. 28.10.1913. b. 17.10.1917
d. 20.1.1985 d. 14.7.1998

Charles Romer-Lee = June Isabel Thornycroft
b. 30.6.1909 d. 19.3.1999
d. 14.9.2000

(1) Sheila Atkins = Peter Thornycroft Romer-Lee b. 15.1.1939 = (2) Lynne Turnbull b. 2.2.1948

Daniel Romer-Lee = Diana St Aubyn
b. 14.7.1944 b. 16.11.1945

Robin Knyvett Romer-Lee = Annette Brocklehurst
b. 22.10.1942 b. 23.1.1941

Kirsten Smith = Richard Peter Romer-Lee
b. 6.8.1971 b. 9.7.1965

Katherine Tully = Anthony James Romer-Lee
b. 23.12.1968 b. 27.2.1967

Christopher Daniel Romer-Lee = Alexandra Bollen
b. 25.5.1972 b. 28.11.1971

Serena Isabel
b. 20.3.1974

Benjamin Knyvett Romer-Lee = Iona Montgomery
b. 3.4.1971 b. 18.6.1972

Edward Evelyn Romer-Lee = Katherine Pavry
b. 19.12.73 b. 13.6.1976

Max Humphrey Romer-Lee
b. 18.5.1997

Kristin Sonja
b. 27.8.1999

Jessica Charlotte
b. 19.7.2002

Josephine Charlie
b. 17.11.1999

Georgina Mae
b. 9.6.2002

Orson Hayward Romer-Lee
b. 31.7.2005

Arthur Knyvett Romer-Lee
b. 15.6.1999

Isla Elisabeth
b. 8.3.2002

Thomas Peter Romer-Lee
b. 8.3.2002

(3) Anne Harriet
b. 10.1.1978

(4) Sarah-Jane
b. 12.6.1981

= Joshua Alexander Fairley
b. 23.4.1975

Caroline Susan
b. 17.6.1941
d. 28.6.1996

(1) Nicholas Carter = Ann = (2) Paul de La Grange Jordan de Sury
b. 29.11.1942 b. 25.2.1943 b. 3.12.1936

(1) Sally Hill-Brooks = James Seymour LEE = (2) Hannah Lennon
b. 15.7.1947 b. 20.11.1945 b. 2.1.1954

Maxillian Hugh Carter = Merilese Alexandra Bates
b. 19.6.1965 b. 22.8.1967

Emma Louise = John Edwin Sims-Hilditch
b. 17.10.1966 b. 14.2.1965

Sophie Ann = James Hyslop
b. 1.3.1968 b. 11.3.1966

Adam James Louis Carter
b. 6.12.1977

Orlando Spencer Seymour LEE
b. 7.2.1968
d. 29.3.1981

Imogen Jemima
b. 18.4.1996

Guy Alexander Hugh Carter
b. 27.9.1998

Daisy Louise
b. 13.12.1991

Betty Hannah
b. 30.5.1993

William John Sims-Hilditch
b. 27.2.1997

Ottilie Ann
b. 7.12.1995

Eloise Felicity
b. 31.5.1997

John Archie Hyslop
b. 25.6.2000

Edward Joseph Seymour LEE
b. 26.2.1985

Grace Olivia Seymour
b. 15.6.1986

Jack Illtyd Seymour LEE
b. 12.8.1989

Florence Daphne Seymour
b. 13.7.1993

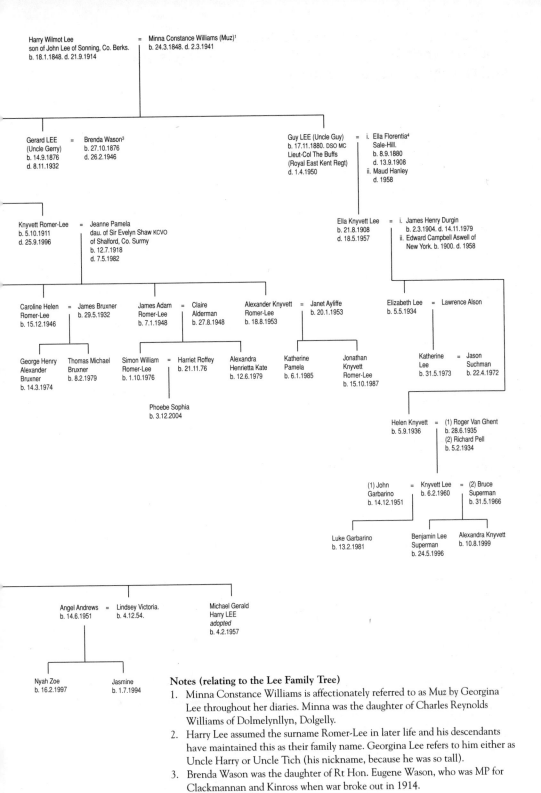

Notes (relating to the Lee Family Tree)

1. Minna Constance Williams is affectionately referred to as Muz by Georgina Lee throughout her diaries. Minna was the daughter of Charles Reynolds Williams of Dolmelynllyn, Dolgelly.

2. Harry Lee assumed the surname Romer-Lee in later life and his descendants have maintained this as their family name. Georgina Lee refers to him either as Uncle Harry or Uncle Tich (his nickname, because he was so tall).

3. Brenda Wason was the daughter of Rt Hon. Eugene Wason, who was MP for Clackmannan and Kinross when war broke out in 1914.

4. Ella Sale-Hill was the daughter of Gen Sir Rowley Sale-Hill, KCB.

The Descendants of Henry William Banks Davis RA and Georgina Harriet Lightfoot

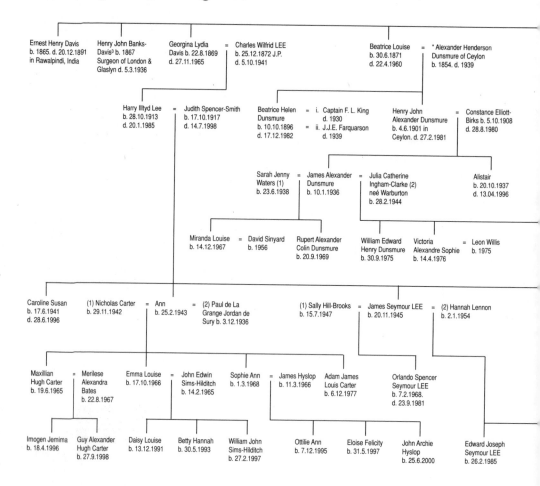

Notes (relating to the Davis Family Tree)

1. Henry William Banks Davis RA lived from 1862 to 1901 with his family at Le Château de la Barrière Rouge, St Etienne au Mont, near Boulogne. It was here that Georgina Lee and her siblings were born. Today this handsome country house, which dates back to the Second Empire, is occupied by the Huguet family and known as Les Quesnelets.

2. The mother of the diarist, Georgina Harriet Davis, died in 1879. She was buried in the graveyard of Rhayader 35 years later. See diary entries for the first week of December 1914.

3. Henry John Davis adopted the surname Banks-Davis, but was the only one of his siblings to do so.

4. After the marriage of Arthur Davis to Audrey Clive, the couple adopted the surname Clive-Davies.

5. Philip Osorio changed his surname by deed poll to Probert.

6. Both Dunsmure brothers served in the Cameron Highlanders. They were killed within a few months of each other. 2/Lt Colin Dunsmure was 21 only a few days before he left England. He was last seen alive at Loos on 25 September 1915, when his devoted servant H.P. Thompson tried to carry him into shelter, but was killed doing so. See diary entry for 12 October 1915 – when conflicting telegrams were reaching his Mother – and for 5 January 1916.

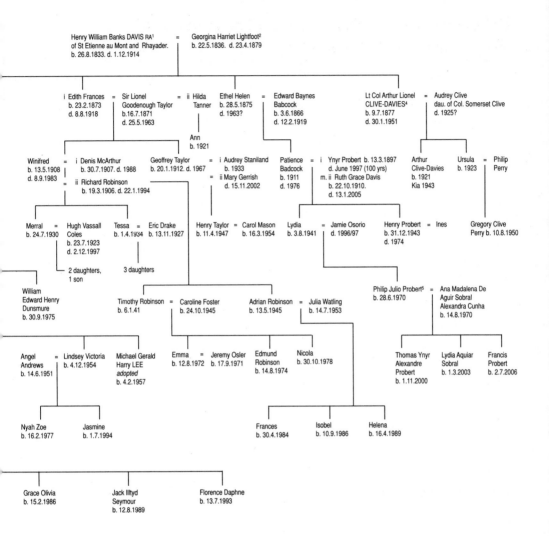

Henry William Banks DAVIS RA[1] = Georgina Harriet Lightfoot[2]
of St Etienne au Mont and Rhayader.   b. 22.5.1836. d. 23.4.1879
b. 26.8.1833. d. 1.12.1914

i Edith Frances = Sir Lionel = ii Hilda   Ethel Helen = Edward Baynes   Lt Col Arthur Lionel = Audrey Clive
b. 23.2.1873   Goodenough Taylor   Tanner   b. 28.5.1875   Babcock   CLIVE-DAVIES[4]   dau. of Col. Somerset Clive
d. 8.8.1918   b.16.7.1871   d. 1963?   b. 3.6.1866   b. 9.7.1877   d. 1925?
                d. 25.5.1963   d. 12.2.1919   d. 30.1.1951

Ann
b. 1921

Winifred = i Denis McArthur   Geoffrey Taylor = i Audrey Staniland   Patience = i Ynyr Probert b. 13.3.1897   Arthur   Ursula = Philip
b. 13.5.1908   b. 30.7.1907. d. 1988   b. 20.1.1912. d. 1967   b. 1933   Babcock   d. June 1997 (100 yrs)   Clive-Davies   b. 1923   Perry
d. 8.9.1983 = ii Richard Robinson   = ii Mary Gerrish   b. 1911   m. ii Ruth Grace Davis   b. 1921
             b. 19.3.1906. d. 22.1.1994   d. 15.11.2002   d. 1976   b. 22.10.1910.   Kia 1943
                                                                             d. 13.1.2005

Merral = Hugh Vassall   Tessa = Eric Drake   Henry Taylor = Carol Mason   Lydia = Jamie Osorio   Henry Probert = Ines   Gregory Clive
b. 24.7.1930   Coles   b. 1.4.1934   b. 13.11.1927   b. 11.4.1947   b. 16.3.1954   b. 3.8.1941   d. 1996/97   b. 31.12.1943   Perry b. 10.8.1950
               b. 23.7.1923   d. 1974
               d. 2.12.1997

         ⌐ 2 daughters,   3 daughters
           1 son

William   Timothy Robinson = Caroline Foster   Adrian Robinson = Julia Watling   Philip Julio Probert[5] = Ana Madalena De
Edward Henry   b. 6.1.41   b. 24.10.1945   b. 13.5.1945   b. 14.7.1953   b. 28.6.1970   Aguir Sobral
Dunsmure   Alexandra Cunha
b. 30.9.1975   b. 14.8.1970

Angel = Lindsey Victoria   Michael Gerald   Emma = Jeremy Osler   Edmund   Nicola   Thomas Ynyr   Lydia Aquiar   Francis
Andrews   b. 4.12.1954   Harry LEE   b. 12.8.1972   b. 17.9.1971   Robinson   b. 30.10.1978   Alexandre   Sobral   Probert
b. 14.6.1951   adopted   b. 14.8.1974   Probert   b. 1.3.2003   b. 2.7.2006
                          b. 4.2.1957   b. 1.11.2000

Nyah Zoe   Jasmine   Frances   Isobel   Helena
b. 16.2.1977   b. 1.7.1994   b. 30.4.1984   b. 10.9.1986   b. 16.4.1989

Grace Olivia   Jack Illtyd   Florence Daphne
b. 15.2.1986   Seymour   b. 13.7.1993
                b. 12.8.1989

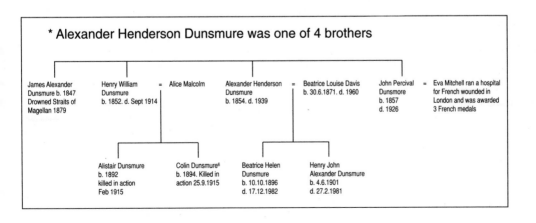

* Alexander Henderson Dunsmure was one of 4 brothers

James Alexander   Henry William = Alice Malcolm   Alexander Henderson = Beatrice Louise Davis   John Percival = Eva Mitchell ran a hospital
Dunsmure b. 1847   Dunsmure   Dunsmure   b. 30.6.1871. d. 1960   Dunsmore   for French wounded in
Drowned Straits of   b. 1852. d. Sept 1914   b. 1854. d. 1939   b. 1857   London and was awarded
Magellan 1879   d. 1926   3 French medals

Alistair Dunsmure   Colin Dunsmure[6]   Beatrice Helen   Henry John
b. 1892   b. 1894. Killed in   Dunsmure   Alexander Dunsmure
killed in action   action 25.9.1915   b. 10.10.1896   b. 4.6.1901
Feb 1915   d. 17.12.1982   d. 27.2.1981

1914

What had the Belgians done, that their country should be invaded and ravaged?

Sir Edward Grey

BOOK I

JULY 30 – AUGUST 29, 1914

THURSDAY JULY 30

15 Neville Street, South Kensington

You are nine months old, my little son, when I begin this Diary. We are parted at present, at what cost to the joy of the house, only your Father and I know. You are too small to understand. You are happy as the day is long at Glaslyn* with a Grandfather who adores you while Daddy and I remain alone in London. Your Grandfather's message today says 'Baby is a real little Hercules – He seems to think I am there on purpose to joke and laugh with. As soon as I appear he entices me to play.' Your Nannie, a quiet, placid Somersetshire woman, who sings to you all day, writes 'The mountain air is doing Baby so much good that his cheeks are as firm and rosy as apples.'

But there is one solemn reason that makes me start my Diary tonight. Grave rumours of a possible terrible conflict of Nations are on everybody's lips, and have been gathering for some days past. If indeed the dread that is in all our hearts is justified by future events, my little boy will have some idea of what War means to our Country. Except for the Boer War, thousands of miles away, we have been at peace with our neighbours for one hundred years. If we fight, it is because we shall have been dragged in through loyalty to our friends abroad.

---

*   Home of Georgina Lee's father, Henry William Banks Davis RA, near Rhayader, over-looking the River Wye.

Sir Edward Grey, the Minister for Foreign Affairs whose name will go down as one of the most patient Peacemakers the world has known, is failing to reconcile the quarrel between Serbia and Austria, with Germany, lusting for War, at her back to make peace impossible.

The murder of the Crown Prince (and his Consort) of Austria by Serbians is the excuse for provoking war. If Austria declares war on Serbia, Russia must help Serbia as they are all brother Slavs together. Germany is Austria's ally, and France must help Russia if attacked – we are France's friends, and cannot allow her to be crushed.

Therefore, my baby, whose dimpled hands, however eager, cannot yet grasp a weapon for the honour of your country, we must wait and see what the next fateful days bring forth.

FRIDAY JULY 31

This being Bank Holiday weekend, Daddy and I had arranged to spend it at Cossington.* We were to start from Paddington at twelve. But at breakfast, we saw in the papers that Germany has flung down the gauntlet. She is taking as a pretext the preparations for war Russia is making on the Austrian frontier. Worse still, breaking all conventions, she is marching to invade the neutral state of Luxemburg. This is an open menace to France.

There is such a panic on all the money markets on the Continent, that to protect itself our Stock Exchange has closed for an indefinite period. Bad as this is, it saves the country from a worse catastrophe, for it prevents foreign securities from being dumped on our market, it saves a panic rush on our banks, and chaos. But it causes the sudden ruin of many stockbrokers,** and a feeling of terrible depression throughout the country.

One has heard of well-known City firms being 'hammered' the last two days, but now all the offices are closed, and behind the closed door each firm is reckoning its losses. I heard something of it as I sat for an hour at Paddington waiting for our train. A sense of impending calamity hanging over everyone, overcame the ordinary reserves of English people. Tongues were loosened, people spoke of their experiences.

An elderly man sitting by me in the waiting room told me in listless tones he had been on the Stock Exchange forty years, and had never known it close in a crisis, nor seen so many failures in a few hours. The room was crowded with holiday people and children making the best of the absence of the trains which should be taking them to the seaside. They played with their spades and pails on the dusty floor of the waiting room.

To add to the general disorganisation, the shunters of the Great Western had seen fit to go on strike a few hours earlier. Paddington was getting every moment more congested by would-be travellers finding the platforms packed by people who should have departed some hours previously.

---

*   A small village in Somerset, a few miles west of Glastonbury.

**   *The Times* of 30 July announced the failure of seven firms and next day two more were 'hammered'. The New York Stock Exchange, after a day of 'wild excitement and utter demoralisation', also closed indefinitely.

We wired to Aunt Ethel that there was a strike at Paddington and we did not know when we could arrive. We finally did board a train, that took us straight to Taunton, twenty-five miles beyond our destination, but that was a trifle, since we reached Aunt Ethel at 8 o'clock instead of 5.

Your cousin, wee Patience, rushed into the hall and suspended herself by both arms from my neck. Patience is five, a little fairy with large grey-green eyes and long dark lashes. With her tiny fingers she models the most astonishing little objects out of plasticine, nothing too minute, even a string of monkeys climbing up a tree, the whole thing not more than 2 inches high. She is the cleverest little girl I know.

SATURDAY AUGUST 1

The papers at breakfast announce the official declaration of war on Russia by Germany, and so, my son, the Emperor, or Kaiser, Wilhelm II, has thrown off at last the mask of peacemaker he has worn for ten years and shown himself in his real light. There was no reason for Germany to meddle in Austria's quarrels with her vassals. The Kaiser has long thirsted for an opportunity to hurl his gigantic army and his fleet, at the whole of Europe.

For the last ten years our country has looked with suspicion at the continually expanding German Fleet. Yet friendly relations have increased between the two countries. Until just lately the German papers were congratulating themselves that the two peoples had at last reached a good understanding. Now that the German Army is invading Luxemburg, these illusions are fast vanishing. Yet we must be patient, and not jump at once to the worst view.

To revert to more peaceful topics. We spent the day at Cossington walking about the neighbourhood which is very picturesque, but so busy were we, discussing the chances of war in all its aspects that we scarcely noticed the scenery.

Uncle Baynes* was chiefly concerned as to whether England would join in. The mere possibility that she might not, filled him with disgust. With our Navy at the very height of its strength and efficiency, and our aeroplanes ready to do such splendid service, it would be a mighty pity if we did not have a go at the Germans. Uncle Baynes' views are I think, shared by the majority.

SUNDAY AUGUST 2

No newspapers to be had today in Cossington, but as we intend to motor to Taunton this afternoon, we may get them on the way home. Taunton, my baby, and its neighbourhood was the home of some of your ancestors. Your great-grandmother was a Corfield, and many are the tales she told us when we were children, of the home of her girlhood in sunny Somerset.

Having delved into the peaceful recollections of a century ago, we remembered the great excitement of the war, and made for a newspaper shop in Taunton. Imagine our

*   Edward Baynes Badcock was married to Georgina Lee's youngest sister, 'Aunt Ethel'.

shock of surprised excitement on reading that Germany has invaded French territory without even declaring war and while the German Ambassador is still in Paris! So far there has been no collision, but Germany's brutal threat to 'blot France out from the map of Europe' shall not be realised, please God, as long as England is there to help.

MONDAY AUGUST 3

Today has been very wet. Heavy showers pouring on the little garden enclosed by high walls, make it a gloomy abode in bad weather. Most of the day we have sat in the sheltered loggia, discussing Belgium's appeal to King George to help her against Germany's brutal invasion.

In 1839, Germany had pledged herself, with other Powers, to respect the neutrality of Belgium. Yet an attack on France through Belgium is her avowed plan of campaign. Having reckoned on the compliance of Belgium, she has insolently threatened her if she attempts to resist; if however she submits to the desecration of her territory, Germany promises to leave her intact when peace is signed.

To this 'infamous proposal', as Asquith stigmatised it in his great speech in the House, the King of the Belgians gave an indignant refusal.* Having appealed to King George to stand by him, he prepared for a vigorous defence at Liège.

Sir Edward Grey also delivered a great speech, laying before the house his attempts to secure peace, and declaring that 'England cannot stand aside if France is to be attacked'. He explained how Germany had appealed to England not to interfere, promising that if our Navy leaves Germany alone, Germany claims she will not interfere with French territory along the coast!

TUESDAY AUGUST 4

We had to leave Cossington very early, at 7.30, to get back to town by midday for Daddy to be at Westminster. The Archbishop and the Bishop of London did not leave London, owing to the crisis, and their presence means much more work for their Legal Secretaries.**

The thrilling news we found at the station was that Sir Edward Grey, has delivered an ultimatum to Germany, 'If by midnight tonight Germany has not pledged herself to respect the neutrality of Belgium, England will declare war' – meantime the British Army has begun mobilising. Of this we had ample evidence on our journey up. Already trains full of soldiers were at every station. When we reached London soldiers and officers in khaki were everywhere.

*   King Albert I had succeeded to the throne in 1909. He reaffirmed Belgian neutrality in the summer of 1914 and assumed personal leadership of the Belgian Army when his country was invaded.
**   Charles Lee, Georgina's husband, a solicitor by profession, was Legal Secretary to the Bishop of London, the Rt Revd Arthur Winnington-Ingram. His family firm, Lee, Bolton & Lee was – and still is – based at 1 The Sanctuary, next door to Westminster Abbey. See Appendix.

Daddy came home from the Sanctuary in the evening saying there was no cash to be had anywhere; not even at his club could they change a £5 cheque. The Banks are to remain closed until Friday, and the Government has ordered a 'moratorium'. This means no debts can be recovered by law until a date is fixed. The tradespeople have not sent in their weekly books.

Your Uncle Gerry came to dine with us.* He is on the Stock Exchange and, as he explained to us quite cheerfully, is ruined for the time being. His kindness and liberal generosity to those in need of help, are untold. His only fault is an excess in this direction. This puts himself at present in a tight corner, when he should have ample resources. He left us at 11 pm to go to his club, White's, to await the news of Germany's decision.

Awakened soon after midnight by shouting in the street. We guessed that war was declared and were a long time going off to sleep again after that!

WEDNESDAY AUGUST 5

We are in for it at last. But there is not one of us in the country who is not thankful at heart that the great fight is to take place at last. The strain has been too great for many years. We all marvel at the reckless audacity of the Kaiser who, with Austria, has Russia, France, England and Belgium to fight. Italy has declared she will remain neutral.

This has been a day of emotion and new experiences. Having promised to see Uncle Gerry off at Paddington in the morning, I started with him in a taxi. The first unusual sight we met with was at the Powder Magazine in Hyde Park. Our taxi was held up by the manoeuvres of a whole fleet of motor buses, in the hands of soldiers, who were bringing out cases of ammunition and removing them. All was quiet at Paddington, though the railways are taken over by the State from today, for the transport of troops.

We were surprised to see the platforms filled with poorly-dressed men whom we took for unemployed come there to make a disturbance. But after the departure of our train we saw our error and made mental reparation for hard thoughts. Numbers of weeping women began to file down towards the exits, accompanied some by a small son or an old man trying to console them. For the first time I realise what these scenes mean that are going on round London in every station and all day. All reservists are being called up.

Uncle Gerry was loth to leave London during these stirring days, but he is badly needed at Gelligemlyn** where your darling Gran is very, very ill. It is one of Mummy's greatest griefs that you will never know your Daddy's Father, a man beloved by all who know him, rich and poor. For 3 months now he has been hopelessly ill, and all we can do is to stand by and give him all the affection in our hearts.

---

*   Georgina's brother-in-law, Gerard Lee. See Lee Family Tree.
**   Gelligemlyn, home of Harry Wilmot Lee, Georgina's father-in-law, was a country house outside Dolgelly, with beautiful grounds running down to the River Mawddach. See Plate 2.

Later in the day, I had to go to the Army and Navy Stores to get in provisions. But what a state of affairs I found! The grocery and provisions departments had been under siege all day, from customers anticipating a sudden shortage of supplies.

All the men behind the counters were absent. Only a few foremen walked about, displaying a patience worthy of the Order of Merit. But nothing was sold over the counters. Long tables were littered with order forms and pencils, and here everybody had to write out his own order with no guarantee as to delivery or prices. Articles will be charged at the price current on day of despatch, perhaps a fortnight hence. They had had 7,000 orders for groceries that day and were overwhelmed.

People have lost their heads, and are all seeking to hoard food. This is a fatal mistake, as it creates a famine. Also an enormous rise in prices, which is most unfair for the rest of the community. I hear of one woman who ordered £500 worth of groceries at Harrods, and another who actually bought over the counter £45 worth. Her chauffeur stood by, carrying off parcels in relays to her motor car.

On coming in at 7 pm I could have cried with vexation. Your Aunt Edie, who has been staying at Sheringham on the East Coast, telephoned from Paddington to say she was there with little Winnie (6) and Geoffrey (2½) with Uncle Lionel and Nurse. She had wired me to meet her, and wondered why I hadn't turned up. She hoped to reach Bristol some time tonight.

Now this is terrible. The railways are dislocated, their house at Clifton is closed, with no servants and no food in it. I had written to Aunt Edie to tell her I would put them all up here. But she never received my letter, because of the disruption of postal arrangements. It seems to me inconceivable, though, that her hostess should have allowed her to travel on the first day of the war and go right across the country with two little mites!

At 10.30 tonight another wire, this time from your Uncle Romer, your Godfather, asking us to put him up tomorrow, as he has his orders. We are to get him a sleeping valise and cork mattress at Harrods.

I am very, very tired tonight, and yet my brain is so excited, I don't think I shall sleep much. Lord Kitchener has been made Secretary of State for War.

THURSDAY AUGUST 6

There isn't a sleeping valise to be had in all London. This is the result of our efforts, begun at 9.30 am at Harrods, to buy one for Uncle Romer. The Camp Equipment Department at the Army and Navy Stores was besieged by officers and relatives trying, like Daddy and me, to procure campaigning requisites. However, we did secure a cork mattress. We made a dash for one and Daddy shouldered it for fear of losing it. He and I then marched back with it to his office. Nobody minds what he does these days.

The forts round the city of Liège are so invulnerable that the enemy cannot get through. The Belgians are suddenly the heroes of the hour, for their splendid stand is playing havoc with the German plan of campaign. This serious check is giving time to England to send her army across to join the French and Belgian forces.

The general indignation against Germany is bearing dangerous fruit. All the nations are turning against her and towards England who is championing the cause of a small people and a great ally threatened with disaster. The Americans are vehement in their praise of England and abhorrence of the German 'mailed fist'. Japan has offered her navy's services, and all the colonies are offering assistance.

At sea, several German reverses are reported. The great Hamburg-Amerika liner *Königin Luise* was sunk yesterday by a light cruiser, the *Amphion*, while laying mines in the Channel.*

Sir Edward Grey is the most popular man in England today. We feel proud of this statesman who has steered the country so honourably through the biggest crisis in our history. I am reminded of the prophecy of our German Governess when my sisters and I were children. 'The German Empire will fall under the reign of an Emperor with only one arm and who mounts his horse from the wrong side.' The German Kaiser has a withered arm, and mounts from the wrong side.

Your Uncle Romer arrived at 9 at night. He is on the Headquarters' Staff of the Mounted Division, Central Army of Home Defence, and will be at Bury St Edmunds for the present. His staff appointment pleases us all.**

FRIDAY AUGUST 7

Every hour makes the situation more thrilling. Astounding developments occur. I grudge every moment spent indoors, out of sight of the fresh crops of news posters that spring up continually. London seems to be all turned into streets, which are seething with human beings. We had a good experience of this driving right across the city to Liverpool Street Station with Uncle Romer, in full uniform and accompanied by baggage and kit, to see him off to Bury.

The taxi crawled from the moment we reached the Law Courts. There seemed to be thousands of men in cabs. As we moved slowly forward our footboard was boarded every minute by newsboys thrusting special editions in our faces. Your Uncle Romer who to his splendid physique and lion's heart adds the calmest disposition possible, only smiled at the invasions, and thanked them every time in the same polite way.

But your Daddy, I'm afraid, is not so gentle. These continual noisy interruptions got on his nerves. In his already strained state, he spoke so sharply and looked so fierce, that from that moment we were left alone. The crush at Liverpool Street was terrible. Numbers of natives, too, were returning to India from that station as well as soldiers to the East Coast.

---

*   Ironically, the *Amphion* then struck a mine laid by the *Königin Luise*. The loss of life was one officer and 168 men, of whom 18 were prisoners, saved from the German vessel a few hours previously.

**   Lt Col Harry Romer-Lee CMG, DSO (1871–1955) served in the 20th Hussars from 1895 to 1918. He was the diarist's brother-in-law and known as Tich, because he was so tall.

But through the pandemonium our big handsome Staff Officer remained serene and composed, distributing smiles all round even to the porters. He pulled a little aluminium cigarette case from his pocket, given him by Uncle Gerry years ago, and said he had left all his valuables behind. When the train moved off I had such a lump in my throat that I couldn't say goodbye.

Driving home, we saw the Bank of England open for the first time since the 3rd, and queues of people were streaming in quietly to cash their notes.

On coming home at 7 o'clock with Daddy whom I had been to fetch at Westminster, I found a wire from Uncle Romer. He must come back tonight as he has been summoned by his General to a meeting. He arrived at 9.30 pm. Then another wire came from Aunt Clara saying she was also coming to us for the night to see Uncle Romer. So we set to, and made up the bed in your second nursery.

At midnight she arrived overjoyed to find Uncle Romer, as she hardly expected him to arrive till next morning. She was in a frantic state, fearing the summons back to London meant Uncle Romer was to be sent at once to Belgium, so she was determined to see him once more. They sat talking together upstairs until the early hours.

SATURDAY AUGUST 8

Uncle Romer went to his Staff meeting and came back to 2 o'clock lunch. The fare I provided was simple but sufficient for wartime, roast beef and plum tart, as we are told to use the utmost economy in our food. The Bishop of London in a sermon a few days later said nobody, however rich, should have more than two courses for dinner.

After tea Daddy and I went for a walk to see what was going on. Went to Wellington Barracks where the troops are mobilising fast. A long row of horses of all sorts, cart and carriage horses, hacks and hunters, were picketed behind the railings, munching happily at bundles of hay laid out before them. Soldiers were walking up and down with relatives come to say goodbye. Transport wagons were being packed and tarpaulins dragged on the top of those ready to depart.

While we watched, a detachment of men with bayonets fixed and in full campaign order marched out of the gates past where we stood in a big crowd and disappeared in the direction of Waterloo. We then saw two motor cars in which sat two officers of the Flying Corps just ready to go off. A third officer, with a cheery resolute air came out from the gates with an elderly lady and pretty girl speaking very fast. Laughing he caught hold of the girl, kissed her, and jumped into the car which drove quickly away. The poor girl watched the car out of sight with a look of perfect misery.

Today serious measures are being taken to hunt out German spies. All Germans still in England have to report themselves to the police. Several successful raids have been made on suspicious houses and any arms or ammunition was removed by the police.

SUNDAY AUGUST 9

Official news of the seizure of Togoland, Germany's colony in West Africa since 1884. It was their first colony and now seems destined to be incorporated into our Gold

Coast. It was seized at once because it possesses the most extensive wireless station outside Europe.

Daddy and I went at noon to see the 2nd Grenadier Guards march past Buckingham Palace on their way to who knows where? The Prince of Wales has been attached to the 1st Battalion. The Prince, with the King, Queen, Princess Mary and Queen Alexandra, were in the courtyard before the Palace, watching the march past.

The crowds outside must have numbered five or six thousand. A great column of these splendid fellows filed past to the strains of *The British Grenadiers*. Everyone was too affected, I think, to cheer. It was a very stirring sight, but we are getting used now to seeing our regiments go by. Every day we have them trooping down the Fulham Road at the end of our street, bands and pipes playing and followed by a crowd. All the board schools are turned into barracks for the Territorials.

This morning I saw the school in Draycott Avenue besieged by eager little boys climbing up the gates to stare at the soldiers who have taken possession of the class rooms. They were seen leaning on the window sills smoking a peaceful cigarette while they have the chance.

This evening we had hoped to hear the Bishop of London's sermon in St Paul's Cathedral, before he himself goes into camp with the London Rifle Brigade of which he is Chaplain. We had the greatest difficulty in getting on to an omnibus at all. They were all packed inside and out, and when at last we reached Ludgate Hill, we could see the approaches to the Cathedral blocked with people, and large 'Church Full' notices.

It was very disappointing for the Service must have been most impressive, with our Army just on the point of embarking for the Front. We turned away and went to St Bartholomew the Great, the oldest church in the City, and attended the Service of Intercession.

It was a beautiful night, and the crowds filling the City and the precincts of Westminster and the Palace were as great as on Coronation Day.

MONDAY AUGUST 10

The newsboys' shouts seem to have stopped. War news is scanty. With Lord Kitchener at the head of military affairs this is only to be expected. All information as to movements of our Army and Navy is kept out of the papers. Kitchener has appealed to the country for a second army of 100,000 regulars.

The London streets are quietening down, soldiers are much scarcer and seem to be vanishing silently. Food prices are practically normal. 2,000 motorbuses,* with their drivers who are reservists, have gone from London to Belgium to transport soldiers to the Front.

---

*   One of these buses – all of which had an open upper deck – has been retrieved and is now on display at the Imperial War Museum. Thirty vehicles were allocated to each brigade.

TUESDAY AUGUST 11

The town is growing very quiet. But under this calm exterior the public are bracing themselves to face the terrible events we must expect. Everywhere people are organising relief, and making arrangements for temporary hospitals. The Red Cross Headquarters are at Devonshire House. Every district is establishing Committees to work under the direction of the Headquarters Staff, so that no efforts are wasted by working in an inexperienced and useless way.

This morning being the day on which I pay my weekly bills, I went round to the tradesmen who had not sent in the books for a fortnight and asked them to do so at once. They seemed so surprised, but Daddy has just explained that the 'moratorium' ordered by the Government, during which no debts need be paid, still holds good till September 4th. No Bank need cash a cheque over £5, unless it be for wages. Wages are the only legal debt that need be paid.

Paper money is now everywhere in use. £1 notes and postal orders for which no commission is charged, are legal tender.

WEDNESDAY AUGUST 12

Grouse Day! The very best grouse moor in Scotland can be rented today for £5, they say. There is scarcely a sportsman left on the moors, yet the few who are too old to join the ranks and still hale enough to tramp the moors are enjoined to shoot, if only to send the proceeds to the national funds. The Prince of Wales Fund amounted last night to £500,000.

This morning a notice was brought to me by two ladies on behalf of the Kensington Detachment of the Red Cross Society. The Borough has undertaken to equip hospitals for 200 beds, by voluntary contribution. A long list of furniture, utensils, bedding and other requisites was given to me, with a request to mark down those things we would undertake to provide. I must then mark each article and pack them ready to be called for at a moment's notice. I shall give sheets, pillowcases and towels, the folding chairs we use on the balcony, some jugs and a few other items.

Uncle Alex has asked us to put him up for two nights and insisted on paying for his board in these hard times.* I was going to refuse, but shall now accept a donation to produce more articles for the Kensington Hospital.

I lunched with Mrs Dana, a grateful charming woman of American birth, who is married to the Secretary to the Institute of British Naval Architects. She had titbits of news from the naval set to tell me and our fellow guest, Miss Craigie Halkett. Apparently Winston Churchill 'raved like a lunatic for an hour' when the news arrived at the Admiralty that 2 ships we had been hunting in the Mediterranean, the *Goeben* and *Breslau*, had eluded us on leaving Messina and had vanished completely – presumably towards the East.

---

*   'Uncle Alex' was Alexander Dunsmure; who was married to Georgina's younger sister, Beatrice.

I heard that the sudden 'clap of thunder' that mystified London a few mornings ago was in reality the firing of a gun placed on the roof of the India Office in Whitehall. It was discharged to see if the roof would stand the shock. Powerful searchlights are installed on the roof of great buildings, the whole way up the Thames.

Extensive preparations are being made to repel a possible invasion at Harwich, whence Miss Halkett had just arrived. Nobody was allowed to leave the town after 6 pm. Many houses have been pulled down to leave a clear range for our guns; others have been loop-holed for rifle firing. Trenches are being dug and wire-entanglements put up. I suppose the same is being done all along the coast.

You will never realise perhaps what bitter opposition, even hatred, Lloyd George, our Chancellor of the Exchequer, has evoked in the hearts of the Unionists. This is because of the Acts in which he has sought to improve the condition of the lower classes at the expense of the upper. Today a Secretary to the Treasury, himself a Unionist, remarked that Lloyd George's enemies would forgive him everything if they realised the services he has rendered his country throughout this crisis.

To his fertile brain and resourcefulness are due all the measures that have averted a financial catastrophe for England. He has been at work by 5 o'clock for many mornings past. I have promised to join Mrs Dana every afternoon for 2 or 3 hours at a sewing meeting for making bed jackets and pyjamas for the wounded as I am very efficient with needle and scissors!

THURSDAY AUGUST 13

Friendly relations with Austria are broken today and we are at war with her since midnight. I think many of us wondered how long the farce of being outwardly 'at peace with Austria' was going to last.

Now indeed the position of your dear godfather Cousin Rigby Wason, and of his father Eugene, is more precarious. They went off to Marienbad about 3 weeks ago, and nothing has been heard of them for a fortnight. We can only hope that Rigby was able to join Eugene from Bayreuth just before Germany was closed.* But he was to leave Bayreuth the very day war was declared. Eugene's last letter stated that he was blessed if he was going to leave Marienbad before he had finished his cure. All efforts to get news through the Foreign Office have failed.

A week previous to the German declaration of war on France, Italy, being a party to the Triple Alliance, was warned of Germany's intentions. Now Italy, whose alliance did not bind her to take part in a war unless Germany or Austria were attacked, at once passed on the information she had received to the British Ambassador in Rome – who warned our Government at home.

Winston Churchill lost no time in ordering a Naval Review which was nothing less than the mobilising of the Fleet. It was announced publicly that the King would attend

---

* Rt. Hon. Eugene Wason MP. His daughter Brenda was married to Gerard Lee, 'Uncle Gerry'.

the Review, but before the date fixed for the display the King's engagement was cancelled owing, it was said, to the Irish crisis. The Fleet dispersed and took up its position in the Channel and North Sea.

Uncle Alex read us a letter from Colonel Campbell who writes from Harrietsham (Kent) 'The airship *Delta* flew over our house yesterday going towards the coast, and just clearing our roof by 20 feet. She was taking risks in flying so low to conceal her flight. Her engines made such a noise that they terrified cattle who stampeded in a field below our house. One horse died of fright'.

Olympia is being used as a concentration camp for Germans, and camps are being pitched for them in various open spaces out of London.

FRIDAY AUGUST 14

In spite of heavy losses the Germans continue to advance steadily through Belgium hoping no doubt to split the junction between the Allied forces. By sheer weight of numbers they are pursuing a new plan of campaign after their failure in taking the Liège forts.

The manager of the Ritz Hotel has been forced to resign under dramatic circumstances this morning, amid the lamentations of the visitors.* They said they had never had such a pleasant manager to deal with: *un si charmant homme, bon comme du pain*, as an incredulous French lady explained to Mrs Dana.

This afternoon I went with Mrs Dana to the sewing party in Onslow Gardens. Mrs Doughty had had her larger drawing room cleared of all furniture except sofas and chairs, and a number of small workmanlike tables on which were sewing machines, piles of flannel shirts and hospital garments of all shapes and colours. There were about 20 ladies all hard at work. Mrs Dana and I took one of the tables and I was given a shirt, a coat and an operating jacket to finish off. But the work on these was so bad that half my time was spent unpicking and correcting mistakes.

When time was up, I had to hand in the shirt knowing that the opening was so short that the man would scarcely get his head through it, certainly not a bandaged head; while the neckband would have just fitted a boy. However some women were working like professionals. Mrs Dana was. Tea was served in the dining-room and everybody was very pleasant.

Uncle Alex came in before dinner with a report that the Black Watch have suffered severely in an engagement. His sister-in-law had had a letter from a Belgian who wrote that 'wounded men dressed in petticoats had been carried into the hospitals from the Front and the towns people marvelled at their dress, which they had never seen before.'

---

*   Theodore Kroell had been manager of the Ritz since 1909. He was sacked because of his Germanic origins.

SATURDAY AUGUST 15

Uncle Alex went back to Hengwrt* this morning and you are to go and stay there, my darling, because your Gran is too ill for you to be in the house. So we shall have to spend our holidays apart, except that we shall somehow contrive to see you each day. Daddy's little worn-out Vauxhall will still be able to take us the three miles to see you. It is worse for Daddy even than for me, to be parted from you as he looked forward to seeing you properly.

Uncle Alex is also hard hit. The Rubber and Tea Estates from which three-fourths of his income are derived are not expected to pay dividends for some time as they are not at present shipping cargoes. He takes this sudden cessation of income very calmly and with great pluck, although Hengwrt is a large establishment to keep up and Henry is just going to Eton this term.

A friend coming from South Africa, Tom Gladen, told us that they heard of the declaration of war when half-way from Cape Town. The news was not credited by the Germans nor the English on board, who in some cases had become great friends. Tom himself was invited to go and stay at Hamburg. When they reached Plymouth however, they quickly found that things were serious when the Germans found themselves under arrest and were marched off to a place of safety.

The Times today published the plan of Kitchener's campaign to raise a second army. Our illusions as to the short duration of the war are rapidly vanishing. Today we are being prepared for the probability of its lasting two years, perhaps more. The object of this new Army is to have in six months, or a year's time, a fresh and well-trained force to bring into the field. 35,000 recruits have already joined.

It is now announced that Germany is detaining as prisoners of war all Englishmen under the age of 65 trapped in the country by the sudden outbreak of hostilities. So your dear Cousin Rigby's chances of getting home are now practically nil. No news of any sort has been heard of him or his Father in spite of the steps taken through the Foreign Office. The worst part will be hearing nothing but the untrustworthy German war reports.

SUNDAY AUGUST 16

My baby, if ever you read your Mother's diary in years to come you will probably be bored by the details I give of the military aspect from day to day. A few years hence it will not matter a jot where the armies happened to be on August 16 1914. All that will matter to you some day is the result of the terrible suspense we grown-ups are now going through. It is of thrilling importance to us to study the sporting chances of the

---

*   Former stately home of the seventeenth-century antiquarian Robert Vaughan (*c.* 1592–1657) in Merionethshire, 3 miles south of Gelligemlyn. The Hengwrt Chaucer MS found its way into his remarkable library and is now one of the greatest treasures in the National Library of Wales. In the Great War, Hengwrt became the home of Alexander and Beatrice Dunsmure.

players in this awful game. So no wonder we pore over war-maps and articles on the military situation for hours at a time.

Later on, you will be more interested to know what was happening to the population in the invaded regions. Liège itself is now in the hands of the enemy, though the forts have not fallen. Accounts of the townspeople's experience during the terrible attack on the forts are appalling. The women and children, terrified out of their senses at the continual bursting of shells on the roofs of their houses, took refuge in their cellars, while the streets above them were made hideous with accumulating debris and ruins.

But when I can get away from thoughts of such horror, it interests me enormously to follow the military situation. Germany's original plan for annihilating France was to attack in a rapid movement which would bring her army to Paris and France to her knees in little more than a fortnight.[*] But the essence of success for this coup was rapidity, and the German Government never doubted that the French Army would crumple up.

Meantime the German High Seas Fleet remains safe in Kiel and behind Heligoland, their steel-clad island bristling with forts. In reality Admiral Jellicoe is besieging their fleet as effectually as the Japanese laid siege to Port Arthur and their merchant shipping is being gradually strangled.

Lord Kitchener's new Army of 100,000 is mustering rapidly. On Saturday there were already 40,000 recruits and this morning we saw a large detachment, not yet in uniform, filing into St Mary Abbot's for morning service.

In a few years' time it may seem incredible to you, my son, that we only had enough Regulars, when the war broke out, to make up the Expeditionary Force now in Belgium, and that the country would be left in the hands of the Reserves and Territorials. Rightly or wrongly it has been the country's policy so far to depend upon our Navy. But this policy has been more and more violently attacked by the Unionist Party ever since the South African War.

Lord Roberts has protested continually against the inadequacy of our Army. He has advocated conscription, or some measure to enforce the military training of every man physically fit. The Liberal Party had always been opposed to a large Standing Army, as being a menace to the liberties of the people. It did not enter their minds that we might be called upon to take a decisive part in a Continental War.

Kitchener's object in training a new Army is the future welfare of our country. Unless England has done her full share on the battlefields, she will not be entitled to hold out for advantageous conditions of peace. When the spoils of war are divided, we shall be able to stand out for our own terms. The Territorial, who will next be called upon to serve abroad, is at liberty to state now whether he is willing to enter the ranks intended for foreign service, or whether he prefers to remain for home defence. And there is to be no odium placed upon those men, who elect to remain in England.

---

[*]   This was the so-called Schlieffen Plan, which Germany used, with significant modifications, at the outbreak of war. The intention was that Germany would defeat first France, then Russia – and thus avoid having to fight a war on two fronts simultaneously.

Aug. 16

faith in their final mastery of the Sea —

Lord Kitchener's Appeal.

100,000 MEN REQUIRED FOR THE WAR.

NO MEN will be REFUSED who are PHYSICALLY FIT for Active Service and between the ages of 19 and 30.

OLD SOLDIERS UP TO 42.

Late N.C.O.'s of Regulars and Ex-Soldiers URGENTLY NEEDED.

The New Army.

TERMS OF ENLISTMENT FOR THE PRESENT WAR.

The following communication is issued by the Official Press Bureau:—

As some misapprehension still appears to exist, the Army Council desir to make known that ANY MAN enlisting in the Army under the present conditions will be DISCHARGED WITH ALL SPEED POSSIBLE THE MINUTE THE WAR IS OVER, whether this lasts three weeks or three years.

Should the war last over three years their continuance of service will be OPTIONAL.

Lord Kitchener's new Army of 100 000 men required to serve abroad is mustering rapidly On Saturday there were already 40 000 recruits and this morning we saw a large detachment, not yet in uniform, filing in to S? Mary Abbot's for morning Service —
In a few years' time when the British regular Army may be much larger than

Lord Kitchener's Appeal.

MONDAY AUGUST 17

Japan has sent an ultimatum to Germany that she must withdraw immediately her men of war and armed vessels of all kinds from Japanese and Chinese waters. She must also deliver not later than September 15th to Japanese authorities without compensation the entire leased territory of Kiaochow. The answer to this must be received no later than August 23rd. So Germany has another declared enemy.

Another epoch-making announcement is that the Tsar has sent a proclamation to the Poles of Russia, of Germany and of Austria – about 21 million souls. He is promising that their ancient country will be restored to its independence, with freedom of Government, language and religion, if Russia and the Allies defeat Germany and Austria.

Today we are being urged to carry on with our daily business, and return to our usual shopping, expenditure and employment of workers, in order to save the country from the risk of ruin. People were so panic-stricken, at the outset of war, at the idea of losing all their income, that trade has suffered considerably.

It seems to me that England can go on with her industries undisturbed (only hampered by the loss of so many workers gone to the Front). England must see a great increase in her industrial output because of this crisis.

TUESDAY AUGUST 18

At last today the veil of mystery that had hidden the movements of our Expeditionary Army, has been lifted. The last unit, the Field Hospital, has sailed, and there are thrilling accounts of the landing of many of the regiments at Boulogne. Now your Mother knows Boulogne, every cobble of its uneven old streets, like her pocket. She and your Aunts were born five miles out of Boulogne in an old house dignified by the name of Château de la Barrière Rouge. This is a house which your Grandfather kept for over 30 years, as he loved that part of the world as a painting ground. Boulogne, therefore, was our town, and there your Mother was educated for four years, in a Convent.

Now imagine what it is to me to read of the great transport ships gliding in and out of the small harbour, and of the regiments landing on the same quays where we have ourselves embarked and disembarked scores of times. I can see the enthusiasm of the fisher-people, the *matelots* of Boulogne, a distinct race, warm-hearted, impulsive, shrill-tongued and sharp-witted. I can see these *matelots* giving and claiming resounding kisses and shouting words of welcome and the polite and correct official world coming forward to receive the brothers-in-arms who have come to fight side by side with them. The enthusiasm of the Boulonnais is unbounded. As regiment after regiment marched through the town to their camp on the hills above, they were escorted by the populace amid exclamations of admiration at their soldierly bearing and good looks. Our men were singing and laughing all the way, repeating incessantly these words to a certain rhythm: *Are we downhearted? No-o-o-o-o. Shall we win? Y-e-es.*

This Boulogne contingent appears to have landed, the last of them – yesterday 17th; but others were landed at Calais and Dunkirk. The whole transport was effected without a single casualty. This will be a disappointment to those German papers who stated that the English force would not cross the Channel for fear of submarines and mines.

The King's Message to his Army.

This landing of our troops without hin-
drance is due to the secrecy observed by the
Press. Indeed so loyal has the Press been,
that Kitchener has issued his public thanks
to them. This is the greatest compliment, for
Kitchener has always been celebrated for his
stern methods in curbing their indiscretions.

Each soldier in the Expeditionary Force
carries in his Active Service pay-book a letter
signed by Kitchener. It is an inspiring
message, in the very best traditions of our dear
country. It is by showing themselves men of
that stamp that our race has won its honoured
name all over the world and planted the
British flag on half the land of the earth.

But the culminating excitement at
Boulogne was the landing of Field Marshal
Sir John French, Commander in Chief of our
Forces, on the ship *Sentinel* with all his staff.
The local population squeezed itself on the
piers, quays and in the broad open spaces
about the harbour, while the Military
Governor of Boulogne, Daru, a grey-haired
man, surrounded by the officials, military
and civil, received him at the landing stage.
Sir John French and Daru spoke to each
other, each holding his hand at salute, for a few moments. Then our Commander in
Chief said laughingly 'We are very glad to be here, but have you left us any places to
fill?' Daru answered smiling 'I have no doubt you will make your mark very quickly'.

Then Sir John and his Staff went off at once by train to Paris, and at the Gare du
Nord they met with a delirious welcome. A Guard of Honour of Marines was provided
for him, and as he made his way to his car, the crush of cheering people was so great
that the car could not move. He was pelted with flowers all the way to the British
Embassy, amid shouts of *Vive le général French!*, *Vive le roi Georges!* and *Vive la France!*
From the Embassy he went to the Elysée where he was received by President Poincaré,
and most of the ministers. He left Paris in a motor car at 7 o'clock next morning, by a
secret route and for an unknown destination.

Likewise the troops at Boulogne have gone off in train loads, nobody knows where.
They are not allowed to write to any relatives except a postcard to say if they are well or
in hospital. No postmark is stamped on the card.

THE KING'S MESSAGE
TO HIS ARMY.

The King sent the following inspiring message to the troops leaving England:—

BUCKINGHAM PALACE.

You are leaving home to
fight for the safety and honour
of my Empire.

Belgium, whose country we
are pledged to defend, has been
attacked, and France is about
to be invaded by the same
powerful foe.

I have implicit confidence
in you, my soldiers. Duty is
your watchword, and I know
your duty will be nobly done.

I shall follow your every
movement with deepest in-
terest, and mark with eager
satisfaction your daily progress.
Indeed, your welfare will never
be absent from my thoughts.

I pray God to bless you and
guard you, and bring you back
victorious.

GEORGE R.I.

Aug. 9, 1914.

It appears that the embarkation from Southampton was carried out under the same conditions of absolute secrecy. The inhabitants only saw regiment after regiment march down towards the quays. There they embarked silently at night in the great troopships and by next morning the ships had vanished. The ladies of Southampton had established a free buffet so that any hour day or night the troops could be served with hot coffee, cigarettes, tobaccos and chocolates. Not even the skippers knew, until they were 20 miles out, what port they were heading for.

This is the very first time an English Army has landed in France to fight for France. In the past we have always come as enemies.

The Prince of Wales's Fund amounts to £1,250,000 already.

WEDNESDAY AUGUST 19

Today I have had the first shadow of news of your Cousin Rigby. It is a faint little ghost of news, but on August 4th, the very day of the Declaration of War, he was travelling from Bayreuth and managed to get across the German frontier into Austria with scarcely a minute to spare. So he has been able to protect his old Father, unless he has been arrested as a prisoner of war. We hear of a number of Englishmen up to the age of 60 being detained as prisoners of war.

Sir Edward Grey and Lewis Harcourt, the Colonial Secretary, are declaring a trade war against Germany. They have a scheme by which England is to regain the trade all over the world, that Germany has acquired during the last ten or fifteen years. The cheap wage for which a German artisan or labourer will work has enabled Germany to flood our markets with goods far cheaper than anything we can produce. This has been of the greatest benefit to our poorer classes who have had comforts they never could have afforded otherwise.

This theme was the cause of many lamentations the first morning of the war. 'It's all very well, Mum, but I like them Germans. Where are we going to get our boots now, I want to know, we can't afford English boots – and look at my kitchen clock! I gave eighteen pence for it four years ago, and it's never cost me a farthing to keep going.' Hamley's, the fashionable toy dealers, admit that there'll be no toys for Christmas this year. They had just sold their last train and engine, German made, for 3/6, and had nothing cheaper than 25/- British made.

The Kaiser has arrived at Mainz to take personal direction of affairs. As he is so overbearing, this decision does not promise well for the success of his Army.

THURSDAY AUGUST 20

This morning I went to the offices of the Ragged School Union on the way to Islington to offer my services. This is in answer to an appeal on behalf of the poor children of London who will suffer more than usual, through so many fathers being called to the Colours. I went over the wonderful offices, with one of the Lady Superintendents, and was taken to the department where the clothes are stored. There I learnt all about the class of garments needed. They cover the whole outfit not only for girls and boys, but also for their fathers and mothers. So now I shall be busy. I met there Sir John Kirk, the Secretary who had published the Appeal in the papers. He has a benevolent face, a middle aged man with kind grey eyes and a serene smile.*

Today the Belgians are abandoning Brussels. It is not fortified. Its open boulevards and broad streets would be difficult to defend and the Army has retired to the strong fortress of Antwerp. We can only imagine the agony of the inhabitants at seeing themselves open to the desecration of the Germans, who will show no respect for the beautiful undefended capital of their enemies. But it is not to be considered, we are told, as a defeat for the Allies. Napoleon's message to Murat** is quoted: *There is no glory in entering the undefended capital of your enemy.*

A pathetic event announced today is the death of Pope Pius X from a broken heart, they say, at his inability to prevent the War. One of the kindest, gentlest, most straight-forward rulers the world has ever known.

FRIDAY AUGUST 21

You are to stay on another fortnight at Glaslyn for your Grandfather absolutely refuses to part with you. He says he has more pleasure out of you than the whole lot of us put together. A few days ago, for your Grandfather's peace, I settled you were to go at once to Hengwrt, but evidently you must now remain until I fetch you.

Poor beautiful Brussels. It is wide open to the Germans, and no doubt they are marching in there already. It is only natural that they will do so, if only to revictual their army, but one's heart bleeds to think that gallant Belgium should be thus plundered and made to bear the brunt of the horrors of war.

A long letter from your Grandmother telling us of her motor dash to Anglesey with Uncle Gerry to catch Uncle Guy on his way from Fermoy join his regiment.† They heard from him at Gelligemlyn 3 mornings ago, saying to land at Anglesey at such an hour, would his mother go and say goodbye? She and Uncle Gerry got into the car, and covered the 70 miles in less than 3 hours, arriving just as the first ship had been sighted. Uncle Guy turned up in the second and they had two or three hours with him. He is a Staff Captain.

The eclipse was very slight in London and we should scarcely have noticed it had it not been a very sunny day. It was total in the North. The following verse appeared today:

* Sir John Kirk (1847–1922) was a great philanthropist, who had a special interest in child-cripples. He was Treasurer of the Shaftesbury Society and the Ragged School Union from 1879.
** Murat served under Napoleon in Italy, in the Peninsular War in Spain and with the ill-fated Grande Armée in Russia. Promoted marshal in 1804, he married Caroline Bonaparte and became King of Naples in 1808. Attempting to return to his kingdom in 1815, he was arrested in Calabria and shot.
† Captain Guy Lee was on his way to join 1st East Kents (the Buffs), which were part of 16th Infantry Brigade. He was the youngest of Georgina Lee's three brothers-in-law.

> *The War Lord has lately begun*
> *To fancy that Providence trips;*
> *He asked for a place in the sun,*
> *He's getting a total Eclipse.*

Zeppelins have been very active over Belgium. One or two have flown over the Dutch frontier, presumably by mistake,* and have been fired at by the Dutch, where upon they flew back across the frontier to Germany.

The Belgians, it now appears, suffered very heavy losses before retreating on to Antwerp, three regiments, the Guides, Third and Ninth of the Line, being annihilated. An Englishman, motoring along the road to Ghent, gave a lift to a woman who was crying bitterly. '*Tenez*', she said, pulling out of her dress a blue cap with yellow facings marked '3', '*voilà la casquette d'un de nos braves petits soldats, mais il n'en reste plus rien, du troisième.*'

SATURDAY AUGUST 22

The Germans have levied a war-tax of eight million pounds on Brussels! A loan for this, by the bye, is being raised in England. Otherwise their entry into Brussels was made without firing a shot. The Cavalry took possession of the city after a very short parley with the Burgomaster who sallied forth to meet the German Commander, to say they would offer no resistance. The German replied that he would bombard the town if there was the slightest act of hostility.

Oh! it makes one boil with fervour in the knowledge that England will exact a heavy reckoning for this. Kitchener will not let go until he has seen the war through to a successful end, as he did in the Khartoum and South African Campaigns. What one can't get over is the lack of all feeling of decency in trampling down a gallant little country whose misfortune it is to stand between the aggressor and her prey.

The ultimatum of Japan to Germany ends at 3 am tomorrow morning (English time). If the Germans have not delivered over Kiaochow and removed all their warships, Japan will begin to bombard Tsingtao Port.**

This afternoon, Daddy and I went for a walk on Wimbledon Common to get a breath of fresh air and fill up Saturday's free hours. Poor Daddy, who loves the country so devotedly, eats his heart out in London on Saturdays and Sundays, thinking of the river and his rods lying idle.

Putney Heath and Wimbledon Common were crowded with little children, and happy families picnicking and making the most of a lovely summer afternoon and the really beautiful country in which they can roam about so freely. Blackberries were just beginning to darken on the tangled bushes.

---

*   As Holland was neutral.
**   The port of Tsingtao served the coastal province of Kiaochow and had been seized by the Germans from the Chinese in 1897.

We both had a shock too, on our way to Wimbledon, as we passed the grounds of the football club, to see young, able-bodied men swarming in thousands to the grounds to watch a match. Those are the men we want so badly now in our Army. God grant they may not be called to realise this through our disasters.

At last we have news, a little more direct of Cousin Rigby. It came in an open communication, a postcard (a letter might not have come through) to his mother and is dated August 3. It reads:

Marienbad
Well, here we are, and here we remain, days, weeks or months. Last train gone. Anyway we won't budge, unless we have a good chance of getting to England. We are in one of the safest places in Europe, and not much chance of food getting scarce – so don't worry about us. The de la Rues and James Wilsons are here, so we have company, but little to talk about save rumours. I am sure many who bolted from here will be stuck in Germany and much worse off. Love to all
R.W.

This of course was written before we declared war on Germany and Austria.

A relief fund for Belgium is being started in England to help those made destitute by the invasion. Besides this England is raising an immediate loan of ten millions to enable Belgium to meet her losses and France is doing the same. Later, when peace comes, Germany will be made to repair the damage she has caused by paying for it with interest!

The Japanese ultimatum to Germany has expired and no reply has been received. War has been declared.

MONDAY AUGUST 24

Latest edition tonight: A terrible disappointment, Namur has fallen! The French were holding the banks of the Sambre and Meuse in large numbers, and it is a serious loss if they have been driven back. The telegrams add that British troops were engaged around Mons all yesterday (Sunday) right till after dark and that they held their ground. Not happy news about Namur, to go to bed with!

TUESDAY AUGUST 25

A new and strong appeal is being made for more recruits. Kitchener's 100,000 are practically collected, but clearly many thousands more will be needed. The war is going to be very long, it seems plain now. If the Germans carry all before them and reach Paris, then it will take us a very long time to bring her to her knees. We shall do it. The small size of our Army is the great obstacle to bringing the war to a rapid conclusion.

Very oppressive day. Can think of nothing else but the battle that is raging not much more than 100 miles away. Worked hard all day at the clothes I am making for the little

Ragged School children. Aunt Amy came to tea and I enrolled her services for knitting jerseys for the children. She refuses to make shirts for the Red Cross, because everybody has gone mad on that, and nobody is thinking of the poor who are made still more destitute by the war.

Later, 7pm: Have just taken Aunt Amy round to South Kensington Station. The posters there announce 2,000 British casualties during Sunday's fighting.

Lord Kitchener held a midnight meeting yesterday at his own house, which lasted till two in the morning. Winston Churchill was present. At 8 o'clock this morning he called on Asquith and afterwards on Sir Edward Grey. Today Asquith announced, when the House reopened after a fortnight's closure, that he had received Sir John French's report on Sunday's fighting. 'Our troops had fought with the utmost gallantry, and, though hard pressed by the enemy all the time, had succeeded in removing to their new position. Sir John French estimated our casualties at over 2,000.' Think of it, 2,000 British casualties alone in one action, as many as Magersfontein and Colenso put together!

The investment by the Japanese of the port of Tsingtao has begun. The Kaiser has sent a message to the garrison at Kiaochow to hold his possession by whatever means. The German Governor* has had the Chinese villages in the vicinity razed to the ground and all the tall buildings in Tsingtao dynamited, as they might give the range to the Japanese.

A story of General von Emmich's chivalry is being told. As this is the first report of German chivalry that has reached us, it is worth noting, though it is open to doubt! When one of the Liège forts was reduced to ruins, the Germans discovered, half smothered among the debris the heroic defender of Liège himself, General Leman.** Being treated with great deference, he was taken to General von Emmich's quarters, where the aged Belgian hero handed his sword to the German Chief. The latter handed it back to him, with courteous words and bade him keep it in honour of his brave defence.

A letter from your Grandmother gives news today of Uncle Guy, Staff Captain to the Brigade (6th Division) and seconded from the Buffs for service on the Staff. He is at Cambridge, waiting to go to the Front. She writes:

He has been inoculated for enteric, and he insisted on the General being done too, though he stoutly refused. But Guy told the Doctor to come up and he had his needle into the General before he knew it! So like Guy! They are having all their meals under a tarpaulin.

---

*   Capt Clemens Meyer-Waldeck, the naval officer acting as Governor, eventually surrendered the garrison on 7 November.

**   The veteran Gen Georges Leman was in command of the Belgian Third Division, defending Liège against the German assault. He was heavily outnumbered, but held on to the forts ringing the city for eleven days. Having delegated command of his division, he chose to stay behind, but the ammunition chamber of the fort he was occupying was hit by a shell and he was captured unconscious.

Both Uncle Guy's and Uncle Romer's names are up on the Archbishop of Canterbury's special list for prayers, in the Chapel at Lambeth Palace. They were both gazetted in *The Times* for special appointments during the War.

WEDNESDAY AUGUST 26

My baby, it seems so natural to me to address all this writing to you as though you were already a sensible, understanding creature, instead of a young innocent, who is blissfully ignorant of your country's stress and anxiety. How can I tell even whether the story of the struggle will excite anything more than a perfunctory interest in you? You will then be enjoying the freedom and security won for your generation and the succeeding ones through the blood and misery of the present. How little we realised, only a month ago, what it is to feel that security trembling beneath our feet.

For a hundred years we in this island have been living immune from danger, thanks to our Fleet and to the power of our nation, though this power has been dearly bought by the sacrifices of our forefathers. We believe in the ultimate result, for the nation is determined to go on fighting until victory is achieved. But what suspense there is from day to day, as to the fate and movements of our Army.

Today at last we have some news of the terrible struggle that lasted all Sunday and far into the night. The details were announced by Kitchener in the House of Lords and by Asquith in the Commons. The meagreness of details given in the Press is the subject of much criticism. We get most of our news from the French and Russian War Offices who are much less reticent.

This misplaced reticence on the part of our War Office is having a bad effect on recruiting, for the nation is losing interest in a war of which they see and hear nothing. If accounts came through of the severity of the fighting, men would realise the seriousness of the situation. A new mode of driving it home has just been started. All taxicabs and motor buses have large placards printed in red letters, urging men to enlist for the war.

The Germans have occupied Tournai and Malines. These are two beautiful old towns of which Aunt Ethel and I have such happy recollections from the tour of Belgium we made together in 1907. During the Belgian retreat the Germans bombarded Malines for two hours, damaging the lovely old tower of the Cathedral. They threatened the inhabitants to come back again soon in greater force, which they did.

Old Count Zeppelin, now seventy-six years old, is said to be taking command of one of his airships.* He went through the war in 1870 as a Lieutenant in the Hussars. A German Governor of the conquered area of Belgium has been appointed, Field Marshal von der Goltz. He has already proceeded to Brussels.**

---

*   Graf von Zeppelin (1838–1917) was the pioneer builder of these lighter-than-air airships.

**   But he was not there for long. Posted to Turkey in November 1914, von der Goltz commanded the Turkish Sixth Army and laid siege to Sir Charles Townshend's forces in Kut. He died in Baghdad, perhaps from cholera, some ten days before the surrender of the British garrison on 29 April 1916.

In the House today, Asquith strongly supported Lord Kitchener's appeal for recruiting. 'It is a mistaken impression', he said, 'that only 100,000 men are wanted. We want all the men we can get.' Still, no compulsory measures are to be taken, not yet at least, to recruit the half million needed at once.

THURSDAY AUGUST 27

An amusing incident is the 'mutiny' of the Irish Guards in London. On being ordered to move to another depot, they began to shout 'we want to go to the Front, not any more — depots!' Mounted police had to be recalled to quell them, but order was finally restored on their being promised that they would go to the Front, when the right moment came. Kitchener has ordered that each Tommy at the Front is to receive two ounces of tobacco free, every week.

Winston Churchill announced today in the House that the German liner *Wilhelm der Grosse*, was sunk by our cruiser *Highflyer*, after all the men had been taken off. She had been arresting traffic between the Cape and England. One feels some sympathy for the German commander for he behaved very courteously to the liner *Galicia* whom he held up only 2 or 3 days ago.

Our liner was proceeding home from Cape Town when she was arrested by the *Wilhelm der Grosse*. The *Galicia's* wireless operator immediately began sending the SOS message and had just got as far as Gal . . . for the ship's name, when the German commander shouted 'Stop your wireless. I blow up your bridge if you send another letter.' As our liner was unarmed it had to give in. The Germans boarded her, immediately wrecked the wireless and removed two British Army officers as prisoners of war. For the rest, they behaved very well, apologising for the trouble caused, and would not even accept cigarettes without payment saying 'We don't want it said that we robbed your ship'. They then let the *Galicia* proceed on her way.

One is pleased to be able to record acts of courtesy on the part of our enemy, given the accumulating list of outrages they perpetrate on land. They have admitted openly in the Reichstag that they have been forced to commit acts in Belgium, 'the frightfulness of which has been intentional', in order to bring home to the people the necessity of non-resistance.

I can't help fearing that the Germans will get through to Paris. The retirement of the Allies is gradual, but continuous. The Germans get more and more confident as they advance. The next day or two must decide whether they can be checked, or whether the flood will be let loose on poor France.

FRIDAY AUGUST 28

The situation looks black in the north of France. A report says advance parties have penetrated as far as Arras – and the probability of their occupying the northern ports, Dunkirk, Calais and Boulogne is freely contemplated. If this is so, our communications are severely menaced. In fact we should have to shift our base to Le Havre or Cherbourg. Oh! for a bigger British Army! The appeals for recruits in all the papers are desperate. It is openly stated that all the men under 30 who do not enlist are open to the imputation of cowardice. The age range is now extended from 19 to 35.

Your Grandmother writes from Wales that the Welsh will not enlist; they ask 'Why should we fight for England?' They don't realise the situation. Olive Barneby comes to me this morning from Hereford with the same story. The Western Counties are so apathetic. Meetings are being organised all over the country, with good speakers to open their eyes to what German masters would mean.

Daddy is going to join the Public School Corps and will offer his services as Special Constable when we return from Wales in a few weeks. He is too old to join the new Army being over 40. But it may well come to his being needed, and all those like him.

A terrible act of vengeance is the total destruction of the ancient city of Louvain, the Oxford of Belgium. Louvain is now a heap of smoking ruins. The immediate cause was a Prussian mistake, when one body of Prussians fired on their own side.* This was taken as an excuse, the Germans declaring they had been fired upon by the citizens of Louvain. The destruction of the city with its treasures and priceless manuscripts immediately followed.

The day ended up more cheerfully for us here in London than it began. The evening papers gave a glorious account of a stand made on Wednesday 26th by our British Army, in the proportion of 1 Britisher to 3 Germans. Greatly cheered by this news, Daddy and I went to dine with Theo Barneby and Olive at the Automobile Club, finishing the evening at the Alhambra. It was the first time since the beginning of the War that we had felt in anything like a mood for laughing.

The house was draped in red, white and blue, and the performance was much leavened with patriotic display. A poem calling all the men to arms was recited and the *Marseillaise* was sung by the House, everybody standing. But our surprise and joy were suddenly excited to a high pitch by the unexpected appearance on the screen of war telegrams announcing a first naval engagement against the German Fleet behind Heligoland. These signals rolled out on the screen:

The enemy's cruisers were engaged by the British cruisers. The 1st Light Cruiser Squadron sank the German cruiser Mainz.

The 1st Battle Cruiser Squadron sank one cruiser Köln *class, and another cruiser disappeared in the mist, heavily on fire and in a sinking condition.* **

The cheering and clapping grew to intense excitement. Yet no undue demonstration took place. Everyone soon became calm, for we all bear the shadow of the perilous position of our small army.

---

* It was said that a runaway horse caused the German sentries of the occupying forces in Louvain to panic and open fire. Not only the ancient university, but a large proportion of the houses were burnt, churches were damaged and civilians executed.

** This was the Battle of Heligoland Bight. In all, four German cruisers were sunk, at a cost of thirty-five British dead. Seven hundred Germans were killed or drowned.

SATURDAY AUGUST 29

The news of the naval victory in the North Sea does not, alas, blind us to the dire position in North France. The scene of war is shifting nearer and nearer to the surroundings of my childhood.* I can visualise the preparations that are being made there to meet the invasion. They consist of evacuating all the military from Boulogne, which is unfortified. The Military Governor and his garrison have departed, so as to avoid the bombardment of the town. The enemy has penetrated as far as Abbeville, which I remember is only about one hour's journey by slow train from Boulogne.

About 40,000 fresh troops are leaving England now for the Front. The German fury, as displayed by their destruction of Louvain, may be partly due to their fear of the advancing Russians. These are making such progress in East Prussia that so far nothing has checked them. They are marching on Danzig.** We can afford to wait.

I wonder if our tactics would be to leave Paris open to them, as Moscow was left in 1812? What could they do if no defence was offered, and the town cleared before their arrival?

An Englishwoman, who arrived here from Belgium, via Boulogne, said it was heartrending to see Lille deserted and left open to the enemy. Calais and Dunkirk are prepared for defence, and they also have the means of flooding the district around. But the Germans seem to be making straight for Abbeville to cut off our communications with the sea. Uhlans have already been seen there.

One very cheering thing is the great wave of loyalty sweeping over India. The people are burning with desire to fight for the Empire, and the hill regiments of the north, Gurkha, Sikhs etc. are to be employed. One Rajah has given 50 lakhs of rupees (£300,000 to £400,000) for their war effort, and there have been many other gifts. The Secretary for India, Lord Crewe, announced this in the House of Lords, reminding the peers that the French are employing the Turcos (native regiments from Tunis) very effectively. Indian troops will fight side by side with the British.

India's loyalty makes all the greater impact in view of Germany's attempts to raise, through Turkey, an Islamic Holy War against us in India and Egypt. Turkey is being warned of the extreme danger to herself in listening to Germany's interested advice.

---

*   Georgina Lee had spent many of her formative years living at St Etienne au Mont, Boulogne, where she and her sister Beatrice attended a convent. Hence her deep concern that the town she knew well from childhood days was about to be invaded.

**   But they would never reach it. On this very day, the 1st and 2nd Russian Armies were suffering catastrophic defeats at Tannenberg and the Masurian Lakes. The Russians were driven out of East Prussia and 30,000 were killed. Gen Ironside described Tannenberg as 'the greatest defeat suffered by any of the combatants during the War'.

Book II

August 30 – October 7, 1914

SUNDAY AUGUST 30

My baby, not even the thought that I shall have you in my arms in two days time can take the load off my heart tonight. Indeed, the very fact of that happiness to come fills me with added sorrow for the terrible shadow that hangs over our country. I feel as though any joy is out of place while so many mothers are suffering untold miseries today. This much I can promise. In return for my immunity at present from all anxiety concerning my son, he shall be taught to understand the debt he owes to the brave compatriots who have given their lives in this great cause. All honour and peace to the brave dead.

Meanwhile we are eating our hearts out with anxiety to know the worst. The Press Bureau is silent. No list of casualties has been published since our troops first went into action a fortnight ago. All this time nobody knows where their relations are fighting, nor what their fate is. If only our Army had not been so ridiculously small for the task.*

MONDAY AUGUST 31

If I were not so pleased I should be very angry with *The Times* correspondent who wrote from Amiens on the 29th and gave Daddy and me such a night of anxiety as to the fate of our Army. That they have been, and still are, in great peril, is true. But we have this morning Lord Kitchener's blessed statement to the Press Bureau that our Army is unbroken. Only those guns were lost whose horses were killed. Since Wednesday there has been no fighting except with cavalry, the Germans being forced to rest and halt after their fearful losses.

As for the story of the 3 days fighting from Saturday 22nd to 26th, it is one long record of honour for the British Army. They have retired an average of 6 or 7 miles each day, fighting fiercely the whole time and keeping the line unbroken. So the Germans have not yet won the decisive victory they are panting for.

---

*   The British Expeditionary Force had gone to war with five divisions. Maj Gen Spears states that the total ration strength in August 1914 was about 110,000. By contrast, the French had seventy-two divisions. E.L. Spears, *Liaison 1914*, p. 478.

TUESDAY SEPTEMBER 1

Glaslyn

My first peep at you, as I stole into your room at 7 o'clock tonight, showed me a baby grown out of all recognition, fast asleep. It was lovely of you to remember me after 5 weeks. I had to lift you up, at Nannie's request, to feel how heavy you have grown, and you are an armful now!

Little Geoffrey and Winnie were tucked up in their beds but wide awake, of course, to see Auntie.* You are all three fast asleep, bless you little innocents, little knowing how your Mothers have sat up late tonight talking over plans and changes made necessary by the war. It is for this reason that Aunt Edie with Winnie and Geoffrey have come to live for a while at Glaslyn.

Asquith has asked all the Ministers to address meetings throughout the country to encourage recruiting. Lloyd George is to speak in Chamberlain's great stronghold, Birmingham, and will encourage friends to enrol themselves in the same group.** Thus the eligible employees of certain firms are enlisting, to serve together. 500 men were thus netted in one great firm. Most of the good firms are keeping their places open for every recruit, and paying their families half-wages during their absence.

WEDNESDAY SEPTEMBER 2

It has been quite a relief today to see no paper of any sort till tea-time. There was much to be done, domestically, during my one day at Glaslyn. Of course you were my first business today, my son. To carry you into the garden and see your little accomplishments were the first thing to attend to. Already Grandfather is telling me that he can't let you go tomorrow – everybody else can, but not you! Very pleasant for all the rest of us.

In Central Russia, the battle is now raging fiercely round Lemberg. St Petersburg is from henceforth to be called Petrograd, the old name savouring too much of the German. Grad is the Slav word for town, and Burg is the German for it.

THURSDAY SEPTEMBER 3

I shall never forget the face of your dear old Grandfather when he came in to breakfast this morning. He looked so feeble and old. He had just come from your nursery where he had been to say goodbye to you all alone. He is eighty one years old now. I am so thankful you have brought him sunshine during these weeks which have brought anxiety to most of us. His attitude towards the war is one of undaunted confidence. 'My dear,' he said to me, referring to the Kaiser, 'he will have his Villa on the Thames, you'll find, before very long – and be thankful he's got that.'

---

*   Geoffrey and Winnie were the children of 'Aunt Edie', Edith Taylor (née Davis), one of Georgina Lee's younger sisters.

**   These groups were known as the Pals Battalions. They joined up together – but did not realise that they would die together.

When I left you in the evening to come to Gelligemlyn, you were very busy fingering the sweet pea designs on the nursery wall from your bed. Gelligemlyn looked so peaceful in the lovely warm evening light when I arrived at 6 o'clock. Grief and trouble seemed so out of place in such surroundings. But the illness of your dear Gran on one side and the war on the other, are very real facts and one cannot forget either for one moment.

Your Lee grandfather has altered very sadly during the month since I saw him last. His beautiful face is so drawn and emaciated that it is really the ghost of its former self. He is very weak, and now only moves out of his bed for an hour or so occasionally. He likes us to sit with him one at a time, but not to talk. The first thing he said was: 'How is Baby? I am very sorry I couldn't have him in the house, dear little chap.'

Paris is preparing for siege. Numbers of citizens are leaving, and the Government is prepared to move to Bordeaux. But not only is the capital getting ready for a vigorous defence, but the whole country is determined to fight on and on, if necessary, for years to rid itself of the enemy. And so is England.

At last the first casualty list since the beginning of the war is out. Several glorious feats of arms took place during last week's fighting.

Captain Francis Grenfell, of the 9th Lancers, ran forward at the head of his men to rescue two of our guns whose gunners had been struck by shrapnel. The horses had been left under cover some distance away. 'We'll get the guns back' cried Grenfell, and having managed to push out the guns – one over dead gunners – they got them away. After this he went off to hospital to have his wounds seen to.*

FRIDAY SEPTEMBER 4

The removal of the French Government from Paris to Bordeaux will be historic. The event was announced to the French people by the President of the Republic, Poincaré. The spirit which animates France in 1914 is so different from the noisy, bragging, mismanaged France of 1870. The situation in France becomes more fraught every moment. The Germans are getting very near Paris. But the Allies are in position between the Seine and Marne rivers. East of Paris the British Army is on the line of the Marne, while on its flank a huge array of French troops is massed along the Marne and through the Champagne country.

Colonel Abdy whom I saw this morning, and who is busy recruiting among the Welsh, with no result so far, told me that our position in France is splendid. He spoke most mysteriously, as do the papers, who have a quite confident tone, in spite of the Germans being just outside Paris.

The situation is so full of fateful and frightful possibilities. I am strongly reminded of the closing chapter of Anatole France's *L'Ile des Pingouins*, which is a fable and a satire on the history of the French people. In the process of evolution the French nation comes to a point where it can progress no further. The nation is decadent, suffering from

---

*   For this deed of valour Grenfell was awarded the Victoria Cross.

over-civilisation and the evils resulting from loss of qualities implanted by Nature. It finally comes to achieve a fresh start by the blowing up by degrees of the whole of Paris. Anatole France is such a philosopher and can think so far ahead, that his dream might be coming partly true. But not quite in the circumstances, nor from the causes he imagined.*

Just an amusing little incident of recruiting in Wales. Colonel Abdy has not succeeded in netting a single man from the mines and quarries in the neighbourhood. Partly the Welsh do not understand why they should 'fight for the English' whom they dislike and distrust. However this morning Daddy was going round Dolgelly with Mr Cox, helping to find willing fighters, and they did at last get hold of one. 'Hooray, we've got a Welshman at last!' cried Mr Cox. But when he was taken to the office to give his name and particulars, he turned out to be a citizen, until lately, of the 'Parish of Lambeth in the County of London'.

SATURDAY SEPTEMBER 5

Asquith made a speech yesterday at the Guildhall on the war, to plead for more recruits. Almost 300,000 men have now answered and yesterday the authorities had to let intending recruits stand by for the present, with a retainer of 6d per day, until sufficient instructors have been collected.

To return to Asquith's speech, he warned the nation that this is going to be a long struggle in which we shall need all our patience, energy and resources. Bonar Law, Leader of the Opposition, who spoke after Asquith, quoted from Cromwell's words 'We know what we are fighting for, and we love what we know'.

'Rather than be a silent witness', said Asquith in words which will be historic 'which means being a silent accomplice of this tragic triumph of force over law and freedom, I would rather see this country of ours blotted out of the page of history. What would have been our condition as a nation today if we had been base enough through timidity or perverted calculation, through self-interest or a paralysis of a sense of honour and duty, to be false to our word and faithless to our friends?'

Leading men of all parties in the House were on the platform, all animated with one same spirit of determination to fight this war out to the bitter end. It is one of the inspiring consequences of the war, that all differences are sunk in the one great devotion to the cause. 'Whichever way we look, we have abundant cause for pride and comfort' said Asquith yesterday. With these comfortable words deep in my mind, I go to bed.

SUNDAY SEPTEMBER 6

Tonight we had the telegrams of the war news sent out from Dolgelly. There is one disaster for us, the light cruiser *Pathfinder* has been sunk by a submarine in the North Sea – only twenty miles off the East Coast.

---

*   Anatole France (1844–1924), journalist, satirist and man of letters, was the author of several novels. He was noted for his dislike of extremes, his clarity of thought and elegant melodious style. He was awarded the Nobel Prize for Literature in 1921.

The three Allied Powers, England, France and Russia have covenanted with each other not to sign a peace with the enemy except with the consent of all three Powers. France, therefore, cannot accept any terms on her own.

MONDAY SEPTEMBER 7

The liner *Runo* was sunk by a mine 22 miles off the East Coast. Most of the crew and passengers were saved, but 29 lives, mainly Russian emigrants, were lost. The Admiralty also announces that a German squadron of two cruisers and four destroyers have sunk fifteen of our fishing trawlers in the North Sea. A quantity of fish was taken and the fishermen taken to Wilhelmshaven as prisoners of war.

The Admiralty has formed a new Royal Navy Division available to serve with the Army, or Navy as required. After providing for all possible requirements of the Navy, there still remains a large number of men of the Royal Marines and Naval Volunteers.

Tonight after tea, Daddy and I motored over to see you. I sent Daddy up to the nursery first. When I went in ten minutes later, I found you sitting up in bed in your nightgown, with red cheeks and shining eyes, having no end of games with Daddy. So there was no need of my diplomacy here to effect a reconciliation!

On our way home we passed a telegraph boy going to Gelligemlyn, and having taken the telegram from him, we found it was from Uncle Guy. It ran:

We leave tonight 9.30. Love to you all darlings. Goodbye.

It was dated Cambridge 5.30 this evening. We knew this meant a great grief to Granny, already so racked with your Grandfather's illness. We gave it to her, trying to break the blow, but in her nervous and strained state it produced a dreadful breakdown. She had hoped so much he would not have to go just yet.

We tried to remind her that the fact of his being a Staff Officer made his position rather less dangerous. But it was all to no avail, and we had to let her alone for awhile. One piece of good news we had today is a wire from Aunt Nell Wason, stating that Cousin Rigby and his Father have reached Geneva. I am thankful for that. The idea of being parted from your Godfather till the end of the war was a very real grief.

TUESDAY SEPTEMBER 8

The news today is decidedly inspiriting. The First German Army after leaving Paris on its right, has moved in a south easterly direction, and the opposing armies have engaged in a huge battle.* The German advance has at last been brought to a standstill.

Daddy and I saw you this morning at Hengwrt and met you in Dolgelly this afternoon in your pram, waving a silk Union Jack which had been given you by Tom Roberts the Ironmonger, a staunch friend of the family. Nannie was wheeling you about very proudly. Daddy and I were on our way to Penmaenucha. Old Nannie Woods had

---

*   This was the Battle of the Marne, which crucially halted the German advance.

come into Dolgelly with us, and was dying to see you after several weeks' absence. You waved your flag at her and flapped it against her cheek, much to her satisfaction.

WEDNESDAY SEPTEMBER 9

At last today there is a distinct turn of the tide. The Allies today are taking the offensive. The German right has been driven back towards the river Aisne. The British force has this particular action to its credit and Sir John French is evidently administering further severe punishment to the First German Army.

The French centre has been the cause of some anxiety, as it has been the object of a tremendous onslaught of 3 German Armies, under the Crown Prince, General von Bülow and General von Hansen. But the news from that quarter is reassuring. There has been violent fighting, yet the French have held their own, and at Vitry the enemy have lost ground.

Your Grandfather here is weaker today. His dear face is beginning to look pinched, and his nose has a thin, delicate appearance, but looks beautiful.

THURSDAY SEPTEMBER 10

Lord Kitchener's surprise for the enemy turns out to be the loyal Indians. 70,000 Indians with their own Prince headed by the veteran of 70 years of age, Sir Pertab Singh, are now due to land almost immediately. The 6 Maharajahs, 3 Nawabs and The Malik Umar Hazat have showered gifts in money, jewellery and metals. They are sending arms, cavalry, infantry and sappers. Yesterday in the House the telegram from Lord Hardinge, Viceroy of India announcing in detail all India's gifts to the Empire was read out by Asquith. Then a member cried out amid much laughter: 'Send a copy to the Kaiser!'

At all events, the Dalai Lama has shaken off the mist of sublime indifference, which usually obscures from his exalted view what is going on in the world outside Tibet. He is supposed to be always a child, the supposition being that he is not allowed to get old. He has offered gifts of money and men, while seven hundred Princes of more or less exalted rank in India have placed their resources at the disposal of the Mother Country.

No less stirring a response has come from the great Dominions – Canada, besides her valuable contingent of troops has sent great hoards of wheat. Australia and New Zealand are sending their troops, even a little Barotse chieftain of Northern Rhodesia has offered his services.

A letter has come from Uncle Arthur who retired from the Gordon Highlanders on his marriage last January, when he was Captain.* He volunteered for service in Belgium but was first employed raising recruits in South Wales. A few days ago he received orders to go to France, but as he was embarking at Southampton, his orders were cancelled. He has been given the command of the 10th Service Battalion, Gordon Highlanders, in Kitchener's New Army.

---

*   Capt (later Col) Arthur Davis, the youngest of Georgina's three brothers. He and his wife, Audrey Clive, had been married for only six months when war broke out.

He has 800 men at present, one other officer, a Territorial, and two non-commissioned officers. He has to convert these into a fighting force in the shortest possible time, and then they will go abroad. For his poor wife, too, it is a respite. He says that to his dying day he will never forget the sight of her as she left him to get into her train to go back to Portsmouth while he went to Southampton. He is terribly grieved over the disaster to the Gordons in Belgium. The 1st Battalion was almost wiped out, only 5 officers and 170 men were left. Many of the officers were among his greatest friends.

Tonight Daddy and I went to a meeting held in Dolgelly for the purpose of inducing the eligible young men of Merionethshire to recruit. So far this has been the worst county in Great Britain for enlisting. Now that Lord Kitchener has called for another 500,000, making one million in all, great efforts must be made. They had 400,000 men already towards the first half-million. Sir Osmund Williams, Lord Lt of the County, was in the Chair. Sir Watkin Wynne was near him and then a number of Welshmen, Ministers of the Church, professors of Aberystwyth, School Inspectors etc. spoke most eloquently.

But as these all spoke in Welsh, their orations were lost on us. They are natural orators, Welshmen; they speak in very soft low voices, with telling gestures and never hesitating for a word. The first Welshman, Professor Morris, was excellent, for he spoke half in Welsh and half in English. But as he warmed to his theme he dropped the English and confined himself to Welsh, much to our disappointment for his imagery was most picturesque. We all await the result on recruiting tomorrow, in Dolgelly!

FRIDAY SEPTEMBER 11

Lights out in London!
The City is requested to do without brilliant lights such as arc lights, illuminated fronts to theatres and shops, advertisements etc. This is to render more difficult the identification of particular parts of London. Also the citizens are warned not to be alarmed at the sight of airships which will soar over London for the next few nights, in order to observe the London lighting.

We were in Dolgelly this afternoon after going up to Hengwrt to have a peep at you. We found you basking in the sun in the old garden, just on the point of going to sleep, but you were very soon roused and had a game with Daddy. We found on going to Dolgelly that not one single recruit had enlisted, after all the eloquence expended in the town last night!

SATURDAY SEPTEMBER 12

Today for the first time the Allies can claim a victory in France, or what amounts to it. The Germans have now been pushed back behind the river Aisne, their right wing being hotly pursued by the British. General von Kluck, who harassed the British in their retreat from Belgium, is now hard pressed and is being pushed against General von Bülow's Army. These two Generals have had to retire 40 miles in four days.

Winston Churchill made a most cheering speech yesterday at the London Opera House. He announced that the Admiralty are so rapidly building great ships now, that in the next twelve months the number will be more than double the number which will be completed for Germany. The Fleet is doing all we want it to do so far without fighting, the sea is absolutely open to our ships and German warships are nowhere to be seen. In due course we shall have our sea fight, if the German fleet won't come out of their haven, perhaps we can shell their harbours! Another Hamburg-Amerika liner, the *Bethania*, has been captured, and with her 400 men, now prisoners of war.

Yesterday at Cape Town, in the House of Assembly, General Smuts endorsed General Botha's motion to send our King a loyal message. He said but for the Royal Navy, South African overseas food supplies would be endangered. So it was for the House to decide whether they meant, or not, to do their duty to England. He recalled the Peace of Vereeniging, after the Boer War. 'By that peace South Africans secured the fullest liberty, thanks to Great Britain. The Government knows that Germany's intention is to acquire British South Africa for herself. It is against this German Government and the military caste that South Africa, in common with the rest of the Empire, is at war.'

I quote this now, as additional proof of the extraordinary loyalty there is throughout our Colonies for the Mother Country. They all use their freedom to help us to the utmost of their ability, though unasked. It is a glorious thing for our little country that these huge dominions, some so lately added to the Crown, should forget so quickly the bitterness of conflict.

Today I took your godmother, Gertie Wykeham-Musgrave, a dear and valued friend, to see you at Hengwrt. She is staying for 2 days at Tyn-y-Groes Inn with a friend on a motoring tour. Gertie's only boy, a dear middy of 15, is now on the North Sea. He and his mates went straight from Dartmouth College on to a cruiser, the *Aboukir*, and they have already had 'some fun' in chasing German destroyers.

MONDAY SEPTEMBER 14

The news today is so good both in the West and in the East that it is difficult to see how the Germans are going to retrieve their fortunes. In the East, the Russians are having even greater successes than the Anglo-French forces. An Austrian Army has been cut off in Galicia, and is in danger of total annihilation unless it surrenders.

The French are fighting splendidly. How different is the spirit of the French Army of today, so calmly heroic, full of endurance and zeal, while in 1870 it was discontented, undisciplined and lacking in confidence in its incompetent chief. They have vigorously pursued the retreating Germans and now, by avenging the humiliation of Sedan, they have regained their old confidence.

The letters written home by English Officers and men at the Front contain details of horrors they themselves have witnessed. In one case a young officer saw an Uhlan Officer mutilate with his sword a young Belgian girl of 18, and shot him dead at 300 yards range. The poor girl who was very pretty was brought into our trenches, with several other girls who had been grossly ill-used, 'but', added the writer, 'I fear she will die'. He wrote that he had given his shirt to one of the victims who hadn't a garment, and all his rations he divided amongst the 3 poor girls who were starving.

TUESDAY SEPTEMBER 15

As this is the first war in which aircraft have been used for military purposes, these little paragraphs from *The Times* are interesting. They show the state of efficiency our Flying Corps has attained, although so little display and fuss was made of our military aviation before the war. In fact, the impression was that the British were very behindhand in the art of flying. Our judgement once again was at fault. This war has been one of surprises.

TRIBUTE TO AVIATORS

Quite one of the features of the campaign, on our side, has been the success attained by the Royal Flying Corps. In regard to the collection of information it is impossible to over-estimate the value of the intelligence collected.

That the services of our Flying Corps, are fully appreciated by our Allies is shown by the following message from the Commander-in-Chief of the French Armies, received on the night of September 9 by Field-Marshal Sir John French:

'Please express most particularly to Marshal French my thanks for services rendered every day by the English Flying Corps. The precision, exactitude, and regularity of the news brought in by its members are evidence of their perfect organisation and also of the perfect training of pilots and observers.'

To give a rough idea of the amount of work carried out, it is sufficient to mention that, during a period of twenty days up to the 10th September, a daily average of more than nine reconnaissance flights over 100 miles each has been maintained.

We never dreamt of the small Belgian nation stemming the flood of the German invasion and they kept it in check for days. We never supposed the German Fleet would leave the North Sea free of their presence, and remain invisible behind their forts and harbours.

WEDNESDAY SEPTEMBER 16

Evening is closing in over a stormy sky, ragged black clouds are passing across the valley. Cadir Idris is completely shrouded in mist. Across the terrace, the flower beds that were brilliant with colour a week ago are dark and dank from heavy rain. It is a sad landscape and if it were not for the knowledge I have, that behind the spur of that dark hill lies Hengwrt, and in a cosy nursery at the top of the old oak staircase a lovely baby is sleeping, I hope, in his cot, it would seem a very dismal outlook indeed.

As I write, your poor weary Granny has dropped asleep in the armchair at my elbow and I am thankful to see her lost for a few moments to her cares. Your Grandfather had a very miserable night, struggling against the weakness which is stealing over him.

A wire was sent to Uncle Gerry today suggesting he comes home tomorrow from London, instead of waiting till Saturday.

Meanwhile, Belgian refugees are pouring into England in thousands and are being received with open arms. At Folkestone the organisation for dealing with them is very extensive, and hospitality is being offered from all parts of the country. Everything is being done to bring a little sunshine into their lives after the horrors they have been through.

FRIDAY SEPTEMBER 18

A letter from Aunt Nell Wason says that she must go to London at once to meet her husband and son, who have wired that they reached Paris yesterday. The cross-channel service has 4 trains daily from Paris to Le Havre, not Boulogne or Calais yet, so they will be here today or tomorrow. The idea of having Rigby back safe and sound, when we expected him to be detained through the war, is a great joy. How they got from Marienbad to Geneva we don't yet know.

Lord Kitchener made another speech in the House of Lords yesterday, in which he stated that 'the tide of battle has turned'. His speech was very hopeful in tone, and he said the response to the call for recruits had been magnificent. But he was certain that the war will be a long one.

SATURDAY SEPTEMBER 19

I haven't been able to write this evening for when I came home at 5 o'clock I found that your dear Grandfather had taken a change for the worse, and was sinking. I saw him for a little in the evening, but he didn't know me. We sat up till after midnight and wanted to sit up with Muz* all night, but she wished most determinedly to be left alone with him. So we went to bed.

SUNDAY SEPTEMBER 20

Dad is still living, but doesn't know us. Thank God he is in no pain. Muz is wonderful; she has done everything possible for him and is so brave. In spite of occasional breakdowns, she is as calm and collected as she can be.

The old Grandfather's clock at my elbow ticks a most tuneful but continuous dirge and in the future the ticking of this clock will remind me of Dad's last illness more than anything else. To my dying day I shall see his dear emaciated face lying on the pillows, when I hear the ticking of the old metal ringing against the mahogany case, sounding like a musical instrument.

---

*   Minna Constance Lee, Georgina Lee's mother-in-law, who lived at Gelligemlyn, was affectionately known in the family as Muz.

Later: At one pm we were all hastily summoned to Dad's room. The nurse thought him on the point of collapse. We five, Muz, Daddy, Uncle Gerry, Auntie Bobbie* and I stood round the bedside for over an hour. His breathing was so irregular, stopping entirely for some moments, that we several times hoped he was gone, for it has come to that, we hope for his immediate release. However, he rallied and this evening, he is much in the same state, unconscious, or at all events unable to convey to us his feeling or wishes.

To turn from this lingering death to death on the battlefield, going on now by the thousand, is like turning from darkness to light. Death on the field seems beautiful.

MONDAY SEPTEMBER 21

This morning Dad is still in the same condition. Muz has been sitting at his side all night, holding his hand, as she was doing all yesterday. We hardly ventured into the garden, expecting the end at any moment.

Rheims Cathedral is in flames! This is like burning Westminster Abbey. It was the Coronation Cathedral of the Kings of France of the earlier dynasties, and has survived through centuries of warfare. Clovis, the Pagan King, was baptised there 1400 years ago.

I have had a letter from Arthur's wife. She is with him at Aldershot, and tells me of his work, training his new regiment, 10th Battalion Gordon Highlanders, for active service. The men, she says, are mostly in rags, their uniforms are not yet ready. They have to sleep 12 in one tent, with only one blanket apiece. Arthur works night and day and is so pressed that he 'hasn't even time to change for dinner!'

* * * * * * * * * * * * * *

At 11.30 this morning, I was sitting in the sun on the terrace, when Brenda beckoned to me hurriedly from the window above. The last summons has come, Dad was lying motionless, his breath coming so faintly that it was scarcely perceptible. I knelt down by the bed at Muz's side and kissed his dear arm, while Muz said aloud the hymn *Abide with me*. He breathed his last just then, in perfect peace and without an effort.

It was a beautiful end to the last phase which has been very distressing to us. Yet his indifference to our grief as we knelt at his side – he who could never endure to see any of those he loved in tears – was the most poignant thing of all. So ends one of the noblest and best of lives.

TUESDAY SEPTEMBER 22

The destruction of Rheims Cathedral seems to be complete. It was done as an act of revenge by the Germans after they had had to evacuate it. When the French took

---

*   Brenda Lee, wife of Gerard (Uncle Gerry).

possession of it again, the town was shelled by the enemy and now there are only the four walls and part of the towers left standing. The Cathedral was 1500 years old, one of the wonders of Gothic Art by the time it was completed in 1200 or thereabouts. It was intimately connected with French history and French Kings were anointed there. Joan of Arc had Charles VII crowned there* after her victories.

The battle of the Aisne has now gone on for eleven days. The Allies seem to be winning inch by inch, capturing a village here or a ridge there, at infinite cost, yet on the whole we are progressing. I expect we shall have a great surprise and sensation in a day or two when the action is decided. We are burning to hear that the Allies have got behind the Germans.

These few days I can take no interest in what is going on outside. I feel unsettled and unhappy and long to get away to a quiet corner by myself.

Saddened by the death of her father-in-law, unsure of the outcome of the battle raging in France, Georgina, in a rare moment of intimacy, takes refuge in her diary to express how unsettled she feels. She turns away from the war news and goes on to describe closely the character of her husband, Charles Lee, and her concerns about him. He is the 'only quiet, reserved one in the whole family circle', whereas his brothers are all extroverts. They are all directly involved in the war on active service, while he is not – a factor which must have become all too apparent next day at the family gathering after the funeral of their father. Perhaps it is the fragile nature of Charles's character which persuades Georgina loyally to remain with him in London – rather than look after her baby son Harry in the safety of their Welsh haven. This is a dilemma which persists for the duration of the war. At this fraught time, she turns to her diary for comfort and, as always, addresses her remarks to her beloved son:

Your Father was born delicate through the imprudence of his mother. To her it is due that his constitution is different to his brothers. From his birth he has needed more care and he is of a highly-strung, anxious disposition, always busy with 'things that must be done' before he can sit down and enjoy himself. The whole of the fortnight (when we became engaged at Christmas in 1909–10) that I spent with the family at Horton, he was busy answering his letters of congratulations, instead of putting it off till my departure! This has always been a little joke in my own heart against him. He is the most devoted, self-sacrificing Husband, but he is never quite comfortable even with me if there is any little business left undone.

His brothers are quite different. They do enjoy life whole-heartedly. Daddy doesn't enter into this letting themselves go. In spite of their very deep affection for him, I think they enjoy themselves better without him. He becomes more reserved than ever when in their midst. I throw myself as much as possible into their fun and chaff, so as to be the connecting link. Besides this, I love them dearly all three. But Daddy is the eldest son and I want him . . . not to be overlooked.

---

*   In 1429, during the Hundred Years War.

Your Father also is the poor one of the family at present. His father did the very best for him, put him into the family firm and watched over his interests till he was able to stand on his own feet. But he is limited at present to £700 a year, which barely meets our expenses, since you came to us, my treasure. My small income just meets my dress expenses, though it will be more later. So Daddy has to live very carefully, spending nothing on luxuries, very little on entertaining, just a few quiet dinners occasionally. He runs his little ten-year-old car, a relic of bachelor days, which he has to clean and tinker up himself, while his brothers run their smart cars with chauffeurs, entertain liberally and do mostly what they like in the way of amusement.

* * *

Three British cruisers have been torpedoed in the North Sea, and the first on the list is the *Aboukir*, Kit Wykeham-Musgrave's ship. Kit is the only son of your godmother. No list of casualties is out yet and my anxiety on her behalf is intense. To make it more pathetic, a letter from her has just reached me. She left the inn here in a hurry last week to see Kit whose ship was to put in at Chatham for a few hours. The *Hogue* and the *Cressy* are the other two cruisers sunk. Going to the rescue of the *Aboukir* which was torpedoed first, they met with the same fate.

THURSDAY SEPTEMBER 24

A lovely day, warm and brilliant. The sun was streaming into the room where Dad rested, when Aunt Brenda and I came in early, to arrange the flowers around him. A tiny wreath of white pansies and ivy marked 'from Baby Harry' was placed at his feet and rested on the coffin while it was being borne to its last home. At half-past eleven, the open dog cart drawn by old Pugh came to the front door.

It was transformed into a flower carriage. When the coffin was placed there, exquisite flowers were hung all over it and the three sons (Daddy, Uncle Romer and Uncle Gerry) followed immediately behind, then his brothers and brothers-in-law fell in, and lastly the men on the premises. We followed half an hour later in three cars, and came upon a number of cottagers and farmers, from long distances up the valley and from the hills, who had wished to pay a tribute of respect to the best-loved man in the neighbourhood.

The service was simple and very beautiful. Then we followed our Dad to the grave-side and saw him lowered into his bed of moss and flowers. The sun streamed into the bower of sweet-scented flowers as he was laid to rest. God bless his spirit. The presence of so many relatives and friends has softened the blow for Muz. She is very brave and concerns herself about everything that goes on. Uncle Romer Williams and Uncle Gerry, the two irrepressibles of the family have even supplied an element of gaiety to the gathering afterwards.

Meanwhile Uncle Romer (Tich) has told me several very interesting facts. If you refer to General French's first report which I have kept for you in full, you will see that he curtly refers to General Sordet's refusal to send us much needed reinforcements when we were retreating from Mons and when the small English force was holding fast in spite of overwhelming numbers. General Sordet's horses 'were too tired to move before the morrow'.*

The war has taken a new development, for our naval airships have attacked Germany by air, dropping bombs on to the Zeppelin sheds at Düsseldorf from Antwerp, their base.

Better than all news comes a wire from Gertie Wykeham-Musgrave saying Kit is among the saved from the *Aboukir*. I have written to her at once, sitting down as soon as we came home from the Church.

SATURDAY SEPTEMBER 26

A wonderful account of the escape of dear little Kit Wykeham-Musgrave appears in today's paper.** The torpedoing of the *Hogue* and *Cressy* who went to the rescue of the *Aboukir*, has caused an order to be issued from the Admiralty. In future any ship struck by a torpedo or a mine must be left to its own resources just as though it were in action. In other words no big ships must go to the rescue, as it only risks much greater losses. Only small ships are allowed to go to rescue survivors.

Asquith announced yesterday in the House that the First Division of the Indian Army landed yesterday at Marseilles. Another German Colony, German New Guinea, has fallen into our hands. The Australian Expeditionary force under Admiral Sir George Patey, has occupied the town and harbour of Friedrich Wilhelm, the capital of Kaiser Wilhelmsland.†

SUNDAY SEPTEMBER 27

A German aeroplane has dropped bombs on Boulogne! But without doing damage.

Fritz Kreisler, the finest violinist now living (in my humble opinion)‡ has been wounded in the right arm while fighting in Galicia. He is a lieutenant in the Austrian Landsturm.

---

*   But there was truth in this. The French horses were exhausted by the unaccustomed and constant roadwork. Hew Strachan writes: 'In the opening month of the war, Sordet's cavalry had covered 1,000 kilometres and by August 10 the (cavalry) corps had already needed 15,000 new shoes.' *The First World War*, Vol. 1, *To Arms*, p. 260.

**   After sliding down the side of the sinking *Aboukir*, he swam over to *Hogue*, which was then torpedoed. Picked up by *Cressy*, he had to abandon ship again when she was torpedoed. He was rescued three hours later by a Dutch trawler. 'It was a perfect miracle how I was saved.' *(Letter from Kit Wykeham-Musgrave (aged 15) to his grandmother.)*

†   After a few days of only token opposition, Australian troops had captured German New Guinea and the Solomon Islands on 15 September.

‡   Also a brilliant composer. Fritz Kreisler (1875–1962) was a star in the firmament of violin playing all over the world through the romantic charm of his melodies. Today a prize is awarded each year in Vienna to the winner of the International Fritz Kreisler competition.

MONDAY SEPTEMBER 28

We see in the papers that two officers of the Buffs have been wounded. One is Major Finch-Hatton who came to shoot partridges at Horton several times, from Canterbury where the Buffs Depot is. I remember him well, a quiet, distinguished man, who complimented me, by the way, on the agility I displayed in getting over fences, ditches and other obstacles. Aunt Bobbie and I always walked with the guns, as your Grandfather loved having us with him.

The Germans are making great preparations now to capture Antwerp since the Belgian Army's frequent sorties have had most harassing results on the German communications. They cannot ignore Antwerp any longer.

Antwerp is so far the only Belgian town which has not suffered from the German presence, though the effects of war are everywhere visible, in the cutting down of avenues of trees; and the rich cornfields are bare of crops. Beautiful houses on the outskirts have been razed to the ground to give the gunners uninterrupted range, and do away with cover for the enemy.

The King and Queen of the Belgians are the leading spirits of the defence. The King is everywhere in the trenches. The Queen is always on some errand of mercy, visiting hospitals and providing for the necessities of the citizens.

TUESDAY SEPTEMBER 29

Today has been an exquisite summer's day and we have done one of the most beautiful excursions possible. We went in two cars, Muz, Aunt Nell, Gerry and Brenda, Daddy and I to Bedgellert, just under Snowdon. The country we went through is unsurpassable in beauty, and the lovely colouring of the autumn heather and golden bracken, with blue sky and fleecy clouds making purple shadows on the mountains made the scenery glorious.

If only I hadn't the prospect of having to part from you completely again in a week's time for another three weeks I should have enjoyed it enormously. But it's quite terrible to go off again and leave you behind. Your little ways fascinate and hold me so strongly that I see nothing but them when I am with you, and it is simply cruel to me to have to tear myself away. I can never again submit to this separation – never.

THURSDAY OCTOBER 1

The intrepid Mayor of Brussels, Monsieur Max, whose resourceful courage saved the city from destruction, has been marched off to a fortress in Germany. This must be an unbearable provocation to the Belgians who worship him for safeguarding their welfare as far as possible under the impossible conditions at present existing.

FRIDAY OCTOBER 2

A vivid account is given of the landing on September 26th of twenty troopships of Indian forces at Marseilles.*

A letter came from Uncle Guy today, a quite short one, saying he and his men were just going into action. So far all was well, 'It is difficult', he writes, 'to think of little Gelligemlyn amid the roar of the guns'. The letter was dated September 19th.

SATURDAY OCTOBER 3

Another letter from Guy today in which he says he has been 'knocked down by a shell' which killed an old woman close by and wounded a soldier at his side. He himself only felt the concussion. The loss of life on both sides is immense. As we all sit together reading the papers in the evening before dinner, every day there are exclamations of dismay from one or other of us at the sight of a known name, a friend or connection, among the list of casualties. Many of the young war brides, married before their men left for the front, are widows already. Yesterday we saw that a young Meiklejohn in the Camerons, married to the niece of Daddy's old friend, Fred Stewart, is killed. She is only eighteen.

Over and over again we, or the family, have had letters saying 'so far, our beloved Jack or Harry is safe', and next day we have seen his death reported in the papers. What the relatives of those reported 'Missing' must go through, God only knows. In so many cases, such as Colonel Gordon VC (Gordon Highlanders) for instance, men have been given out as killed and are only wounded, but have fallen into the hands of the enemy.

MONDAY OCTOBER 5

15 Neville Street
Our journey up to London was quite amusing. At Birmingham, a lad was being accompanied to his compartment next to ours by a very poor but nice-looking man, and four or five neatly dressed but poor women. He was a recruit. The boy looked so keen, and the family so devoted and full of concern, that I spoke to the old lady nearest to my window. Yes, she said, he was going off and she told me a long story as to how he had always wanted to be a soldier from childhood. I made Daddy pass him a little tip through the carriage window, and then the old lady came back and told me that the boy was 'temperance', and had had great difficulty in separating himself, on the way to the station, from fellow-recruits who were stopping at public-houses. Daddy laughed at me because I told the Father that we were all proud of the lads who went to serve their country and I held out my hand to shake his. He came up smiling, but confused, showing a hand very black from machinery, but I shook it in spite of his apologies, poor fellow.

---

*   'The force is composed of the flower of the Indian Army, with a certain proportion of troops drawn from the British garrison in India . . . Never before in history have Indian troops fought on the soil of Europe . . . Hour after hour fully a score of steamships discharged their cargoes and I am certain happier fighting men never landed in a country where death or glory was to be their goal.' *The Times*, 2 October 1914.

But the adventure of the day was when two French refugees, well to do middle class, got into our carriage at Leamington, chaperoned by an English lady. They were comfortable looking bourgeois, a provincial hotelier, and a very pretty daughter of nineteen. They began at once to chatter in French. As they were in trouble about a sheet of paper to write upon, I placed at their disposal my travelling writing case. Then the mother and I began talking and we talked for two hours. She came from Vitry-le-François, which was earlier in German hands. She was sent away from home to Paris by her husband a week before the Germans reached Vitry.

She told me a number of stories of German horrors which I cannot repeat, but they had happened in her neighbourhood. She had come over to England from Paris to fetch her daughter who had been staying here, but they are now returning to Paris to be nearer home as soon as the Husband writes that it is safe to return.

We were glad to get back to our dear little house, where we found everything in beautiful order, and a warm welcome from devoted Mrs Marsh. But the place seems so empty without you!

TUESDAY OCTOBER 6

London is a city of the French and Belgians by day and of darkness by night. Streets and buses and underground trains are full of chattering and laughing foreigners, smart young women and small children, who recount to each other their adventures. I listened to a group of young girls with an elderly man, on my way to Westminster this morning. One said 'Oh, as for me, I am now indifferent to everything. Each noise I hear I imagine is something exploding or blowing up.'

London is being made darker than ever from tonight onward by an Order in Council. In Onslow Square there is about one lamp left. All lamps in the streets have to be darkened at the top by shades, so as to be invisible from the sky. All shops have to reduce their lighting to a minimum. On the other hand powerful searchlights sweep above the city and precincts from all quarters, searching for airships. Every precaution is being taken against an aerial invasion of London by a fleet of Zeppelins and aeroplanes. As the days close in and nights get longer the chances of this are greatly increased.

I spent three hours this morning taking Mrs Marsh's daughter, who is married to a German, to various Funds to obtain relief. Her husband, an ex-waiter from the hotel Cecil, was placed in a camp at Newbury as a prisoner of war, leaving his wife and baby quite unprovided for. If the child can be put out somewhere, she can find work to keep the baby and herself. After trying at a number of offices and finding she was not eligible for any of these funds, we finally struck Sir Ernest Cassel's Society for giving relief to all aliens.* They have promised to send a visitor tomorrow to investigate the circumstances at her lodgings and she will be helped if they are satisfied.

---

*   Himself an 'alien', Sir Ernest Cassel (1852–1921) left Germany for England aged 16. He
made his fortune as a banker, much of which he devoted to good causes. He founded the
Cassel Hospital for psychological casualties of the war in 1921.

London Lights.

I was frightfully tired after trudging around, mounting so many flights of stairs and not coming home for lunch till 3 o'clock. But I was so pleased with the success of the morning in Finsbury Pavement that I soon forgot the fatigue! Also there was a great deal to excite one's interest and pity at the bureaux we went to. There were so many Germans in distress, men and women of all sorts waiting to be helped out of their necessities. One woman had a tiny baby.

WEDNESDAY OCTOBER 7

Nothing of interest to record. We went out to dine at the Albemarle Club with Aunt Nell Wason and Rigby, and found the streets very dark. The few lights left have the upper half of the glass globe painted black to make them invisible from the sky. Powerful flashes from the searchlights on the Arch at Hyde Park Corner were lighting the sky when we passed at 7 o'clock. But at 10 o'clock on leaving the Club, the moon being bright, the searchlights were not working. Through dinner Rigby told us of the narrow escape he had from being detained in Marienbad. He was only let off at the last moment through a very timely and generous subscription given by Rigby's Father to the Red Cross at Marienbad, which was being collected by the wife of the Commandant.

We talked much of the future, and of the impoverishment everybody will suffer for years as a result of the war. We shall all have to alter our mode of living; but one great boon to mankind will be the disappearance of the terrible amount of luxury and pleasure and frivolity which has been growing steadily for some years now. We shall return to more simple tastes and mode of living.

BOOK III

OCTOBER 9 – DECEMBER 10, 1914

FRIDAY OCTOBER 9

Today I saw marching through the streets two separate columns of recruits of Kitchener's New Army, such young-looking fellows, and many of small physique, conspicuously so. Daddy says they must have been the Territorial Section, as the Regulars are chosen from a higher standard of physique. They had no uniforms; many wore tweed Norfolk jackets and were well-dressed.

Thousands of refugees have left Antwerp and are flooding England. They are coming to Folkestone, where pitiable scenes are witnessed as the boats come in. The people are mostly women, many with tiny infants as well as the aged and infirm. A very large house just round the corner from here, 78 Onslow Gardens, flying the English and Belgian flags, was being rapidly prepared yesterday for the arrival of a good many from Antwerp. I saw nurses with Red Cross badges putting up curtains. I went in to see if there were any small things they needed which I could provide. As they required at once two more camp beds for that evening, I couldn't give them those, so I came away.

London is full of French and Belgians. They seem to do a good deal of shopping, as one hears French all around in the shops.

SATURDAY OCTOBER 10

Daddy and I and Aunt Nell Wason travelled to Blair Atholl, a long day's journey, but we were so busy reading the papers that it was not tedious. The news is terrible today.

Antwerp has fallen! It has succumbed to the bombardment of 200 big guns, and the result of the shelling is awful. The Belgian Army evacuated the town yesterday.

The Commandant of Antwerp, General de Guise, sent out a proclamation two days before Antwerp fell, warning everybody to leave the town. Thousands and thousands of men, women and children have fled by all roads towards Holland, and the steamers in the docks rapidly filled with refugees for England. Four boats with a thousand refugees on each, landed at Folkestone yesterday alone.

One of these fugitives describes the terrible panic that spread among the inhabitants when watchers sped through the streets at dead of night, ringing bells, and calling upon the people to get up and leave the town.

As First Lord of the Admiralty, Churchill had set up the Royal Naval Division in August. But this force was insufficient. Many of the 8,000 men in the division, among whom was the

*poet Rupert Brooke, who were sent out on 4 October to stem the German advance on
Antwerp, were recent volunteers, untrained in the use of either firearms or trenching
equipment. Also the regular British division of 22,000 men which had crossed to Ostend
would not move forward without French support, but the French had stopped at Ghent.
After two days of heavy bombardment of the city by 17in Austrian howitzers and with
Belgian troops on the run, Antwerp could hold out no longer and capitulated on 10 October.
At home, it was felt that the fall of Antwerp brought the German Army that much closer to
British shores and raised the spectre of a German invasion. In the extract which follows,
Georgina Lee reflects the widespread alarm and apprehension in England at this time and
reports the new measures taken by the Government under DORA (the Defence of the Realm
Act).*

The fall of Antwerp makes a raid to England much more possible. This is now openly
discussed in the papers. The German press declares that *war with England will be waged
at the end of October*. This means the invasion by air of a fleet of Zeppelins, in
conjunction with the submarine attack.

That the Government views this possibility quite seriously is shown in a variety of
ways. Notably in these far more stringent regulations concerning the lights of London.
The words *such lighting represents under certain circumstances a source of danger*, are
ominous.

THE LIGHTS OF LONDON
OFFICIAL WARNING

*Under Section 7a Defence of the Realm Act, it is deemed advisable to call public
attention to the following points:*

*All external private lighting not needed to secure the safety of traffic should be
discontinued.*

*Some business and other establishments are still maintaining interior lighting
which is of too great intensity and illuminates the road way.*

*The Commissioner of Police is advised that such lighting represents, under
certain circumstances, a source of danger to the particular neighbourhood and to
the community at large.*

*The police have been given directions to take the action necessary to ensure that
the orders restricting lighting are carried out both in letter and spirit.*

E.R. HENRY,
Commissioner of Police of the Metropolis, New Scotland Yard,
Oct. 9, 1914.

SUNDAY OCTOBER 11

The news is gloomy. The fall of Antwerp is a catastrophe, although the papers make the best of it and say it was expected. It is not, I suppose, as bad as the fall of Paris, but Antwerp gives them such a strong position.

2000 of our men belonging to Marine and Naval Brigades out of the 8000 we had sent to Antwerp had to lay down their arms by crossing the frontier into Holland in the retreat from Antwerp.* We had lent 3 brigades of Marines in answer to an appeal from Antwerp, to help the Belgians. For two days they kept the Germans off, but at last the Belgians gave way on our right and retreated before overwhelming numbers.

It is said that not very much damage has been done to the beautiful old buildings in Antwerp. The Antwerp authorities had given a map of the city to the German General von Beseler, begging him to spare the historic monuments, which they did. They have however posted a proclamation threatening the citizens with the destruction of the city, if they show any hostility.

I am thankful that Antwerp Cathedral has not suffered much. I have twice stayed in Antwerp, once for a week with Father, then with Aunt Ethel. There is something so impressive and 'seizing' to one's emotions in its exterior, that I never could stand before it without the tears coming in my eyes. The painting of the *Descent of the Cross* by Rubens in the Cathedral completed the impression.

TUESDAY OCTOBER 13

Blair Atholl
There is nothing special to record. We spent a very quiet peaceful day, driving with the old ponies this morning, and motoring to Girvan in the afternoon. We miss terribly our London papers, neither *Times* nor *Morning Post* have come and it's so difficult to gauge the importance of the events we read of in the local papers. One chafes at the inactivity one is forced into here. The one thing that soothed me this morning was the news that your first double-tooth, cut three or four days ago, doesn't worry you in the least.

WEDNESDAY OCTOBER 14

Still no London paper. Are the newsagents in league? Ours in Sussex Place is a naturalised German and I don't trust him!

After breakfast, waiting for the post to come in at 10.30, we amused ourselves, pinning a Union Jack over the portrait of Bismarck which, burnt into the wood in 'poker work', adorns the oak overmantel in the dining room, together with Mr Gladstone, Longfellow and Tennyson.

---

*   1,600 of these men were interned in neutral Holland under Dutch surveillance until the end of the war. During the siege of Antwerp fifty-seven had been killed.

THE GHOST OF BISMARCK : *Yes, Sire, there's plenty of "Blood and Iron"— but where are the Brains?*

A Ghostly Counsel.

The news in the *Glasgow Herald* is not very cheery, except that a meeting in London was held between Kitchener, Winston Churchill, Lloyd George and other ministers yesterday. This means no doubt important measures are being taken in view of the new developments taking place just across the Channel.

The Germans are making furious efforts to establish themselves along the coast from Antwerp to Calais. Ostend is in imminent danger. The Belgian Government, together with the British and French Ministers to the Belgian Government have left Ostend to take up their residence at Le Havre!

THURSDAY OCTOBER 15

Ostend is in German hands, so they have practically the whole of Belgium in their possession. 300,000 Belgians are already in Holland and 150,000 in England. Here, they are being sent in batches of a thousand or more to large towns such as Glasgow.

I met today three sweet and pretty Belgian girls; two of about twenty years age with a dear little sister of eleven. They are daughters of a doctor in Antwerp who remained at his post all through the bombardment. I spoke to them for about an hour, and they were delighted to find somebody to speak French with, as it was like being at home again. The only news the poor children had had of their parents ever since the fall of Antwerp, was a telegram from Rosendaal, saying they were safe across the border.

The little girl, who had large velvety eyes with long dark lashes and a very merry way with her, gave me her account of the Zeppelins' visit to Antwerp when they were in bed one night. She said the noise of the engines was like a hurricane sweeping over their heads and rattling iron. When the bombs began to crash, their father ordered them all down to the cellar.

These Belgians are filled with gratitude for the kindness they are meeting with every-where, and especially from their Scottish friends who have taken the six of them in, for an indefinite period. This is only one instance of what is going on all over England.

FRIDAY OCTOBER 16

The Times discusses the probability of an invasion of our shores by a force of Germans. It comments on the necessity of an able Commander to take the command of defensive operations, as Lord Kitchener will have enough to do at the War Office. The German Fleet is intact, and is expected to emerge and engage our Fleet, while an Expeditionary Force starts from somewhere else, perhaps Antwerp, and slips through. It sounds impossible. But preparations are being made for all eventualities.

Owing to the darkness of the London streets at night and the reluctance of people to be out, the theatres are altering the hours of their performance. These now occur every afternoon instead of evening, and the 'matinées' on Wednesdays and Saturdays now take place in the evening. Notices also appear in the papers from the managers of theatres enjoining ladies to 'Bring your Knitting'!

People knit everywhere, dining out at night etc. We here, Aunt Nell, Granny, Aunt Brenda and I, never go into a meal without our knitting. My knitting, I must confess, has lately been for you, my son, soft Shetland vests. But once these are done, I shall revert to the work for the poor children of soldiers and sailors. In France and Germany the knitting mania is the same, we hear. Socks, body belts and comforters.

SATURDAY OCTOBER 17

Another of our cruisers, HMS *Hawke*, has been sunk by a torpedo in the North Sea. 73 survivors out of 540 men were landed at Aberdeen. The Germans are clearly trying to carry out their policy of reducing our fleet by these tactics but the Admiralty announced today the completion of five new battleships. Although the Germans are building ships now at Kiel, we can build twice as fast as they can in time of peace. Now, hampered as they must be by the shortage of materials thanks to the blockading of our Fleet, their rate of progress will be still slower.

Letter from Uncle Guy this morning, from the northern bank of River Aisne. He says the men are undergoing a frightful strain, but they are wonderfully cheery. Some of his men's trenches are only 180 yards from German trenches, and they shout out to the enemy such things as 'Come out and fight, you sausages', while the Germans reply 'We have thousands of English prisoners behind us'!

These witticisms generally end in a fierce fusillade. When he wrote, the men had been in the trenches for five days. The wounded and dead could only be removed at night, for the moment a head moved above the trench it was immediately blazed at. As he wrote, on his knees, the shells were whizzing incessantly over his head. Two French ladies working with the wounded in a cottage close by had been blown to bits by a shell the day before.

To my intense shock, I see in the evening paper that the Captain of the *Hawke* was a very old friend, we knew in our girlhood, my sisters and I. Tudor Williams the son of our neighbours near Rhayader, was a great admirer of Ethel. He was a brilliant officer. I am writing to his poor mother.

WILLIAMS – CAPTAIN H.P.E. TUDOR WILLIAMS. Royal Navy, HMS *Hawke*, only son of Colonel and Mrs Williams, of Rhayader, Radnorshire and dearly-loved husband of Phyllis Williams. 'Greater love hath no man than this: that a man lay down his life for his friends.'

SUNDAY OCTOBER 18

Thank God! there is something today to avenge the loss of the *Hawke*. Four German destroyers have been sunk in a brilliant engagement off the coast of Holland. Capt. Fox, who was Captain of the *Amphion* when she was sunk by a mine at beginning of the war, led the expedition in the new cruiser *Undaunted*.

The week ends on a far happier note than last week, when the fall of Antwerp filled our minds with bitterness. Then came the removal of the Belgian Government to Havre, and the German occupation of Ghent, Bruges and Ostend. But no further.

TUESDAY OCTOBER 20

The stream of Belgian refugees is still continuing. German spies are seizing this opportunity to get into the country. Forty spies were captured landing among the Belgians. So the Government have prohibited the housing of any refugees on the East Coast, whence they could transmit signals to the enemy.

Martha Ciselet, the pretty little Belgian, came to lunch today with Miss Ingles whose parents have taken the six young brothers and sisters in from Antwerp. I am hoping to get this one a home for the winter with the Barnebys.

THURSDAY OCTOBER 22

The German Cruiser *Emden* which has been at large ever since the war, doing much damage in the Indian Ocean, including the shelling of Madras where she destroyed the oil tanks, has sunk five more British steamers, three of them being liners. The *Emden* transferred the crews and passengers to the steamer *Egbert* and sent them to the nearest port, Cochin near Madras. So far the *Emden* has eluded the British cruisers sent to capture her. Altogether she has sunk or captured 15 merchantmen and liners in less than three months.

Sensational discoveries have been made with regard to espionage. The most glaring followed the police raid on a firm of German music publishers, Röder, at Willesden. The floor of a warehouse was solid concrete six feet thick with an armoured roof, to take guns. The position commands the Crystal Palace.

FRIDAY OCTOBER 23

The Germans are making a desperate dash for Calais. The battle which is going on now is the most critical and important of the war so far.* The German Press states: 'the whole fate of the campaign in France depends upon our reaching Calais. It is a matter of life and death to us.'

SATURDAY OCTOBER 24

Travelled back to London from Blair, leaving at 8.30 and arriving St Pancras 8.15.

The battle on the Belgian coast gets more and more critical. The Germans have brought up huge numbers of reinforcements to try and push through, but with no success so far. These reinforcements consist of young men and old men, raw soldiers or those past the age. It looks ominous.

On our way from St Pancras, the streets were so dark our taxi had to go very slowly, especially down Shaftesbury Avenue and Piccadilly. The effect was like a heavy overhead fog, the upper half of the few lamps being painted black.

SUNDAY OCTOBER 25

Uncle Gerry came this morning to tell us of his experiences as an able-bodied seaman! He has enlisted for service with one of the naval gun posts on the roofs of Public Buildings. His post is on the Crown Agents' Office in Whitehall. They are all gentlemen on his post, twenty four of them. He has to wear a dark blue uniform, like a yachting suit, and spends six hours at a time, wet or fine, on the roof, drilling and learning to handle the gun.

Every now and then they are rung up by the Admiralty and told that an airship (friendly) is coming down from such and such a direction, and they are to train their guns on it. The searchlights are then turned on in that direction, and as soon as it is 'sighted' the manoeuvre of aiming at it is gone through.

---

* This was the start of the First Battle of Ypres. Had Ypres fallen, the route to Calais and the other Channel Ports would have been wide open, putting the main supply lines of the British Expeditionary Force at risk. Ypres did not fall and the Anglo-French line held, but the four weeks of intense fighting cost the British Army 8,000 dead and 40,000 wounded.

Daddy is considering the best work for him to take up for the nation's service. He is tied up at Westminster from 10 till 6, but he can give a few hours out of the twenty-four. He may apply for a billet on the searchlights staff.

MONDAY OCTOBER 26

In tonight's paper there is the first mention of our Indian troops. The Sikhs and Gurkhas charged the enemy and are reported to have caused widespread casualties.

The streets are full of soldiers. We see a good many wounded, convalescing and being driven in cars for an airing, or taken for a walk in the Park. London is very full, but it is hard to believe that so few miles away this terrible fighting is going on now, now, now at this moment.

TUESDAY OCTOBER 27

Aunt Ethel and I went to Mrs Armour's huge house in Harley Street to work for Uncle Henry's West London Hospital. They have fortnightly afternoon sessions. We sewed hard at shirts or one shirt between us, Aunt Ethel and I, and chatted to the other ladies, but I hurried home soon after five.

Today I had a startling letter from Nurse Mayer who is looking after your dear Grandpapa at Glaslyn, saying that there had been a fire in his bedroom which might have burnt the whole house down. He was dozing upstairs in his armchair in the evening; the lamp (a heavy reading lamp) had just been placed on the mantelpiece. Nurse was putting coals on the fire, when suddenly the marble chimney piece fell forward, the big mirror above was dragged down too, the lamp broke and flames shot up just by Grandpa's armchair.

Nurse flung a rug on the top and dragged Grandpa away downstairs into the garden. She then flew back, but found the flames had made such progress that she couldn't cope. She shouted for Rose and fortunately Hughes was in the garden. He could not enter by the door, but he got in by a ladder through the window and by dint of water buckets being passed through he got the fire out in one and half hours.

Poor old Grandpapa was calm and so far is none the worse for the shock, but it was a narrow squeak! We have all dreaded an outbreak of fire with those lamps which are carried about,* though Grandpa made a rule that no lamp should be carried by any woman in the house and the maids were under pain of dismissal. But as he went on carrying them himself until quite lately, Uncle Henry made a rule that he must henceforth leave them alone.

WEDNESDAY OCTOBER 28

Your first birthday, my precious one. You have had so many presents, you spoilt little boy, a guinea from Auntie Minna, five shillings from Grand-Aunt Louisa and all sorts

---

*   Probably paraffin oil lamps. It is unlikely that electric lighting would have reached this rural part of Wales by 1914.

of woolly dogs and a squeaking elephant. And today for the first time I have refused on
principle to give you things you asked for, so that you should realise that you cannot
have everything you want!

There are signs today of a weakening of the German attack on Ypres. They have lost
heavily without making any progress. The casualties among our men are very high.
Many sons of the highest families are killed and today it is announced that Prince
Maurice of Battenberg, our Princess Beatrice's son, is among the killed.*

THURSDAY OCTOBER 29

Aunt Ethel and I have just come back from Aldershot where we spent the day with
your Uncle Arthur and Aunt Audrey. He is now a major in the 10th Gordon
Highlanders, and is doing grand work in drilling the recruits into an effective force.
They are doing splendidly.

We had a very interesting day. From the train, we saw, passing through Brookwood,
sappers of Kitchener's New Army building a bridge and making a road.

Audrey met us at Aldershot Station in the car. The house is a big one and stands in a
park, Aldershot Manor. We drove later on to the camp to fetch Arthur home for lunch.
It was an extraordinary sight. The whole of Aldershot, those straggling miles of
dwellings, barracks and military buildings, is devoted to the training of Kitchener's
million men. Companies of these were seen in every direction for miles and miles over
the beautiful undulating country, among the bracken and heather slopes, or the
downtrodden, hard-stamped soil, bare of even a blade of grass.

Along the horizon, as far as one could see, were columns of men drilling and
manoeuvring. Men in all sorts of clothing; dark blue serge uniforms, the old scarlet
uniform and some in khaki. A large percentage of recruits were so small and looked like
boys. It was bitterly cold. The wind swept over the bleak unprotected open spaces
where the tents were pitched, and in spite of heavy motor-coats, we were all blue with
cold. The men must suffer intensely at night.

Even more interesting to us was the great camp for German prisoners, about ten
miles beyond Frimley. There must have been thousands of these in the rows and rows of
tents pegged down close together behind the wire entanglements. Outside the railings
were raised platforms with watch towers for the sentries who are there with fixed
bayonets and loaded rifles. The wire entanglements have a strong electric current
passing through them and this is turned on at night.

Several prisoners have been found glued to the wire, dead, in the morning, after a
fruitless attempt to escape. The German soldiers are resigned enough. They look very
unkempt and their queer-toned khaki, a blue grey different to anything else, looks dirty.
They were great strong-looking men and the cavalrymen we got nearest to were fine
fellows. We saw some of the famous Prussian helmets, with the spike covered in khaki

---

*   Princess Beatrice (1857–1944) was the youngest daughter of Queen Victoria and Prince
      Albert.

to hide the glint of it. One is not allowed near enough to speak to them and the spies enclosure is even more closely guarded.

The spy section gives the sentries a great deal of trouble. The guard shook his head doubtfully as he told us that they were 'brewing mischief' even there. He kept one eye on his charges all the time and said he'd be thankful to be quit of them! Some of them looked perfect devils, but they were unwashed and unkempt. They are the German waiters and civilians who were interned on suspicion.

There was a great clamour going on and the men were all crowded together in huge clusters. But when we asked two English soldiers the meaning of the shouts or booing, one said the prisoners were receiving rations and the other said the spies were up to some mischief! The soldier prisoners give no cause for anxiety.

There was a roll-call going on in the spy section, a hoarse-throated individual was shouting out in guttural tones teutonic names such as Ernst Schmidt, Karl Bauer, etc. I saw among the cluster two men having a fight – at least, one was showering blows on another.

We got home late for dinner but after a very enjoyable day.

FRIDAY OCTOBER 30

Prince Louis of Battenberg, First Sea Lord, has resigned, as a result of the campaign against him because of his German birth. Public opinion was dead against the First Sea Lord being of German origin and the Government has accepted his resignation.* Lord Fisher, the founder of the Dreadnought and maker of our present great battle Navy takes his place. He is looked upon by the public much as Kitchener is in his own sphere.

SATURDAY OCTOBER 31

There has been a disaster to a hospital ship *Rohilla*, which went on to the rocks near Whitby while on her way from Leith to Dunkirk, to evacuate wounded. She had a large staff of doctors and nurses on board. Lifeboats rescued 146 from the wreck, including Capt. Neilson and all the nurses, but 83 have perished.

War with Turkey may yet be averted for the impression seems to be that she was forced into the shelling of Odessa by the Germans.

The King's sons were in the Park two days ago and stopped to have few words with you.

---

*   In fact, Prince Louis had been born in Graz, Austria. He had served in the Royal Navy for forty-six years and had taken on British nationality in 1861. But this was not enough to save him from the current wave of anti-alien hysteria. Malcolm Brown writes: 'At a time when allegedly some patriots thought kicking a dachshund in the street a major step towards the winning of the war, he clearly had no chance.' *The Men who went to War*, p. 111.

TU L'AS VOULU, DINDON!

THE TEMPTER: *Come along and be an Eagle, and help me fight the Lion and the Bear!*

The Kaiser Tempts Turkey to join the War.

SUNDAY NOVEMBER 1

A lovely bright day.

Thanks to the flooding of the Yser Valley caused by the Belgians opening the dykes, the Germans have had to retreat back behind the Yser. When the Belgians turned on the water from the sluices, the Germans were done for. It is extraordinary that the Germans risked this inundation, for every military map shows that the country is below high-water level. The German trenches were so placed that when the sluices were open they were in 6ft of water. The floods have ruined miles and miles of valuable cultivated beet-land (sugar) which had been reclaimed after generations of toil and labour. Thus the Germans have failed so far in their attacks on Paris, Warsaw and Calais.

On the other hand one of our aircraft-carriers, the *Hermes*, which was carrying sea planes has been torpedoed. It happened in the Dover Straits as she was returning from Dunkirk, but nearly all the officers and men were saved.

Although the prospects seem good, the fighting is of a terribly fierce character and the casualty lists are appalling. The young brother of my friend Verena Barneby, a 2nd Lieutenant in 10th Hussars, has been killed. She and Theo came up to London three weeks ago to see him off to the Front.

MONDAY NOVEMBER 2

Sybyl Lee, Daddy's first cousin, has wired him for a special licence. She is to be married tomorrow morning at Grimsby, the port which he will put into for a few hours from the North Sea. He is on a submarine and was recalled to his ship two days before the day fixed for wedding at the beginning of war. She came up from Bury St Edmunds to see Daddy, and the wedding takes place in the early morning.

The Germans have a pitying contempt for the Belgians, an ordinary enmity for French and Russians, but their fury with us for spoiling their game, for *bringing about this bloody war*, as they put it, finds vent in proclamations such as that below.

"ANNIHILATE THE ENGLISH."
ANOTHER ROYAL GERMAN ORDER.
BAVARIAN CROWN PRINCE'S COMMAND.

We reproduce herewith from the "Frankfurter Zeitung" of Thursday, Oct. 29, the "Army Order of the Day against the English," issued by the Crown Prince Rupprecht of Bavaria. The news is communicated to the "Frankfurter Zeitung" (and to other German papers of the same date) in a telegram from Munich, where the Army Order was published in the "München‑Augsburger Abendzeitung," a newspaper which enjoys semi‑official connections with the Bavarian Government.

**Ein Tagesbefehl
des Bayerischen Kronprinzen.**

W München, 28. Oktbr. (Priv-Tel.) Die „München‑Augsburger Abendzeitung" veröffentlicht folgenden Armee‑befehl, den Kronprinz Rupprecht von Bayern als Kommandierender der 6. deutschen Armee an seine Sol‑daten gerichtet hat:

„Soldaten der 6. Armee! Wir haben nun das Glück, auch die Engländer vor unserer Front zu haben, die Truppen jenes Volkes, dessen Neid seit Jahren an der Arbeit war, uns mit einem Ring von Feinden zu umgeben, um uns zu er‑drosseln. Ihm haben wir diesen blutigen, ungeheuren Krieg zu verdanken. Darum, wenn es jetzt gegen diesen Feind geht, übet Bergeltung gegen die feindliche Hinterlist für so viele schwere Opfer. Zeigt ihnen, daß die Deutschen nicht so leicht aus der Weltgeschichte zu streichen sind. Zeigt ihnen das durch deutsche Hiebe von ganz besonderer Art. Hier ist der Gegner, der der Wiederherstellung des Friedens am meisten im Wege steht. Drauf!"   Rupprecht.

"Soldiers of the Sixth Army:
"We have now the good fortune to have the Englishmen on our front, the troops of that country whose envy for years has been at work encircling us with a ring of foes, in order to throttle us. It is that country which we have, above all else, to thank for this gigantic, bloody war! Therefore, when we have to do with this foe, TAKE REVENGE AGAINST HIS HOSTILE IN‑TRIGUING FOR THE MANY HEAVY SACRIFICES WE HAVE TO MAKE. Show him that the Germans are not so easily to be erased from the world's history! Show him this by inflicting German blows of a very special sort! Here is the enemy which chiefly blocks the way in the direction of restoration of peace!
" *At him!*
"RUPPRECHT."

Annihilate the English – *Frankfurter Zeitung*

The Turkish Ambassador in London was today handed his passports. He went to the Foreign Office and paid a long farewell visit to Sir Edward Grey. He seemed downcast on leaving. He had done his utmost to preserve peace. In Constantinople, the peace party viewed the shelling of Odessa by so-called Turkish ships (the *Breslau* and the *Goeben*) with consternation. They look upon the event as a catastrophe to the Ottoman Empire.

Florence Younghusband dined here tonight and told us about her son Frank who has been in action off Nieuport. His ship, the *Viking* accompanied first the three monitors, then the *Venerable*, on their recent exploits. For the first few days of the war Frank had the best fun of his life. Though only 20 he was doing First Lieutenant's work and had to go on board to seize many of the prizes of war. For days the German merchant ships, not fitted with wireless, knew nothing of the declaration of war. They steamed on cheerfully, flag flying, towards the ports where they were challenged by the little destroyers who were zig zagging over the seas. Frank always boarded the ships himself and had infinite delight in hauling down the Kaiser's flag and hoisting the King's.

TUESDAY NOVEMBER 3

Tonight I am less optimistic about the war. Not that I have any doubts as to the ultimate issue. But I have an idea that we shall see some disasters before it is over – I mean, disastrous days. The German people too, are just as confident as we Britishers, that the war will end advantageously to them. So we have dreadful things before us with such an unscrupulous foe. For instance the blowing up of our merchant ships means that somehow the Germans have sown mines around the coasts of Ireland and the North Atlantic route.

The Admiralty have met this by declaring the Channel and the whole of the North Sea a military area. So ships trading with Norway, Sweden, Denmark and Holland are advised to come up Channel and avoid going round the Hebrides and north of Scotland. The Admiralty guarantees safety to all vessels strictly adhering to the routes given. They warn them that any straying even for a few miles from the course indicated may suffer fatal consequences.

The main trade route between America and Liverpool has been indiscriminately mined by these wretched Germans. They don't care whether they blow up an American liner with passengers or not. The *Olympic* narrowly escaped disaster.

WEDNESDAY NOVEMBER 4

The police came to Daddy's office in the Sanctuary tonight requesting that all the blinds should be drawn down at nightfall because of its proximity to Westminster Abbey. All windows must be in darkness.

News comes of the magnificent fighting our British Army has put up lately. The terrible nature of it sickens one. It seems so hopeless for our small numbers to withstand for ever the onslaught of those hordes of Huns. Nor is the recruiting going now half so fast as it should, the men do not realise the situation. We haven't enough men to give ours a rest.

Uncle Guy writes, in a manner which makes one realise the absolute exhaustion they are all in. The lack of sleep, he says, is torture. If only he could have a few hours sleep! He had lain down on some straw with his General, he writes, a few nights ago, hoping for a rest, but half an hour later they were heavily shelled.

May Barneby, who came to tea, told me her cousin, Major Slater-Booth, now home, wounded, said that the most horrible thing he had been through was when our guns had to be dragged over our own wounded.

The casualty lists are terrible. In today's there are two pairs of brothers killed. This battle for Calais* has been most bloody; it has lasted twenty days already. It becomes more and more clear that legislation must be made to compel men to serve, if only during this war. Our Army will be extinct if it is not reinforced. Press censorship and current methods of recruiting are blamed for the shortfall. Now that the first million men have joined up, the next half-million is dribbling in too slowly. Much more should be published about the real state of affairs. Recruiting should be carried on more picturesquely, with musical displays etc, so as to appeal to our stolid fellows.

This morning I took you to the Park in your pram with Nannie to see the parade and departure of the Sportsmen's Battalion for their camp, preparatory to going abroad. This splendid corps is composed of athletes and sporting men up to the age of forty five, who can shoot, ride and do other sport. They were such handsome big fellows, there are gentlemen and non-gentlemen, trainers and jockeys too. There was a big band to accompany them on their march to Liverpool Street Station.

When the band struck up, as they left the Parade Ground, you got very excited, my pet, and waved your little gloved hands. Your pram was very soon left behind in the crowd, for your Mummy started marching alongside the battalion. Granny came too, and she and I accompanied the men from the Knightsbridge Barracks Parade to Hyde Park Corner, Mummy's eyes streaming all the way.

I can't see a column of men marching through the streets without feeling emotion. Especially impressive were the new recruits battalions, marching in their plain clothes, Norfolk jerseys, tweeds or dark serges. Each one different to the next, but all animated with the same fine spirit. I always feel a lump in my throat.

THURSDAY NOVEMBER 5

Tonight Daddy came home late, 7.30, and told me he had enlisted in the Veterans section of his old Corps, the Inns of Court. The active Corps composed of the young members, is in camp in the country and many have been given commissions in Kitchener's Army. The Veterans Corps is composed of former members who are now too old to enlist in the Regular Army. But if, as seems probable, every fighting man will have to go to Belgium, then the defence of our country will fall upon those who are training now to fit themselves for defence, i.e. nearly everybody.

*   Now known as the First Battle of Ypres. It raged from 19 October to 22 November.

Daddy was very efficient as a volunteer before. He passed as a first-class marksman with a rifle. I am so glad this Corps is being resuscitated and that Daddy has got into it once more. He has been so eager to do something to help the country, yet his time is so taken up at Westminster, he can't give up the whole of his day. He really is the most hardworking partner in the firm.

FRIDAY NOVEMBER 6

Daddy and I have just come home from Pelham Street where we went after dinner to see your Uncle Romer. He is up for the night from Bury St Edmunds on his way for a weekend with his wife and children. He told us that an important raid is expected on the East Coast very soon. Kitchener expects it, and is going down there on Monday. Uncle Romer explained that the invading force would have a bad time of it before it could get inland from the shore.

He was chuckling with delight at the prospect, and so he and his fellows are eagerly looking out for the raid; they will be dreadfully disappointed if nothing happens. He thinks that good regular troops are much needed in England, in spite of the prevailing opinion that every good fighting man should be sent to Belgium or France.

SATURDAY NOVEMBER 7

This morning it was announced that Tsingtao has fallen. Tonight we learn that the forts, after eleven weeks' siege by the Japanese, were finally carried by a bayonet charge by the Japanese and some British. This success is all the more fortunate just now as it frees the Japanese Fleet to join us in hunting down the few remaining German fast cruisers which are doing such damage. The *Emden* has not been heard of for some days.

Our British troops have been locked in terrific fighting for the last few days, but in spite of the fierceness of the German attack they have by sheer doggedness held on to Ypres. This is the town which the Kaiser has said must at all costs be taken by the end of October.*

SUNDAY NOVEMBER 8

The first thing I saw this morning was a poster announcing *British Raid in the Persian Gulf*. My heart flew to my mouth, for the whole family has been very anxious on cousin Cathcart Wason's behalf. The reason for our nervousness was the fact that Cathcart was given such an antiquated tub for this job in the Persian Gulf before war broke out. It was said he would not dare fire his guns on the *Odin*** for fear of sinking himself.

But to our delight, we found that the *Odin* has been playing a prominent part in the outbreak of war against the Turks. So we ran into the telegraph office and sent a wire of

---

*   Ypres was not yielded to the Germans. By the end of the war, the defence of the Ypres Salient had cost the lives of more than 200,000 British and Imperial troops.
**   The *Odin*, launched in Copenhagen in 1872, was 42 years old, hence his apprehension.

congratulation to Cathcart's wife, who is now at Aberdeen. Our wire will probably be her first intimation, poor dear. She is so plucky and I am very fond of her.

After this we went and lunched with the Barnebys at 34 Wilton Crescent. Theo was up for 24 hours, off duty, but had to return to his Yeomanry at Shrewsbury. Poor Verena, looking so pretty in her mourning, told me of her brother's death, young Turnor. He had only been out a fortnight at the Front and the 18th Hussars had had a very hard day, dismounted, in the trenches. But towards dusk, the German shells which had come over incessantly, ceased.

Rashly, Turnor and his neighbour Sir Frank Rose both put their heads above the trench and instantly both were hit. The Germans have snipers to catch the unwary after the shelling has ceased. The two young fellows were buried together in a little church yard. The place where they lie was marked, so that Verena can go there one day. It was near Ypres.

MONDAY NOVEMBER 9

Glaslyn

10 pm – Hughes has just been telling me about the fire which all but burnt Glaslyn to the ground a fortnight ago. He cannot speak of it, and his old Master's wandering in the rain round the house outside, with the smoke and flames pouring from his bedroom window, without tears in his eyes. When your poor old Grandfather had been rushed out by the nurse, he tried to come in again and met Hughes stumbling downstairs who cried out 'It's all up, sir, there's no chance!'

After a while Hughes was able to get into the room, and fling out of the window the burning rugs and clothes. The sofa was on fire underneath, but he managed to turn it upside down and poured water over it. Twice he thought he was suffocating and staggered to the window for breath, but still he held on, till the burning mattresses, sofa, armchair, blankets etc. had been extinguished. Hughes and his wife are perfect heroes.

I found Father very altered. The shock of the fire has upset him considerably. Tonight he told me he was always dreaming about it and going back on the horror of what might have occurred.

TUESDAY NOVEMBER 10

I have been busy all day going into the fire business, interviewing the valuer and the builder. I was able to make a very satisfactory claim for compensation for Henry who was too busy to come from London. The builder starts repairs, re-painting and papering on Monday. I shall have to see to new curtains, covering of ottoman etc.

Last night poor Father had a bad night. At 3 o'clock his bell went and I jumped out of my sleep to go in next door. He wanted me just to sit by him and talk of anything that came into my head. I told Nurse to go back to bed, wrapped myself in the eiderdown and stroked his hand. After awhile he excused himself for not talking and dozed off. All he wanted was not to be left alone, the state of his heart makes him feel apprehensive.

How terrible it is that man must go through this failing of everything during old age. Why should his last years be made miserable through discomfort and disease?

Lord Kitchener in his Guildhall speech yesterday, testified to the magnificent work of our Army, but asked for another 350,000 men immediately.

WEDNESDAY NOVEMBER 11

The *Emden* has been destroyed at last! After eluding British, French, Russian and Japanese warships, she was at last tracked down to the Cocos Islands by the Australian cruiser HMAS *Sydney* and forced to fight. Out of her 326 men she lost 115 killed and 56 wounded, the rest including her gallant Captain Karl von Müller and a young nephew of the Kaiser, Prince Josef von Hohenzollern, were taken prisoner.

The Captain however was given back his sword for the chivalry he has shown all through his glorious but short career. He had sunk a Russian Cruiser, a French Destroyer and 15 merchantmen, but all his prisoners have testified to his kindness and consideration to them.

Here at Glaslyn I have had a busy day putting things in order, and repairing damage done by the fire. I have not been out at all.

THURSDAY NOVEMBER 12

The Germans have made progress on the road to Calais, thanks to enormous reinforcements. They have taken Dixmude which brings them within 42 miles of Calais.

FRIDAY NOVEMBER 13

The Germans have not got beyond Dixmude. Our troops have repelled the enemy in their fiercest attacks, in particular they have driven back the famous Prussian Guard.

An American who has been at Hamburg and visited Kiel, tells of the great liners and transport ships he has seen in those ports already filled with soldiers ready for the invasion of England. But one of the Officers to whom he spoke said: *We should be such fools to attempt the raid now. The weather is too unsettled for the Zeppelins to accompany the Expedition. It will be for the Spring.*

I went to Llandrindod today with Mrs Clark in her car to see about the repairing of an armchair damaged by the fire. Father has been very feeble these two days. We could hardly prevail upon him to get up today. His mind seems confused. He rang his bell several times in the night without needing anything. He was not conscious of where he was or what was happening. It is pitiful.

SATURDAY NOVEMBER 14

I have no time to write tonight for I am 'on duty' with Father. He had a bad night yesterday with delusions and nightmares. He woke up in a terror imagining his nurse had stood by staring at him, suddenly gone mad. He would not let her come into his

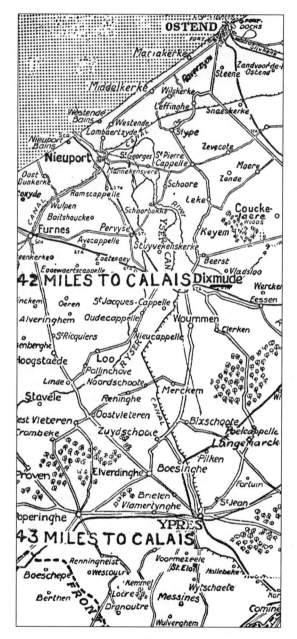

Three Routes to Calais.

room. I had to send for Hughes and nothing else would pacify him. All today I had to keep nurse out of his sight. She was to go away at once. Since then poor nurse has been crying all day at her sudden and undeserved dismissal. She was so upset at the upheaval and rapid preparations for departing, that she had a racking headache. So I sent her to bed at 7 and told her not to reappear till tomorrow morning.

SUNDAY NOVEMBER 15

I can't get home to you and Daddy before at least Wednesday. It is in any case awful my leaving Father in this feeble state. He is better today and quite reconciled to his nurse. She is a most devoted, conscientious woman and I'm thankful she is staying.

I have been very busy all today, packing china and silver to send up to Uncle Henry for his new house and writing heaps of letters to the family.

TUESDAY NOVEMBER 17

Your Grandfather had a very bad night. He told me this evening he did not see how he could last like this much longer. It is dreadful to see the wreck that age and disease make of a great man.

The Great Field-Marshal Lord Roberts is dead. His death was worthy of his gallant life. Though 82, he had gone across to France by Boulogne, then on to the Front, at General French's suggestion, to visit the Indian troops, who worship him. He spent a whole day visiting them in their trenches, at the headquarters of several of the Maharajah chiefs.

But a biting north-east wind was blowing. He had refused to wear his greatcoat, because he heard that the Indian troops would not have their coats on, only their field dress. He returned to General French's headquarters at 4 feeling chilled, and had a cup of tea. Instead of dining with General French, he went to bed. At midnight he was very ill, and the Commander-in-Chief's doctor found he had pneumonia. 24 hours later he passed away, being semi-conscious to the last.

The German Press pays tribute unanimously to Lord Roberts' greatness. One paper says: *There are moments in war when the warrior salutes with his sword instead of striking with it. Such a moment came with the death of Lord Roberts.*

The battle of Ypres is still raging, but in spite of the Prussian Guard's desperate attempts, the Germans have not broken through.

WEDNESDAY NOVEMBER 18

Lloyd George has brought out his War Budget. The main features are 3d a pound tax on tea, 1/2d on every glass of beer and income tax doubled. Whereas Daddy's income tax has up till now been 9d in the £ – his being an earned income – the tax will now be 1/6.

It comes heavily on us, as our income is *just* above the line at which one is liable. However, it is an easy way indeed of paying our debt to the country.

Then there is a great War Loan offer by the Treasury at 3½ per cent. Those who invest at once can purchase at £95, but £100 is the minimum one can buy. There is a great rush on the shares. The hope is that the War Loan issue of £350,000,000 should meet the war expenses of the first year.

THURSDAY NOVEMBER 19

I have been anxious about a possible invasion of England by the Germans while I was here. I would then not be able to get back to you in London, because of the railway being taken over, for moving of troops. Happily, these fears have not yet been realised.

Your Grandfather is very ill today, and I have wired for a second nurse. I do not feel able to cope with the responsibility nor the care he needs, during the day. Thank goodness Uncle Henry* is coming tomorrow. I am at my wits' end to know what is best to be done.

FRIDAY NOVEMBER 20

Henry arrived this morning, and the second nurse in the evening. Henry is shocked at the great change in Father.

9 pm: Have just had a distressing scene. Father had suddenly realised Nurse Mayer was in attendance. He was angry with me for having left him with 'that dangerous

---

*   Henry Davis was Georgina's surviving elder brother. Her eldest brother, Ernest, had died in 1891, aged 26.

woman' and became violent saying he would leave the house if she didn't. Henry and I had great difficulty in pacifying him. He was so agitated, Henry had to give him an injection of morphia. But we have to keep Mayer out of his room tonight.

SATURDAY NOVEMBER 21

5 pm: We have just had a most painful hour to go through with Father who was in delirium. It was as much as we could do to keep him in bed. With it all, his fine indomitable spirit was quite unbroken, he defied us all, and battled with his hands, talking the whole time. It is extraordinary the strength he has. The morphia injections had not the slightest effect. It is terrible to see all this and Henry and I are much upset and unnerved.

SUNDAY NOVEMBER 22

Sent a wire to Daddy early this morning to say I would like him to be here with me and to come tomorrow if possible. It will be a comfort to have him. Uncle Henry wants him too. Aunt Beatrice and Aunt Ethel suddenly appeared at 4 o'clock, having motored from Hengwrt.* After staying two hours they went on to Glanrhos where they are putting up at Mrs Clarke's invitation, as there is no room for them here. The big double-bed room is in workmen's hands after the fire.

10 pm: Darling Father is lying very peacefully and talking affectionately to everybody, his nurses included. It's such a relief to see him so. He does know me, though he talks only half-sense.

WEDNESDAY NOVEMBER 25

The achievement in the Persian Gulf, in which Commander Cathcart Wason distinguished himself (HMS *Odin*), has been much greater than at first supposed. British forces have captured the town of Basra, on the Persian Gulf, between the Tigris and Euphrates rivers. This is the terminus of the great Turkish Railway, built by German influence and German money, to join Constantinople and the Persian Gulf. Not only have the British taken Basra but we have also taken possession of the railway from Basra to Baghdad.

This is a great blow to Germany and has created a profound impression on India and the Eastern countries, as Basra has been a stronghold of the Turks for 250 years.

FRIDAY NOVEMBER 27

A battleship, HMS *Bulwark*, has mysteriously exploded in Sheerness Harbour, where she was taking in ammunition. Her total complement of 805 men, with the exception of twelve survivors, went down with her. The cause of the explosion is not yet

---

*   Two of Georgina's three younger sisters. See family tree.

ascertained, but it is thought that one of her magazines exploded. Naturally there was a suspicion that a submarine or mine had done the deed.*

The Russian advance in Poland is significant.** Kitchener alluded to it in his speech in the House of Lords two days ago, when he summarised the situation for the last month. He said that the Germans had sustained heavier losses than ever before.

MONDAY NOVEMBER 30

Father still lies unconscious. Edie arrived by the 3 o'clock train. Ethel and I went to meet her and brought her home. She found Father very altered. She is staying at Glanrhos tonight. We are passing very sad days, Henry, Ethel and I. We cannot settle down to anything, cannot take in what we try to read, have nothing to do but watch and wait.

Sir John French has sent home an important despatch describing the operations from October 3, when the BEF was moved from the Aisne to the North, in order to bar the road to Calais. It is a story of extraordinary pluck and indomitable endurance, without which the enemy would have forced its way through to the Channel ports with, French adds, 'disastrous results'.

TUESDAY DECEMBER 1

Father's big spirit passed away at 5 o'clock this morning. As it was leaving, a flash of lightning lit up the windows and the far rumble of thunder was heard. It was a most beautiful deathbed. Ethel, Henry and I had been with him all night, because last evening we saw the end was near.

A beautiful full moon was shining straight on to his face which was turned towards the window. For the first time for three days he opened his eyes, fixed them straight in front of him, pushed his head back slightly and stopped breathing altogether.

A few moments later, the sky became quite black, a sudden gale sprang up and a heavy patter of hail beat against the window. It was a most impressive tribute of Nature to the passing of the spirit which had worshipped Nature. The river Wye below his windows was very full, swishing past with a sound of music, and shining in the moonlight.

This morning in the full daylight he is lying there, with an inscrutable expression of peace, and 'contempt for all the paltriness in life' on his fine features. Poor Hughes goes about broken-hearted, unable to speak. Last night he came in alone to say goodbye to his old master.

WEDNESDAY DECEMBER 2

Daddy arrived at 6 o'clock in the morning. He had travelled all night to come and help Henry through the ordeal of the last preparations and accompany him back to London for the cremation tomorrow.

---

*   These suspicions were unfounded. The Germans had nothing to do with this major disaster, which was caused by a massive internal explosion.

**   In Austrian Poland (Galicia), the Russians drove back the Austrians 150 miles and reached the Carpathians.

Aunt Beatrice arrived by the 4 o'clock train from Hengwrt. So we four sisters are together in our old home for the first time for many years. The studio has been prepared by us and Hughes to receive the coffin for Father's last night in his home. It is very simple. On the east side stands his last big Academy picture, the one he was not able to finish for the last exhibition. In front of the picture, on the low stool I remember all my life, his palette just as he left it, with his brushes, palette knives and the little linen apron I made him, which he wore while painting.

9 pm: The scene of the removal of Father's dear remains to his beloved studio for his last visit is deeply stamped on my mind.

A wild night, rain pouring in torrents, the wind howling round the house. A group of silent sombrely clad men clustering in the porch, candles flickering, and we sisters with Henry and Daddy taking a last look at Father lying majestic in his white drapery.

Then the last journey downstairs, Hughes jealously holding the head of the coffin, and the weird transit into the pitch-black night, the pelting rain and sobbing wind, across the lawn to the studio. I remember the faint white gleam of the coffin gliding through the darkness, and how Uncle Henry, Aunt Edie and I, who followed, slipped mechanically into the spaces between the men, and helped to carry him to his studio.

In the studio were the others waiting to receive him. Gently he was laid down facing east. There after awhile we left him.

THURSDAY DECEMBER 3

At ten o'clock Mr Evans, our former Vicar at Llanwrthwl, for whom we have a great regard, came and performed a touching and beautiful little service in the studio. There were only ourselves and the servants, only Hughes could not bring himself to come in. When it was over, Father was taken away to travel to London where he is to be cremated tomorrow, according to his wish.

His other wish cannot be carried out during the war, that he should be taken to France to lie by his wife's side in the plot of ground belonging to the Davis family in the churchyard of St Etienne au Mont, Pont de Briques, near Boulogne.

As the war makes it impossible to take Father's ashes to France at present, they are to be laid in a vault in the churchyard at Llanwrthwl. Some day Uncle Henry may remove them to St Etienne, a mile of so from the old house, Château de la Barrière Rouge, where I and your Aunts and Uncles were born.

Daddy and Uncle Henry went up by the midday train to London for the cremation, leaving us four sisters to await the arrival of the sacred urn to be laid to rest at last.

FRIDAY DECEMBER 4

Today we sisters have been alone. The two nurses left this morning and, devoted as they have been, it was nice to be alone. We filled our time turning out cupboards and making up bundles of clothes to present to the hospitals in France. They are needed by British soldiers, who have no clothes to be brought home to England in, after they have lain wounded on the battlefield.

We opened the old writing desk belonging to our Mother. It was locked up among Father's things and he left directions it was to be opened by us. He had never opened it since her death in 1879. In it there is a diary written from 1857 to 1861, covering the period just before her engagement almost up to her marriage. It is delightful, so simple, yet full of fun, and sentiment.

The King has gone over with the Prince of Wales to France, and has met at Ypres King Albert of Belgium, Lord Kitchener, General Joffre and General French, and together they visited the troops. His visit has had a very inspiriting effect on the men. He then went to the Headquarters of Sir Douglas Haig, where he presented 4 DSOs about 20 Distinguished Conduct Medals and 1 Légion d'Honneur.

Uncle Henry told us about the cremation ceremony at Golders Green. The President of the Royal Academy, Sir Edward Poynter, was present.* A beautiful, simple laurel wreath, the tribute from the Royal Academy, was laid on the coffin in the Crematorium. The service was read by a clergyman, and then the coffin slid through the opening doors and disappeared. Uncle Henry went through into another chamber, to see the coffin consigned to the actual crematorium. He just saw the furnace seize the coffin, that is, the glow of white heat surround the coffin which immediately burst into flame and then everything was hidden from view.

Afterwards he saw the ashes, which were silky white, sifted, and placed into a porcelain urn. Daddy and Uncle Lionel stayed with him to the end. Then the urn was handed over to Mr Pritchard who is bringing it home for burial at Llanwrthwl on Monday.

SUNDAY DECEMBER 6

Ethel and I went to church this morning. It turned out a wretched day by one o'clock and so wet that we did not stir out in the afternoon. I answered a great many personal letters of condolence.

MONDAY DECEMBER 7

Today we laid Father's ashes to rest in the little churchyard at Llanwrthwl. The casket, with the flowers, was taken down in a carriage. The vicar met us at the gate of the cemetery; Henry carried the casket (about 2ft long and 12 inches wide, made of polished oak). It bears a brass plate engraved with Father's name and dates:

> **H.W.B. Davis R.A.**
> Born August 26 1833
> Died December 1 1914

---

*   'He was probably, with the exception of Alfred Stevens, the most versatile and accomplished academic draughtsman the English school has ever produced.' *The Times*, 28 July 1919.

And we four sisters followed, carrying the flowers.

The rain was pouring all the time we stood by the grave as it has done nearly every day since Father died. It seems as though Nature was weeping for him. A small brickwork chamber, lined with cement, had been prepared, and the casket was lowered and fitted into it when the words *Ashes to Ashes* were said. A thick stone slab was finally laid and cemented above the casket. So we left him.

After life's fitful fever he sleeps well

At 10.30 pm when the moon was coming up over the hills and across the river, Henry, Lionel, Edie and I went on to the bridge. We stood looking down at the same scene from which Father had painted a lovely moonlight effect some years ago. Then, Henry threw down upon the water a handful of his ashes which he had kept back. The wind took the little handful of white dust, it looked very white in the moonlight. We watched it go for a few seconds till it vanished in the mystery of the night.

TUESDAY DECEMBER 8

Henry and I travelled back to London by midday train, arriving Euston at 9 o'clock. As soon as I reached home I rushed upstairs to the nursery and found you just settling down to sleep after your last bottle. You turned sharply in your cot without making a sound. As soon as you saw Daddy at my shoulder you smiled at him. I didn't disturb you any more.

THURSDAY DECEMBER 10

There is good war news today. A British squadron has avenged the loss of our two cruisers, the *Good Hope* and *Monmouth** (sunk in the Pacific some weeks ago) by sinking four of the five German cruisers that sank ours, viz: the *Scharnhorst*, *Gneisenau*, *Leipzig* and the *Nürnberg*. The *Dresden* escaped, but is being pursued.

Our British Squadron under Admiral Sturdee sighted the German Squadron off the Falkland Islands. It is supposed that Admiral von Spee went down on the *Scharnhorst*, our Admiral Cradock's death being thus 'avenged', as if this is any satisfaction or consolation to anybody.

---

*   These two cruisers had been sunk on 1 November by Admiral von Spee's Far Eastern Squadron off the southern coast of Chile, near Coronel. Fifteen hundred British sailors perished.

BOOK IV

DECEMBER 13, 1914 – MARCH 3, 1915

SUNDAY DECEMBER 13

Daddy and I went to see Briton Rivière today.* He advised us to have soon an exhibition at the Fine Arts Gallery of Father's studies, sketches and drawings and to leave the important pictures for an exhibition at some future period when the depression caused by the war has lifted. He said that the Academy would certainly have asked us to lend Father's pictures for the Winter Exhibition at Burlington House if it had not been for the War Fund Exhibition they have arranged there in January.

MONDAY DECEMBER 14

There has been a most daring exploit by our submarine B11 – commanded by Lieut. Commander Norman Holbrook RN. He entered the Dardanelles, dived under five rows of mines and torpedoed the Turkish battleship *Messudiyeh* which was guarding the minefield. Although pursued, the B11 returned safely, after being submerged on one occasion for nine hours. When last seen the *Messudiyeh* was sinking by the stern.

WEDNESDAY DECEMBER 16

The first German shells have fallen in England. This morning at 8 am some German cruisers were sighted off Whitby, Scarborough and Hartlepool. A few minutes later they started shelling the three towns causing many casualties and damage to buildings and property. The general impression this evening is excitement. Everybody seems to think it a pity for those who have to suffer, but a very good thing for the country generally, which will at last be roused to the seriousness of the situation. The cruisers bombarded for half an hour, then, on sighting British patrol vessels, they disappeared in the mist.

THURSDAY DECEMBER 17

The shelling of the three towns is more serious than was reported yesterday. Altogether 40 people have been killed and several hundred wounded, all civilians, including children and babies.** Whitby Abbey, a priceless old monument, was much damaged.

---

*   Briton Rivière RA (1840–1920) was an English painter descended from a Huguenot family. He produced a varied mix of contemporary genre, classical and animal subjects.
**   This was the first time since 1690 that civilians had been killed in Britain by enemy action. Martin Gilbert, *First World War*, p. 110.

It is mortifying that the German cruisers were able to come 400 miles, to bombard three cities and return to Kiel, without any of our fleet being there to stop them. How did they get through? On their way back they sowed mines in the North Sea which have already sunk three of our merchant steamers.

FRIDAY DECEMBER 18

The most satisfactory news today is that England has assumed the Protectorate of Egypt which henceforth ceases to be the vassal of Turkey. The Khedive, who has thrown in his lot with the Sultan, has 'left Cairo for Vienna and Berlin'. One could almost feel sorry for Turkey who has been made the catspaw for Germany. But she was thoroughly warned beforehand.

SUNDAY DECEMBER 20

Today I went with Muz to the service in the Chapel of Chelsea Hospital. It was most touching to see all the old pensioners, many-medalled veterans of former wars, sitting at peace in the haven of their old age. While the young generation are fighting the Empire's battles so few miles away.

My mind wandered a good deal to the old flags, some dating from Marlborough's wars, hanging over our heads. It seemed such a pity that they were all grey black with London grime and were hanging unprotected in this atmosphere.

We had tea with dear Mrs Kenyon Slaney, so lively, good looking and sweet, but stone deaf. Still, we get a lot of pleasure in seeing her, she is so warm-hearted. Her brother, Mr Schooles, told us that the whole coast round Hythe is one vast camp and is strongly entrenched. Also that Romney Marsh is ready to be submerged by the sea at a moment's notice in case of invasion, as was done in Belgium.

MONDAY DECEMBER 21

Today I went with Verena Barneby to Bedford College to offer our services for teaching the elements of French to the Tommies. The lady who attended me began by asking if I had ever taught French. I said: never. She looked surprised, so I added 'but I can speak French'. She then addressed me in French and found me on my own ground there! But apparently they have plenty of helpers, more helpers than willing students, so my name and address were taken and I shall be contacted if required.

TUESDAY DECEMBER 22

There is a long account in *The Times* of the terrible plight of France's great manufacturing city, Lille. This has been in German hands for three months. Prince Rupprecht of Bavaria is one of three German Commanders in Lille and the extortionate quantities of food he squeezes out of the starving population are scandalous. All the flour has been seized and the people are only allowed to buy black bread. All personal property left in houses, from which owners have fled, has been seized and sent to Germany. Looting and theft everywhere.

WEDNESDAY DECEMBER 23

Today I went to buy some toys for your stocking, as those I chose you some days ago never arrived from the shop. There seems to be nothing attractive to little ones. Clumsy wooden animals with joints that move only when you push them up or down, no mechanical or spontaneous movement and where are the dolls? Heaps of hard-stuff dogs, cats, teddy bears, etc, but you don't care a bit about them. I have seen no mechanical toys sold in the streets yet. So the great German toy invasion is one we mothers can only regret, until British manufacturers replace it.

Still, as you love making a noise and nothing pleases you more than to hammer and clatter and bang, I got you a very nice horn to blow, to go with your drum. Also some soldiers made like skittles for you to knock down with a ball.

It is horrid cold weather. We are doing practically nothing in the way of Christmas presents, only for the children, nieces and nephews, children at Glaslyn Lodge and our servants and some tips. No family presents.

The French Prime Minister made a most stirring speech in which he declared France was determined to fight to the bitter end. True to their glorious pact with England and Russia,* he stated that France would never make peace, until Belgium was completely indemnified for all her losses; until Alsace-Lorraine was restored to France, and until Prussian militarism was crushed.

FRIDAY DECEMBER 25

A foggy Christmas morning, just the weather for an air raid.

At 8 am you were brought into our bedroom with rose face, and bright eyes, to play while Nannie went to Church. After breakfast you came down to empty your stocking and find some fascinating animals, including an inflatable rubber frog that leapt up and down. But you were entirely absorbed in the bright green cardboard box in which the frog had come from the shop! This satisfied you completely, you tiresome creature!

I went to Church with Muz at the Chelsea Hospital. There we had a very affecting short sermon, from the Army Chaplain, Mr Moseley. Daddy and I had lunch at Minna's and dinner at Aunt Nell Wason's where there was a big family gathering. You had your first Christmas dinner downstairs with the servants (you little son of the house!) and had a crumb of Christmas pudding. The two sons of Mrs Marsh, the cook were there, one a fine young gunner just enlisted, waiting orders to go abroad.

Although it was agreed no presents were to be given, Daddy had a cheque for £15 from his Mother, I had a beautiful fur coat given me by Muz, Aunt Nell and Minna, and various smaller gifts. All day I kept expecting a Christmas greeting from the Germans, but nothing of the kind occurred.

---

*   The Triple Entente.

We had a family gathering at Aunt Nell's tonight. Although this Christmas is so full of sadness and anxiety, we determined it should be a happy family occasion – and in many ways it was.

SATURDAY DECEMBER 26

Today there is a fine account of the naval action off the Falkland Islands. Only it made me groan involuntarily when I read about the actual sinking of the *Scharnhorst* and the *Gneisenau*. It seems to me inconceivable that such bravery, skill and seamanship as the Germans showed should all be wasted. 'They must perish or else we', seems so cruel in the world's history. To attain such a degree of efficiency, only to have to succumb, in the first collision with Great Britain, seems a strange fate.

This battle is another triumph for Lord Fisher's policy of heavy guns and big ships, as opposed to Sir Percy Scott's submarine policy. It seems such a short time ago since Sir P. Scott's letter, now famous, appeared to the effect that submarines and destroyers would be the only ships needed in future warfare. In each naval engagement since this war broke out, victory has remained with the heavier guns.*

SUNDAY DECEMBER 27

A respite in the 'soak' weather of which we have had so much. A pale sun came through a watery blue sky and lit up the stately old Chelsea Hospital Chapel, while Daddy and I were there, so that the singing suddenly became more fervent and joyous. Daddy perked up too at my side. We walked across the Park after lunch to see friends.

MONDAY DECEMBER 28

Today there is more exciting news. An air-raid, the boldest of the war, was made by seven of our hydroplanes, escorted by cruisers, right into the Bight of Heligoland, where they dropped bombs on the German warships lying in the roads off Cuxhaven. Our ships, consisting of the two cruisers *Arethusa* and *Undaunted*, a destroyer flotilla and submarines, escorted these seven sea planes while the latter delivered the attack.

But while waiting, they were themselves attacked by Zeppelins, German sea planes and submarines. Our ships beat off the attack and succeeded in picking up six out of the seven sea planes. The seventh sea plane was later seen in a wrecked condition off the coast of Heligoland. The fate of its pilot, Flight-Commander Francis Hewlett, is not known.** All this was going on at dawn on Christmas Day.

WEDNESDAY DECEMBER 30

Today I travelled to Gelligemlyn with Muz, she and I alone, but Daddy joins us tomorrow. We have come down for ten days to get the pheasants shot, and this is the

---

* At this stage, the potential of submarines was underestimated by many, though not by Lord Fisher, who was in favour of using them for coastal defence.
** He survived, and received a telegram of congratulation from the King.

last year there will be any real covert shooting at Gelligemlyn for some years to come. We had great difficulty in getting any guns for the two days shoot. All the young men are away, and the old ones are limited! Uncle Gerry cannot leave his anti-aircraft gun in London even for a day, Uncle Romer cannot get leave, and Uncle Guy is seeing fierce fighting at the Front.

Later in the evening, Uncle Hugh Lee came to see us and to meet his fiancée, Hilda Blagden. I am fond of her, and am very pleased at the match. They both went up to your nursery and found you standing up in your cot in your nightgown. There you stood with flaming cheeks and twinkling eyes laughing at us all and doing your little tricks, saluting etc. while I simply stood by bursting with silly pride.

I left you this morning to the possibility of a Zeppelin raid over London in my absence. Nannie and the servants have explicit and simple instructions as to what to do if they awake at night to hear explosions. Seize eiderdowns, rugs, coats and go below at once to the basement. Our house is well adapted for a Zeppelin raid, as the basement has two exits, back and front, to the outside, street and garden so there is little fear of being trapped underground, even if the house did partly collapse.

I wonder if it will strike you as strange that I leave you alone in London with the bare chance of a raid. It is typical of the prevailing state of mind over here. Nobody alters their plans for the chance of a raid; we all face it quite calmly and in a spirit of fatalists. What is to be, will be. I know you to be well cared for with your Nannie and Daddy wishes me to come here with him and it is not right to sacrifice his wishes.

THURSDAY DECEMBER 31

While at breakfast this morning a telegram was brought in. Thinking it was news of a missing plum-pudding and mince pies from Harrods, Muz opened it jauntily. But it was from Aunt Brenda, saying that Uncle Gerry is going off to Dunkirk tonight attached to one of the anti-aircraft guns, like the one he has been working at in London on the roof of the Crown Agent's office.

Muz was frightfully upset to think of his going off to the Front without her seeing him again. But her alarm was greater still, when on opening the paper, we saw that there was a great air-raid upon Dunkirk yesterday, in which fifteen men were killed and fifty wounded.

Daddy arrived this evening and gave us the latest news. Gerry was asked by the Admiralty yesterday if he would go to Dunkirk today, with two other men of his section. He said yes, went off to the Admiralty and at once was medically examined, certified fit, and flew off to get his kit. He then came home to dine with his wife and telephoned to Daddy who was eating his solitary dinner at home. Daddy went round to Pelham Street and found Uncle Gerry and Aunt B finishing their bottle of champagne.

Gerry is off tonight. He will take just as much kit as he can carry and no more, for his is only an AB (Able-Bodied Seaman) and takes rank as a private in the Army! He belongs to the RNVR – Royal Naval Volunteer Reserve. His great wish was to go to the Front with the faithful James, his chauffeur, in charge of an armoured motor-car.

1915

Here we are, in the centre of it all and I would not be anywhere
else for a million pounds, and the Queen of Sheba
Julian Grenfell (died of wounds, April 30, 1915)

FRIDAY JANUARY 1

Gelligemlyn
The New Year has opened with a sou' westerly gale and rain, as befits the troubled year
we are likely to have.

I read that on Christmas Day there wasn't a shot fired across the trenches between
Germans and English. The men fraternised and exchanged greeting. The Germans, too,
love the cartoons of Big and Little Willie and call out for the copies of the *Daily Mirror*
to be sent to them. As no one ventures across with them, our Tommies weigh the
papers with stones and throw them across to their trenches, where the adventures of
the Willies provoke much merriment.

Cousin Monier Williams and his handsome daughter Angela arrived this evening to
stay for the shoot.

SATURDAY JANUARY 2

The New Year has begun with a naval disaster. Our battleship *Formidable* has been sunk
in the Channel and it is not yet known whether by being torpedoed or by striking a
mine.* Seventy one survivors so far have been rescued by a light cruiser, and it is hoped
that others may yet come.

Flight Commander Hewlett, the naval airman who led the sea-plane attack on
Cuxhaven, has been rescued at sea (where he remained 6 hours on his damaged sea-
plane) by a Dutch trawler and has just been landed in Holland. He is returning to
England. He had to remain seven days on the trawler, and had to go through the
terrible storm of last Monday and Tuesday. But the skipper gave him the best of
treatment, and landed him at Ymuiden where he went straight to the British Vice-
Consul. Before leaving his sea-plane he destroyed the motor and sank the machine.

SUNDAY JANUARY 3

Today has been celebrated throughout the Kingdom with an intercession service in
every Church. A beautiful form of prayer for the success of our troops was gone through
and prayers were said on behalf of our wounded and sick enemies as well. Here in little
Llanelltyd Church a service was also held.

---

*   She did not strike a mine, but was torpedoed off the South Devon coast on New Year's
Day. Two hundred members of the crew survived.

LETTERS FROM THE FRONT.

MORE TALES OF THE TRUCE.

CHRISTMAS GOODWILL.

FRIENDLY MEETINGS WITH THE ENEMY.

An officer in a Highland Regiment writes on December 28 :—

You need not have pitied us on Christmas Day; I have seldom spent a more entertaining one, despite the curious conditions. We were in the trenches, and the Germans began to make merry on Christmas Eve, shouting at us to come out and meet them. They sang songs (very well); our men answered by singing "Who were you with last night?" and of course "Tipperary" (very badly). I was horrified at discovering some of our men actually had gone out, imbued more with the idea of seeing the German trenches than anything else; they met half-way, and there ensued the giving of cigarettes and receiving of cigars, and they arranged (the private soldiers of one army and the private soldiers of the other) a 48 hours' armistice. It was all most irregular, but the Peninsular and other wars will furnish many such examples; eventually both sides were induced to return to their respective trenches, but the enemy sang all night, and during my watch they played "Home, Sweet Home," and "God Save the King," at 2.30 a.m.! It was rather wonderful; the night was clear, cold, and frosty, and across to our lines at this usually miserable hour of night came the sound of such tunes very well played, especially by a man with a cornet, who is probably well known.

Christmas Day was very misty, and out came those Germans to wish us "A Happy Day"; we went out, told them we were at war with them, and that really they must play the game and pretend to fight; they went back, but again attempted to come towards us, so we fired over their heads, they fired a shot back to show they understood, and the rest of the day passed quietly in this part of the line, but in others a deal of fraternising went on. So there you are; all this talk of hate, all this fury at each other that has raged since the beginning of the war, quelled and stayed by the magic of Christmas. Indeed, one German said, " But you are of the same religion as us, and to-day is the Day of Peace"! It is really a great triumph for the Church. It is a great hope for future peace when two great nations, hating each other as foes have seldom hated, one side vowing eternal hate and vengeance and setting their venom to music, should on Christmas Day, and for all that the word implies, lay down their arms, exchange smokes, and wish each other

MUSICAL HONOURS.

An officer in the North Staffordshire Regiment writes on Christmas Eve :—

We had been calling to one another for some time Christmas wishes and other things. I went out and they shouted " No shooting," and then somehow the scene became a peaceful one. All our men got out of their trenches and sat on the parapet, the Germans did the same, and they talked to one another in English and in broken English. I got on top of the trench and talked German, and asked them to sing a German Volkslied, which they did; then our men sang quite well, and each side clapped and encored the other. I asked one German who sang a solo to sing one of Schumann's songs, so he sang " The Two Grenadiers " splendidly. Our men were a good audience and really enjoyed his singing. Then I walked across and held a conversation with the German officer in command. One of his men introduced us properly, he asked my name and then presented me to his officer. I gave the latter permission to bury some German dead who were lying in between us, and we agreed to have no shooting until 12 midnight to-morrow. We talked together 10 or more minutes—Germans gathered round. I was almost in their lines within a yard or so. We saluted each other, and he thanked me for permission to bury his dead, and we fixed up how many men were to do it, and that otherwise both sides must remain in their trenches.

Then we wished one another good night, a good night's rest, and a happy Christmas, and parted with a salute. I got back to the trench. The Germans sang " Die Wacht am Rhein." It sounded well. Then our men sang quite well " Christians awake," and with a good night we all got back into our trenches. At times we heard the guns in the distance and an occasional rifle shot. I can hear them now, but about us is absolute quiet. I allowed one or two men to go out to meet a German or two half-way. They exchanged cigars or smokes and talked. The officer I spoke to hopes we shall do the same on New Year's Day. I said " Yes, if I am here." Of course, no precautions are relaxed, but I think they mean to play the game. All the same, I think I shall be awake all night so as to be on the safe side. It is weird to think that to-morrow night we shall be at it again hard. If one gets through this show it will be a Christmastime to live in our memory. Am just off for a walk round the trenches to see all is well. . . . We had an absolutely quiet night in front of us, though just to our right and left there was some firing going on. In my trenches and in those of the enemy opposite to us were only nice big fires blazing and occasional songs and conversation.

This morning after réveillé the Germans sent out parties to bury their dead. Our men went out to help, and then we all both sides met in the middle and in groups began to talk and exchange gifts of tobacco, food, &c. All the morning we have been fraternizing, singing songs. I have been within a yard, in fact on to their trenches, and have spoken to and exchanged greetings with a colonel, staff officers, and various company officers. All were very nice, and we fixed up that the men should not go near their opponents' trenches, but remain about midway between the lines. The whole thing is extra-ordinary. The men were all so natural and friendly. Several photos were taken, a group of German officers, a German officer and myself, and a group of British and German soldiers. The Germans are Saxons, a good-looking lot, only wishing for peace, in a manly way, and they seem in no way at their last gasp. I was astonished at the easy way in which our men and theirs got on with each other. We have just knocked off for dinner and have arranged to meet again afterwards until dusk, when we go in again and have songs until 9 p.m., when " war " begins again. I wonder who will start

Letters telling of the remarkable Christmas spent in the trenches — Dec. 1914.

Letters from the Front: the Christmas Truce.

The accounts that have come to us in letters from the Front published in *The Times* etc. are so remarkable and display such an unexpected turn of events on Christmas Day, that I cannot do better than insert the documents themselves. It speaks well for both sides, that neither betrayed the confidence of the other. Of course there was mistrust which at least a few of our officers felt for the overtures made by the enemy. But the same curious interchange of comradeship and Christmas gifts took place on the Belgian lines between Belgians and Germans.

Another little incident of the war is so typical of the spirit with which Englishmen make war – even war does not extinguish their love of sport! Your cousin Charlie Romer-Williams, who, as despatch-rider had four horses shot under him, and was slightly wounded twice, came home for a few days to collect beagles to take over to Belgium.

BEAGLING FOR OFFICERS AT THE FRONT

The good stock of hares on Belgian soil has been too much for the sporting officers of the Cavalry Brigades, and Lieutenant Charles Romer-Williams, of the 4th Dragoon Guards, has accordingly obtained a pack of beagles, which are now at the Front. He returned home to Newnham Hall, Northamptonshire, last week, and was fortunate in securing the loan of the pack of Mr Ernest Robinson, of Liscombe, Leighton Buzzard, who, as soon as he heard of Mr Williams's requirements, offered to lend his beagles, expressing the hope that the officers and men at the Front would enjoy good sport with them. Lieutenant Romer-Williams was once Master of the Eton Beagles, and the borrowed pack could not be in more capable hands.

Morning Post, January 3, 1915

MONDAY JANUARY 4

The *Formidable* was the victim of a submarine. She met her doom off the South Devon coast and it is awful to think that a German submarine could get so far west without being detected. The *Formidable* went down ¾ hour after being struck, but such a furious sea was raging that many men were doomed from the first. Out of the few who got into a boat which was not swamped, several died from exposure.

WEDNESDAY JANUARY 6

This morning we had news of Uncle Gerry from Dunkirk. He reached the port safely with the other ABs,* and they are very jolly and happy together. He had not had his clothes off since he left England several days earlier and life is rough, to say the least. They all sleep together at very close quarters in one room, on straw, and have plentiful rations of bully-beef, biscuits, tea, condensed milk and jam.

---

*   Able-bodied Seamen.

Water is very scarce and it all has to be boiled. There is none to wash with, or very little! Mr Binks the naval instructor, is a great pal of his now, and shows his friendship by valeting Gerry. This valeting consists of washing Gerry's tin plate and seeing that he has plenty of straw to sleep upon. He is the only one of the section who is not a gentleman by birth.

Great indignation has been aroused not only throughout Belgium and among the Allies, but at the Vatican, at the arrest of the brave Archbishop of Malines, Primate of Belgium, who has been confined to his Palace, under military guard. The German Military Authorities took umbrage at the Pastoral Letter he issued for the consolation of his countrymen, as a protest against the sorrows inflicted on his people.

The Archbishop, Cardinal Mercier,* after enumerating the outrages the Belgians have been victims of, has reminded them that they must do nothing to avenge their own wrongs. He also tells them that they owe no allegiance to the conquerors, their allegiance belonging only to the King and Government.

This exhortation made the military authorities so furious that they gave orders for the seizure of every copy of the Letter, while soldiers were posted in every church to prevent the reading of it by priests. Besides the Cardinal a number of priests and people connected with the publishing and printing of it have been arrested.

This step is regarded by many as an unpardonable blunder. The German Catholics are indignant at the 'sacrilege' committed on the person of the great prelate. The Pope and his Council are protesting against his arrest to the Kaiser and demanding his instant release.

FRIDAY JANUARY 8

In spite of continual rain, Angela and I are out most of the day. Too misty and wet to do the Precipice walk today, so we walked to the grand and lovely falls of the Upper Mawddach, two miles up the glen from the bridge over the Eidon.

The Upper Mawddach simply dashes down over a precipitous hill-side of rock, through which it is by degrees cutting itself a deeper chasm over the shoulder between two steep hills. It was a lovely walk, but it poured all the way back, about three miles. But Daddy came to meet us in the car to save us the long extra walk along the high road. He is always so considerate in those ways.

FRIDAY JANUARY 15

Kensington

I was coming home at three o'clock this afternoon, when standing on our doorstep was an officer in khaki. I called out 'Guy!' flew across the road and Uncle Guy's arms were round me in a moment and he was kissing me on both cheeks in the very middle of

---

*   Cardinal Mercier, Archbishop of Malines (1851–1926), had become a highly popular figure, through his militant stance against the German Occupation and sterling defence of his fellow-citizens.

Neville Street! He had left the trenches at Armentières at seven last evening and was already here straight and hot from the firing line.

He was here half an hour and we telephoned through to Granny and I told her someone wanted to speak to her. She came and Guy altered his voice to speak, mystified her completely and finally told her in his own voice that he was dying to see her. He and Granny are coming to dine here tonight with Daddy, while I, unfortunately am tonight, of all nights, dining with Mrs Gerald Paget who has a 'hen' dinner party. Guy has been given a week's leave. He looks so well and handsome, but thinner. He went up to see you and was so amused, for in spite of your cold, you saluted him properly!

Mrs Paget's dinner party was most amusing. We were seven, and by the time we dispersed our throats were so hoarse that we could hardly speak. There were Mrs Guest, a very handsome, stately rather sad looking woman, Mrs Whately, Verena Barneby, Mrs Ivor de la Rue, Miss Stewart, myself and our hostess. Mrs Paget is a *grande dame* if ever there was one, and with it all she is as lively and joyous as a girl of 18. Very witty and intellectual. We met at Saltmarshe when I was there in June, and we used to have great arguments and fun together. I made friends with Mrs de la Rue, who was introduced as half-saint, half-devil. She proved charming and full of ideas.

SATURDAY JANUARY 16

We dined at Aunt Brenda's to meet Captain Claude Hamilton and Mrs Hamilton. He has just returned wounded from the Front. He was shot in the head by snipers, while giving instructions to the artillery. The bullet made a bad wound and gave him concussion, but he is getting over it.

The trenches he and his men (Sherwood Foresters) occupied had been captured from the Germans and were in a terrible state, dead Germans had just been placed under the sods of earth. You couldn't, he said, drive a pickaxe anywhere in the earth without digging into a corpse. The conditions were too awful to describe. Nobody could really want to return to such scenes. In spite of that he talked quite gaily of returning there himself, as soon as he gets over his constant desire to sleep.

Uncle Guy told us many strange things too. About 60 yards away from the trenches occupied by the Buffs, was a position occupied by Saxons. The Saxons' trenches becoming untenable from water, they proceeded to erect earthworks with sand bags etc, and occupied them instead of the trenches, increasing the threat to the Buffs' trenches. A Saxon officer stepped across with a flag of truce, and harangued the Buffs, telling them that they were Saxons and we Anglo-Saxons, and they didn't want to fight us at all.

He advised the Buffs to get out of their trenches and build earthworks, as in a few days he and his men, Saxons, would be replaced by Prussians whom they hated. If the Buffs set to work quickly, they, the Saxons, would not fire or interfere. So, said Uncle Guy, when he left the trenches last Friday, the Buffs were hard at work making high earthworks, on a level with the Saxons who were sitting smoking their pipes, watching our men at work.

But before he left, orders had come from Headquarters enquiring why there was such a complete cessation of firing? Whereupon there was an impetuous fusillade, all aimed in the air, and no more hobnobbing. Uncle Guy added, in an undertone to Daddy, that an attempt would be made to quietly persuade the Saxons, 500 or 600 of them, to walk over to us and surrender, as they hate the war. When Guy returns next week, he will find the hateful Prussians occupying the Saxons' position.

MONDAY JANUARY 18

Dined with Uncle Hugh Lee to meet Monsieur and Madame Brunel de Montpelier, the Belgians whom he has had living with him for weeks. Their big château de Kemmel, near Armentières, was sacked by the Germans in October, who made it their head-quarters. It is now the headquarters of some of the British. I sat near M. Brunel, a middle-aged man, who was delighted to find me speaking French like a French woman, and we talked the whole evening. They had to leave their château at half an hour's notice, travelling in an old van, as they dare not take their car.

They left home at 10 pm and reached the frontier at 4 am, with the old mother and a young daughter. The son went to join the Belgian Army. M. Brunel escaped only just in time as he would probably have shared the fate of his cousin, a big landowner nearby. He was requested to hand over 100,000 frs (£4,000). This he could not do, though he gave them what money he could lay hands on. He was tied to his own gate posts, prodded with bayonets and finally shot.

M. Brunel is leaving tomorrow to go to Armentières and see what the Germans have left. He has been told that there is not a pane of glass left in the windows, that the Germans tore up the dresses of his wife and daughter and scattered them, pillaging the house-linen and everything they could carry away. Mme Brunel, a dark handsome woman of about 50, or more, vivacious and pleasant, took a liking to me and asked if she might come and see me. I begged her to do so.

WEDNESDAY JANUARY 20

An airship raid over the East Coast last night. Three Zeppelins or other airships dropped bombs over Yarmouth and Sandringham village. A good many buildings were damaged and so far the number of deaths ascertained is three.

THURSDAY JANUARY 21

We never came home to bed till 12.30 last night, Daddy and I having had a night out with Uncle Guy before his return to the awful war tomorrow. After the theatre we went to his club, the Naval and Military,* and sat there over a light supper.

Uncle Guy's view of the Retreat from Mons is novel, to me and startling. He called it a 'page to be wiped out of English history'. It was a rout, a débâcle; our troops, left in

---

* Then situated at 100 Piccadilly, formerly the London residence of Lord Palmerston.

the lurch by the French, unsupported by reinforcements, misled by false intelligence as to the German forces, retired at a run for four days. It was at Le Cateau that they made their first big stand, when the German pursuit slackened a little and gave us the opportunity which began to turn the scales in our favour.

I lunched with Verena Barneby and went with her to the Royal Academy to see the War Relief Exhibition. All artists of note in the United Kingdom have been asked to send small works, which are being sold for the Red Cross Society, one third of the sum realised going to the Artist. There was a delicious bronze life size head of a baby boy called *The Dawn of Thought*, by Willis Ward, so exactly like you in features and expression, that you might have been the model. Verena exclaimed 'It's just like Harry!'

I walked up to the clerk with the sale catalogue to enquire the price, in a wild impulse to buy it if possible. It was £25 and little as that is for such a lovely little effigy which might be your head, I had to smile and say 'I must think it over'. I learned from the clerk that a sum of between £5,000 and £10,000 has already been realised for the Red Cross.

FRIDAY JANUARY 22

An awful day of snow, slush and brown half-fog. Poor Guy left early this morning for the war, at 7.30 am. We all spent his last evening together at Aunt Nell's, and he was the life and soul of the party.

I spent the morning working hard at the Kensington Square Workrooms to help supply hospital necessaries to the French and Belgian hospitals.

MONDAY JANUARY 25

Splendid news in this morning's paper. A patrol-squadron of our battleships sighted, early yesterday morning a German squadron of battle-cruisers including the *Blücher*, on their way to bombard our coast. Our ships, led by the *Lion*, Admiral Beatty's flagship, sank the *Blücher* and seriously damaged two battleships.*

TUESDAY JANUARY 26

I spent this morning in Kensington Square working at the War Hospital supply depôt, and this afternoon working for the West London Hospital wards, making flannel garments in each case. This afternoon's work party was in a beautifully furnished house in Kensington Court. The home of Lady Plender – Lady Splendour – as I called her once (not entirely by mistake). The rooms were indeed gorgeous, gilt and bright colours and flamboyant curios everywhere, and splendid lace curtains, cloths, sofa backs etc etc!! A big splash in fact.

We dined last night with Minna Crombie to say goodbye to Eugene before he sails for France. He ought to be still at Winchester, if he were doing his last year there.

---

*   This was the battle of the Dogger Bank on January 24 – and the first battle between Dreadnoughts. Morale at home was boosted considerably by the news of the sinking of the *Blücher*, with the loss of 29 officers and 841 ratings.

WEDNESDAY JANUARY 27

I went today with Olive Barneby to Queen's Hall to hear one of the famous Hilaire Belloc lectures on the War. He is the man who two years ago wrote articles predicting what would happen when the great collision came with Germany. His forecast of Germany's attack on Belgium and her strategy was borne out absolutely by subsequent events. Since the outbreak of war, Belloc has been writing in *Land and Water*, and giving lectures.

I hear he is coining in money at the rate of £20,000 a year and gets £6,000 from *Land and Water* alone.*

The Hall was packed, not a vacant seat and men, many wounded, or on leave, were in the majority. Muz came with us, but she found it too technical, poor darling, and I think she napped at intervals! It was difficult to catch all he said when he faced the screen on which were lantern slides. These showed local maps of fiercely contested regions, such as Soissons and Rheims. At the end Belloc told us it was a grievous mistake now to assume that Germany would be defeated, for at any moment she might regain the initiative.

THURSDAY JANUARY 28

We had a small dinner party tonight, Verena Barneby with Olive, Rigby and Henry. I told them their fortunes by cards after dinner, always a great source of jokes and fun.

FRIDAY JANUARY 29

The first sunshine we have seen for weeks. Perhaps the Germans will take this opportunity of flying over with their Zeppelins, as Count Zeppelin is supposed to have sworn that he would be in London by the 30th January.

SATURDAY JANUARY 30

Last night after dinner, I rang up Brenda to hear when Gerry was expected home from Dunkirk, as he had only volunteered for a month at a time. She replied in great excitement that he had just arrived! So Daddy and I slipped on fur coats and went round at once.

We found a very sailor-looking Gerry in heavy leather boots up to his hips (he had never had them off, I believe, since he left England, and certainly his clothes had never been off). He was looking very cheery, thin, and hungry and doing justice to his dinner having had nothing but bully beef, cold, for a month. He had had a far more exciting time than he expected, being continually turned out at night to repel aircraft attacks.

The British airship *Beta* was outside Dunkirk and Uncle Gerry's section had to guard her and her air-shed. Also Gerry's position was continually receiving the shells destined

---

*   Hilaire Belloc's prestige was such that his lectures were fully reported in *The Times*. Nowadays he is better remembered for his humorous verse, such as *Cautionary Verses*.

for the German aeroplanes fired by the other anti-aircraft stations. But he escaped all injury. He has come home with a shocking cold and cough, though, caught outside one night during an alarm. Without greatcoats, they rushed from their straw to their gun stationed on the tower 80ft high, fully exposed to the east wind and there they were for three hours.

TUESDAY FEBRUARY 2

The merchant ship *Dacia*, a former German merchantman bought by the Americans and carrying cotton, has sailed from Galveston. She has been made a test case. If she is allowed to sail free, then all the German ships interned in American Ports can be bought by Americans and used for trade. England, France and Russia have declared that they will not allow this transaction, so the British have notified America that, if the *Dacia* falls into our hands, she will have to go through the Prize Court. Great excitement has been caused over the case.*

WEDNESDAY FEBRUARY 3

Am quite tired tonight having spent long time at the Stores ordering Uncle Henry's linen for his house, and doing without lunch. I came home about 4, had tea, then had you immediately after for over an hour. You are no rest, let me tell you – here, there and everywhere, seizing every opportunity to dash across the fender and hearth on all fours to catch hold of the flames or glowing coals. Or striving, with closed eyes and clenched teeth, to pull down on top of you the electric candelabra. I can't lose sight of you for a second, and you are only 15 months old.

I wonder whether you or your generation will ever be able to make friends with Germans, or trust them. A document, photographed from the one found on a German soldier, shows how the order was given by his Brigade 'to shoot all Frenchmen, wounded or otherwise, who fell into the soldiers hands, as no prisoners were to be taken'.

German submarines have been torpedoing merchant ships on our west coast near Liverpool. Great dissatisfaction is expressed at the leniency of McKenna, Home Secretary, towards spies in England.** Spies are said to be at the bottom of the wretched successes the Germans have had against our merchantmen.

THURSDAY FEBRUARY 4

Today I spent with Mrs de la Rue at Hackney, in the far East End, visiting children from the County Council School. Or rather we were visiting the mothers of all those that

---

*   In the Prize Court, the legality of the capture of vessels at sea was determined. In particular, could merchants send goods from the USA to Germany, when not intended for the government or for the armed forces? The British government were strongly opposed, realising that, if approved, this ruling would undermine the naval blockade. Edwin J. Clapp, *Economic Aspects of the War, 1915*, chapters 4–6.

**   Reginald McKenna succeeded Lloyd George as Chancellor of the Exchequer in May 1915.

needed treatment for defective eyes, teeth, hearing etc., and arranging about it. It was very tiring, for we tramped for miles. I came home very tired at 4.30, having left home at 10.

FRIDAY FEBRUARY 5

The German Admiralty has declared a blockade of the British Isles starting from February 18. From that day any British ship in the Channel or North Sea will be destroyed without warning and 'it may not always be possible to save the crews'. Neutral ships will be exposed to the same danger, and a narrow route is left open for them round the North of Scotland.

SATURDAY FEBRUARY 6

Today Granny and I lunched with Daddy at *Le Rendez-vous*, Dean Street, Soho, a cheap and quite excellent lunch for 2/- each! Then Granny and I went to dear old Gray's Inn Square to see Daddy drill with his Corps, the Inns of Court. Daddy, looking spare and slender, was quick and altogether martial in his bearing. I recognised several legal friends among the four companies. They have no uniforms or rifles yet, but they do all sorts of marching manoeuvres. We were very entertained watching for over half an hour.

Germany's declaration of a blockade against England has provoked a storm of indignation and ridicule in America. The Americans are protesting against Germany's lawlessness in sinking neutral vessels. German diplomacy goes on blundering more and more. The result is that the neutrals are gradually inclining towards the Allies and the Germans will not have many friends left.

SUNDAY FEBRUARY 7

Went to church at Chelsea Hospital with Muz. Uncle Romer, on leave for the weekend, joined us there with Aunt Clara. Then they came and lunched here with us. Dined with Uncle Gerry.

TUESDAY FEBRUARY 9

Today I had a jolly little lunch party, Mrs Paget, Verena Barneby, Aunt Ethel and Aunt Clara and we laughed very much. The war was taboo, except for a few passing words. Mrs Paget's mother being German, it is natural that she does not take quite the same standpoint as the rest of us.

Last night we dined at 91 Onslow Square to help Rigby entertain the Belgian lady living there. Minna is away and Rigby finds intercourse hampered by his inability to talk French and hers to speak English. She told me of the dreadful pressure the Germans are putting upon the people in Brussels, where she owns property.

For her house, she will have to pay on March 1st a tax ten times as heavy as hitherto to the Belgian Government. She has to find 3000 francs but is totally unable to get money. If it is not forthcoming, first her furniture, then her house will be sold by the

Germans themselves. Being very hard pressed for cash, her husband decided to go to Brussels to get money out of his bank, where he had deposited his securities and cash, in a private safe. He was allowed to open his own safe only in the presence of a soldier with a loaded rifle and to withdraw 500 frs (£20), and no more.

Meanwhile, think of the iron tyranny to which the Belgians are subjected, and imagine an Englishman handling his own money under the menace of a German rifle and only thus! I am afraid both your Grandfathers would have been felled to the ground by the butt-end of the rifle under like circumstances!

THURSDAY 11 FEBRUARY

Spend the day at Hackney with Mrs de la Rue, visiting the children's mothers for the Care Committee. Most depressing, disheartening work, because it is so inadequate in relation to the misery one sees. All we visitors have to do is to hunt up the mothers and see that they take the children marked out at the school as requiring treatment to hospital to be attended. We are not allowed to help in any way personally, by giving anything. When I came home tonight, I was ashamed to see my own fat, lovely, healthy, easy baby, surrounded with every possible care and attention and to think of the disadvantages the poor little babies I saw today have to struggle against.

FRIDAY FEBRUARY 12

America has sent two notes, one to Germany and one to England, warning them that Germany will be demanded complete satisfaction for any damage done to American shipping, or to any of her citizens. England is warned that complications may arise if she makes use of the American flag, as a substitute for the Union Jack. This refers to the incident of the liner *Lusitania* substituting the American for the English flag last week, during her journey from America. The Union Jack was lowered when the ship was a day's journey from Ireland, as a precaution to ensure the safety of the passengers. America took friendly exception to this, pointing out that her flag would be prejudiced, in the sight of Germany, if the British made frequent use of it.

The incident aroused much comment and has no doubt provoked Germany to adopt a still fiercer and more determined attitude.

MONDAY FEBRUARY 15

Uncle Hugh Lee's wedding with Hilda Blagden. Paper souvenirs were being sold outside the Church, and as you were stationed in your pram just by the bride's door (next door to the Church at the back of our own house, St Peter's, Cranley Gardens) to wave good luck to her, I obtained a copy for your diary. I am sorry to tell you the bride never noticed you, as she brushed past you up the steps of her home, but she was very amused when I told her what she had missed.

She looked very elegant, graceful and beaming with happiness. It has been quite a romance, as she cared for him from the time he became a widower. She is a dear, very feminine creature.

This ridiculous fashion of selling 'souvenirs' of the wedding was started, for anyone below royal rank, three or four years ago for the marriage of Lord Stafford. Now at all fashionable weddings it is done, as a speculation on the part of street hawkers, who get hold of the particulars. Copies are sold for 6d.

The blockade of Britain by Germany is to begin on Thursday, and the Kaiser is expected at Cuxhaven on that day. Germany is not at all abashed at the indignant protests and warnings she has received from neutral countries. Her tone is more truculent than before, and America has been informed that Germany will not be diverted from her new policy in the war zone.

A most important announcement was made in the Commons today by Lloyd George on the finances of the War:

1. The accumulation of Gold in this country is now larger than it has ever been in the history of our country.
2. The Allies' expenses will be £2,000,000,000 and England will spend more than France or Russia.
3. The British Government can finance the war for five years out of the proceeds of investments abroad, and France for about two or three years.
4. England has advanced 32 million pounds for purchases made by Russia here and elsewhere.

TUESDAY FEBRUARY 16

I spent a long day out, visiting the family and acquaintance laid up with catarrh in the eyes, the form that influenza seems to be taking this year. First I went to find Olive Barneby at her request and found her in bed; next Aunt Louisa up at Highgate,* she was recovering from the same, lastly Aunt Ethel. They have all suffered acute pain in the eyes.

WEDNESDAY FEBRUARY 17

Another great air-raid, in which 40 aeroplanes (including 8 French ones) took part, was undertaken by the British yesterday afternoon. 240 bombs were dropped over Zeebrugge, Ostend and other Belgian Coast towns in an attempt to complete the destruction done in the raid a few days ago and to destroy the submarine bases.

THURSDAY FEBRUARY 18

Today is the first day of the Blockade of England by Germany! The cross-channel service to France is suspended, to give time for all our destroyers to be ready to escort our transport across. Last night I went with Aunt Clara to hear Hilaire Belloc in another lecture on the progress of the War. The gist of it was that the next week or two

---

*   Louisa Davis, her father's youngest sister.

will be critical. The main interest lies on the eastern side where Germany is desperately trying to break through at Warsaw, so as to get command of the only railway system to St Petersburg.

More important still, Germany is trying to prevent Russia spreading her forces into the great Hungarian plains which are the granary of the Austrian Empire and also of Germany. As long as Germany and Austria can command the corn of Hungary they are more or less independent of the food blockade. But if Russia gets possession there, this great source of food is cut off from the Central Empires and their position becomes precarious.

FRIDAY FEBRUARY 19

Daddy and I came today to Newnham Hall (Northampton) to stay with Uncle and Aunt Romer-Williams. We travelled down by the 5 o'clock train and met Armorer Nicholson's husband, who was coming down too by that train. Nicky was invalided home from the war some months ago, having fractured a leg during the retreat from Mons. He is still lame, and is at present quartered in Dublin, on the reserve, until he is well enough to go back to the Front.

We were lucky to find Armorer and Nicky staying here on short leave from Dublin. Armorer is so beautiful; she is very quiet and sweet, in continual anxiety lest Nicky should be sent back to the Front.* Florence Younghusband and Kraussie are here.

The house, which belongs to our old childhood friend, Hal Bromfield, has been much added to by Uncle Romer. He has also filled it with beautiful furniture, pictures, prints and miniatures, china, enamels etc. Then I prolonged the evening by sitting in Florence's room gossiping and having my hair brushed!

SATURDAY FEBRUARY 20

Lovely sunny day. Daddy and I went for a long walk with Kraussie to the old Church, 13th century, but walls and tower out of the perpendicular and subsiding in places. There we saw tablets to the memory of some of the Bromfield family. Spent a very pleasant day, played duets with Kraussie, and laughed a good deal. The war news is not very exciting.

SUNDAY FEBRUARY 21

Florence came home from Church with the exciting news that British warships have bombarded the forts at the mouth of the Dardanelles. This is news of the utmost importance. If we get through, we can run in reinforcements and equipment to the Russians. Turkey's joining in has simply opened a door for our fleets in the Dardanelles, which otherwise we should have been compelled by our treaties to leave closed.

Florence showed me a letter she had just opened from 'Jack' Younghusband (General Sir George Y), who is at present commanding at Ismailia a division of mixed Indian and British troops against the proposed Turkish invasion of Egypt.

---

*   He was – and was killed in action in 1917.

Jan. 26. 15   Copy   Ismailia
                              Egypt.

My Dear Florence,   NEWNHAM HALL.
                         —DAVENTRY.—

Many thanks for yours about Alexandria.
If I am that way I will certainly look
up your friends. At present we are
busy guarding the Canal against the Turks
who vigorously urged thereto by Wilhelm
II are coming on in great numbers.
It is a desperate venture & few ought
to return to tell the tale. We bumped
into them yesterday about a dozen miles
out from here and the aeroplanes had
quite an exciting day. One was flying
low because of the mist when it suddenly
got it at 300 yards from a Turkish
battery. He made a streak for the
moon or thereabouts & got off with a
few holes in his wings. The other airman
was just over the Turks when his
engine failed and down he had to plane
hotly pursued by cavalry. However
just before they came up he got her
going again & flopped off, but only
got a mile or so when down she came
again. Again he just got her up in time
but she wouldn't rise more than 300 feet
and at that range he got peppered by
every damn fellow he passed. However

Letter from Gen. Sir George
Younghusband to his wife.

he got back safely, but with
three bullets in his machinery.
They have given it out in all the
mosques in Syria that Wilhelm II
has become a Mahomedan, & he is prayed
for under the strange title of "Emperor
Guillaume Mahomed." Good old
Wilhelm, he is really a very funny
fellow. All the German officers
profess Mahomedanism & it must
be great fun seeing a fat Major in
a tight uniform rubbing his nose on
the ground and doing the 32 genuflex-
-ions on a marble floor.
Well good bye, my dear, & for the
sake of all you dear people at
home may we soon have Wilhelm
by the beard and process up the
Unter den Linden. Best love.
    Yours affectly
        Jack.
(General Sir George Younghusband)
                      KCSI. CB.
commanding a division mixed British &
Indians at Ismailia. —

TUESDAY FEBRUARY 23

The Germans have sunk several more neutral ships, one or two Norwegian and the American ship *Evelyn*. On the other hand two of their submarines are two days overdue at Cuxhaven.

WEDNESDAY FEBRUARY 24

The little Folkestone and Boulogne Channel steamer, in which we so often crossed backwards and forwards, was attacked by a German submarine yesterday four miles from Boulogne harbour. But the torpedo passed 30 yards in front of the ship! There were 92 passengers on board. A third Norwegian ship has been sunk by a torpedo, but the crew escaped in their own boats. Also another American ship *Carib* been sunk by a German mine.

The Russian counter-offensive to the German attack north of Warsaw has been successful. A week has passed since Hilaire Belloc told us that if the Germans did not take Warsaw, or 'get astride' of the Warsaw-Petrograd railway within a fortnight, it would look as though this last violent effort was to succeed no more than the previous ones.

FRIDAY FEBRUARY 26

I was shocked this morning to hear that Alistair Dunsmure has been killed, a boy of 20, in the Cameron Highlanders, first cousin to your first cousins Henry and Beatrice. His father only died four months ago, and he went to the Front just before his father's death. His younger brother, also in the Camerons, is out there too.

I hear also today that Eugene Crombie has arrived at the Front, within sound of the guns, and he expects to be in the trenches in a day or two. Henry Bolton's boy of 22, who only joined the Sussex Territorials a few weeks ago, has also just arrived at the Front. The losses are awful these last few days. The 16th Lancers have had six officers killed and five wounded and Lord knows how many men.

I met yesterday pretty little Mrs Rattray, wife of an officer in the 60th Rifles. She told me that, out of his regiment of 1000 men, there are only 250 left. The regiment has twice already been made up to its full fighting force. But now there are no men to take their place and there will be none left of the original lot.

To think of that awful despotic maniac the Kaiser, plunging Europe into such wholesale slaughter! What can be done to him when it is all over? Think of the flower of our nation, these splendid young fellows being butchered for his lunacy.

SATURDAY FEBRUARY 27

British and French warships have entered the Dardanelles, bombarding the forts. All our thoughts and hopes are centred on this phase of the war. The German submarines have not achieved a 'coup' so far, yet our transports are now taking thousands of troops across to France, to say nothing of the stores, equipment and ammunition for our

Feb. 27 th

lunacy.

Saturday Feb. 27 th The British & French warships have gone 15 miles up the Dardanelles, bombarding the forts, without being even hit by the Turkish guns.

All our thoughts & hopes are at present centred on this phase of the war. The German submarines have not achieved a "coup" so far — yet our Transports

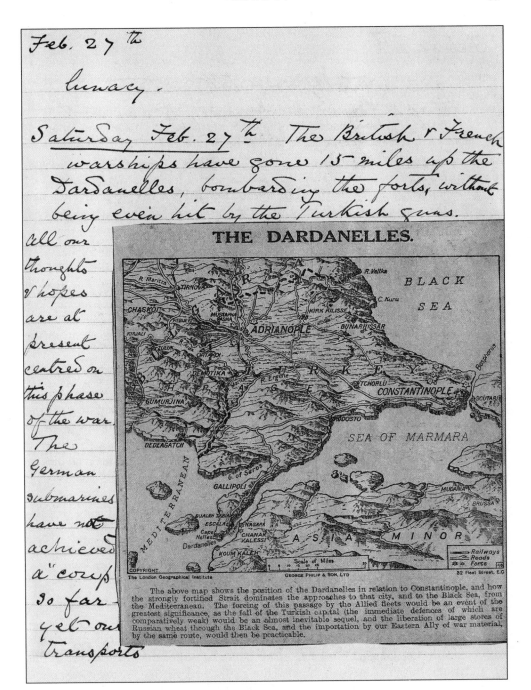

THE DARDANELLES.

The above map shows the position of the Dardanelles in relation to Constantinople, and how the strongly fortified Strait dominates the approaches to that city, and to the Black Sea, from the Mediterranean. The forcing of this passage by the Allied fleets would be an event of the greatest significance, as the fall of the Turkish capital (the immediate defences of which are comparatively weak) would be an almost inevitable sequel, and the liberation of large stores of Russian wheat through the Black Sea, and the importation by our Eastern Ally of war material, by the same route, would then be practicable.

Map of the Dardanelles and Gallipoli Peninsula.

Allies. Lionel Taylor,* up for the day from Bristol, came in to tea today and told me that ships are leaving Avonmouth daily.

MONDAY MARCH 1

Today Daddy was late at the office (a rare thing for him) because he stopped to watch the newly-formed Welsh Guards marching to mount guard at Buckingham Palace. It was their first appearance in public. In honour of St David's Day, they had a real leek, root and all, stuck into each man's cap. It is not yet settled what distinguishing badge they are to wear.

The Admiralty's 'surprise' to the world in the Dardanelles is the presence of the new super Dreadnought *Queen Elizabeth*, which was not known to be afloat and finished. She is fitted with 8 new monster naval guns, 15 inch, firing shells weighing a ton each, with a range of 20 miles! No wonder the four forts guarding the entrance to the Dardanelles have been heavily shelled with the *Queen Elizabeth*, the *Irresistible*, *Vengeance* and others to do the business. The French warships also took part. It is all going splendidly.

The *Queen Elizabeth* is the first of the ships to be driven by oil-fuel alone and her speed is about 25 knots instead of 21 knots. So she is a great improvement on the earlier Dreadnoughts in speed, gun-power and self-protection.

TUESDAY MARCH 2

The Government, through Asquith, has announced its policy in response to the German blockade. No ship of any sort is to be allowed in or out of Germany, she is to be completely isolated. No goods are to go in, none are to come out.

The one blot on our Country's wholehearted response to the call made on all men to rally round and keep the flag flying, is the strike of the wretched workers, engineers, on the Clyde, for an extra farthing an hour. The strike is most serious. It is stopping the supply of ammunition and equipment on which not only our own Field Force, but the Allies depend.

An interesting fact is that two-thirds of the undergraduates at Oxford and Cambridge are serving either at the Front or in the Army here, as officers, privates, or in some capacity. Eighty out of eighty-nine 'Blues' are serving.

WEDNESDAY MARCH 3

The Americans don't like our blockade of Germany as it destroys their trade completely with Germany. But England is resolute and is not to be turned from her purpose in this life and death struggle. American ships are not confiscated, neither are the goods; nor is the liberty of the crews infringed. Only the merchandise is not allowed to enter any port destined for German use; nor is any German merchandise allowed out. It is terrible for the German people, but better than prolonging the war.

---

*   Georgina's brother-in-law, married to her sister Edith.

BOOK V

MARCH 4 – MAY 30, 1915

THURSDAY MARCH 4

I have just been reading the story of the Battle of Ypres. It thrills me so deeply that I want you to read it too, my pet. It shows you what Englishmen can do by their heroic perseverance and determination. Truly the impossible can be achieved with perseverance.

The heroic captain of a small British collier has had the honour of ramming and sinking a German submarine. Seeing the periscope of a submarine a short distance off, and then the wake of a torpedo coming towards him, the master of the *Thordis* steamed at full speed towards the periscope, went right into it and tore it away. Oil immediately rose to the surface and no further trace of the submarine was seen.

On reporting the occurrence to the Admiral at Plymouth, the *Thordis* was ordered into dry dock to see if the Captain's claim was justified. The state of the damaged collier was such as to satisfy the Admiral. The Captain was awarded the £500 reward for being the first merchantman to sink a submarine.

FRIDAY MARCH 5

I had a full and tiring day but did nothing worth recording. I went to bed at 10.30 with a splitting headache and yet had done no real good to compensate for the waste of energy. What finished me was taking Beatrice to the Coliseum, after being on my feet the rest of the day. I am disappointed to find I cannot get any sustained work done, either visiting among the poor or helping for the war. You and the house take up so many of my hours; and I get too tired from much standing.

SATURDAY MARCH 6

Another German submarine has been sunk, this time by a destroyer, and the crew of 29 officers and men were landed at Dover as prisoners. It is significant that no English or neutral ships have been torpedoed this week, so the German blockade of our coast is so far rather a farce.

SUNDAY MARCH 7

We dined with Minna tonight to help to talk with her charming Belgians, M. & Mme Dries who will persist in not speaking English. So it rather relieves Minna if I am there to help her out.

TUESDAY MARCH 9

This afternoon while at the work-party I go to, for the West London Hospital, I talked to a pretty young woman, Mrs Pardoe. She was in trouble over a young nephew in the Gordon Highlanders, now a prisoner in Germany, taken in the disaster to the Gordons during the retreat from Mons. This is poor young Lt Neish. He says their state is dreadful and they do not expect ever to get back to England.

He managed to get a letter through somehow, without its being censored by the Germans. They are being starved, he says; he never knew till now that it was possible 'to live on air'. He tells his people not to send out any more parcels because he has never received one as they are all taken by the Germans. His Uncle, Colonel Neish, also a prisoner, has been separated from him and sent he knows not where.

But what they hate most are the lies told them about England. London is a mass of ruins; the British are suffering heavy defeats; the Germans have brilliant victories. 'For God's sake', he writes, 'tell me the truth about the old country'. To get the truth in the letters written to him, he has arranged a code. If the worst has happened to England they are to write 'Old Aunt Victoria is very ill, or dying'. Needless to say, his relatives have written 'Aunt Victoria is well; indeed she never has been ill'.

WEDNESDAY MARCH 10

I was writing the other day that the Germans has sunk none of our ships for over a week. Today it is announced that they have torpedoed three merchantmen without warning and without attempting to rescue the crews who were drowned. But tonight it is officially announced that we have sunk their submarine U20, taking prisoners and rescuing the crew.

Belloc's lecture was again packed, not a vacant seat. He told us that the man – we do not yet know who he is – who conceived the idea of forcing the Dardanelles and taking Constantinople, will, if it proves successful, go down to history as the one who deserves the gratitude of Europe for deciding the issue of the war.

He pointed out the complete change which would result from the fall of Con stantinople. Not only would the present blockade of Russia cease, i.e. her huge reserves of corn and oil would be open to us, and she would get the ammunition and equipment she is gasping for. But Turkey would be open to the Allies for taking Austria in the rear and the Balkan States, freed from Turkish menace, would be free to join us.

What is keeping the war in abeyance is the lack of ammunition to feed the monster War. We really need every available man to be working at full pressure, manufacturing shells. But this is the time a lot of men have chosen to go on strike.

The necessity is so great, that Lloyd George has framed a Bill, proposed yesterday in the House and rushed through today, empowering the Government to commandeer any and every factory needed for the manufacture of shells and bullets.

THURSDAY MARCH 11

The British forces on the Western Front have made an important advance, taking the village of Neuve Chapelle. Every trench and every position within a mile from the former British line was captured.

FRIDAY MARCH 12

A further British advance is reported by Sir John French in tonight's news. So it looks as if we are really moving forward at last. When Uncle Guy was home on leave a few weeks ago, I asked him what the general scheme was for the campaign when the new Army went out. 'Oh, just advance', he replied, 'It will mean a horrible slaughter but it is the only thing to be done.'

SATURDAY MARCH 13

The Paris paper *Matin* speaks enthusiastically of the success of the British troops at Neuve Chapelle and calls it the most important advance made for many weeks.

A German submarine has torpedoed an armed merchant cruiser of ours, *Bayano*, off Ailsa Craig, as she was leaving the Clyde. 195 lives were lost. Another British ship, going from Belfast to Ayr (the very stretch of sea Daddy and I used to gaze at from Blair last October), came upon a lot of wreckage and lifeless bodies and two rafts upon which 26 exhausted men were clinging. The *Balmarino* rescued these men and took them into port at Ayr. They stated that the *Bayano* went down in three minutes.

TUESDAY MARCH 16

The German cruiser *Dresden* which escaped being sunk in the battle of the Falkland Islands, has just met her doom off Valparaiso. She was sunk by the *Kent* and *Glasgow*, after all her crew had surrendered. It is rather amusing, because the Captain had boasted that he would fight to the last man when he met the British warships. But after five minutes action, the white flag was hoisted. After the Captain and crew had been taken abroad, the fire which was already raging on the *Dresden* reached her magazines and she blew up and sank.

Kitchener has spoken in the House of Lords on the difficulties of supplying munitions. The great trouble at present is that the workmen in the north get such high pay that they will only work two or three days out of the six and the rest of the time they drink. It is too maddening to think that such a successful offensive as the Neuve Chapelle battle is only possible with vast supplies of ammunition and that until these arrive our men are lingering and waiting in the trenches.

The men who have loyally continued to work in the factories are fit to rank with the soldiers who have earned their medals in the field. Those who have deserved well of their country will receive a Labour Medal at the end of the war. This should be prized by their descendants as a great memento of the biggest crisis in our history.

WEDNESDAY MARCH 17

There is an awful casualty list today, including 156 officers, 46 of them killed, the rest wounded. Uncle Guy's words are coming true, 'we shall just advance but the slaughter will be appalling'. And the descriptions we hear of the effect of the big guns on the trenches sicken one. Eugene Crombie writing to his mother yesterday says 'I watched the shells bursting, and saw one fellow blown right up into the air, still holding his spade. He came down again, but as ill-luck would have it, another shell burst just in the same place and I saw him vanish noisily and completely in bits.'

THURSDAY MARCH 18

A new move is being made by the Government to supply the labour field. The Government is appealing to women of all classes who are willing to work. They are to register themselves, thus placing themselves at their country's disposal.

Another ominous sign of what we still have before us, is that many more nurses are likely to be wanted for the large increase in casualties expected during the coming months. If only I could help in this way! I am longing to do some useful work.

FRIDAY MARCH 19

A Zeppelin came over Calais yesterday and dropped a bomb which fell on a train and killed seven refugees.

Today we took you in Minna's car to be seen by an old girl-friend of hers and mine, Mrs Macintyre, who has a nice baby of 5 months. After we got home Lord Caithness came to see me to talk over Miss Reeves's affairs. We soon dismissed that and then discussed the war and mutual friends. Nobody does anything else nowadays.

SATURDAY MARCH 20

There is news enough today. Three battleships have been sunk in the Dardanelles, the *Ocean*, Captain Hayes Sadler's command, the *Irresistible* and the French ship *Bouvet*, all struck by floating Turkish mines. The French *Bouvet*, which had engaged the forts in action most gallantly, was sunk in three minutes as her magazines blew up.

Many of the crew of the *Ocean* and *Irresistible* were saved. The *Inflexible* lost many of her crew by shells fired from the forts, but four of the forts were silenced. The squadron was doing splendid work in bombarding and reducing the forts. The loss of the *Bouvet*'s gallant crew is very great. New measures are to be adopted to cope with this menace of the floating mines. I can imagine the Turks putting them down by thousands after this success.

Uncle Tich, whom we saw last night, strongly deprecates the policy of the Government in keeping so many reverses from the public, as it keeps us all in the illusion that all is going well. As the Germans know from their reverses, no good is gained by keeping the country in a Fool's Paradise.

As a nation, we are strong to bear reverses; they serve to brace us and bring out our best qualities. But all along we have been given too rosy a view of the war and made to understand that all was going well. Here I have been laughing at the German blockade and now I am told this!

MONDAY MARCH 22

Enormous casualty lists keep coming in from the Western Front. It is an appalling human price to pay for perhaps two miles of territory gained. Seeing what Neuve Chapelle and St Eloi have cost us in a week, one can imagine what it will entail when the Germans have to be cleared out of Belgium.

The moral of these casualties is being driven home to our workers in England by Kitchener, and every wise man who writes or speaks these days: 'More shells, shells, shells!' Spend the shells and spare the soldiers is the chief theme. With our new heavy guns the artillery men can destroy the enemy's trenches from afar. But with a shortage of shells, the murderous trench-warfare has to go on.

Many of the recalcitrant workers have fallen into line, after Kitchener's appeal. But still there is a lack of labour. So women are being enrolled for the manufacture of equipment and munitions of war.

TUESDAY MARCH 23

This evening Aunt Edie and I were watching you getting ready for bed, when Sybil Scott and her fiancé Charlie Wynne-Jones, were announced! There was an excitement for he was supposed to be in the trenches at La Bassée. Down I flew and found Sybil looking very pretty, calm and excited all at once, and the good looking young man with charming manners, who is to be married to S. by special licence on Friday.

It appears that Charlie W.J. only arrived from the Front last night. He has been given a few days leave at a quarter of an hour's notice. He jumped into a car, came straight to Boulogne and wired to Sybil from Folkestone. Sybil, who was in Cornwall, took the first train up to London and arrived late last night.

This morning she rang up Daddy at Westminster.

'Charlie, will you do something for me?'

'Yes, I will', said Daddy, 'now, what is it?'

'I want you to get me a special licence to be married on Friday; my Charlie has just arrived from the Front and has to go back Sunday.'

'Come down both of you to me at once', said Daddy, and he took them straight to the Faculty Office in Knightrider Street in the City.

The preliminaries were gone through, then Uncle Hugh Lee went to the Archbishop to ask for the Special Licence. The Archbishop said it would be all right as Uncle Hugh knew the girl and her family and the Arch. himself knew the Dean of St Asaph, the bridegroom's father. But he would not actually hand over the document until he had a letter of approval from the Dean.

The Archbishop, Randall Davidson, is exceedingly strict about these hurried marriages. He insists on every investigation being carried out, to ensure that the marriage is above all suspicion. Sybil is 25 and heiress to a large property near Gelligemlyn and her marriage would normally be the occasion of great rejoicings.

Now it seems so strange to see her so simple and sedate, caring for nothing but to become the wife of the boy who has been in love with her for years. And in two days they will be parted. Her wedding is only one of hundreds, even thousands, of the soldier and sailor marriages going on and the State encourages these unions for state reasons!

Charlie Wynne-Jones is in the 17th Lancers and as the Cavalry have nothing much to do just now, some of them are being sent home for 3 or 4 days. He told us his division was in the reserve trenches behind the firing line at Neuve Chapelle, ready to charge the Germans and pursue and rout them if they had been 'got well on the move'. Unfortunately one of our divisions arrived 1½ hours late, so that the success already achieved could not be turned into a much greater victory.[*]

WEDNESDAY MARCH 24

The fall of Przemsyl liberates a large army of Russians to move on to the siege of Cracow. It also disposes of a substantial portion of the Austrian Army.

Sir George Younghusband, your cousin, whose letter from Egypt I copied and inserted in this diary four weeks ago, is in the papers today as having dispersed a Turkish force 1000 strong, detected near Suez two days ago.

FRIDAY MARCH 26

Daddy and I left the house at 10.30 this morning for the Church in North Audley Street. A very few intimate friends were there to see Sybil Scott's wedding. She looked very pretty and slim in her satin gown and soft folds of tulle like a cloud about her dainty little figure. The ceremony was over before 12, after which we just went into Lady Trotter's house in Eaton Place, to wish the young couple good luck. It would have been a very affecting little wedding if Sybil herself had not been so radiant and bright, oblivious to the trials awaiting her, for he has to return to the Front on Sunday.

I brought back a piece of white lilac from her bouquet and took it straight to your nursery where you were eating your dinner in the high chair, with the little pink bib tied under your chin. You sniffed at the lilac, and finding it nice, went on sniffing and sniffing until it was a very parched and bruised bit of lilac indeed.

---

[*]   Thus a great opportunity was missed. In his later despatch, Sir John French states that, by 11 am on 10 March, Neuve Chapelle and roads northwards were in British hands. No further advance began until 3.30 pm. *Massacre of the Innocents – The Crofton Diaries, Ypres 1914–1915*, p. 201.

SATURDAY MARCH 27

The Dardanelles operations are being resumed, the weather having cleared after a week's gales. But there are naval critics who deplore this delay stating that the essence of Nelson's success lay in the fact that he never waited. Once having started his operations he rushed them through before his enemy had time to turn round and take measures for his defence.

This delay of a week has enabled the Turks and Germans to repair the damaged forts and mount new guns so that the Fleet will find its task harder than before.

MONDAY MARCH 29

We have all been packing for our departure for Glaslyn tomorrow. We are going to Glaslyn to see to the valuing of all the pictures and drawings left by your grandfather. This must be done before we can prove the Will. Aunt Ethel is coming too, to help Uncle Henry and me, who are executors.

It is very sad to me to remember that just a year ago you went to Glaslyn for the first time and delighted your Grandfather so completely. The place is so bound up with him that I cannot imagine it without him. His personality was so strong.

TUESDAY MARCH 30

Travelled down to Glaslyn, Granny, Aunt Ethel, you, Nannie, our parlour maid and I. The place was looking lovely in the evening sun when we arrived; the garden looking so trim.

THURSDAY APRIL 1

Daddy and Uncle Henry arrived at 7 o'clock this morning, having travelled all night. Aunt Ethel, Uncle H and I spent the morning in the studio preparing the pictures for the valuers coming tomorrow from London.

TUESDAY APRIL 6

Glaslyn
For the last few days I have had nothing to say, except that Aunt Ethel and I have worked all day at dividing into six all the lovely sketches and studies of your Grandfather's which have not been selected to go to London to be valued by Agnew's. Altogether we sorted about 280 into categories. We selected six in each category for the six legatees, a terribly difficult job. We sorted them into Moonlight Studies, Highland Studies, River Thames etc. making each of the six canvases in each category as fair in value or merit as we could. Sometime later, we must all meet and each pick out a picture in turn.

All the larger, more important works, together with his few old Masters inherited from his father, comprising a rare and valuable van Goyen, two lovely David Coxes, one Samuel Prout, *Hulks at Plymouth*, and eight fine proofs of etchings by Rembrandt (bought by your Great Grandfather at the celebrated 'Stowe' sale of the Duke of Buckingham in 1833), all these were taken up in a large van to London today by Agnew.

Some of them must be sold for Death Duties, but our object is to keep all we can in the family. Added to this, the War is fatal to picture-selling. People will not spend a penny on luxuries, and we do not want to expose his beautiful works to the humiliation of being sold at knock down prices.

We parted today. Aunt Ethel going to London; Daddy, Granny and I coming to Gelligemlyn for a week. I left you at Glaslyn which is more bracing for you, and to save Granny trouble here, as we are only picnicking for a few days. You suddenly have taken to walking so much better, but your most amusing trick is 'doing the Frenchman'. You carefully lay down anything you are holding, then spread out your hands and made such an amusingly perplexed face as though you were saying 'Que voulez-vous?'

We arrived at Gelligemlyn at about 3 o'clock and have been all round the premises and for a walk over the hill. The garden is in very good order.

The campaign against drink has started with the King. From today he has stopped all alcoholic drink in his household; he and his guests have barley-water or aerated or plain water; in the steward's rooms and kitchens only plain water is allowed. Lord Kitchener has done the same, and this example will no doubt be followed throughout the land, possibly rendering prohibition by law unnecessary. The Tyneside workers are said to be responding to the King's grave appeal to all men, in this our Country's crisis, to give up all drink until the war is over.

SATURDAY APRIL 10

A long letter from Uncle Guy this morning to his Mother. He described a very narrow escape he had just had. He was superintending the making of bombs (the hand-grenades they are throwing across the trenches) and seeing to the wire detonators being fitted and the fuses. 800 of these were ready and he had them spread out in rows on the floor of a store room. Suddenly one of his men shouted 'look out, one of the bombs is alight!' At the same moment the man picked up the bomb and threw it across the room away from the others.

The fuses are timed to explode the bomb in 6 seconds. Guy shouted 'down on your faces all of you', a command they all obeyed, except one man who stood staring, fascinated, at the fizzling fuse. Guy jumped at him, threw his arm about his neck and dragged him down. For the few seconds, that seemed like years, there was deathly stillness, then the explosion came. That end of the place was wrecked, but a moment later the men were all on their feet, laughing at their marvellous escape.

MONDAY APRIL 12

We leave tomorrow for Neville Street at 8 am and I am all excitement because I shall meet you at Shrewsbury. Daddy will have to go straight on to get two or three hours work at Westminster, while I await at Shrewsbury the arrival of your train from Rhayader. I wonder whether I shall find you again saluting every man in khaki who goes by the window.

Yesterday we had quite an event. Daddy and I drove to Ganllwyd in the little car and found the whole village on their doorsteps. 'Are you going in pursuit too, Sir'? they cried to Charlie. It then appeared that the two German officers who escaped from the prisoners' camp at Denbigh a week ago had been seen in the mountains a few miles away. The constables in the district, as well as the soldiers in camp at Trawsfynydd had all turned out to join in the chase.

Today we hear the two fugitives were captured at Llanbedr, near Harlech, where they were run to earth. They were exhausted having wandered in the mountains for a week.*

TUESDAY APRIL 13

Returned safely to Neville Street after meeting you at Shrewsbury. Train full of soldiers and I found your carriage so packed I got the ticket examiner to find us another place, so he put us into a first class to Euston. You enjoyed yourself thoroughly and laughed every time we caught sight of each other in the mêlée.

THURSDAY APRIL 15

Yesterday evening a recruiting meeting was held at Blyth, in Northumberland, and the streets in this collier town were thronged with people. The orator, speaking in the market place, had been enlarging upon the treatment the Germans would mete to the English if they got a footing in England. Just at that moment, a real live Zeppelin came in sight, flying high. 'Here is a visitor for you', quoth the speaker, 'this should be an inducement to recruiting.'

It was about 8 o'clock. Six bombs were dropped at Blyth, and others at neighbouring villages, within a radius of 35 miles from the coast but very little damage was done. One civilian killed and several hurt. More damage would have been done, were it not for the splendid way that the whole South East of Northumberland went into utter darkness within a few minutes, all lights being extinguished.

Only one Zeppelin arrived this time. The commander had apparently lost his bearings, his objective probably being the great armament works at Elswick, and the ship building yards at Newcastle.

The full list of casualties for the battle of Neuve Chapelle is double the losses for those we had at Waterloo. Of officers we had 190 killed, 359 wounded, 23 missing. Missing very likely means buried alive in the trenches, for in this hideous warfare whole sections of trenches become obliterated or filled up by mine explosions, and the men are literally buried alive. There were 2337 men killed; 8174 wounded; 1728 missing. The total number of casualties up to April 11 was 139, 347.

---

*   On 1 May these two officers were tried and sentenced to 28 days' imprisonment.

FRIDAY APRIL 16

There has been another Zeppelin raid, early this morning, on the East Coast, at Lowestoft. But again no damage was done. It looks as though they were trying their wings for an attempt on London.

We heard today of the death of another young officer, Captain Johnston, Eugene Crombie's first cousin. His pretty little wife was with Minna, two or three months ago, seeing her husband off. She adored him and though very plucky, she hardly knew how to get through the days for her anxiety.

Daddy brought me home tonight this paper he had to fill in, as a Volunteer of the Inns of Court. I have got him to procure a duplicate copy of the form, so that you may see how your Daddy answered his country's call when he was needed. He drills every day at 4.30, and on Saturdays he is out all the afternoon with his Corps, route-marching and manoeuvring between Putney and Richmond.

Inns of Court Reserve Corps.

Home Defence Service.

Form to be filled up and returned at once to the Hon. Secretary, G. Nugent Bankes, 123, St. George's Road, S.W.

Please answer all the questions fully.

1. Are you prepared to do Patrol Work locally at night? *not night work*

    (a) What evenings of the week?

    (b) At what times?

2. Are you prepared to do Patrol Work locally by day? *Yes*

    (a) What days of the week? *Any day*

    (b) At what times? *Any time*

3. Are you prepared to go away for
    (a) A week at a time? *A week twice a month*

    (b) A few days (state number) at a time? *Three days each week*

    (c) At what intervals of time? *in every week*

    (d) At your own expense *Cannot afford the expense.*

4. In case of Invasion, in addition to service near your home, would you be prepared to serve in any part of your Country? *Yes*

5. In case of Invasion, would you be prepared to serve in any part of the United Kingdom? *Yes*

Signature *Charles W Lee*

Address *15 Neville Street SW*

If allotted to a Platoon, please state its number *Platoon No: IV*

Charles Lee's Inns of Court Reserve Corps Form.

*** HOLD AVAILABLE ***

Item ID: 204521832R
Author: Lee, Georgina
Lydia, 1869-1965.
Title: Home fires burning :
the Great War diaries of
Geo
User name: Lawy, Helen
(Mrs)
Pickup By: 19/10/2018
User ID 0300790496

Today I went with Florence Younghusband to offer to help on the Chelsea Branch of the Belgian Relief Committee. It has its headquarters at Crosby Hall on the Embankment close to here. They were very glad of the offer and I am to be employed in a day or two.

TUESDAY APRIL 20

The Bishop of London has returned from the Front, where he went for a fortnight at Easter to speak to the men in the trenches and hospitals. Daddy, who is devoted to the Bishop, cherished the scheme of going out with him as his secretary. But at the very first hint he gave of his secret desire to the Bishop's private secretary he was told it was quite hopeless. Nobody who was not in a military or ecclesiastical capacity would be allowed in the lines. Daddy has a great deal to do with him in his official capacity as Registrar to the London Diocese.

WEDNESDAY APRIL 21

Heard today that another young relation of the Wason family, Walter Andrews, has been killed in the war. Also Eugene Crombie has had the narrowest of squeaks, when a bullet tore his cap to ribbons. He had been told to report on the state of the enemy's barbed wire entanglements and just raised his head to have a peep over the trench. Instantly the sniper's bullet found him. This is how most of the young men are being killed.

There has been another very severe action at St Eloi. Several German trenches were carried and altogether the British advanced about 800 yards. But in a day or two the terrible casualty lists will be appearing again.

FRIDAY APRIL 23

After several weeks of silence from the Dardanelles (and of tense anticipation on the nation's part) we hear that British and French forces are landing there. Sir Ian Hamilton has command of the expedition. Von der Goltz, late German Governor of Brussels, is now Commander-in-Chief of the Turkish Army.

Alexandria is being used as the base for our large bodies of troops, French and English, where Allied troops have been amassing for days, waiting for the signal to embark.

Today I went with Miss Hood to see some of the wounded Tommies at the West London Hospital. They were all in one ward and looked very cheery and patient. They had been wounded at Neuve Chapelle and Ypres. Wipers, as they called it! I was so sorry I had no cigarettes or sweets with me as my visit to the hospital was really intended for the babies' ward; but I promised I would bring them some in a day or two, and I will.

They were amusing and sarcastic over a Royal Visit they had had the day before. Princess Arthur of Connaught having announced her intention of coming, they were all kept inside in the ward, instead of going out to take the air. When she appeared, she said to one Tommy mysteriously 'Here, take this' and she gave him two oranges, much to his disgust. 'I've had enough of Royal Visits', he told us.

I asked one Tommy what brand of cigarettes he preferred. He got red and muttered something, so I said 'I suppose the best brand of all will be just good enough for you, won't it?' He laughed with me, so now I must find out what brand a Tommy likes best!

SATURDAY APRIL 24

This evening the papers are full of the Canadians who have 'saved the situation at Ypres' by recapturing four 4.7 guns which we had lost in a sudden advance the Germans made yesterday.

It appears that by means of the horrible expedient of asphyxiating gas bombs a section of the trenches occupied by the French colonial troops north of Ypres have been lost. The Germans made a considerable advance, as nothing could live in the atmosphere created so the French retired. This sudden attack of the Germans is another desperate attempt upon Calais. They have had no scruples in breaking the rules laid down by the Hague Convention against the use of asphyxiating gas in warfare.

I went to see Aunt Louisa today. She, dear soul, is always thinking of the Tommies. She had just been sending off 9lbs of sweets in a large parcel to the sailors of the *Inflexible* who were in the Dardanelles and saved many men from the *Ocean* and *Irresistible*. Her faithful maid Lizzie's brother is gunnery instructor on the *Inflexible* and was wounded in that action.

SATURDAY APRIL 25

Eugene Crombie has suddenly come home wounded, a bullet wound through his chest, but looking as well as possible! Late last night his mother had a wire to say 'slightly wounded'. This morning a wire from Eugene from Dover said he was sent home for a fortnight. He was sent to a home first, but his mother was allowed to fetch him in the car and bring him to Onslow Square, as his wound is healing so rapidly.

He was walking to his trench Friday night when he was suddenly knocked over flat by a blow on his chest. The bullet has pierced sideways, a glancing shot, and come out again three or four inches further. He showed me the exit hole of the bullet and the bullet itself. It is an inch long, very pointed, no thicker than a pencil, and makes a clean wound.

Daddy and I were asked by Minna on the telephone to go round and see Eugene after 3 o'clock, so we went about four and found him just washed and freshly dressed in his bedroom surrounded by his mother, his former Nannie and Fenella! Eugene says our papers are always too optimistic. The Germans have so entrenched themselves as to make their position practically impregnable.

TUESDAY APRIL 27

The second battle of Ypres is raging furiously in Flanders, but it seems the crisis has passed. The Germans had made elaborate preparations for asphyxiating the Allies all along the front they meant to attack. When the Canadians pressed home the counter attack to the German trenches, they discovered numerous pipes laid down in front of German trenches, connected with cylinders containing the gas. Our men first saw pillars of greenish-yellow smoke rise slowly to a height of six or seven feet, and then, caught by the favouring breeze, these were wafted across to our lines. Some men who got the fumes worst died asphyxiated, others were seized with dreadful nausea.

THURSDAY APRIL 29

An appeal is launched to all the women of England to make respirators, thousands and millions of them. They are pads of absorbent cotton wool laid between another cover of gauze, 5½ inches long by 3½ wide, to cover mouth and nostrils and to be fastened round the head by elastic.

I went today to the Press Private View of Royal Academy with Lionel Taylor to see your dear Grandfather's last exhibit at the R.A. It is the picture he tried to finish for last year's exhibition. But he was broken-hearted and discouraged because he had not the physical strength to do the last three or four days' work it needed.

SATURDAY MAY 1

Yesterday morning there was another Zeppelin raid over Bury St Edmunds. Fortunately Uncle Tich and the staff had left for Norwich a few days ago! Several houses were set on fire but nobody was killed.

SUNDAY MAY 2

Now that the full accounts have come out of this second battle of Ypres, we realise that the Germans did make a significant advance. But for the heroism of the Canadians, it would have ended in a catastrophe. We are now face to face with the fearful struggle before us.

The Germans are a long way from being reduced to the defensive. Months ago it was said that Kitchener on being asked 'When will the war end?' replied 'I don't know when it will end, but it will begin in May'. Now it seems that we are only just beginning the serious struggle, but our full resources are not nearly ready.

Germany is taking advantage of the lessons these last nine months have taught her. Her scientific skill enables her to create new weapons to outdo ours, as this horrible asphyxiating gas method has shown. So all our hopes of the war ending this autumn are shattered again.

It is best to have no delusions, but to brace ourselves for the sacrifices we should one and all make for our country. My one deep regret is that I personally am suffering so little when others are giving all.

TUESDAY MAY 4

Yesterday the Roll of Honour contained 200 officers killed and wounded. Today's contains another 200. How can the supply of officers keep up to these enormous demands?

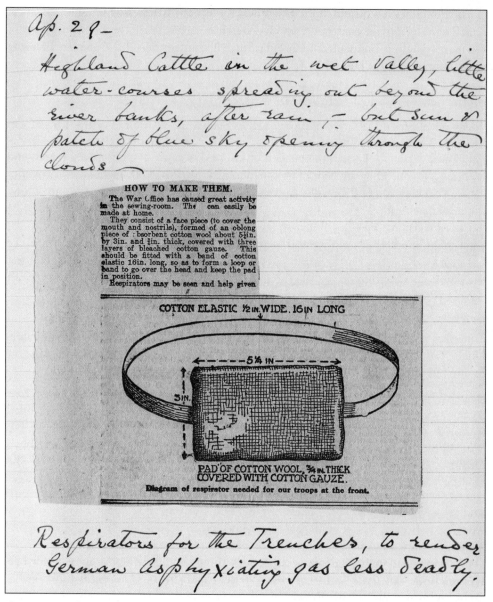

Ap. 29 —

Highland Cattle in the wet valley, little water-courses spreading out beyond the river banks, after rain, — but sun & patch of blue sky opening through the clouds —

HOW TO MAKE THEM.

The War Office has caused great activity in the sewing-room. They can easily be made at home.

They consist of a face piece (to cover the mouth and nostrils), formed of an oblong piece of absorbent cotton wool about 5½in. by 3in. and ⅜in. thick, covered with three layers of bleached cotton gauze. This should be fitted with a band of cotton elastic 16in. long, so as to form a loop or band to go over the head and keep the pad in position.

Respirators may be seen and help given

COTTON ELASTIC ½ IN. WIDE. 16 IN LONG

5½ IN

3 IN.

PAD OF COTTON WOOL, ¾ IN. THICK COVERED WITH COTTON GAUZE.

Diagram of respirator needed for our troops at the front.

Respirators for the Trenches, to render German asphyxiating gas less deadly.

Gas respirator diagram.

THURSDAY MAY 6

Last night we went to the first dinner party except with the family we have been to since the war started. It was given by Mrs Gilbert Mellor, whose husband is at the General Headquarters at St Omer. The other guests also said this was their one and only dinner party. Everybody seemed dull and distrait. I myself found it hard to keep the ball rolling, so pre-occupied are all one's thoughts.

I hear we have a foothold in the Dardanelles, but very little is said about it. Salvation must come from that quarter apparently, because in the West the position is one of stalemate. Neither side can do anything, though the Germans have gained a footing once more on terrible Hill 60.

FRIDAY MAY 7

Today an old friend of my childhood, David Sladen, now Colonel of the Kings Own Scottish Borderers came to see me with his sweet wife. David was badly wounded in the arm, and is home on leave. He looked very aged and worn and anxious. He told me he was wounded an hour after the big fight began for Hill 60. There is not one of the original officers of his Regiment left. He said they are nearly all killed, at all events none are left to fight. He said he had always found hitherto that things never turned out as bad as he had imagined, but this war surpassed his expectations. Worst of all was when shells burst near him, and their hideous results were there under his eye.

I forgot to say that Daddy and I went last Sunday to see Major Fred Reeves at Miss Keyser's home. He has had his leg off, poor fellow, after having a terrible wound inflicted by shrapnel.

SATURDAY MAY 8

The English-speaking world is shuddering at this latest German horror – the sinking of the great liner *Lusitania* yesterday off Old Kinsale Point, Ireland.* So far 1195 souls are reported either drowned or killed by the explosion of a single torpedo fired at her. Last week a notice appeared in the New York papers warning Americans that they travelled to England on the *Lusitania* at their own risk. Many of the influential Americans, Mr Vanderbilt for one (he is missing), received mysterious telegrams warning them not to embark. The warning was disregarded as nobody could seriously believe that the Germans would sink a ship laden with non-combatants and many women and children. This is the result.

SUNDAY MAY 9

All the neutral countries especially the Dutch, are horrified at this cowardly act of piracy which sank the *Lusitania*, without giving her a chance of saving her passengers. At 2 o'clock, while most of the people were at lunch, two explosions suddenly occurred, and the vessel sank in twenty minutes.

The Dutch, a people bred in all the traditions of a great seafaring race, speak of the crime as one against all the laws, written and unwritten, of naval warfare. It is the premeditation of the act which makes it so execrable. Just think of what it means, hundreds of innocent people, blown up, killed, injured or drowned, including women and babies. Among the dead were 94 children.

---

*   In the USA opinion was outraged, as among the dead were 140 Americans.

GERMAN THREATS.

THE NEW YORK EMBASSY ADVERTISEMENT.

AN "AMAZING NOTICE."

The sinking of the Lusitania was, it will be recalled, preceded by a number of specific threats.

A week ago to-day the following advertisement appeared in a number of American newspapers :—

TRAVELLERS intending to embark for an Atlantic voyage are reminded that a state of war exists between Germany and her Allies and Great Britain and her Allies; that the zone of war includes the waters adjacent to the British Isles; that, in accordance with the formal notice given by the Imperial German Government, vessels flying the flag of Great Britain or any of her Allies are liable to destruction in those waters; and that travellers sailing in the war zone in ships of Great Britain or her Allies do so at their own risk.
IMPERIAL GERMAN EMBASSY, WASHINGTON, April 22.

At the same time that this notice appeared many of the passengers who intended to embark in the Lusitania received telegrams of warning signed "John Smith" or "George Jones." One in particular, addressed to Mr. A. G. Vanderbilt, said :—"Have it on definite authority Lusitania is to be torpedoed. You had better cancel passage immediately."

Imperial German Embassy warning to intending travellers on the *Lusitania*.

MONDAY MAY 10

A verdict of 'Wilful Murder' has been returned against the Kaiser and the German officers of the submarines in the case of the *Lusitania*. The effect of the sinking of the ship has been to arouse a fierce anti-German feeling throughout the country against all the naturalised English Germans and Austrians. These were turned out bodily from the Stock Exchange yesterday by fellow members. Strong measures, such as wholesale internment, are clamoured for by the whole country. There are 20,000 people of German origin at large in London alone, and they constitute a real danger.

A Zeppelin came over Southend at the mouth of the Thames this morning and dropped 100 bombs, killing some people and destroying houses.

TUESDAY MAY 11

There have been riots in various parts of London today against the Germans. At St John's Wood, a housemaid came in very excited and saying she couldn't get through the crowd near the house. A German was being molested, and his house attacked. He had six carrier pigeons there. The police had to protect him. Many such scenes occur everywhere and thank goodness the people are fighting this danger themselves, instead of waiting for the Government to take slow measures.

More news comes in of the invasion of Gallipoli, which is causing frightful casualties on both sides. It has cost us dearly to get astride the Gallipoli Peninsula. But there is no finer tale in our history than that of the deed done on Sunday April 25th by the Australian, New Zealand and British troops supported by the officers and men of our warships.

WEDNESDAY MAY 12

The anti-German riots in the East End are assuming big proportions. Even your peaceful Mummy cries hurrah! Today the dentist advised me to have in the house respirators against the German gas-bombs as they are said to be about to throw these down at us from Zeppelins shortly!

The masks now used by our men at the Front seem to be working well. Although the Germans are still using gas as a preliminary to all their attacks, the men can hold their own till the gas goes by. It is very heavy and sinks down to the ground and is blown along the ground by the wind.

The French have made a very notable advance north of Arras, so the evening papers say. Joffre's first real success in this spring campaign.

THURSDAY MAY 13

The Commission appointed by Asquith last December to look into alleged German atrocities in Belgium and France, has at last published its report. As the members, headed by Lord Bryce, Chairman, are seven of the most distinguished men in law, diplomacy and history, their findings carry great weight. All the evidence has been sifted with the greatest impartiality.

You can imagine the grim fury and determination such reading excites in our people. It is to protect us from such horrors that our men are enlisting with more determination than ever. The loss of the *Lusitania* resulted in a great rush for recruiting.

Meanwhile the outbreaks all over London against the Germans need serious measures. There is a regular hue and cry against them. Some of the most prominent of the naturalised English Germans in London Society have deemed it advisable to protest their abhorrence of German methods by public letters to *The Times*, like those overleaf for instance.

I have started my visiting of four refugee Belgian families all of the middle-class. I am struck with the resignation of them all and their adaptability. Three of them having children with them, all healthy and cared for by the Committee, seemed happy and

May 13th

to protest their "abhorrence & detestation" of German methods by public letters to the Times, like these for instance:

> TO THE EDITOR OF THE TIMES.
>
> Sir,—I am an Austrian by birth but have resided in this country for the best part of my life—in fact, for the last 45 years, during 40 of which I have had the privilege of being a naturalized British subject. From the day that I swore allegiance to Queen Victoria I have been a loyal subject, and all my thoughts and all my actions were directed towards the welfare and towards the happiness of my adopted country.
>
> When this terrible war broke out, I exclaimed, I wish I had not lived to see it, and since the moment I saw how it was waged by Germany, nothing but feelings of disgust and abhorrence at the unheard-of crimes committed by the enemy were aroused. I wish to let everybody know that my sentiments of loyalty are and will always remain unabated, and it is my pride to say that I am a member of the British family.
>
> Yours obediently,
> E. F. SCHIFF.
> 1, Carlos-place, W., May 12.

> TO THE EDITOR OF THE TIMES.
>
> Sir,—As we belong to a family which has been settled in this country for more than a century and has taken some share in its public life and commercial development, we have hitherto assumed that our attitude with reference to the many breaches of international law and to the atrocities committed by the German military and naval forces would be taken for granted; but as there seems to be a general wish for an expression of opinion on the part of all British subjects of German extraction, we have no hesitation in saying that we entirely share the feeling of indignation and horror which now pervades the whole British Empire, and that we look with amazement upon the fact that the German population tolerates methods of warfare which at all times have been looked upon as unworthy of civilized nations. On previous occasions we have already expressed our conviction that the present war was brought about by the deliberate action of the German Government, and we are at one with our fellow-citizens in their determination to support every step which will lead to a final and decisive victory of the British arms, and will prevent the recurrence of acts such as those which we have witnessed. One of our sons has already fallen in fighting for this cause; all our other sons and all the other male members of our family who are of military age are serving with his Majesty's forces. We ourselves have always been and are now ready to give every service that it may be in our power to render, but having shown our loyalty and devotion to this country by unmistakable signs we hope we shall in future be relieved from the necessity of having to make a public declaration of these feelings.
>
> We are, Sir, yours faithfully,
> ERNEST J. SCHUSTER.
> May 12. FELIX SCHUSTER.

I have started my visiting of refugee Belgian families and have four of these, all of the middle-class. In seeing them, I am struck with the resignation of them all and of their adaptability to their circumstances. Three of them having their children with them, all healthy & cared-for by the Committee

Letters from naturalised British citizens of Germanic origin.

contented enough, as they have their own little 'interior' provided for them and they manage for themselves.

But the fourth case is pathetic. I found a pretty young woman, no older than 24, in one single big room with a pretty little boy of four. Her husband, after depositing her in safety over here, returned to Brussels five months ago. She has had not a word of news of him since. She was evidently unaccustomed to doing anything for herself, but now she is becoming more expert with her materials and little gas stove.

I asked if there were anything I could do for her, as I am there, to befriend and help her. She wouldn't say for some time. Then she admitted she needed underlinen, and something cool for the boy to wear. Poor little man, his only garment is a very thick, heavy jersey and the weather is getting hot. They all wanted clothes, poor things, having come to an end of what had been provided for the winter. Fortunately I can probably get clothes for them, as a Committee for clothing is formed and I can go and choose garments for my protégés.

The work done by this Belgian Refugee Fund is wonderful. Here in Chelsea alone, supported by subscriptions and gifts, they have housed in furnished flats, forty-four families, who get an allowance of food, meat, vegetables, bread and groceries given to them three times a week. Doctors are provided in case of sickness and clothes are also given.

Besides these 'flat families' of which I am a helper, there are dozens of others living in hostels free of charge, and in tenements. The greatest kindness is shown to these innocent victims of war.

FRIDAY MAY 14

Today all the German aliens are being interned by Government order at last – but the people have led them to this. The rioting all yesterday was very severe and ugly. Tonight, while we were at dinner we heard rough voices on the pavement outside this house. Mary the parlour maid returned a few seconds later saying 'a man has been taken away from the street'.

We jumped up and went to the front door to find all the maids standing at the area gates down the street. The commotion was coming from the grocer post office shop at the corner, which bears the nasty name of 'Klosz'. The Teutonic name had almost caused the beginning of a riot, but the police had just stopped it in time. Old Nannie who came to see me, said 'They are rioting everywhere, the little baker's shop near us has been looted'.

But why, I ask, are there such hundreds of German butchers and bakers in London?

MONDAY MAY 17

I haven't written the last two days, I have been too busy. Today I went to work at the Hospital Supply Depot to help make waterproof bags for the gas masks or respirators our troops urgently need. The masks are saturated in a solution and keep moist a certain time in these bags. The Depot has already turned out 20,000 in one week with the help of lady workers.

Uncle Henry, who dined here tonight, told us that a perfectly efficient solution to counteract the gas is nothing more nor less than man's own natural water! If the mask or respirator is saturated in it, as soon as the gas sweeps by, it decomposes the 'water' and turns the natural element into ammonia which acts as an antidote to the poison gas and makes it innocuous. In this manner, our poor fellows are not likely to run short of their preservative!

The death caused by the poison is a terrible one. It creates a frothy fluid which gradually rises and 'drowns' the lungs, so that the victim suffers all the horrors of drowning which lasts several days. He gasps for breath, swaying to and fro in an agony of breathing.

TUESDAY MAY 18

A horrid cold wet east wind day. I spent all the morning of it at the hospital depot stitching waterproof bags for the soldiers' respirators. And every day this wretched wind remains in the East, and we know this means the Germans can continue using their poison gases against our men. The east wind is always detestable, but it has never been as odious as this year.

Eugene Crombie came up to see you just as I had put you into your cot. Again you were too impressed at the sight of a 'tolier' (soldier) to move. But you retained enough presence of mind to salute on being reminded. Afterwards you couldn't take your eyes off him, you were deeply concerned about the sporran of his Gordon Highlander kilt!

WEDNESDAY MAY 19

Visiting the Belgians is not altogether easy. I got into hot water, without knowing it, by signing an order for too many clothes for one family who needed new outfits entirely. When my order was presented to the Secretary at Crosby Hall for endorsement to obtain forthwith the necessary garments from the clothing depot, Mrs Childers, the Secretary, 'n'avait pas l'air content, et a dit que Mrs Lee demandait trop à la fois.' It was indeed too much for the resources of the clothing depot. Instead of new undergarments and suits and frocks for Father and Son and Mother and Daughter, there was one chemise given for the Mother, of such coarse, voluminous make, that it was only suitable for a very stout peasant. Also a few garments of like make for the little girl, nothing else.

So I am trying to collect the requisites together myself. I was able to give clothing of my own to the pretty young Mme Liedt, whose husband went back to Belgium five months ago after placing her in safety. She has had no news of him since. She is rather helpless in her one room where she has everything to do for herself and child of five, for she knows nothing of cooking or housework. I gave her practical advice on making porridge, cooking macaroni etc. to make nourishing dishes and eke out her slender allowance of meat and food. It seems certain that Italy will declare war on Austria at any moment now; though Austria is doing everything she can to avert this by offering free and full terms to Italy. But the whole country is burning for war.

Tomorrow we are taking you to Littlehampton, Granny and I, to be with Daddy who is going to train at Arundel for a week with the Inns of Court Reserve Corps.

THURSDAY MAY 20

Littlehampton

Your first glimpse of the sea! We took possession of our rooms on the sea front at lunch time, awaiting the arrival in the evening of Daddy. He is going to sleep here, instead of being billeted like the rest at Arundel.

Rather foggy and misty, but we took you out on the sea front in your go-cart and you were very excited at the waves. There are many small children with their nurses here; it is a splendid place for children.

FRIDAY MAY 21

In England there is grave trouble brewing in our Cabinet caused by crises in the Admiralty and the War Office. The first is the open quarrel between Lord Fisher, First Sea Lord, and Winston Churchill, First Lord of the Admiralty. The public has long been annoyed at the constant interference by Churchill who is after all only a politician, with the greatest living Admiral, Lord Fisher. The public wants Churchill to move on to something else. His impetuosity has caused some of our naval disasters, it is said, and, whenever he has interfered, something bad has resulted.

The other crisis is that Kitchener is charged with the 'tragic blunder' of not providing enough high explosives. He has pinned his faith on shrapnel shells as used in his South African campaign in preference to high explosive shells. Without sufficient high explosives, our troops have had to suffer frightful casualties.

Now the crisis has come and changes have to be made. It is urged that Kitchener should remain as organiser of the Armies, but another Minister should have the task of supplying the munitions. A new Coalition Cabinet is being formed including Unionists as well as the Liberal Party.

Uncle Guy writes from Armentières intimating that our men at the Front have lost all feeling of respect for their enemy. No quarter is given. He writes that 200 Germans left their trenches unarmed to surrender, shouting out 'We are the counter attack' (meaning that they were ordered to counter attack but that they wouldn't do so, if they were spared). Uncle Guy adds 'not one of those men will ever shout again, no not one. The fighting is desperate and to the death.'

SUNDAY MAY 23

There was a terrible railway accident near Carlisle, yesterday; the biggest there has ever been in England, three trains being in collision.* A train full of troops ran into a local train, and while the dreadful struggle to get out was going on, an express crashed into

---

*   The catastrophe happened at Quintinshill in Dumfriesshire and was caused by a signalman's error. The troop train was carrying some 500 Royal Scots Leith Territorials, en route for Liverpool Docks and then Gallipoli. It took fire engines three hours to reach the wreckage, in which 227 soldiers were killed and 246 injured. Jim Minnoch, 'The Worst Train Wreck in History', *Stand To!* No. 66, January 2003.

the wreckage. Everything caught fire. 160 bodies have been taken out so far from the debris, and about 250 other passengers injured.

Everything is so peaceful in this brilliant sunshine here in Littlehampton that it is impossible to realise, looking at the smooth opal sea that just across the Channel war is raging with its terrible results. There is no sign of shipping within sight of the coast, nothing to suggest that the submarines are at their deadly work. I sat with you on the grass among the buttercups and daisies, this afternoon, and a more peaceful scene altogether could not be imagined.

The controversy against Lord Kitchener and the Government, entirely started and led by the *Daily Mail*, still continues, but most of the papers have indignantly refuted attacks on Lord Kitchener. A public demonstration was made by the Stock Exchange Members, when Lord Northcliffe's *Daily Mail* was burnt on the floor of the Stock Exchange and a vote of loyalty to Kitchener was unanimously passed.

MONDAY MAY 24

There is no decision yet regarding the new Cabinet. But Lord Fisher has resigned and taken himself off to Scotland – leaving Churchill in charge at the Admiralty pro tem.* He is not likely to remain there, however, as the whole trouble has arisen because of the 'landsman's' interference with the seaman. It is freely said that it was Churchill who insisted on first attacking the Dardanelles by the Fleet alone, against Fisher's better judgement. Incalculable harm was done by this abortive adventure because it gave the Turks several weeks to prepare a defence with German aid on a large scale while we were mustering our land forces.

Italy has at last declared war on Austria. The greatest enthusiasm prevails in Rome and the whole of the country. The Germans are furious at the 'infamous disloyalty' of their late ally in the Triple Alliance,** but declare that it will make no difference to the war or at least to their success. The German nation still seems confident of their ultimate victory.

Today Granny and I went to lunch with the family cousins, Lady Maud Barratt and her sister Lady Ellen Lambart. Maud has a house here and a home for illegitimate babies at Rustington, a mile from here. She has 48 babies there now. She looks after them from their birth and keeps them until they are 3 years old, when they are put out to other institutions. She has been asked by the Belgian Government, for she has applications to take in some of the poor little babies of the Belgian Nuns whom the beastly German soldiery ill-treated. There are about 150 of these poor Nuns expecting to be mothers.

---

*   Churchill had written to Asquith three days earlier, resigning his position as First Lord of the Admiralty.

**   In a furious speech to the Reichstag Chancellor von Bethmann Hollweg denounced his erstwhile ally: 'Italy has now inscribed in the book of the world's history, in letters of blood which will never fade, her violation of faith.' *The Times*, 29 May 1915.

TUESDAY MAY 25

We had a delightful morning at Arundel, starting with Daddy by 9 o'clock train to see him on parade with the Inns of Court Reserve Corps before they started the day's manoeuvres. It was a glorious day and the beauty of the place, with the imposing pile of Arundel Castle towering magnificent and stately above the town, was a revelation.

On the platform at Arundel Station we met one of Daddy's comrades, Reginald Smith KC, but a mere private like Daddy. We walked up to the town together, Granny and I and the two Inns of Court Reservists. They left us in the square to fall in with the others, after showing us the spot where the parade was to be. We made our way to this and sat down under the lime trees shading the road, between the river and one of the castle gates which you see in the photo.

Soon they came down in platoons, about 200 of them, and we saw them drill for ten minutes or more before they were ordered off on their duties. We were anxious Daddy shouldn't be overtired for he had had a very heavy cold, and we made him skip yesterday's duty, because he was too seedy. Granny has parted from him with the injunctions 'not to dig too deep at the trenches, not to get too hot, to do as little as possible while appearing to do a great deal' and suchlike.

While we were watching a man from the town photographed the platoons, so Granny went up and asked him to snapshot Daddy's line. He is to send us the result. It really was quite inspiriting to see these men, all more or less distinguished in the legal profession,* donning uniform and coming out of their offices and chambers to do the hard work preparatory for Corps Home Defence. Many of them had grey hair and were between 50 and 60. They all have to be over 40 and beyond the age limit for regular service. Most of them look very smart and soldierly.

Later Granny and I drove out to Rustington to see Lady Maud's home for little babies. It was both a delightful and pathetic sight. Delightful, to see fifty or so sweet little creatures from a month or so to three years old, rosy and happy and well cared for. But pathetic, to think that most of them will never know their parents and that they will always have a slur on their birth and be made to feel it, poor mites. Some of them were gentlemen's children and you could see it.

The matron told us that the children born illegitimately are much more precocious and sensitive than those born in wedlock, as the result of the mental strain and often misery of the mothers before their birth. It is a terrible injustice to bring children into the world so cruelly handicapped in the struggle for existence.

When I saw the older ones whom we had seen having tea in the garden run in with their little pink smiling faces upturned towards us to be petted and talked to, the tears suddenly rushed to my eyes. There was something so piercing in the sudden realisation of the wrong done to the poor little unsuspecting creatures and of the parents' love that was so cruelly withheld from them.

---

*   Not all were lawyers. One of the Inns of Court Reserve Corps companies was commanded by Sir Owen Seaman, the editor of *Punch*.

WEDNESDAY MAY 26

Today is our last day at Littlehampton. The sun has shone brilliantly and we have had a restful change. Tomorrow we go back to the strenuous life in London and to the responsibilities we have taken up – perhaps also to the first Zeppelin raid on London. I must get some protective masks for the household. It is expected that the Germans will, if they come, throw down asphyxiating gas bombs upon us. Scotland Yard has already issued a warning to house-holders to shut doors and windows instantly in case of a raid *especially those on the lower floors to keep out the poison fumes.*

THURSDAY MAY 27

We arrived safely in London at about five this evening. London looked brilliant and beautiful in the sunshine with the bright fresh green trees of the parks and gardens. In spite of the real danger of Zeppelins, I felt happy to be in our own pretty house. Not even the placards put up everywhere of another Zeppelin raid at Southend depressed me. Two women were killed and one child badly wounded. They were incendiary bombs, so I suppose these raids are just trial trips to give the crews practice for the big incendiary raid they mean to make on London.

SUNDAY MAY 30

Lord Fisher's post of First Sea Lord has now been filled by Admiral Jackson, one of Fisher's most trusted men, and a 'master of strategy', it is said. Very little is known of him so far. So Balfour[*] and he take the place of Churchill and Fisher. It is a mighty pity these two had to resign because their masterful minds took opposite views and neither would give in. But they are splendid men, full of courage and driving power, just the qualities we needed in such a crisis, and they have both rendered splendid service.

I have always trusted and admired Churchill's genius, because of his courage, originality and extraordinary energy. But he has many enemies, and the public lose sight of his splendid feat in mobilising the Navy before war was declared. He thereby saved the country from the surprise *coup de main* which the Germans had hoped to achieve.

[*] Arthur James Balfour, 1st Earl of Balfour, Conservative Prime Minister 1902–6, was favoured by Churchill as his successor. But Fisher declined to serve under either and resigned. Earlier (22 May) he wrote to Jellicoe : 'Balfour and Winston are inseparable and have been so since the mad gamble of the Dardanelles was first mooted. Balfour is really more to blame than Winston.' Martin Gilbert, *Winston S. Churchill*, vol. 3, p. 46.

BOOK VI

JUNE 2 – SEPTEMBER 27, 1915

WEDNESDAY JUNE 2

The Zeppelins came to London last night!! But no one was aware of it until we opened our papers at breakfast. Not a word has leaked out as to the parts of London they passed over. But I was having tea with Mrs de la Rue just now. Her sister told us she had heard, while slum-visiting in the north-east, that they had been over the City Road, the Angel Islington, and at Shoreditch.

SATURDAY JUNE 5

I have been in bed these two days with a sharp attack of laryngitis. The persistent east wind is causing throat trouble, besides helping the Germans in their gas-attacks. I made myself worse by going to a late tea with Mrs Lionel Lambart. Her husband, Captain Lambart RN, is in the Dardanelles on a Staff appointment. He was on the *Ocean* when she sank, and on another of those sunk since, but he seems to escape unscathed. He is a fearless, high-spirited fellow and a keen and reckless polo-player.

She is an American, and a delightful woman, very self-possessed and full of character, quiet and observant. She is taking up nursing the wounded and will help in the hospitals here. We talked so much for over an hour that it finished me! My throat, already sore, gave out suddenly in the night. I awoke feeling choked, with a burning bar across my throat that prevented my breathing properly.

Przemysl, the great Galician fortress which the Russians captured after a prolonged siege some time ago, has been retaken by the Austrians and Germans. This big set-back to the Russians is entirely due to lack of shells. This news comes just at the right moment to promote the campaign Lloyd George started yesterday as Minister of Munitions. In a brilliant speech he made at Manchester, he told the country the real truth – it is touch and go whether we win this war or not.

The fall of Przemysl shows that fine leadership, superiority in numbers and dauntless courage are of no use without shells. 'If,' said Lloyd George, 'we had been in a position to expend shells as the Germans did in this last battle for Przemysl, 200,000 in one hour, the Germans would be driven out by now from France, from Belgium and would be defending their own country against our invasion.'*

---

*   In his speech, Lloyd George declared that his short experience as Minister of Munitions had shown him that the country had not yet brought one half of its industrial strength to bear on the war. *The Times*, 4 June 1915.

Lloyd George's speech, full as it is of plain speaking, is yet so buoyant, so confident and high-spirited, that far from depressing the nation, it makes everyone boil to go and work. It just strikes the right note. I think this speech explains the eminence he has attained in the control of the country.

A little Welsh solicitor, he was hated by the upper classes for his socialist or radical ideas which he was strong enough to force upon his party. But now the whole nation believes he can achieve the most important issue in this war, namely the adequate supply of high explosives. He has an extraordinary quickness in grasping fresh problems, and adapting his powers to the needs of the moment. I remember the contempt lavished upon him at the time he introduced his new schemes for the taxation of the rich. But above all when he delivered an indiscreet and insulting speech at Limehouse against hereditary peer-dom. This has become a byword as 'limehousing' (i.e. stigmatising in scurrilous terms the Lords). When I remember all this, I can hardly realise that this was the same man as the now high-spirited statesman and patriot whom the whole country trusts in her hour of peril. It also discloses, in its frank good humour, the strong personal charm he is credited with, even by his strongest political opponents.

SUNDAY JUNE 6

Audrey has just come in, having rushed up from Glaslyn with Uncle Arthur where they had gone for a few days' leave before he went for France with his regiment, 10th Gordon Highlanders. They had hardly arrived at Glaslyn when Uncle Arthur had a wire announcing that he had a splendid Staff appointment given him for the Dardanelles, as DAAG.* He is to be at the base at Alexandria. He sails on Tuesday. She will go out to join him as soon after as she is allowed. It is a great stroke of luck for her and for us, his not being sent to France.

TUESDAY JUNE 8

We have scored a splendid achievement over a Zeppelin that came on Sunday, on its return journey. While it was in full flight between Ghent and Bruges, a young British airman, Flight Lieutenant R.A. Warneford, who is only 22 and only qualified for flying in May, attacked the Zeppelin from above, dropped six bombs on to it, causing it to crash to earth, killing the 28 occupants. But he himself was blown upwards by the explosion which turned his machine turtle. He kept his head and his seat, and after looping the loop, came down to the ground. But in enemy territory! However, he got his engine started, rose up and got home safe to his aerodrome!

So this is a feat to be proud of. He is the first airman to have bagged a Zeppelin. I hear tonight that the King has telegraphed to Warneford his 'hearty congratulations on his splendid achievement' and has conferred on him the Victoria Cross.

---

*   Deputy Assistant Adjutant General.

WEDNESDAY JUNE 9

The second son of Daddy's partner Henry Bolton, a boy of 18, just out of Dartmouth has been killed at the Dardanelles. It's terrible. He had been out there barely a month. All the boys are being killed. His father, a dry, reserved, delicate-looking little man, is a brick. He joined Daddy's Corps months ago, though his two sons were out at the Front, and insisted on giving his services to the Country, though he works like the indefatigable creature he is, all day at Westminster.

THURSDAY JUNE 10

I went early this morning to see Uncle Arthur off at Paddington for Devonport where he sails tonight for Alexandria in the *Benares*. God grant that he may escape torpedoes, though of course the warships and transports are escorted by destroyers. When I arrived at the Paddington Hotel, Audrey was just stuffing into the top of his bag a life-jacket, in case his ship is torpedoed. We all had a pull at the straps to get the bag closed. He looked very smart in his staff-cap, and the pair of scarlet tabs on his tunic.

Poor Audrey, in spite of the pangs of parting, was proud and excited as we all walked down the platform to see him into the Cornish Express. She is going out to join him in about a month.

FRIDAY JUNE 11

Uncle Guy has just come home suddenly from the firing line for four days. His men and one or two officers having been sent to the rear for a few days rest from the trenches, some of them have come home. Daddy went to meet him at Victoria and was with him five minutes. He asked Guy how things were going out there, and Guy replied 'It's rotten. If the Government don't hurry up with their shells we shall get the biggest licking England has ever had. There are no shells for our artillery, or nothing like enough, and all we can do is to hold the Germans for a while. But we can't advance and we are losing many more men than we ought.'

MONDAY JUNE 14

Daddy has just come in and tells me that his Corps, together with the other Volunteer Corps are going to be employed guarding railways and communications and also guarding German prisoners. So he, with his fellows, will be required to give up a week at a time on these duties.

Last night we gave a family supper party in honour of Uncle Guy who returns to the horrible Front tomorrow. He is remarkably cheery in spite of the unlimited time he has to go back for. He says that the Germans will never pierce our lines now, but the question is *shall we ever pierce theirs?* However we hope that a deluge of British shells will soon begin to flow.

SATURDAY JUNE 19

The saddest news is the death of the air hero V.C., Lieutenant Warneford, who destroyed the Zeppelin single handed. He was testing an aeroplane at Versailles and, when at a height of several hundred feet, the machine was seen to crumple up and he was hurled to the ground.

MONDAY JUNE 21

The French are doing splendidly. They have taken 10,000 prisoners during the last few days and no doubt are aggrieved because we English are doing so little to support them. In fact I hear they are furious at the system which has left us so short of shells and munitions.

In France every man is either fighting or working day and night to provide munitions; in England such a thing as this is possible. A workman was summoned for assaulting and grievously injuring another workman because the latter was turning out more shells during work hours than he himself chose to do. I am glad to say the magistrate gave him the maximum penalty, 6 months hard labour and a very heavy fine. He further told him that, had he been a German or a Frenchman, he would have been taken out and shot in those countries.

THURSDAY JUNE 24

This morning in *The Times* Uncle Guy's name is gazetted. He has been awarded the Military Cross. In yesterday's *Times* his name also appears in Sir John French's despatches. So he has distinguished himself, the dear fine fellow.

On the doctor's advice, we left London today. You still have a stiff neck, a swollen gland caused by a horrible tooth, and are fretful and unhappy. So we picked up, you, Nannie and I and set out for Wales.

Hengwrt

Hengwrt is looking so beautiful; I do love this place. It is just now at its best, with the splendid old trees in their early summer foliage, and the ground beneath the spreading boughs carpeted with red and white foxgloves.

WEDNESDAY JUNE 30

Aunt Beatrice and I went to lunch at Penmaenucha with Sybil Wynne-Jones. We found her very excited and happy as she is off to London tomorrow to see her husband. He is coming home from the Front for seven days. As they were only together two days at the marriage, this is a new little honeymoon. We had a very pleasant few hours with her.

Our time there was in such a contrast to the depressing tea we went to afterwards at Mrs Cox's. Mrs Cox is an American and, like so many Americans, is nervy, faddy and fussy in the extreme. At present she fusses over the war, thinks everything England does is wrong. She says we are to blame for the war; we attacked and Germany is defending herself.

England's sin is to try to be a democracy, which accounts for her unpreparedness. England tried to copy America . . . 'I beg your pardon', I put in, 'England was there long before America' and so on. I got so angry that I ceased to be genial. It makes me furious when Americans sneer at England, and yet show such alarm and terror at England being beaten. If they really think us so stupid, why will they come and live here?

THURSDAY JULY 1

A National Register is at last to be taken of every man and woman between the ages of 15 and 65, irrespective of class, in Great Britain. The main questions to be asked are

1. What is your employment?
2. Are you able and willing to undertake any other employment besides your present one, to aid in the supply of war material?

So at last the war is going to make a difference to everyone and we shall all have the joy of feeling that we have a chance of being assigned work in the service of our dear country.

Meanwhile the need for economy in household expenditure and food is being urged by the Government. Meat only once a day should be the limit for each household. All this is carried out here at Hengwrt. Aunt Beatrice has placed her household on a war footing and dinner at night consists of soup, a light dish of fish or eggs, vegetables and light pudding.

No lamb or veal is to be killed throughout the Country. Now that the Russians are being pushed back, the end of the war is indefinitely postponed. They have lost practically all that they gained at the beginning.

FRIDAY JULY 2

A nasty wet day and you have been rather miserable. You are still fretful and seedy and we don't know what to do with you, but we have put you on a diet of milk and sago. Uncle Alex with all his experience of tummy-trouble in the Eastern climate recommends sago. Your poor Nannie shakes her head and says you will get so thin especially as you dislike milky food and want bread and butter. But we must be firm and not listen to your poor little cries.

SATURDAY JULY 3

Thank God you have been more your dear little self today. The light sago diet has already worked wonders. You talked and laughed more and imitated the rooks and crows cawing in the great trees overhead. We took you in the car when we drove up the beautiful glen of the Upper Mawddach, and the awful road running up the gorge, in some cases overhanging the deep narrow chasm of the river. You loved the drive, but slept most of the way home. My heart is beginning to tighten at the thought of leaving you in two days to go back to London, but how much better for you to be here than there!

SUNDAY JULY 4

My last day here and tomorrow I return to Daddy and to much threatened poor old London! I have received an odd document, an appeal for my aid to help the Committee at Crosby Hall to keep the moths out of their wool! Presumably wool being knitted into socks for troops by Belgian refugees!

TUESDAY JULY 6

I came up to London yesterday from Hengwrt and found Daddy in the Sanctuary, deep in the Probate papers, relating to my Father. We want to invest a couple of hundred pounds* out of Father's estate in the Great War Loan which is a fine investment besides being a great help to the country. 4½% interest, but investors cannot touch their capital until 1945. The Government reserves the right to pay it back in 1925.

This morning I went to help with the wool! Bale upon bale of wool has been sent over as a gift by America to Crosby Hall, to be knitted by the Belgians for the Allied Armies. We have to go through these thousands of skeins of wool, wrap them in parcels with a moth preservative and store them. I worked for two hours cutting string to the right lengths, and waiting on three other ladies who were making up the parcels. It sounds an absurd pastime, but this is a sample of the many ways in which women are helping.

WEDNESDAY JULY 7

Worked all the morning at the Hospital Depot in Manson Place close by. Many women I know go and work there so I meet a friend each time. Much talk of German preparation for a tremendous new offensive on Calais with great reinforcements of troops sent over from the Russian Front.

FRIDAY JULY 9

Uncle Lionel is staying with us for two nights and has brought us some sensational gossip. But as there is never any smoke without fire, I must repeat it! Sir John French is captivated by the beautiful actress, Maxine Elliott,** and having absented himself in her company on various occasions, has caused General Joffre such dissatisfaction that the latter has complained.

Complaints also are aimed at Sir J. French's Staff. They are accused of remaining so far behind the firing line that they are out of touch with the real situation at the Front.

---

*   Georgina Lee's investment of £200 would be roughly equivalent to £11,600 today. In terms of purchasing power, one pound in 1914 equated to £58.18 in 1998. *Whitaker's Almanac, 2004.*

**   The American actress, Maxine Elliott (1873–1940), was celebrated for her feminine charm and beauty. She left the stage during the war to nurse wounded soldiers in France. There she devoted her own personal fortune to equipping and staffing a barge as a floating hospital.

Asquith and Lord Kitchener have gone over to France to confer with Joffre. It will be interesting to see if Joffre secures the recall of Sir John French. He has already dismissed some of his own Generals, who have shown themselves to be incompetent.

Lloyd George has publicly reprimanded his old colleague, Haldane, the ex-Minister of War, blaming him for the shortage of War Supplies. The general feeling is that Haldane is being made a scapegoat.

SATURDAY JULY 11

The great news today is that General Botha, Commander-in-Chief of the Union of South Africa forces and President of the Republic, has finally defeated the Germans in South-West Africa. The German colony now comes under British Control. Kitchener has cabled his congratulations to Botha. The official text is:

We shall warmly welcome you and the South Africans who can come over and join us.

Today I had quite a social day, for the first time for months. I lunched at Princes' with Colonel Reeves and Mrs Morrell, then we all came back here to tea. Colonel Hanham and Colonel Reeves provided an almost unheard of masculine element in these dreadful days when all the men are fighting or working. Colonel Hanham was only on leave for three or four days. I forgot to say that Gerald Graham-Clarke, home on three days leave from the Front, came with his mother to lunch with us on Saturday. After lunch he took her off to a matinée to keep her thoughts busy during the last fleeting hours of his leave. But he begged me to go round at 6 pm just before he had to start out and remain with his mother. I arrived and found him eating some poached eggs and tea, his last meal in England!

At 6.15 he shouldered his haversack, kissed his mother and went off without looking round. We watched him through the window, walking down Victoria Street to the station. Then I turned to her, made her put on a hat and coat and took her for a brisk stroll in St James' Park. These partings are so awful. Gerald has been in the firing line at Ypres for over three months and has had hair's breadth escapes.

WEDNESDAY JULY 14

Today being the fête of the French Republic,* the French flag was flying from all public buildings and many houses. Girls in white with tricolour ribbon were selling favours and tiny flags for the benefit of the French hospitals.

The wretched Welsh coal miners have actually had the face to declare that they will strike tomorrow if their demands are not met. This could paralyse the Navy, to say nothing of the production of war munitions.

---

* Celebrating the storming of the Bastille Prison in Paris on 14 July 1789, and the start of the French Revolution.

So the Government has stepped in and a Munitions Act has been put into force. This makes the strike illegal. Every man going on strike will be fined £5 for every day or part of a day that he keeps away from work; while the penalty for inciting any one to strike is £50.

FRIDAY JULY 16

I had a letter from Uncle Lionel today which gave me an interesting account of a visit he had just paid to the German prisoners camp at Dorchester.

You can see them, he writes, *playing games. They also have opportunities for work in the fields and on roads and get paid 2½d per hour. They put in good work for the benefit, as they say, of a German province.*

Historically the place is interesting, as French prisoners 100 years ago were interned near the same camping-ground and planted long avenues of trees along the roads. The German camp intelligence is amazing and baffles even their guards, to whom they gave information of the sinking of the *Lusitania* and the riot in the German camp on the Isle of Man. They get their news some hours before it reaches Dorchester in the newspapers.

SATURDAY JULY 17

The coal strike in Wales is serious. About 300,000 miners are idle. The men have not budged from the position they have taken up. As the Munitions Act cannot be carried out instantly, the time lost is crucial. The iron works are closing down, and every industry for war will be impeded. It is a disgrace that such a state of affairs is possible. The French were already very impatient at our shortage of munitions and disgusted at our impeding their advance and now this is the limit.

On the other hand, I saw today a very inspiriting sight, the procession of 50,000 women through London, petitioning to be allowed to work for munitions and other war-work, as a recognised labour force. They marched in sections carrying red, white and blue flags, first a red section then a white, then a blue, so that at a distance, as they moved down the incline in Oxford Street, I saw the section form a monster tricolour.

Then came sections of Allied flags. Between each, large banners were carried by women with such legends as:

MEN MUST FIGHT AND WOMEN MUST WORK

WOMEN MUST WORK TO DEFEAT THE ENEMY

WOMEN'S WORK WILL SAVE MEN'S LIVES

After marching through the streets, starting from the Embankment, past Clubland, through Oxford Street, Park Lane and Regent Street, the procession reassembled on the Embankment where, from the wall of the new Munitions Office, Lloyd George replied to the Women's Deputation.

He said that nobody who had witnessed this most impressive procession could fail to appreciate the organising capacity shown by women. He himself attached 'enormous importance to the subject'. He went on to state that already in England 50,000 women were being employed in war factories, but in Germany there were 500,000 at least and in France about the same.

He promised that the women would be employed in unlimited numbers as they were wanted, but that it would take a little time to organise a totally new labour-army. The National Register was the first step in that direction. He promised *that women should be paid the same price as men for piece work*. But he explained why it would not be fair to pay them at the same rate as men for time work. Being untrained and unskilled, they could not get in as much work, of as good quality, in the same time as men.

Mrs Pankhurst, he said, had asked for the latter as well as the former, but it could not yet be complied with. Mrs Pankhurst here replied to Lloyd George that she had asked for this to prevent any possibility of women being sweated for cheaper labour.

I take the trouble to write about this because I believe this Women's Demonstration and Lloyd George's acknowledgement mark a new departure in the Women's Movement. It is, apart from patriotic motives, a clever stroke by the leaders of the Women's Suffrage Movement. They have seized a glorious opportunity for women to show what they can do, if properly organised and if allowed to compete with men in spheres hitherto closed to them by law and prejudice.

I saw Mrs Pankhurst, marching with three other suffragette celebrities in front of the procession. I was surprised to see her look so active after her terrible prison and hunger-strike experiences of the last two years previous to the declaration of War, when a truce was called between Suffragettes and the Government.[*]

MONDAY JULY 19

The coal strike is still going on, to the everlasting shame of Wales, and Lloyd George is going down there tonight to bring the men to reason.

SATURDAY JULY 24

The coal strike has been settled by Lloyd George, but in favour of the men so the employers are not pleased. The general public is too relieved to give much sympathy to the coal-owners.

Today Daddy went to a big parade of his Corps at Richmond. They were inspected in Richmond Park by General Bridgeman who addressed them and complimented them on being 'wonderfully steady on parade'. He added that he had 'no idea there were so

---

[*]   Both Emmeline Pankhurst and her daughter Christabel had been imprisoned before the war.

many eminent men in the Regiment, and that the next time he inspected them, he would expect to find the Lord Chancellor beating the drum'.

On Monday I am going down to Gelligemlyn with Muz to help her settle into the house for the summer. I am longing for the train to steam up the platform at Dolgelly and see your lovely mischievous little face looking out for Mummy.

SUNDAY JULY 25

Today saw a great Intercession Service on the steps of St Paul's Cathedral, in the presence of nearly 4,000 troops of London Territorials. Vast crowds stretched all the way down Ludgate Hill, and along the side streets. Muz and I went to the offices of the London Diocese Registry. Daddy and Uncle Hugh are Joint Registrars to the London Diocese, and their office windows look straight over the great space and steps in front of St Paul's. We reached the office by back ways so as to avoid the great crowds.

We had not long to wait before the Mounted Police appeared at the head of the procession. First the Clergy and the Bishop, then the fine troops in khaki, all London recruits, and these ranged themselves symmetrically in semi-circles at the foot of the steps. The Bishop stood on the steps supported by the Clergy, the Staff Officers and the massed bands, and the service began with O God our help in ages past, sung by the whole assembly.

It was a most impressive sight, especially when the western sun lit up the group of white-robed figures on the platform, the scarlet cassocks of the two Bishops, and the multitude of khaki-clad warriors below. A special War Litany was read, the responses being made by the soldiers.

MONDAY JULY 26

Muz and I arrived at Dolgelly at 4.50 this evening. I could hardly contain myself with impatience at the train's delay, for I knew my little boy was waiting for me at the station. When at last we did arrive, I jumped out and I saw a sedate little figure in a smart pink tunic with white leather belt and white hat come towards me led by Nannie. Very solemnly you lifted your face to be kissed and after a while you thawed considerably and made little attempts at conversation.

On the journey I read in the Daily Sketch the account of the open air service at St Paul's. I cut out the photo of the general scene because it shows your Mother and Aunt Hilda Lee leaning out the window of the Registry Offices, our white-trimmed hats showing conspicuously.*

TUESDAY JULY 27

Well, the Germans haven't got Warsaw yet!** Hindenburg and Mackensen, the two great sledge-hammers of the German and Austrian Armies are being made to pay a

---

*   See Plate 10.
**   In strategic terms, Warsaw was important because it was a major rail centre in a country where railways were few and far between. But also there was no other crossing place over the Vistula for 200 miles.

terrible toll for every inch of ground. But the Western Allies look to the issue of this fight for Warsaw with intense anxiety.

SATURDAY JULY 31

The news from the Russian front is bad. The Russian Army has retired from Warsaw, removing everything that would be of use to the enemy. This is a terrible disappointment and a severe setback to the Allies. Our lack of readiness has cost the Allies all the present Russian sacrifices and the dreadful anxieties of the immediate future.

MONDAY AUGUST 2

We had been two days without news, just at this critical time. We have no news of the Dardanelles at all, except the daily casualty lists. The Press clamour for conscription becomes every day louder and more insistent. It is urged that if England decided now upon conscription, it would be the best counterstroke to the German success over Warsaw and restore the confidence of the Allies.

WEDNESDAY AUGUST 4

Today is the anniversary of our declaration of war. There was a big Intercession Service in St Paul's which the King and Queen attended. The Archbishop of Canterbury officiated.

SATURDAY AUGUST 7

Daddy was there on the platform at Paddington to meet me and brought me home. We went out again to see Captain Alan Sale-Hill in Sister Agnes' Home. He has a shattered arm and leg. He had only been in the trenches a few days, when he was summoned by his Colonel into the dug-out and a shell burst through the roof, wounding him in the arm, leg and side. He was pinned down where he lay but after a while stretcher-bearers came to fetch him away. He told us he felt three heavy blows, when he was hit, but no immediate pain. Seeing that his cap had fallen from his head, he picked it up and this is all he remembers.

After seeing him, we had tea close by. Then, being by Victoria, we went in to the station to see the departure of trains taking back to the Front officers and men who have been on leave. These trains depart at 5.40 every day, or most days, and it is a moving sight which brings one in close touch with the war raging so very few miles away.

The approaches were packed, not only with relatives but with others who, like ourselves were there to give our brave men a parting cheer. The public were kept behind barricades. But the humorous police were wonderfully patient and good natured with all, and most considerate to the relatives who were present in hundreds.

Young wives with tiny babies, the soldier husband carrying an older child, older mothers striving hard to keep their tears back while the soldier boy was still by, young children, sisters, sweethearts, grey-haired fathers, there were some of every description, but all brave and cheery or trying to be.

The men themselves, bronzed and sunburnt laden up to the eyes in full kit and baggage in war-worn khaki, looked cheery and resolute, as they went quickly along towards the platforms of the two troop trains. Only relatives were allowed on the platforms. They formed a dense crowd, after the men had entrained, in the space between the two platforms.

As the first train steamed slowly out, a great cheer rose up, in which we joined from behind the barricades. God bless them all! It is now 10 pm and they must be nearing the trenches already.

SUNDAY AUGUST 8

I have had a letter from Uncle Guy who has just been singled out for great distinction since he won his Military Cross. They have chosen him out of hundreds of officers to start a school for hand-grenades and bombs.

The Germans have entered Warsaw but they found little of value. For weeks past, the Russians had been steadily removing everything from Church bells, sent to Moscow, to the smallest copper and brass fitting in workshops or private houses. Of course art treasures were removed and all objects of historical interest, including Chopin's heart, which was one of Warsaw's relics. Half the houses were burnt or destroyed, and the city itself was left waterless by the removal of all pumps. The Kaiser, when he makes his triumphal entry into Warsaw, will find it about as comfortable and cheerful as Napoleon found Moscow in 1812.

TUESDAY AUGUST 10

Today I kept shop for nearly 3 hours in the King's Road, Chelsea. I was trying to sell socks knitted (machine) by crippled Belgian soldiers. My only companion was one of these cripples who was knitting hard all the time. When I spoke in French he looked up, smiled and went on working. He didn't understand anything but Flemish. As customers were woefully lacking, I went every now and then on the doorstep inviting in some of the passers-by and appealing for customers to buy socks for soldiers at the Front. But I couldn't persuade anyone to come in.

So I soon had nothing to do but watch the torrential rain splashing on the asphalt road. The lady-helper who promised to relieve me at 1 o'clock had not yet appeared at 1.30. So I left the Belgian knitter in charge, and came home, leaving a written message to say 'no business done'.

WEDNESDAY AUGUST 11

There was a big Zeppelin raid on Monday night over Southend and Hull, in which five Zeppelins participated. They killed 13 women, 9 children and 6 men. Later, Gerry dined here and told us that the Zeppelins had dropped bombs on Folkestone, and very severely damaged the central station. Charlie R's sister who is staying near Folkestone wrote that all our guns along the coast from Dover to Folkestone were blazing away and one Zeppelin was hit amidships. She however righted herself and made for Ostend.

FRIDAY AUGUST 13

There was another Zeppelin raid on the East Coast last night. Uncle Tich was up today from Norwich and he told us the Zeppelins were over Woodbridge, Aldeburgh and Harwich. They killed 6 people, injured 23 and seriously damaged 14 houses. This is the third raid since Monday. Tonight, 9 pm the searchlights are playing all over the sky very keenly. We have been watching them from the balcony.

TUESDAY AUGUST 17

For the first time since the war began we have lost one of our Troop Transports, the *Royal Edward*, and our immunity hitherto makes the loss all the more terrible. The bare news has only come out tonight, but while 600 were saved, 1000 are said to have gone down. It happened in the Aegean Sea,* the disaster being caused by an enemy submarine. The men were reinforcements for the Dardanelles Expedition.

THURSDAY AUGUST 19

A letter from Aunt Ethel who writes from Suffolk. She said 'the night that the five Zeppelins came over the East Coast last week, one of them went right over our house, but we never heard it, though everybody else living around seems to have been up to see it go. They said that our field was brilliantly lit up by the Zeppelin and that the noise was deafening. I was furious next morning, as you may imagine, to have missed it!'

We had three people to dinner last night, Major Charles Richards who is working at the War Office, 'Andy' Cox and Armorer Nicholson. While we were on the balcony after dinner, a great Red Cross vehicle came to a standstill just below. Seeing the car wouldn't move, Daddy went down and found three ladies, two quite young, one of whom was the driver and a third older woman. Daddy found they belonged to the Women's Aid Detachment and that they were just off on their night work to Enfield. Canteens have been started by women all over the country to provide soldiers and munitions workers with food all day and all night.

So these girls, having laden the Red Cross car with cake and other items, were on their way, when the car stopped. They knew nothing whatever of the works of the car and were hopelessly stranded, so it was a plucky undertaking altogether. Daddy called out Andy, and between them they eventually found what was wrong.

Meantime the two girls had had to take a taxi, after filling it up to the roof with cake, to go on to Enfield. They left the older woman behind to look after the car till a mechanic came round to retrieve it. The man turned up at 11 pm, but Daddy and Andy

---

*   Off the Italian Dodecanese island of Kos. 1,185 soldiers perished.

had already repaired the damage themselves and Daddy had driven it round Onslow Square to test his repair!

The volunteer women's work in the canteens is arduous. These women have to take the food on trolleys up and down the lines in the factories and among the shells and rifles which are being made, so they see everything that goes on.

Later: News came in tonight that German submarines have torpedoed the unarmed White Star Liner *Arabic*. It sailed from Liverpool yesterday for New York with a large number of passengers. The ship was sunk at 9.15 this morning in the Irish Sea and 44 passengers were drowned. Oh! These Germans! What, and where will be the end of this terrible war? Each day lately has brought a new and dreadful event. News also of renewed desperate struggles in Gallipoli. We only just forestalled the Turks, in the recent attack. The losses were enormous on both sides and we gained very little.

The disaster to the *Arabic* was not as costly as the sinking of the *Lusitania*, for though the ship sank in ten minutes, most of the passengers and crew got off in the boats and landed at Queenstown. But this makes the German act no less infamous, as the submarine gave no warning. The ship was bound for America, so it was no excuse to pretend that she carried contraband for one of the Allies.

SATURDAY AUGUST 21

I was busy again all this morning working at the surgical requisites depot in Mulberry Walk. I have joined that lately and abandoned the Manson Place depot, because my dear Mrs Dana is in charge of one of the chief rooms. Besides it is by far the best organised of all the workrooms where I have worked.

We sit in a large airy room, opening out onto a charming old-world garden in Chelsea. A flagged space, with chestnut trees growing out of the irregular stones, round seats placed under the trees. We have tea out in the garden. Large door-windows are always open, and the whole establishment has a secluded convent-like appearance.

Brave busy women bend silently over their needlework, their soft white linen head-gear hiding all but the very fringe of their hair and the long white overalls in which they wrap themselves to prepare the surgical dressings. They are very silent; only now and then a merry peal of laughter comes from the pretty superintendent. Something starts off her gaiety, and one hears good-humoured chaff in explanation of new and puzzling bandages, with retorts and laughter from the others.

Some of the women are so pretty. There was one beautiful one sitting in the window opposite me. I couldn't help reflecting what a contrast there is between this poetical side of the war, as represented by the white-robed women in the peaceful Chelsea home, and the poor fellows we are working for in their terrible trenches.

WEDNESDAY AUGUST 25

Oh dear! How we vacillate between high hopes and low fears! Today the tone of the papers is decidedly gloomy, or is it Charles Richards, still staying with us, who is pessimistic? Bulgaria seems to be veering round towards the German influence and Charles says that, if they come in against us 'we are in the soup'.

In Gallipoli we have advanced 800 yards, which is considered a substantial gain. But it goes no quicker than that and the daily casualty lists are simply appalling. Anything between 100 and 150 officers killed or wounded each day, sometimes even 200.

TUESDAY AUGUST 31

The last day of the last summer month! It feels cold and autumnal today. I am busy packing up and sorting out the house before leaving on Thursday with Daddy to join you at Gelligemlyn.

MONDAY SEPTEMBER 6

Gelligemlyn
As usual, as soon as I get here I forget the war for a few days! But until the war is over, there can be no real ease or peace of mind, and the war drags on. Only the casualty lists are always new.

THURSDAY SEPTEMBER 9

Three Zeppelins were over London on Tuesday night. Aunt Amy Marshall, in a letter received by Muz this morning, writes that she and all her household (in Philbeach Gardens S.W.) had been awakened by bomb explosions, five in number. The papers do not state the exact locality, of course, and just mention the 56 casualties. Several fires broke out, but were promptly extinguished.

There has been a change in the Russian Armies. The Tsar has assumed supreme command. As he states in a manifesto to his people, 'now that the enemy has penetrated the inner precincts of our sacred country, it is right for him to be at the head of his Armies'.* The Grand Duke Nicholas has been transferred to the Caucasus, of which he is made Viceroy and Commander-in-Chief.

Later: I was distressed to hear today that Dick Hughes, the 17 year old son of your Grandfather's faithful servant Hughes, has died in camp at Kildare, from spotted fever. The poor boy only arrived there three weeks ago from Wales. He had been so keen on enlisting, but was too young when the war broke out. Poor Hughes went over to Ireland and saw him, but it was hopeless. He has come back to Glaslyn, quite broken-hearted.

---

* This decision hastened the fall of the Romanovs. The Russian GHQ was at Mogilev, 500 miles from St Petersburg. By taking over supreme command, the Tsar was detaching himself from his capital and his ministers. Later, the Tsar became so out of touch that he was unaware of impending revolution, until forced to abdicate in March 1917.

SATURDAY SEPTEMBER 11

There was another big Zeppelin raid on Wednesday. This account I have had from Aunt Louisa's maid Lizzie is so good, as seen at Highgate, that I insert it:

27 Southwood Ave,
Friday 10th September/15

To Mrs Lee

Dear Madam,

As you are up in Wales, I thought you would like to hear about the air raid of Wed: night. The papers are so vague unless one is near you don't get much detail.

On Tuesday night I was woke up just before twelve and the bombs were going off very quickly, we looked out of the window but couldn't see anything only the search lights playing all over the place, I went down to Miss Louisa and got her to see them and they kept on playing till about 1 o'clock. Of course we didn't get much sleep after; so on Wed we all retired very soon after 10. At 11 o'clock we were woke up again by gunfire and when my husband looked out of the window and said 'there it is', I saw the Zeppelin with shell bursting in the sky. I went down to Miss Louisa and found her looking out of the window.

I was terrified. The beastly thing seemed to be quite still for a minute and then slowly sailed over our road or appeared to do so, Miss Louisa stood at her window and watched it as though she was looking at fireworks and was as calm and cool as it was possible to be. Very soon we saw the red glare in the sky of the fires. The thing itself looked like a huge silver cigar.

The gun on Parliament Hill fired at it but it got safely away. One of the shells from the gun crashed through the roof of a mission hall in Archway Road where we wait for the tram. The shell didn't explode but went through a chair right through the floor and buried itself in the concrete. In Wood Lane, Cheapside the fire was still burning last night and part of Liverpool Street Station was damaged. Also in Theobalds Road there are very few houses with their windows in. The penny bank was completely gutted.

A bomb dropped in Grays Inn Square where my husband drills, but it didn't explode; also Leathers Lane is wrecked in several places. It really does unnerve one and now they know they have reached the City, I'm sure they will come again. However, what is to be will be and one can do nothing. I'm thankful Miss Louisa takes it so calmly.

I hope you and Mr Lee are enjoying your holiday and that Master Harry is keeping well.

I remain,
Yours faithfully,
Lizzie

SUNDAY SEPTEMBER 12

Lloyd George has again emphasised in one of his fiery speeches, the gravity of the crisis. 'Nothing but our utmost can pull us through', he says 'are we now straining every nerve to make up for lost time? Are we getting all the men we shall want to put into the fighting line next year, to enable us even to hold our own?'

France, Belgium and Russia can do no more. England is the only ally who still has not engaged her vast resources to the utmost, and she has to do it quickly before it is too late. Lloyd George also declares that 'the course pursued by this country during the next three months will decide the fate of this war'. Every creature in the country should be doing something to help us win it.

WEDNESDAY SEPTEMBER 15

Sir Percy Scott, of naval gunnery fame, has been appointed director of the London gunnery defence against aircraft attack. Thus the defence of London is going to be placed on a very different footing. The anti-aircraft guns, like the one on which Uncle Gerry serves, fire only 1lb shells and these get nowhere near the Zeppelins, which do all their damage unhindered. The difficulty remains the damage and injury caused by our own shells to our own people in the streets.

THURSDAY SEPTEMBER 16

Mr Balfour, now First Lord of the Admiralty, has made an announcement which pacifies to some extent my qualms over the danger of taking you back to London. He says measures are being taken which will meet the danger to which London is exposed from Zeppelins.

Lord Kitchener has also made an important statement in the House on the state of the war. He says that though the response of England to the call to arms has produced 3 million soldiers, he and the Government have to concern themselves over the supply of men for 1916 as a reserve to the existing forces. Recruitment has fallen off during the last few weeks. The result of the National Registration will be open to the Government very shortly now. It is possible that Lord Kitchener is opening the way for compulsory service.

MONDAY SEPTEMBER 20

Glaslyn
Beatrice, Edie and I started a little before 10 o'clock in the car for Glaslyn. We had a glorious drive, through Aberystwyth, right over Plynlimmon and through the Wye Valley, arriving at 1.30. We found Henry, Ethel and Patience still at lunch. Glaslyn looked lovely in the bright sunshine and the foliage very thick and quite green.

We spent the afternoon dividing Father's pictures, casting lots for each series of six. I was so lucky in getting all those I had set my heart upon, actually drawing some, and exchanging others for my favourites.

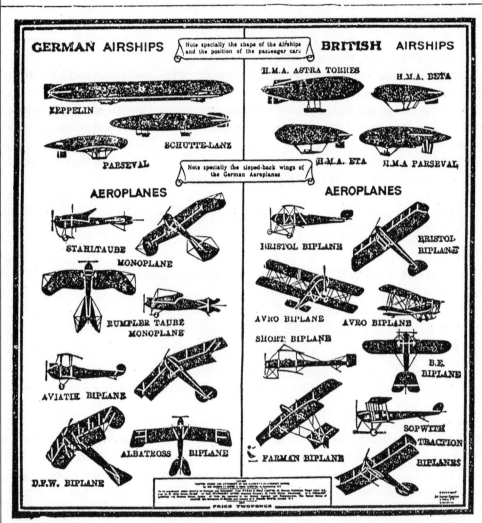

Above is reproduced a poster issued by the Home Office illustrating types of aircraft. The public are advised to familiarise themselves with the appearance of British and German airships and aeroplanes, so that they may not be alarmed by British aircraft, and may take shelter if German aircraft appear. Should hostile aircraft be seen, one should take shelter immediately in the nearest available house, preferably in the basement, and remain there until the aircraft have left the vicinity. The public are told not to stand about in crowds, and not to touch unexploded bombs. In the event of hostile aircraft being seen in country districts, the nearest naval, military, or police authorities should, if possible, be advised immediately by telephone of the time of appearance, the direction of flight, and whether the aircraft is an airship or an aeroplane.

German and British Airships.

I mean to put just two or three into your nursery for you to grow up with, knowing what an impression is made on one's mind in childhood by the pictures one lives with in the nursery.

WEDNESDAY SEPTEMBER 22

Beatrice and I motored back to Gelligemlyn, or rather Hengwrt, in two and a half hours from Rhayader, splendid going.

The new war budget has come out and the taxes are very heavy. An extra 4d on tea, though 3d was put on last year, making 1/- tax altogether on a pound of tea; the half-penny post done away with, so no more half-penny postcards; letters are 1d per ounce instead of 1d per 4ozs; telegrams are 9d instead of 6d; telephones are dearer; petrol is dearer; income tax is 3/4 on earned income instead of 2/6.

I haven't got to the bottom of it all, but the sum the country has to find is 1590 million pounds. But it is only a small price to pay to keep the German menace under control and keep our country free. So we shall pay cheerfully, though we may have to economise.

MONDAY SEPTEMBER 27

At last we have gained victories in the West.* The French have advanced along their fronts and the British have gained 4,000 yards capturing many guns, machine guns and prisoners.

---

*   Georgina Lee is referring to the battle of Loos, which opened on 25 September. 'For the British, Loos was a set-back that caused much heart searching and distress. Of nearly 10,000 British soldiers who attacked at Loos, 385 officers and 7,861 men were killed or wounded.' Martin Gilbert, *First World War*, p. 201.

Book VII

September 29, 1915 – February 12, 1916

WEDNESDAY SEPTEMBER 29

The first accounts of the advance have come through from some of the wounded who have arrived in Paris. When at last the infantry was ordered forward, it was the Colonial French Division which has produced such splendid fighters and achieved such dashing exploits, which took the lead, headed by the famous General Marchand of Fashoda fame. He, poor fellow, was shot down, dangerously wounded by shrapnel in the abdomen.

You will not know, probably, when you read this, who Marchand was, but 15 years ago he was very much the man of the moment. When Kitchener, at the end of the Omdurman Campaign, reached Fashoda on the White Nile, in the marshes and swamps far south in the Sudan, he found this gallant little French explorer had arrived there months before and there he and his little expeditionary party had planted the French flag.

Kitchener, with much diplomatic tact, had to explain to him that England's influence was now paramount in Egypt and the Sudan, and that he, as England's representative could not admit the French flag in this sphere. Poor Marchand had to bow to *force majeure*, but it caused a great deal of bitter feeling in France at the time.

FRIDAY OCTOBER 1

15 Neville Street
Daddy and I arrived this afternoon to a very cold, raw and empty London, at least it seemed empty during our drive from Paddington. This evening too the street is absolutely dark. There is one street lamp, at the Fulham Road end, and it is shaded off by dark blue paint round the globe, so that it makes but the faintest glow on the ground. Very stringent new regulations are in force from today about keeping all our windows dark. Anyone infringing the order is liable to imprisonment and heavy fines. No skylights are to be illuminated and as we have two on our landings we have to cease using those lights.

All day in the train I had the scent of the rose and sprig of verbena you gave me as I said goodbye to you this morning. Little Ella, always ready with gifts of flowers, gave you the lead.* She is very devoted to you although there is such a difference in your ages.

---

*   Ella was Harry's 7-year-old cousin, daughter of Guy Lee, youngest of the four Lee brothers.

1. Georgina Lee with Harry, born 28 October 1913. (*Ann de La Grange*)

2. Gelligemlyn in the early 1900s. From left: Gerard Lee, Minna Lee (Muz), Charles Lee. Stooping over a croquet mallet is probably Harry Wilmot Lee, with Brenda Wason on his right. (*Carol Bruxner*)

3. Georgina Lee with Harry and Nannie at Glaslyn. (*Ann de La Grange*)

4. Harry with Ella Lee, his cousin, at Gelligemlyn in June 1918. (*Ann de La Grange*)

5. Charles Lee, who was Legal Secretary to the Bishop of London throughout the war. (*Ann de La Grange*)

6. Barristers under orders: the Inns of Court Reserve Corps on parade. Charles Lee is arrowed in the back row. (*Daily Call, 11 February 1915*)

THE DAILY CALL, THURSDAY, FEBRUARY 11, 191

The Inns of Court Reserve Corps
BARRISTERS UNDER ORDERS.

Daddy's Corps — Daddy's top hat & collar, are just v̄
in second row where I have placed the arrow

Uncle
Gerry, at
his anti
aircraft
gun at
Dunkirk.

Jan. 1915

7. Gerard Lee (Uncle Gerry) at his anti-aircraft gun in Dunkirk in January 1915. *(Ann de La Grange)*

8. Lt Col Harry Romer Lee (Uncle Romer) and Maj Guy Lee (Uncle Guy) receive the DSO, 2 January 1918.

Honours for Mer ioneth Officers.

Lieut.-Colonel H. ROMER LEE.

Major GUY LEE.

Lieut.-Colonel H. Romer Lee and Major Guy Lee, sons of Mrs Constance Lee, Gellygemlyn, Dolgelley, were both awarded the D.S.O. in the New Year. Lieut.-Colonel H. R. Lee is now A.A. and Q.M.G. of one of the Welsh Divisions in France, where he has been for the past eighteen months. Major Guy Lee, who has been in command of an army grenade school, also in France, is on his way to take up a similar appointment in India. Another grandson of the late Mr C. R. Williams of Dolmelynllyn (Captain C. R. Wason, R.N.), was last year awarded the C.M.G. for his services in the Persian Gulf.

9. Midshipman Kit Wykeham-Musgrave's miraculous survival. See diary entries for 22 and 26 September 1914. (*Ann de La Grange*)

MIDDY'S ESCAPES.

Midshipman W. H. Wykeham-Musgrave, who escaped death three times in the North Sea disaster. He was successively on the Aboukir, the Hogue and the Cressy when they sank, and was finally picked up clinging to a plank. He has been in the Navy only two months.

10. The Bishop of London, surrounded by London Territorials, leads the open-air Intercession Service on 25 July 1915, from the steps of St Paul's Cathedral. Georgina Lee (arrowed) watches the scene from the window of the London Diocese Registry. She gives a detailed description of the occasion in her diary entry for that day. (*Daily Sketch*)

"o sacrifice matters if we win." This was the message that the Bishop of London gave to the nation from the steps of St. Paul's yesterday, when he addressed 4,500 London Territorials after leading them in procession through the mud and the He spoke with a personal knowledge of the noble work our men are doing at the front.—(Daily Sketch Photographs.)

The Intercession Service at St Paul's July 25
Mummy & Aunt Hilda in window of London Registry.

Eugene Crombie in the trenches 1915

11. Eugene Crombie writing a letter in the trenches, 1915. He was killed in action near Arras on 23 April 1917, aged 20. *(Ann de La Grange)*

Mrs Colby – with whom I generally work

The ironing room at Mulberry Walk Surgical Requisites' Depôt – Here the large bandages, – very complicated confections for broken hips, abdominal injuries etc, are ironed smooth –

12. Georgina Lee (left) and Mrs Colby in the ironing room at Mulberry Walk Surgical Requisites Depot. *(Ann de La Grange)*

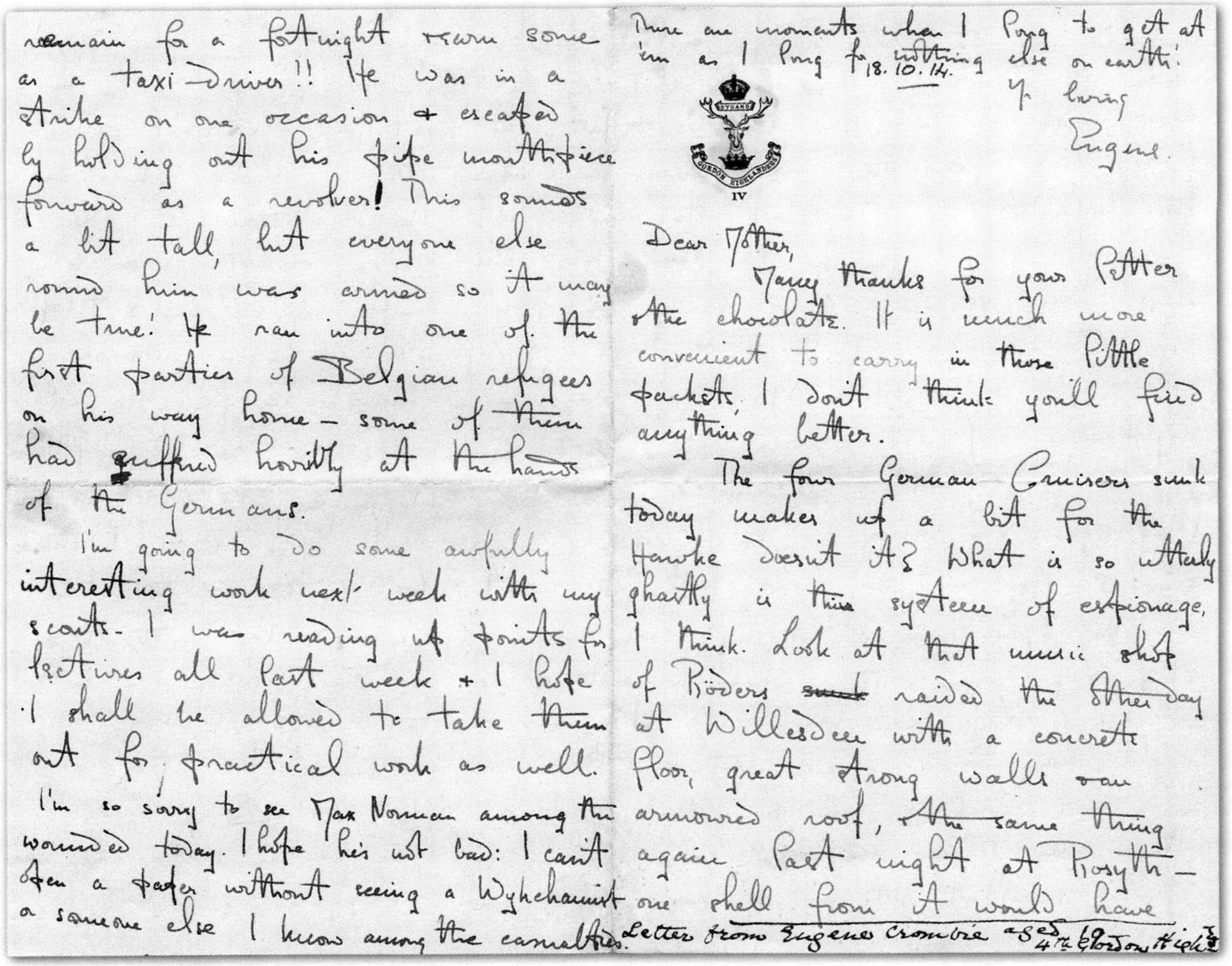

There are moments when I long to get at 'em as I long for nothing else on earth! 18.10.14.
Yr loving
Eugene.

Dear Mother,

Many thanks for your letter & the chocolate. It is much more convenient to carry in those little packets. I don't think you'll find anything better.

The four German Cruisers sunk today makes up a bit for the Hawke doesn't it? What is so utterly ghastly is this system of espionage, I think. Look at that music shop of Röders ~~sunk~~ raided the other day at Willesden with a concrete floor, great strong walls and armoured roof, ~~the same thing~~ again last night at Rosyth – one shell from it would have

Letter from Eugene Crombie aged 19 4th Gordon Highrs

remain for a fortnight & earn some as a taxi-driver!! He was in a strike on one occasion & escaped by holding out his pipe mouthpiece forward as a revolver! This sounds a bit tall, but everyone else round him was armed so it may be true! He ran into one of the first parties of Belgian refugees on his way home – some of them had suffered horribly at the hands of the Germans.

I'm going to do some awfully interesting work next week with my scouts. I was reading up points for lectures all last week & I hope I shall be allowed to take them out for practical work as well.

I'm so sorry to see Max Norman among the wounded today. I hope he's not bad: I can't open a paper without seeing a Wykehamist or someone else I know among the casualties.

13. A letter from Eugene Crombie to his mother, dated 18 October 1914. He had insisted on leaving Winchester College early, in order to join the Army. *(Ann de La Grange)*

14. Audrey Clive-Davies, nursing at Alexandria, 1915. Married to Lt Col Arthur Clive Davis, Audrey was Georgina Lee's sister-in-law. *(Ann de La Grange)*

Audrey Clive-Davies, nursing at Alexandria – 1915-

15. The royal carriage fetching surgical supplies going direct to Queen Mary. Georgina Lee stands second from the left. *(Ann de La Grange)*

The Royal Carriage fetching the weekly Supply of Surgical requisites made by us at Mulberry Walk – The Supplies go straight to Queen Mary who distributes them as she wishes to the hospitals –
standing second from left: Mummy (my white overall raised to carry parcels into Van –
on my right, Mrs Bischoff, then Mrs Dana, the tallest

16. Belgian women, supported by two Scouts, collecting for their M. Max Distress Fund at the entrance to Newmarket racecourse, October 1914. In her diary entry for 1 October 1914, Georgina Lee refers to M. Max as 'the intrepid Mayor of Brussels'. (*Imperial War Museum Q53361*)

17. Tea for 600 Belgian children at Earl's Court. (*Imperial War Museum HU88813*)

18. Alexandra Palace converted into dormitories for Belgian refugees, October 1914. *(Photo Alfieri: Archives Générales du Royaume, Brussels)*

19. The Belgian Surgical Depot at 115 Queen's Gate. Georgina Lee is seated at the table, recording the monthly list of supplies made in the workroom. *(Ann de La Grange)*

March 8th

Off this worst of all winters.
These photos of my Belgian Surgical
Depôt have just arrived —

The Office, G.L.L. making monthly list of supplies made in Workroom.

20. Police hold back the crowds as the General Post Office in the City burns after the explosion of a 112lb bomb on the roof during the air raid of 7 July 1917. Altogether 57 people were killed and 193 injured. Georgina Lee describes the raid in her entry for 7 July 1917 and visited the scene on 8 July. (*Imperial War Museum Q65536*)

21. Zeppelin L48 was brought down in flames at Theberton, Suffolk, on 17 June 1917. Five members of her crew were killed. Georgina Lee records an eyewitness account of this episode in her diary entry for 29 June 1917. (*Imperial War Museum Q58467*)

22. Odhams Printing Works in Long Acre, near Covent Garden, sustained a direct hit during the raid of 28/9 January 1918. Of the men, women and children who had crowded into the basement for shelter, thirty-seven were killed and eighty-nine injured. See diary entry for 29 January 1918. (*Imperial War Museum HO122A*)

23. The façade of the Chelsea Hospital, which was bombed on 16 February 1918. Georgina Lee visited the site three days later and describes the devastation in her diary entry for 19 February 1918. Two children were found impaled on the railings. (*Imperial War Museum HO33*)

24. The memorial plaque to the Ludlow family. (*Gavin Roynon*)

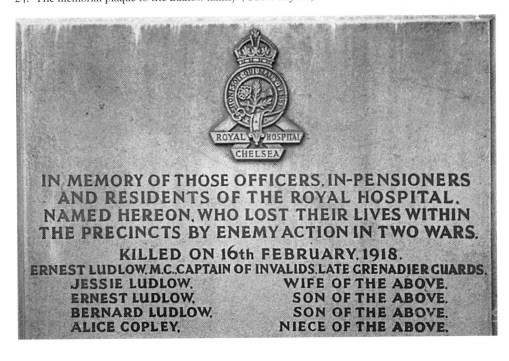

IN MEMORY OF THOSE OFFICERS, IN-PENSIONERS AND RESIDENTS OF THE ROYAL HOSPITAL, NAMED HEREON, WHO LOST THEIR LIVES WITHIN THE PRECINCTS BY ENEMY ACTION IN TWO WARS.

KILLED ON 16th FEBRUARY, 1918.

ERNEST LUDLOW, M.C., CAPTAIN OF INVALIDS, LATE GRENADIER GUARDS.

JESSIE LUDLOW,	WIFE OF THE ABOVE.
ERNEST LUDLOW,	SON OF THE ABOVE.
BERNARD LUDLOW,	SON OF THE ABOVE.
ALICE COPLEY,	NIECE OF THE ABOVE.

25. Harry Lee and his cousins, Charlie and Knyvett Romer-Lee, sell roses on Queen Alexandra's Rose Day, 'when there are millions of roses sold in her name for the hospitals' (diary entry 21 June 1916). (*Ann de La Grange*)

26. British and Dominion troops enjoy a free buffet at Victoria. (*Imperial War Museum Q27835*)

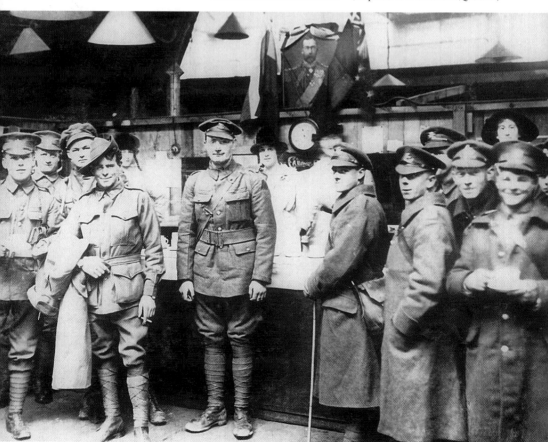

27. London Tank Week, 4–9 March 1918: Beatty and Babs (the actresses Bunny Beatty and Barbara Burns-Norvell), after investing £1,300 at the Chiswick Tank, sang a song that was greatly appreciated. (*Imperial War Museum Q54381*)

28. Marshal Foch, followed by General Weygand, passing the royal box on Peace Day, 19 July 1919. HM King George V is taking the salute. (*Imperial War Museum Q28758*)

29. British troops passing down Constitution Hill, 19 July 1919. Note the high vantage point enjoyed by an Australian soldier. (*Imperial War Museum Q28759*)

The President driving with the King in yesterday's procession from Charing Cross Station to Buckingham Palace. ["*Daily Mail.*"]

30. President Wilson and King George V drive to Buckingham Palace, 26 December 1918.

SATURDAY OCTOBER 2

Our Expeditionary Force which started in the Persian Gulf about a year ago has now penetrated so far up the Tigris that we suddenly hear that it is now only 100 miles away from Baghdad. If Baghdad falls it will create a great sensation among the Eastern peoples, for whom Baghdad is a sacred city and Holy of Holies, just as Mecca is to the Mohammedans.

It is our Indian Army, mixed with British, which has provided troops for this Expedition. When one thinks of the resources of the British Empire, how certain Colonies are entrusted with different tasks all over the world, the Canadians in France, the South Africans conquering German S.W. Africa, the New Zealanders and Australians helping to crack the nut in the Dardanelles, the Indians defending Egypt with the Egyptian Army, and invading Palestine, one wonders that the Germans ever believed that they could overthrow Great Britain.

Today in doing my shopping after a month's absence, I find everything gone up in price a great deal. Butter 1/10 a lb instead of 1/6, tea 2/2 instead of 1/7. Gloves, black ones, almost impossible to get; the small picture I want to give Uncle Gerry will now cost more: the frame 25% dearer owing to a strike among the gold-beaters, and the glass 75% dearer owing to the great rise in the cost of glass.

Bacon is now 1/7 and I remember it 10d some years ago; altogether living costs much more. Though one pays cheerfully any price, when one's country's future is at stake, living becomes somewhat of a problem for limited incomes. Especially when there is a fat baby requiring a first-rate nurse and an extra servant for the increase in the household!

SUNDAY OCTOBER 10

Bulgaria has decided to join the Central Powers, so we now have her in the lists against us. The Germans are jubilant. They are entering poor Serbia from many points. That brave and sorely tried little country is fighting to the death to save herself from annihilation. The treacherous Ferdinand,* it now appears, has been in secret contact for a long time with Germany and Austria to revenge himself for the results of the last Balkan war in 1913.

MONDAY OCTOBER 11

I have just read an article from an American paper which has made my heart sick with apprehension.** For the first time, I ask myself whether the German race with its genius

---

*   First king (1908–18) of modern Bulgaria.
** Some consternation had been caused by an article by Raymond Swing in the *Chicago Daily News*. This was largely reprinted in *The Times*. Swing reported that – under the initiative of Dr Rathenau in the War Ministry – steel and zinc substitutes were being developed by German scientists to replace copper and tin.

for invention is meant after all to have the mastery of the world. For all these months we have been believing that Germany must collapse from exhaustion before we do, chiefly because our blockade of the sea would starve her of the products she needs for manufacturing her war materials.

Now it seems that Germany is daily becoming more and more self supporting. Thanks to her great organiser of industrial resources, Rathenau,* she has substituted for the raw products she can no longer get from abroad, new products from her own inventiveness.

What distresses me so is the thought that the genius of our race is not such as to cope with the German in this respect. Our country is so unorganised, so hopelessly independent, that in a crisis like this, such as has never before happened in our history, one feels the lack of the mighty pull altogether which is our hope of survival.

The Germans are overrunning the North of Serbia. Frenzied discussions are going on in the papers and among the public about the course the Government should pursue.

1. Should a large force be sent to Serbia to check the German advance?
2. Should the Dardanelles Army be withdrawn from Gallipoli, where it cannot advance?
3. Or, should Serbia be left to take care of herself, and all energies concentrated on the Western Front?

We are racked with these new anxieties, harassed with the uncertainty and the hideous possibilities of the future.

I think of you all the time, you are at the back of all my anxieties. Will my boy grow up to a free, great England, as his forebears have done for so many generations, or will the shadow of a great failure cloud the Land of our Fathers?

TUESDAY OCTOBER 12

I have just had a letter from Aunt Beatrice telling me about Colin Dunsmure. He is first cousin of your cousins Henry and Bee. We heard he was wounded at Loos in the advance of September 25. Colin is all that his poor mother has left. Her husband (Uncle Alex's eldest brother) died last autumn and her elder son Alistair, a young officer in the Cameron Highlanders, was killed in the spring. Aunt Beatrice writes:

We have had three days of terrible anxiety about Colin. Telegrams to say he was missing and a final one yesterday to say there was no hope of his being alive. However late last night a fourth wire to say he was alive and on his way home. You can imagine the joy and relief!

---

*   Walther Rathenau was an industrialist. He realised that government direction of national resources would be necessary for victory. As Head of the Raw Materials Department in the War Ministry, Rathenau ensured the conservation and distribution of raw materials essential for the war effort.

But in the morning we had a long letter from the Colonel, Cameron of Lochiel, to Philip Mitford. Colin was commanding No 2 machine gun section on the left. They were nearly all ousted by the enemy's enfilade M.G. fire He was shot in the head and his servant was left with him. We went out next night and found most of the gun team, including his servant, lying dead, but we could not find your cousin. Since then it has been impossible to do any more searching, as the Germans are back again over the same ground. There is, I fear, no doubt in my mind that he is dead by now.

The letter is very long and continues with a wonderful account of the bravery of the battalion (Camerons of Lochiel).

The Camerons advanced over the open ground in perfect line without officers to lead them, amid a hail of shrapnel and machine-gun fire. I hope it may be some consolation to Dunsmure's relatives to know that he died doing his duty. Please convey my deepest sympathy to your poor cousin's relatives. He was a splendid officer and I shall never see better officers than him and the others we have lost.

Yet, in a fourth telegram this poor boy is now said to be on his way home and one wonders how his Mother will find him – convalescent or dying!

Aunt Beatrice has also been very busy giving voluntary aid to the Government in the great National Registration. As Commandant of the V.A.D. nurses for Merioneth she has been sifting out the 'pink forms' which were issued to all men of military age.

She writes:

We've been all the week at the Drill Hall (Dolgelly) working on the Pink Forms. I had to get twelve of the V.A.D. nurses to help with the sorting as it would have taken too long, and tomorrow we shall finish. We began at 9.30 and many of them worked till 7 pm so I am very pleased with them.

It is extraordinary how few men are to be exempted from serving. Those who are not to be 'pressed' have a star after their name. It will be a revelation to most in this district to see how few of them have been starred. Married men with children, up to the age of 40 are just as liable as others, and it is only certain occupations (rather unfair I think) which have been starred. It looks as though the country will be drained of all labour, apart from these few occupations.

This the system by which the Government is finding out all the men who can be taken for service.

WEDNESDAY OCTOBER 13

9.45 pm: I am all trembling with excitement as we have just come in from the pavement outside listening to the guns popping in all directions! Evidently the Zeppelins are paying us a visit tonight, but the whole fusillade only lasted about 6 or 7 minutes, and they were a long way off to the East. Searchlights are playing all over the sky. In an instant our little quiet street had all its inhabitants on their doorstep and people were all talking and laughing.

A postman came round wheeling his red parcel-cart, flashing his little lantern, just as calmly as though nothing was happening, and delivering his parcels. We asked him if it was another raid, and he said that, as he was passing by the Reserves Depot in Cromwell Road five minutes ago, the troops there had been ordered to 'stand to'.

10.15 pm: Uncle Gerry has just answered our telephone and says that a Zeppelin did just pass over Thurloe Square and Onslow Square! So near us, and yet we never saw it. What an excitement to think the Germans have just passed over our heads. Uncle Gerry says it is very difficult to see the airships unless the flashlights are on them. Tomorrow we shall hear what the damage is.

THURSDAY OCTOBER 14

Gelligemlyn
I travelled down to Wales very comfortably, meeting Alex and also Jacqueline Trotter, Sir Henry Trotter's eldest and very pretty daughter, unexpectedly at Paddington. Another lady got into our carriage, who knew all our neighbours. She had been at the theatre last night.

When they heard the bombs and guns, no one moved or showed any excitement. But as soon as the act was over, she and her friend went out to see what was happening. There, quite close to the Savoy was a bomb burning itself out in a huge hole in the roadway. It had killed five people and wounded others. She saw wounded being taken into Charing Cross Hospital. As she walked, her feet in her thin shoes were cut by the broken glass lying all over the pavement.

She spoke to a girl who was in a very agitated state, holding a bundle of clothes. The clothes belonged to another girl she was walking with, who had been badly injured and whom she accompanied to the hospital. This poor distracted girl was not fit to be left to herself, being terribly shaken by her experience.

FRIDAY OCTOBER 15

Daddy sent me details of the raid on Wednesday night:

Damage was done in Fleet Street; the Lyceum Theatre slightly injured. Bomb just missed its roof and coming down on a crowded house. I tried to get down at midday, but the block was so fearful in the Strand, it would have taken hours, and the buses had no room in them for miles. At 1 am they visited Croydon and dropped a lot of bombs there.* Salter (partner) has just come in from Lincoln's Inn. Every house in that locality has its windows broken.

---

*   Five Zeppelins participated in this raid – the heaviest air raid over Britain of the war. Seventy-one civilians in London and the Home Counties were killed.

Mr Walter's office has no roof. Cloisters of Lincoln's Inn smashed. Chancery Lane Road torn up nearly all the way. Belgian Refugees' wooden building in Kingsway in small matchwood. I shall try and get there tomorrow.

SATURDAY OCTOBER 16

I have just come home at 6.15 from a meeting for enrolling Boy Scouts at Caerynwch, but just too late to see you awake! Yet, vexed as I am, as soon as I see your pink face so peacefully lost in sleep, it's an extraordinary happiness that steals over me. To see you safe and well is perfect happiness alone. The nice and very pretty red-haired Florence who has taken over Nannie's place for ten days, has quite adopted you and you her, for the time being. But she said that before going to sleep you were repeating to yourself 'Good-night Nannie, good-night Mummy'.

WEDNESDAY OCTOBER 20

It is announced that Sir Ian Hamilton has been succeeded in the command at the Dardanelles by General Monro, Sir Ian having returned to England 'to make a report'. As long ago, in fact at the outset of the campaign, many people, soldiers especially, said that Hamilton was no use. It is very depressing, though, to find out after months of no progress, yet terrible casualties, that Hamilton is succeeded by another leader.

THURSDAY OCTOBER 21

German cruelty has aroused a storm of indignation all through the world in the case of Edith Cavell, an English hospital Nurse, at the head of the Belgian Red Cross Infirmary in Brussels. Her fame as a heroine will last and her name rank with the Grace Darlings* and Florence Nightingales.

This brave woman had been nursing English, French, Belgian and German wounded with equal devotion. She had helped Allied wounded prisoners to escape from hospital. When confronted by German authorities, she did not deny it. Thrown into a cell, she was then court-martialled.

American diplomats made superhuman efforts to save her, which were ignored. But before an appeal to a Higher Court could be heard, she was executed. Sentenced to be shot by a volley-party, the poor woman was led blindfolded into the garden where the soldiers were waiting for her. Her immense courage and devotion to duty are immensely admired and there is widespread shock at her fate.**

---

*   Heroic daughter of William Darling, keeper of the Longstone Lighthouse, Farne Islands. In 1838, despite perilous seas, she and her father launched their small boat and rescued five survivors from the wrecked *Forfarshire*.

**   A fine statue of Edith Cavell stands at the bottom of St Martin's Lane, just off Trafalgar Square.

TUESDAY OCTOBER 26

Our King George has issued a manifesto to his people appealing for recruits and though it was only published on the 23rd October the response has been magnificent. The murder of Nurse Cavell in Brussels, too, has fired the imagination of men, and has had a very great effect upon recruiting. The Germans have defeated their own object in ordering her execution.

FRIDAY OCTOBER 29

Our King has met with an accident while visiting our troops at the Front in France. He was riding and reviewing a regiment which has greatly distinguished itself in the recent fighting at Loos. The sudden tumult of cheers which succeeded the perfect silence of the inspection frightened his mare. She reared, and, overbalancing, fell backwards upon the King. He is reported 'very severely shaken and bruised' and is to keep to his bed for several days. The Prince of Wales left the Front and came to London, probably to report to the Queen on his Father's condition. We are all trusting that the accident is not more grave than the papers admit.

SATURDAY OCTOBER 30

General Joffre has come to London with several French officers to confer with our Ministers in Downing Street. He is the Guest of Lord Kitchener. This is the first time Joffre has been over here, though Kitchener has been to France several times. Probably the visit is prompted by the situation in Serbia. A few days ago a desperate appeal was published from the Serbian Premier for help.

MONDAY NOVEMBER 1

The King is better and there are no complications, only the pain caused by the bruises.

Joffre has paid a very hurried visit to England. But they say that his quick, alert manner, his emphatic speaking straight to the point, mincing no words, his rising with daylight and wasting not a second, has impressed the Cabinet in Downing Street. He came, it is said, to get a straight answer, yes or no, on an urgent question of policy. In a word, he seems to have woken up some of the Twenty-One of '£4000 a year salaries and long week-ends' and convinced them of the urgency of the situation.*

SATURDAY NOVEMBER 6

Kitchener is absenting himself for an indefinite period on service elsewhere. Meanwhile Asquith has taken the nominal lead of the War Office, with the War Council working under him. Kitchener's colossal work of raising and organising the New Armies (he has under arms a New Army of 2,000,000) is now practically finished. So the great soldier

---

*   This is a tilt at Asquith's Cabinet.

and organiser of victory may be going to direct the fighting machine he has created, out in the near East.

TUESDAY NOVEMBER 9

The Lord Mayor's Show this year has been turned into a recruiting pageant. I went to see it, from the office in Dean's Court by St Paul's. Besides contingents of many overseas troops, there were captured German guns in the procession. Also our anti-aircraft guns, motor ambulances, supply lorries, field forges and a bi-plane on its lorry. It rained the whole time, so the gala carriages, with their gorgeous liveried domestics covered in waterproofs, did not make their usual effect.

The recruits who volunteered on the spot were to march immediately behind the corps they had enlisted in. But there were very few, only a dozen, at our stage in the procession.

THURSDAY NOVEMBER 11

An Italian liner, the *Ancona*, has been torpedoed in the Mediterranean by a German submarine and 194 people were drowned. This crime, a new *Lusitania*, has caused great sensation in the USA, because of the 11 Americans on board who died. Also in Italy which is not yet at war with Germany.

Uncle Guy has written in great distress, 'broken-hearted' he calls himself, because of an accident which happened for the first time at his Grenade School. A grenade exploded prematurely, killing 3 sergeants, 1 officer and wounding 30 officers and men. He himself was in his office at the time. But an officer came at once to report. Guy rushed to the scene, which was like a battlefield. Dead, dying and wounded were lying there, being assisted as best they could be by the uninjured.

Bandages were quickly procured and the wounds dressed, but poor Guy could not get over it. General Plumer, who commands the 2nd Army, sent for Guy and was quite charming and sympathetic. He told Guy to run home for a week's change. Guy won't do this however. He says it is only right for him to stay, though the school is to be closed for a few days to give the staff a rest after the shock.

Daddy's first cousin Dick Lee, who was in the 10th Suffolk Regiment, has just been killed in Flanders, capturing a German trench.

SUNDAY NOVEMBER 14

Churchill has resigned his place in the Cabinet of Twenty-One, because, not being elected one of the five in the War Council, he found that 'he was not able in times like these to remain in well-paid inactivity'. So, in words that will become classic, he has written a letter to Asquith, taking leave of him and his colleagues, and announcing his decision to go to the Front in his old regiment. It is a very dramatic *dénouement*, or rather, phase, in a brilliant career. Whatever may be said by his enemies, and they are numerous, his was the strongest and most far-seeing and energetic personality in the Government.

Years hence he will probably be considered one of the ablest men England has ever had, and no man has ever done so much to make our Navy all-powerful. In spite of this, his rather overbearing way and his self-assurance have created him many enemies. When failures have resulted from his policy, such as the sending of the Naval Division to the relief of Antwerp, and later the Dardanelles Expedition, these failures, which have been failures mainly because the Government did not give him the full support the plans demanded, have been visited on him alone.

No one can believe, though, that his strong and forceful personality is lost for ever in the affairs of the nation; he will probably come back to the fore again once more, a stronger and better man for this chastening episode. They say Asquith has always appreciated and valued his genius, and was anxious to have him in the Inner Five Council.

Winston Churchill, in bidding goodbye to the House, two nights ago, before proceeding to France to join his regiment, made a speech vindicating himself of the charges brought against him. It was frank, and raised the veil on the events which led up to the great decisions, the attempt to relieve Antwerp, the naval action off Coronel which resulted in the destruction of Admiral Cradock's Squadron, and lastly the Dardanelles Enterprise.

Through his words, one could see how his energetic, strong decisions and clear foresight had given the impression that he was leading the Cabinet with the Premier. The speech has caused a *volte-face* of feeling in his favour in many quarters. It is amusing to hear almost everybody who hadn't a good word to say for Winston, veer round and say he was the only strong man in the Government!

Daddy went to Caterham, or near there today, to help his Corps to dig trenches for the defence of the Surrey hills outward defences of London. Whole woods have been levelled to give free range for our guns in case of need. These trenches are only part of a continuous chain of defences between London and the South Coast.

FRIDAY NOVEMBER 19

One of our hospital ships, the *Anglia*, was sunk in the Channel two days ago by a German mine. She carried 384 people at the time and 134 of these were killed or drowned. There were 200 'cot cases' i.e. wounded who could not be moved, on board. But thanks to the rapid rescue by several ships who raced to the spot in reply to wireless messages, many of the passengers were saved. The *Anglia* was the ship which brought the King home after his accident, about a fortnight ago.

I heard today from a friend at the hospital depot where I work every morning, that Sir Anthony Bowlby the King's Surgeon who came home with the King, had told her that if the King had not been riding over a ploughed field (or rather standing in one) at the time of the accident, he must have been killed, when the horse fell back upon him. He himself thought he was done for, and expressed the wish that the Prince of Wales (then at the Front) should return at once to England, because it would be inexpedient for the new Monarch to be out of England on his accession to the Throne.

So the Prince was sent to Boulogne, but there he was delayed by a cable from the Admiralty saying that on no account must he embark until the presence of any mines had been detected in the Channel. So there he had to wait for 24 hours. The King has not yet completely recovered, and the injuries were more serious than the Press had been allowed to say.*

The situation in Serbia is desperate. The Germans have advanced so rapidly that they now cover four fifths of Serbian soil.

SUNDAY NOVEMBER 21

Daddy was out all today at Woldingham, 20 miles south of London, helping dig the trenches for the defence of London. He says the trenches are beautifully made, with dug-outs as big and luxurious as drawing rooms! He came home very muddy in the evening.

Meanwhile Lord Kitchener arrived in Athens and had an hour's interview with King Constantine. He left Athens again in the evening and is said to have gone to Gallipoli.

FRIDAY NOVEMBER 26

I was out early this morning across the Park to York Place, where Alex Dunsmure was operated upon for appendicitis. I arrived before it began and was with Beatrice while it lasted. I took her out for a brisk walk. It was lovely crisp, frosty day, and we were in the Park till nearly eleven. Then we went back and soon after we got in, Uncle Henry, who had assisted Tyrrell Gray, the brilliant surgeon, came and told us it was all safely over.

But they found the appendix in a bad state, brewing up for another attack, so it was removed just at the right time. Aunt Beatrice's husband is a man of such sterling qualities, that we have all felt very anxious since the bad attack he had a month ago at Hengwrt.

SATURDAY DECEMBER 4

I spent this afternoon with Alex Dunsmure at the home, and found him still weak, but improving. We had tea in his comfortable room.

It was a miserable wet day, and pitch dark at 5 o'clock when I started home. It was such a weird sight coming along Park Lane to see the total blackness of the Park on the right, the almost total extinction of the arc lights, the few left burning showing only the tiniest circle of light at the bottom of the globes. All the same the great motor-buses were swinging along in the mud as fast as usual.

---

*   Sir Bertrand Dawson, his physician, wrote: 'Besides the widespread and severe bruising, the pelvis was fractured in at least two places and the pain was bad, the subsequent shock considerable and convalescence tedious.' It was four weeks before the King was able to hobble with two sticks along the balcony outside his bedroom. Thereafter he was never quite the same man again. Harold Nicolson, *George V – His Life and Reign*, p. 268.

But instead of their usual bright lights, small dark blue or dark green glow-lights showed through the glass panes. Altogether the effect is ghostly in the large thoroughfares; the traffic surges to and fro looking only like great black masses carrying glow worms which shed no light, but just enable you to see them. In the far distance all you see is a continual kaleidoscopic change of glow worm red, yellow or green lights.

There is very disappointing news tonight of the retirement of our Mesopotamian Expedition to 100 miles south of our most advanced spot, which was only eight miles from Baghdad. Our forces are not large enough for the very large reinforcements the Turks have hurried up. We seem to botch all our undertakings by always starting with inadequate forces.

SATURDAY DECEMBER 11

It is a week since I wrote and the news has not improved. There is now a huge rush of all men of military age to enlist 'voluntarily' during the last two days of Lord Derby's Voluntary Recruiting. 'Voluntary' in an absurd word, for the men are told that if they don't come now they will be fetched after tomorrow.* Every single clerk in Dad's office has enlisted, even two delicate and married ones of the age of 40.

Of course they will not all be required for a long time, as they will be called up in groups and the single ones go first. I don't know how normal work is to be carried on. If things get too difficult at the office, I shall volunteer to help myself!

Dear Alex is doing well at last today, for the first time. For several days he caused me such uneasiness that I hadn't the heart to write this diary, and hated my At Homes. Only yesterday was there an improvement. He had a setback by having pleurisy a few days after his operation.

MONDAY DECEMBER 13

Uncle Guy came back from the Front on Saturday for the third time since the war began. Daddy and I dined with him at Pelham Street, where he and Granny are staying. He told us all about his Grenade School. He is a wonderful man and I am sure he will have a distinguished career. His Grenade School is a self-contained camp and all his own creation.

There has been another accident there, through the premature bursting of a grenade. Guy found that some were faulty. In one case, on examining a grenade which he had had sliced in half, he found that the walls of the chamber containing the fuse were of unequal thickness and so thin that the explosive lying beyond the wall ignited from the heat sooner than it should have done.

---

*   Lord Derby had been appointed Director-General of Recruiting on 5 October. Under his scheme – intended to be an alternative to conscription, which Asquith hoped to avoid – every man between 18 and 41 was asked to 'attest', i.e. promise to serve when called. It became clear that voluntary recruitment could no longer answer the ever-increasing demands of the Front, and conscription came in, in January 1916.

Daddy lunched with him today, just after Guy had been to the Ministry of Munitions to 'kick up a devil of a row' over the faulty bombs which have so far caused death or injuries to fifty of his men. As luck would have it, the engineer and inventor of the grenades was in the building, and was called in to speak to Guy. Thinking Guy was an officer from the trenches come to complain without knowledge, the engineer, who is also the contractor, was very cool with Guy. He told him that, to talk as he did, he couldn't know much of the grenades, nor how they were made.

'How about this?' then said Guy producing the half section of a faulty bomb from his pocket. He pointed out the defect and when he said that he was Commandant of the Grenade School, the engineer collapsed. Guy told him he was going to report the whole matter to the War Office, taxing him at the same time with charging 6/- a piece for his grenades, while he, Guy, could turn them out for sevenpence at the small factory he commands. So we await developments.

THURSDAY DECEMBER 16

Sir John French has asked to be relieved of the Command in France and Flanders, and is appointed to command at home. He has been created Viscount. He has been succeeded by Sir Douglas Haig.* They say the continual strain of the sixteen months of this terrible struggle is too much for French.

SUNDAY DECEMBER 19

We had a delightful family Christmas Dinner at Pelham Street last night, to say goodbye to Guy. He returned early this morning to his Grenade School at the Front.

Muriel Wason was there. She had just that day arrived from France, where she has been nursing in a Croix Rouge hospital at Foix, in the Ariège. Her accounts of the primitive methods of nursing, devoid of all hygiene and sanitary scruples, were revealing. The roughness of it all was compensated for by the merriness and wit of the French blessés, by whom she and the other English nurses were much loved.

But when you think that by six pm all the nurses are turned out of the wards by a military law which forbids any woman being in the hospital at night, you can realise what it must be like for severely wounded and sick patients to be left to themselves all through the long hours of the night. Also, no screens are allowed, for even the most intimate treatment or necessities, the reason being that 'all sorts of things' and flirtations might be going on behind the screen.

TUESDAY DECEMBER 21

Today we hear that the Dardanelles have been, or are still being, evacuated. Suvla Bay and Anzac Bay, the landing places occupied some months ago and upon which such

---

*   Haig formally became Commander-in-Chief of the British Expeditionary Force on 19 December.

high hopes had been built, turned out to be terribly costly and fruitless. Still, for months they were held, because withdrawal would mean heavy losses. Now, we hear that these positions have been evacuated without the knowledge of the Turks and these forces are going to be used elsewhere. One could weep at the thought of our failure to bring the Dardanelles Campaign to a successful issue and at the waste, the holocaust of precious lives.

WEDNESDAY DECEMBER 22

The withdrawal of our Army from Suvla Bay and Anzac Point has been accomplished with only three casualties and no deaths. Two wounded soldiers and one wounded seaman, the loss of six guns which we destroyed first and a small amount of supplies. This operation so successfully carried out, is considered an 'amazing achievement' according to Asquith, reflecting the greatest credit on the Commanding Officers of both Army and Navy.

The withdrawal is the result of Lord Kitchener's personal visit to Gallipoli a few weeks ago. He decided, with General Monro,* the new C-in-C out there, that the quest was hopeless and that the forces would be more useful elsewhere.

FRIDAY DECEMBER 24

Uncle Guy has been made Chevalier of the Légion d'Honneur by the French Government. This is a mark of recognition which was 'beyond his wildest dreams', so he says in his letter to Muz. As I have mentioned already, his Grenade School has been highly commended by the French Generals in command.

Joffre sent him Officers of his own Staff, and many other Officers passed through his Course of training, so as to enable them in their turn to instruct the French Army in all they need to know about hand-bombs and grenades. Guy's own manual has been translated into French for use in the French Army.

Today is the Eve of the first Christmas when your stocking is to be hung up. You came with great ceremony to hang it up this evening by the dining room fireplace and you shouted up the chimney a message to Father Kips-mus to be sure to come tomorrow. One of Daddy's waders had to be chosen for this, in view of the rather bulky 'presents' awaiting you.

Uncle Hugh and Aunt Hilda are staying here, with just our three selves, with Granmuz for Christmas, a very reduced group compared to the Christmas family parties of past years. Uncle Gerry is too busy on his anti-aircraft gun to get away.

---

*   Lt Gen Sir Charles Monro, who had commanded the Third Army in France, succeeded Sir Ian Hamilton on 28 October. From the start he impressed his staff officers by his decisive approach. 'He was a harder man than the whimsical Hamilton, disinclined to spare the inefficient or incompetent, whatever excuse was offered, but with a refreshing open mind.' Michael Hickey, *Gallipoli*, p. 323.

MONDAY DECEMBER 27

We had a happy Christmas well, *comparatively* happy, that is, none of the family are at present in immediate danger. I have you and Daddy safe and well, and all the brothers are more or less safe for the moment. What you loved most were the two big crackers. After seeing Granmuz and me pull one, you were wild to do the other yourself and then wanted 'more bangers'. You never even blinked at the noise!

Today we had another attempt to get in the first shoot, as we were baulked by the deluges of rain on Friday. Today the rain came on again at 11, and a great gale lashed itself into fury by lunch time. We were all soaked by lunch time and after an excellent lunch in one of the cottages on the top of the hill, we were home by 2 o'clock.

I changed all my things, attended by you and then had to play with you before and after your tea until 6 o'clock. You don't let me off, I can tell you!

FRIDAY DECEMBER 31

The last day of the old year. A long year of waiting and suspense, of disappointed hopes, yet of fears allayed. The hopes of breaking the German resistance are so far disappointed, but what of the German boasts of invading England and destroying London, of crushing England by air, if not by sea? And think of the German Fleet still cowering behind the defences of Kiel.

1916

The rank stench of those bodies haunts me still. And I remember things I'd best forget

Siegfried Sassoon

MONDAY JANUARY 3

Gelligemlyn

Another terrible tragedy like the *Lusitania* horror. This time a P&O liner, the *Persia*, has been torpedoed in the Mediterranean off Crete without warning. Out of about 500 souls, 334 have been lost including 60 women and children. There was no panic, a few boats were lowered, and as the ship went down a few among those washed overboard were taken up into boats, but the great majority were drowned.

Some of the lost are American, including the American Consul for Aden and his secretary. Perhaps this new outrage will at last arouse President Wilson's anger and break his determination to remain patient.*

---

*   It didn't. The USA remained neutral. The American Secretary of State, Robert Lansing, sent a formal protest, but took no further action. Fifteen more months would elapse before the USA entered the war, in April 1917.

WEDNESDAY JANUARY 5

The poor boy, Colin Dunsmure, Henry's first cousin, missing since September 25, has been accounted for at last, and his mother's long agony of suspense is at an end.*

Second Lieutenant Colin Dunsmure, Machine Gun Officer of the 5th Cameron Highlanders, was wounded at Loos on September 25 and last seen alive that afternoon lying 50 yards from the British sheltered trench. He has now been found dead on the field by men of the 6th Queen's Regiment, and buried by them near Hohenzollern Redoubt. He obtained his commission on September 16, 1915, and was the younger son of the late Henry Dunsmure, of Glenbruachy. He was 21 a few days before he left England.

The Times, January 5, 1916

One hears of so many men turning up again after being prisoners in German hands, that it was quite possible he was still alive.

There have been some terrible cases of wounded cripples returning home after months of no news, to find their wives re-married, Enoch Ardens of the war.**

THURSDAY JANUARY 6

Mr Asquith has introduced his Bill for Compulsory Service, the gist of which is that single men must enlist now and go before the married men. But there are exemptions.

Clergy & Ministers
War Workers
Those with Dependents
Conscientious Objectors (Quakers & Others)
Last Sons of Mothers
Territorials & Kitchener Army who earlier enlisted for Home Service only.

Asquith made his statement to a crowded House. A good proportion of the members, about 50, were in khaki, some wounded or back from the Front. But the Bill the Government proposed was that of compulsion for a very limited class: viz: the single young men who had not attested.

But now comes the crux. At the outset of Lord Derby's campaign, it was found that married men were holding back because they found young bachelors abstaining on the grounds that as they had no wives and families to protect, they had less stake in the

---

*   See diary for 12 October 1915.
**   In Tennyson's epic poem, Enoch Arden, 'a rough sailor's lad', is shipwrecked and away for so long that – when he returns home – his wife has remarried. There is no reunion: Enoch chooses not to disturb his wife's idyll with her second husband – and dies forlorn.

country than the married ones, so 'let them defend their families, and let us look after the work and trade'.

The married men on the other hand, saw the danger of leaving their families unprotected in case of death. 'If something had not been done to reassure the married men', said Asquith, 'the whole recruiting campaign would have collapsed entirely.' He then gave his solemn pledge that the married men would not be called up until the single men had been dealt with.

Having received this assurance, married men went freely to the recruiting offices. Now the figures show that the married outnumber the attested single men by 147,000. To redeem his promise, the Prime Minister finds it necessary to adopt conscription which will, after all, only affect the class of unattested bachelors among whom are the shirkers.

There has been one dissentient voice in the Cabinet, Sir John Simon, Home Secretary, who has resigned. Also the whole Irish Party is against the Bill, although Ireland is **not** affected by the Bill!

Asquith's Bill will take about a month to put into action and the voluntary system is still open to all the shirkers or undecided young men who have so far abstained. If they still hold back, then, as Asquith says significantly, the unstarred eligibles will be treated *as though they had done what everyone agrees it is their duty to do for the State in times like these and be treated as though they had attested for enlistment.*

SATURDAY JANUARY 8

Neville Street

We travelled back to London today, you, Nannie and I. The train was very crowded up to Shrewsbury and the only way in which we coaxed you to sleep for half an hour at midday, was by making a nest for you in my fur cloak on the only vacant space in our carriage.

Everyone is reading Sir Ian Hamilton's dispatch on the Dardanelles, covering the period ending in his recall on October 17. It is a heartbreaking yet glorious tale of disappointment and heroism. Several times our troops were on the brink, but the plans failed partly through inertia on the part of some of the commanders. There is a heartrending account of some of the forces gaining a position on a summit from which they could actually see their way through to Constantinople, the Narrows of the Dardanelles, and the Asiatic Coast.

Sir Ian Hamilton, though he seems to have foreseen and provided against every contingency,* notably the terrible water difficulty, lacked firmness in enforcing his orders on, chief of all blameworthy ones, General Stopford, Commanding the Suvla Bay contingent which landed on August 6.

---

* Not so. Owing to poor staff work, the men under his command had not been prepared for the conditions they would meet in Turkey. Nor had the three divisions at Suvla Bay been trained to move at night over open country. They were also totally unused to the relentless heat of the Gallipoli Peninsula in August.

This leader lost precious hours and days in starting the advance, excusing himself by pleading that his divisional commanders declared it was impossible to move the men until they were rested etc. This terrible delay cost the general scheme dear.* After that, the golden opportunity was lost and never occurred again. The Turks strengthened their defences enormously so that operations from that time till the evacuation degenerated from the offensive to the defensive.

Discreditable as the record of the Suvla Bay Commanders is, Sir Ian Hamilton himself incurs a great deal of blame. One cannot help thinking of the Napoleon maxim, that there is no such word as impossible.

MONDAY JANUARY 10

This ghastly but impressive cartoon by the great Dutch artist Raemaekers, 'the Kaiser's most dangerous enemy', stamps for ever the infamy of the German Admiralty's methods at sea.**

I forget whether I mentioned a few days back the explosion, in harbour (locality not published) of HMS *Natal*. This caused the deaths of 380 ratings and 25 officers, including Captain Back, in command. Today Daddy brought back the news which he had heard from a friend of his who knew Captain Back well, that the *Natal* was in Cromarty Harbour. There was a large children's party going on, on December 30, when the explosion occurred. Mrs Back and all the little guests were blown up and killed.

Today the evacuation of Gallipoli is complete. The very last man has been withdrawn and one man has been wounded, the only casualty. It is a wonderful achievement. But people quite lose sight of the reason for this evacuation – the failure of the enterprise.

But we are phlegmatic as a race. This placidity is really a proof of strength and dogged persistence. We know we shall get through all right in the end, in spite of our blunders; and if we are foiled at the Dardanelles, well, we have the chance of trying somewhere else.

SATURDAY JANUARY 15

Went today to see the cartoons on the war by Raemaekers, the great Dutch artist. They are poignant and vivid beyond description, recording for future generations, the misdeeds of the Germans, in indelible strokes and burning into the imagination the horrible sides of war.

---

*   A.J.P. Taylor writes: 'General Stopford, Lieutenant-Governor of the Tower of London, had never commanded in wartime. At Suvla Bay, 20,000 men were put ashore; only a thousand Turks, without machine guns, barred their way. Stopford did not go ashore. Instead . . . he settled down to his afternoon nap.' *First World War*, p. 72.

**   The cartoons of Louis Raemaekers (1869–1956) provided such effective propaganda for the Allies – and were so popular – that the German government placed 12,000 guilders on his head, dead or alive. There were showings of Raemaekers' cartoons in US cities as well as in Britain.

n Tirpitz's rendering of the laws of the sea.—A scathing cartoon by Louis Raemaekers on the sinking of the Persia.

Women and Children First.

Some are masterpieces of satire, such as those dealing with the indifference and placidity of his Dutch compatriots, who have taken the woes of Belgium calmly, out of fear of the Germans. The cartoons are doubly valuable for being the work of a man who comes from a neutral country. The rooms were so crowded at the Fine Arts in Bond Street that we had to move round the narrow lanes in rotation and we were never able to get into one of the rooms at all.

SUNDAY JANUARY 16

Tomorrow we all move to Basil Street to be with Muz until, possibly, Easter. It will be far nicer for us all to be together for a while during this period of anxiety. Muz felt she could not bear to live alone on first returning to Basil Street, since Dad's death. I shall have more spare time for my work in Mulberry Walk to which I go nearly every morning.

TUESDAY JANUARY 25

26 Basil Street

We begin to feel more and more the new conditions caused by the dearth of men. As each group is called up in turn, we have to accustom ourselves to fresh difficulties.

Also certain everyday household requisites have practically disappeared; methylated spirit is frightfully dear and rare; soda, for washing up, cannot be bought. Today I wanted some good *crêpe de chine* for a little coat which needed a heavy make, and all I was shown was a thin papery sample and told there was no other to be had! Silks are very dear. Today I saw a girl of 14 or 15 riding a bicycle delivery-cart for small parcels, such as boys or young men normally use for rapid delivery.

Now we hear that the museums are to be closed for lack of keepers. Only the Reading Room at the British Museum is being kept open.

THURSDAY JANUARY 27

This evening I came home really tired. I am working hard now, every morning at the Depot and lately it has been hard work because I have undertaken the packing of the bandages and surgical requisites. One is up and down all the time carrying parcels and stowing them in their shelves preparatory to their being called for by the Royal Van.

After doing this till lunch time, I spent the afternoon at the West London Hospital, as usual on Fridays, visiting one of the women's wards and changing their reading books. So I came in at 5 o'clock and went straight to the nursery. You looked so happy and cosy having tea, that as Granny was out, I got Nannie to make me some tea and I had it there.

SATURDAY JANUARY 29

A new policy has started, concerning the restriction of imports. The first banned goods are paper, fruit, tobacco and furs. That is, they are either entirely prohibited or very highly taxed.

The immediate result of the paper tax will be thinner newspapers and dearer and fewer books. There is a great campaign against spending and every day we are being exhorted to buy absolutely nothing that is not necessary. We ought all to help the country by living as cheaply as possible, not to save our pockets, but to save the country.

Still, I couldn't help buying you a shilling bunch of grapes this morning!

TUESDAY FEBRUARY 1

I work so regularly at the Mulberry Walk Depot now, where they have made me one of the responsible packers, that I have had to give up the Belgian visiting. I received a letter from the Secretary of the Visiting Committee at Crosby Hall, accepting my resignation.

Daddy has just come in to say that the air raid caused a great deal of excitement last night. We heard at six pm in London that the Zeppelins were on their way, so this accounted for the almost total blackness of the streets. It was so dark when we went out to dine at Pelham Street that we literally could not see the kerbs, nor could the omnibus drivers we hailed see us. Cabs are very scarce. Uncle Gerry knew of the raid and told Daddy, but none of us ladies were told for fear of alarming us. However, the Zeppelins did not reach London.

But all trains to the suburbs were stopped from 6 o'clock, underground trains too. Business people were kept in London till midnight. The tube stations were thronged with people who had bought a penny ticket in order to get down to the platforms for security underground. Fifty ambulances were lined up along the Embankment. Birmingham and Nottingham were both damaged, but the War Office is withholding all news.

FRIDAY FEBRUARY 4

A British trawler fishing in the North Sea came back to Grimsby on Tuesday night reporting that he had seen a wrecked Zeppelin, the L15, sinking in the North Sea. Seven or eight men were on a platform just out of the water and shouted 'Save us! We give good money', and after a while these men were joined by more, making about twenty altogether.

The captain of the trawler realising that the Germans outnumbered his crew considerably, thought it unsafe to attempt to rescue them, so he returned at once to report to the Admiralty, leaving it to the authorities to send assistance. A wise man he is, I consider, for German treachery has been too often displayed to us to suppose that the Germans would have allowed themselves to be brought in as prisoners. There is no news yet as to whether the Zeppelin has been brought in.

SUNDAY FEBRUARY 6

The Bishop of London has preached a sermon in which he says the skipper of the trawler was perfectly right not to run the risk of taking the Zeppelin crew on his boat. Indeed the clergy are preaching very strongly now on the war.

Granny and I go on Sunday to Holy Trinity, Brompton, to hear the Rev. Gough preach his famous war sermons, which people are flocking to hear. He tells us that the text which says that we must feed our enemies and treat them well does not apply to the Germans. They represent the devil and must be destroyed ruthlessly, in fact he is quite mediaeval in his opinions!

THURSDAY FEBRUARY 10

I have had a certificate and a beautiful badge from Queen Mary for which I paid the sum of one shilling for working regularly at the hospital depot in Mulberry Walk. Of course other women give up even more time, afternoons as well as mornings, but I have a house and a very exacting baby and I let nothing interfere, if I can possibly help it, with our hour after breakfast and our hour after tea. Tomorrow though I am tearing myself away from you for four or five days to go and see Aunt Edie at Clifton and her two little ones.

It is an opportunity for me too to leave you and Daddy while you are both under Granny's roof and she can look after you in case of a Zeppelin raid. Isn't it an extraordinary state of affairs that we live in constant danger of bombs being showered upon us? Everybody feels that the chance of a bomb hitting one's own roof is infinitesimal, still it is possible. The horror the bombs do cause wherever they fall is very daunting if one stops to think about it.

QUEEN MARY'S NEEDLEWORK GUILD.

BADGE CERTIFICATE.

Mrs C Lee

of *15 Neville St. S.W.*

having been engaged in voluntary war work for the Q.M.N.G. has been granted the badge of the Guild, which she is entitled to wear during the war, so long as she continues a voluntary worker.

ST. JAMES'S PALACE.

Annie Lawley

Hon. Sec.

Date *Feb 5ᵗʰ 1916*

Queen Mary's Needlework Guild Certificate.

SATURDAY FEBRUARY 12

Clifton

Your cousins Winnie and Geoffrey gave me a great welcome. At tea time they come down, clamouring for Aunt Edie to play the piano, which they both love, and little Winnie dances. She is so graceful and unselfconscious, very merry and sweet-tempered and Winnie is always asking about you, what Harry says, etc. etc.

I found Bristol turned into a real war city, soldiers everywhere and continual streams of ambulance cars or war motors, 40 or 50 at a time, making their way through the streets to Avonmouth to embark for the Front. It is one of the chief ports of embarkation. The streets are darkened but not nearly so stringently as in London.

There is a great clamour among a section of the public for reprisals and it is urged that we should drop bombs on the civilian population instead of confining ourselves strictly to military objectives. Saner experts point out that it is futile to waste our efforts when we can achieve more advantageous reprisals.

The latter urge that our best defence is not to set up anti-aircraft guns and wait for Zeppelins to come here, nor to drop bombs on civilians. But we should work to wrest the supremacy of the air from Germany, as our Navy has done on the seas. We could then attack the Zeppelins as they leave their coast.

BOOK VIII

FEBRUARY 17 – NOVEMBER 28, 1916

THURSDAY FEBRUARY 17

20 Basil Street
This is a fresh diary book, the eighth, I think, since I began at the outset of the war. Who would have supposed that there would have been so much to keep up this little record for? As Lord Kitchener once said 'three years', most of us did not expect the war to be over any earlier. But now the war seems to be spreading further and further away. A decisive result in either East or West seems almost hopeless, so impenetrably strong are the lines on both fronts.

Today the Russians send us splendid news that the troops of the Grand Duke Nicholas have taken the Turkish fortress of Erzerum, the capital of Armenia. It is a point of great strategic importance on the road from the Caucasus to the Bosphorus.

Remember always, whatever part Russia is destined to play later, it is she who averted disaster in August 1914 by drawing off the enemy with a bold offensive stroke in the early weeks.

WEDNESDAY FEBRUARY 23

I haven't written for nearly a week! Paper is getting very scarce and it is well to economise. I was unable to buy any more writing books to match the first six or seven volumes of the diary. We all have to content ourselves with what we can get nowadays, and be thankful to get it! Newspapers are much thinner already.

The French have at last succeeded in bringing down a Zeppelin, which was on its way to Paris. The airship was attacked by an anti-aircraft gun mounted on a motor, firing incendiary shells. A thin red line of flame was seen to spread and the ship began to descend very slowly to the earth. As it touched the ground, the bombs in it exploded. Spectators rushed to the scene, shouting in triumph, and found the charred bodies of some men in the debris. The companion ship of the wrecked Zeppelin turned back and fled.

There is a fierce battle developing on the Western Front. The Germans are making a huge effort to break through the big fortress at Verdun. They have captured up to the second line of French trenches.

It is amusing that my little article has appeared, to stimulate the Bristol ladies to greater effort. When I was at Aunt Edie's, I was struck by the disproportion between the splendid premises of their Hospital Depot and the numbers that worked there. I gave vent to my feelings, and Lionel just asked me to put them in the form of an article for the *Bristol Times and Mirror*. I am anxious to hear whether the workers feel conscience-stricken, as many had given up attending because of petty little jealousies or wounded vanity – or laziness.

FRIDAY FEBRUARY 25

The country is beginning to feel in real earnest what war means. All the single men groups in the Kingdom have been called up, and today it is announced that by July all the married groups will be called up. Such a state of affairs has never before been known in England.

This means that every man up to 41 must go, unless exempt for some reason. But they are very strict with exemptions and few get off entirely. Think of all the businesses that must close down, think of what will happen to people, where the husband, lawyer or other professional man is the one who supports wife and children. All the wife will get, if her husband is a private, is 12/6 a week and 3/6 for each child. No more commissions are to be given. This is what families with income from £500 and upwards will have to live upon, like families of working people!

SATURDAY FEBRUARY 26

London is one vast mud and mire field! Heavy snow, dark grey slush, through which the traffic forces its way, splashing the foot-passengers. The snow is just left to deal with itself as there are no men to clear it away.

As Daddy and I had a free day together we went first to get myself a pair of thick shoes for wet weather. I bought a pair for 25/9, the same kind of shoe for which I paid 16/9 three years ago.

MONDAY FEBRUARY 28

The fighting around Verdun is more and more desperate. This is the big German offensive for which the French have been grimly waiting. On Saturday night the news was that the Germans had completely 'flattened out', with their big siege howitzers, one of the outer forts of Verdun, Douaumont. But today the French news is that the fort, or what remains of it, has been not only retaken, but that the Germans are being rolled back themselves.

These days are most critical, and the strain is terrible – yet we go on with our work as usual. Another liner, the P&O *Maloja* has been sunk by a mine two miles off Dover Pier. 122 people are reported dead. Amongst these are little boys and one baby whose bodies have now been recovered. The frequency of these outrages on passenger boats has partly blunted our horror of them. Think of seeing dead bodies of men, women and children washed up along the shore near Folkestone and Dover, which used to be a favourite picnicking resort for us.

WEDNESDAY MARCH 1

We are laid up with influenza and in bed, Muz, Daddy and I, the result of the dreadful damp and snow of the last ten days. I don't see you for fear of giving you the infection, but I hear your little feet running to and fro overhead, and the babbling little voice, the most delicious of sounds to me. When I hear it I forget the aches and pains of this disgusting influenza.

THURSDAY MARCH 2

Today is the last day of voluntary enlistment. Tomorrow conscription begins for single men. Every man who has not now enlisted will be called.

We are still in bed with influenza, Muz and I, feeling very sorry for ourselves and miserable.

FRIDAY MARCH 3

The one thing I have dreaded since I took to my bed four days ago has happened, although I have kept you away from coming near my room. You have developed a heavy cold. Although you want nobody but Nannie when you are seedy, it is torment to me to lie here, pinned in bed with a temperature, and not be able to go to you.

Daddy who is still in the house after his touch of 'flu, has been with you a great deal, trying to amuse you, and unable to keep away from his poor fretful little boy. 'He's asking for the Cocoa book, where is it?' said Daddy coming into my room and looking for the new *Times Dictionary*. It has coloured plates illustrating dogs or cows of every breed, hats of every age and nationality, birds, plants and minerals and it is a real treasure book to you.

It is a marvel to me how you remember the words when you see the pictures again. Your little way is this: If the word Cocoa has struck you particularly pleasantly, you laugh, and perhaps five or six times you plant your finger on the same picture of a cocoa plant asking each time more forcibly 'What's that?' 'Cocoa', I reply imperturbably and after that you don't forget it!

TUESDAY MARCH 7

Muz and I are downstairs at last, feeling weak and wretched, and now to crown all, Nannie has been sent to bed by the Doctor, with a temperature of 101! We were both so staggered when the Doctor came down and told me just the very thing I feared. I was alarmed at your having been with Nannie up till now.

While we were cogitating, Brenda Lee put her head into my room and offered at once to lend us Florence, the charming maid who looked after you at Gelligemlyn in the summer during Nannie's holiday. On top of all our agitation, a wire came from Uncle Guy announcing his arrival at 5 pm from the Front with his soldier servant. A bed has to be made up for the one in the library, for the other in the servants' hall. Guy has been sent home for a week on a special mission, to visit all the bombing schools in England. He has to report first thing at the War Office tomorrow to get his orders.

WEDNESDAY MARCH 8

The Germans haven't got Verdun yet.

FRIDAY MARCH 10

Aunt Ethel, who always writes very amusingly, has written me from Glaslyn where she has been living for some weeks now. Alluding to conscription in our part of Wales, and to the Tribunals set up locally to enquire into the right of men to be exempted, she writes 'the people are murmuring against poor old Mr Clarke who has the invidious job of being on the Tribunal. Those who can't get exempted say he has kept five men on his own estate, who ought to be taken. I think it is quite unfair for he does want them to go, only they have legal claims not to be taken. Old Mrs Rice is desperate and other farmers' women are furious.

Poor Mr Chas Woosnam who is on the same job, says his life has been made unbearable by the beastliness of the creatures there, who try to intimidate him. His wife says she really thinks his life is hardly safe, so great is the venom of the Builth beauties. But he says he'll do his duty all the same. But isn't it loathsome!'

MONDAY MARCH 13

The Germans have achieved little so far in their 20 days' battle for Verdun. Their losses are estimated at 200,000 in the short three weeks. If they go on losing men at this pace, it is good for us, that the Germans have chosen the tactics that suit us best. The French line is 'eaten into' a little more every day, but the French just fall back slightly and wait for the Germans to come on again. The French defence of Verdun will be one of the glorious passages in French history.

THURSDAY MARCH 16

Guy left us very early this morning to return to his Grenade School in France. It was delightful having him for even this brief visit, because he is so keen on his work and never bored with telling us everything that goes on at the Front. He is the only soldier I know, except Arthur, who tells one anything interesting!

He went to the Investiture at Buckingham Palace yesterday to receive his Military Cross. The King spoke to him for some minutes, observing 'I see you have the *Légion d'Honneur*, when did you get that?' Guy told him, and the King told him 'I congratulate you', and again later 'I congratulate you very much indeed'.

SATURDAY MARCH 18

15 Neville Street
We all came back here today to take up our residence in our own little home. Delightful as it has been being with Muz, still, home is home, and nothing comes up to it. It was lovely to sit down to tea among our beautiful pictures, just Daddy and I. You were equally pleased to be in your nursery again.

I spent most of the morning at the new little Belgian Surgical Depot, of which I have been made the organising superintendent! There are six Belgian paid workers and a paid forewoman, working for the Belgian Red Cross, with funds provided by American contributions.

It is a small affair, but I am going to try and make a big success of it. The forewoman is most capable, she prepares the work, instructs the workers and keeps the hours' book. I keep the expense books, pay the wages and do the business connected with the outside. I called at the headquarters of the Belgian Red Cross, interviewed Mr Maeterlinck the Secretary and got him to promise to call once a month for our parcels of supplies to be sent to the Belgian hospitals. It will interest me enormously to run this little industry.

SUNDAY MARCH 19

Spent most of the morning at the new Depot trying to make our workroom business like and comfortable. We have a beautiful large, airy drawing room, with three big windows, chairs, tables, but no cupboards except one large writing-bureau with glass bookcase. I emptied out all the books, cleaned the old bureau shelves and drawers thoroughly with paraffin (it needed it too!), and had large packing cases placed against the wall. These I shall have fitted with shelves and padlock doors, also have them papered with suitable wall paper, to keep the dust from getting through the chinks.

MONDAY MARCH 20

There was an air raid yesterday at two o'clock by several German seaplanes over Dover, Deal, Margate and Ramsgate. Four of the fourteen victims were small children on their way to Sunday school. The Dutch cartoonist, Raemaekers, has made a striking cartoon drawing to commemorate the murder of these innocents.

To respond to these air-raids, these has been a large raid on Zeebrugge, the German air-base, by a fleet of 65 allied aeroplanes, English, French and Belgian, when considerable damage was done. This is the best way to deal with the Zeppelin menace, to attack the enemy aircraft in their own nests.

TUESDAY MARCH 21

The King has today signed the decree prohibiting the importation of certain luxuries, motor-cars, motor-cycles, gramophones, pianolas and other musical instruments. Mr Hughes, Premier of the Australian Commonwealth, who is in England now, has been making stirring speeches to incite Britain to form a strong league to oust Germany completely from trade with the British Empire, and to replace German products by her own resources and industry.

Today I had an interesting afternoon. I met Mr Walter Baillie-Hamilton at a lunch party at Mrs de la Rue's, and discovered that he had been working for the Belgian Field Hospital (entirely equipped by British funds) during the German invasion of Belgium.

The All Highest
Assassin.

THE ALL-HIGHEST ASSASSIN.—"Well, and aren't they all future enemies of my dynasty?" [Five childre
were killed and nine injured in Sunday's daylight air raid on East Kent.]
Specially drawn for " The Daily Mail" by Louis Raemaekers. Copyrighted in Great Britain by " The Daily Mail" and in France by " Le Journa'

He was at Antwerp at the evacuation and went through all the vicissitudes of these anxious months.

As soon as he heard of our new born Surgical Depot, he offered to come and see us. He has had experience in the running of hospitals. When he came today, greatly to the excitement of our eight workers, he examined all the different bandages and appliances and told us what to make and what to leave alone.

Then he enquired as to the prices we were paying for materials and he found we were paying Harrods far too high a price. Finally we went in a taxi to Mortimer Street, to the Hospitals and General Contracts Company to be given the benefit of their wholesale prices.

I found that we could buy our absorbent cotton wool, of which we shall want supplies by the 100lbs, at 8½d, instead of 1/8d as Harrods charged, so that we shall save pounds in a very short time. This was very satisfactory, and I came home at 5.30 tired, but very pleased with my afternoon's work.

SUNDAY MARCH 26

The first Channel steamer has been torpedoed, between Folkestone and Dieppe. The *Sussex*, filled with military men and 270 women and children was just able to get into port, but 50 passengers died. There was a commotion among my Belgian workers this morning, because a woman very much liked by them all was travelling on that boat. She was planning to go with her child to France to see her husband, who is fighting with the Belgian forces. The ship was towed into Boulogne.

FRIDAY MARCH 31

The little Surgical Industry is coming on very well indeed, and the Crosby Hall Committee seem very pleased with me. I received this acknowledgment of my report, and I insert it here because some years hence it may interest you to see the Committee names of those who were so satisfied with your Mother's efforts!

Last night Mr Baillie-Hamilton came to dine. He gave us many interesting details of his work in poor invaded Belgium. In the first months of the War, he went to one of the organisers of the Belgian Field Hospital, which is run by an English staff and with English funds.

He was all through the bombardment and evacuation of Antwerp, when he and his friends moved the wounded and entire Field Hospital out of the town. For three days during the crisis he and his friends had no sleep at all. Later, and after his health completely broke down, the strain of these terrible days reacted on him. He could never fall asleep without seeing once again the horrors he had witnessed.

Your Uncle Henry whom I was with today has been kindly treating a charming Belgian priest, Father Ingleben. He is a distinguished man, who came over with the flood of refugees and has been devoting his life to comforting his people in their exile. His throat is causing him trouble, so Henry is treating him.*

SATURDAY APRIL 1

A lovely, mild day at last, after six weeks of the most unpleasant weather I can ever remember. Snow, rain, sleet, cold winds, culminating in the big blizzard last Tuesday. This was the biggest gale London had experienced for many years, and much damage was done to buildings.

Today Daddy and I walked across Kensington Gardens to see the trees that had been blown down. The scene of devastation along the Broad Walk and the south side of the Round Pond was extraordinary. About 100 of the fine old elms had been uprooted and lay in all directions. Hundreds of poor children were swarming about the great trunks lying prone, having for once a real taste of the delights of country life.

Many older boys, armed with choppers, were lopping off the boughs and carrying away the wood for firing. Evidently the authorities had given permission to the poor to

---

*   Henry Davis, Georgina's elder brother, was an ear, nose and throat surgeon.

carry off what they could, only too glad to get the work of clearing done somehow, in these days when there are no men available.

The omnibuses now have women conductors; during the last few days they have become general, only elderly men left to represent the male element. The women wear long leather gaiters to their knees, tight dark blue breeches and dark blue short skirts down to their knees, which allow them to run up and down the steps easily.

SUNDAY APRIL 2

Today I had an inspiration while at my Belgian workroom. One of the workers, a young girl lately arrived from Belgium told me of her great disappointment in failing to be taken on as *infirmière* or nurse to the Belgian Red Cross. She hoped to be paid as she has now no means of subsistence.

It struck me how splendid it would be if we could get Belgian girls to be taken on, free, as probationers in London hospitals, to be taught the whole system of nursing. Then, not only would they be maintained free of cost now, but after the war they would form a fine nucleus for trained nursing in the hospitals in Belgium. They would have learnt a profession during their exile, to enable them to earn their living after the war.

It would also afford present employment for a number of young Belgian women with nothing to do here. I am going to bring forward my idea to the Chelsea Committee.

MONDAY APRIL 10

The great anxiety at present is for the British forces under General Townshend besieged in Kut (Mesopotamia).

The British under General Townshend had suffered heavy casualties on 21 November, in the attack on Ctesiphon, only 22 miles from Baghdad. Four days later the retreat along the Tigris to Kut began. Thus, in the wake of Gallipoli, the Turks enjoyed a second triumph over the British. Townshend's army spent Christmas locked up in Kut, where it was besieged from 5 December by 80,000 troops. It was a shock to the British public to learn that, far from capturing Baghdad, one of its armies was trapped.

Georgina Lee now mentions a letter from General Younghusband to his wife. This throws light on the grim ordeal of the troops sent up from Basra with orders to relieve the garrison at Kut. They did not succeed, being frequently attacked as they toiled north and losing 4,000 men killed or wounded at the battle of Sheikh Sa'ad, just a few miles east of Kut. Martin Gilbert, in his First World War, *reports that the medical arrangements were so bad that 'even eleven days after the battle a newly arrived Indian Field Ambulance unit found two hundred British and eight hundred Indian wounded still lying in the open, on muddy ground without shelter and with their first dressings unchanged'.*

After holding out for 147 days and with no relief forthcoming, the British troops surrendered to the Turks (see Georgina's diary for April 29).

General George Younghusband is one of the four generals of the relieving force and his wife told me two days ago that she had just had a letter after many weeks in which he describes the heroism and endurance of the English and Indian troops who are trying to force their way to Kut in the face of unimaginable difficulties and obstacles.

He himself had not had his boots off for three weeks. The weather conditions, the swamps, the flooded Tigris and the impregnable Turkish positions all combined to make this the most arduous campaign, perhaps, of the whole war.

TUESDAY APRIL 11

Today I was at the Mulberry Walk Depot packing hard in the small vestibule, when Princess Christian (sister to King Edward) came to visit the Depot with some of her ladies. She had to pass by my corner, and of course I curtsied as she went by. She stopped, smiled and then came up with extended hand, which I took and bowed over. Mrs Stokes, our Principal, said 'This is Mrs Lee', and the Princess then walked on.

She is a very nice-looking woman, grey haired of course, but with a pleasant, engaging manner rather like her sister the Princess Louise, Duchess of Argyll, whom I used to have an opportunity of seeing. In fact I have dined twice at Kensington Palace, and some day I will tell you of that interesting little episode. It was at the time Aunt Ethel used to be so much with the Princess. I have often thought that this Princess could have taught something in charm and graciousness of manners, in considerateness and simplicity, to many of our society people.

It was quite a revelation to me to see that Royal ladies can be concerned with the entertainment of the least important guests! The first time I went to Kensington Palace we saw the New Year in, and it was on this night that I smoked my first cigarette, she inciting me to it, and laughing at my inexperienced efforts!

THURSDAY APRIL 13

Today Mrs Gerald Paget came to tea with me. I met her at Saltmarshe two years ago, and from that our acquaintance ripened into real friendship. Yesterday she told me she loves me as I always made her feel so cheerful and I must go and stay with her again this summer.

Muz came to tea also and Mrs Francis Anson. When Mrs Paget left I accompanied her, and she said 'What a beautiful woman your mother-in-law is, much more so than you, my dear', she added, laughing very much, 'although I think you are the dearest creature I know!'

FRIDAY APRIL 14

Today we completed our first month's work at the Belgian Surgical Depot. Our result was astonishing, 4054 made articles, some very complicated indeed.

The Secretary of Belgian Red Cross Headquarters in London, M. de Vigneron, came to see our result. He was staggered at the pile of parcels he was expected to remove! After a very pleasant visit, in which he praised the women for their work, he thanked us most charmingly and withdrew.

Soon after, a boy scout appeared with a taxi and a huge hamper. The hamper was filled and put in front of the taxi, and all the rest of the parcels were stacked up inside. After this the ten workers present had a good tea, with Belgian cakes, offered by myself and they did so enjoy the little feast and excitement of the day. They have worked splendidly.

Tomorrow I leave all my work to go to Gelligemlyn with you, Daddy and Nannie. I am very tired and sleepy and it's half-past ten.

FRIDAY APRIL 21

Gelligemlyn
Good Friday – and though Easter is so late this year the weather has not been at all springlike. I never remember such a backward season. Still, we have seen the sun a little today and yesterday. I made the most of it by taking you down to a sheltered part of the river bank, by Gelligemlyn Pool, where you played with spade and bucket in the sand.

SATURDAY APRIL 22

The fighting about Kut has been fierce between the relief force and the Turks. General Townshend's force is still besieged. If he is relieved in time, there will be a wonderful tale of British heroism and endurance to be told both of the besieged garrison and their saviours. The former are in a very critical situation for lack of food.

Daddy brought in five small live trout which we put into the big bath for you to see. I never saw anything so amusing as your expression when you saw the real thing. You grew quite red with astonishment. Later on we caught them again with a small net and carried them in a pail back to the river. I do wonder whether you will be a keen fisherman, like your forebears on both sides.

TUESDAY APRIL 25

The sensation of today is the frustrated attempt of the traitor, Sir Roger Casement, to land arms and ammunition in Ireland, for the purpose of fostering a rebellion there against England. He is an Irishman who has been living in Berlin for the last few months. He was on board a German boat, disguised as a neutral merchantman, but the suspected vessel was sunk. Casement and two of his confederates were taken prisoner.

It seems that the approaches to Ireland were being watched, because a derelict ship, laden with arms had lately been discovered in the vicinity by our patrols. So far this is the only news given. Sir Roger C has shown his enmity to England in every possible way since the war began. He has given the Germans to believe that the Irish would welcome the Germans as their deliverers. Everybody is hoping that he will be shot summarily.

Ninety years on, Sir Roger Casement still excites controversy. He had a distinguished diplomatic career, serving as British Consul in Mozambique, Angola and the Congo, where his report on the appalling exploitation of black labour by white traders led to reforms in Belgian colonial rule. His report on the Putamayo rubber industry while Consul-General in Rio de Janeiro earned him a knighthood in 1912. The outbreak of war revealed the paradoxes in his character and his split loyalties. Born of an Ulster Protestant family, he always sympathised with the mainly Roman Catholic Irish Nationalist cause. In 1914 he openly enlisted the support of Irishmen in the USA for the Irish Volunteer Movement.

From March 1916 he was in Berlin, making preparations for his ill-judged expedition to Ireland. He visited the Irish prisoner of war camp at Limburg-Lahn, urging them to join the Irish Brigade which he planned would rise up against the British Government. But he gained little support either from the Irish or from the German High Command, who had no manpower to spare.

On 21 April the German vessel on which he was heading for the Irish coast was intercepted and sunk by HMS Bluebell and he was put ashore near Tralee. He was arrested and charged at Ardfert Barracks with landing arms and ammunition in County Kerry. In London, where he was confined in the Tower, he was accused under the terms of the Treason Act of 1351 with aiding and abetting the enemy and was sentenced to death. Georgina here reflects the widely held view that he was a traitor. The attempts to gain him a reprieve failed.

The Easter Rebellion in Dublin further blackened his reputation in the eyes of the public and raised the spectre of an unholy Irish–German alliance. Casement had some influential supporters, but the revelations contained in his notorious diaries did not enhance his reputation. He appeal was dismissed and he was hanged on 3 August at Pentonville Prison.

WEDNESDAY APRIL 26

Yesterday was Anzac Day in London, the anniversary of the great landing in Gallipoli of the Australian and New Zealand contingents. The newly-formed army, with no traditions yet made, created a glorious record during the first twenty-four hours of the campaign in Gallipoli.

There was a Memorial Service in Westminster Abbey for the Anzacs who fell in Gallipoli. It was attended by the King and Queen and the great feature of the day was the procession to the Abbey of Anzac Veterans, all of whom had fought in Gallipoli. There was also a contingent of Australian and New Zealand naval men, who had taken part in the destruction of the *Emden*. The most impressive feature was the entrance into the Abbey of a number of blinded heroes, who were seated near the King and Queen during the Service.

The rebellion in Dublin continues. Yesterday the city was partly in possession of the rebels who seized the Post Office and cut off all telegraphic and telephonic communication with the outside. Troops were hurried up from the Curragh. This no doubt is part of the plot in which Sir Roger Casement was concerned, and it has failed just as his part failed. Sir Roger has been transferred to London under military escort, to await his trial. Yesterday in the House Mr Asquith was asked whether Sir Roger Casement would be shot at once. Asquith replied 'That is a question which ought not even to be asked'.

It has been a week of very bad news. First the revolution in Dublin has not yet been quelled, but is spreading to the western counties. Many troops have had to be called up, some being sent from England. This uprising, timed to start with the landing of Sir R. Casement, also coincides with the bombardment of the East Coast (Lowestoft).

SATURDAY APRIL 29

Kut has fallen, after heroic attempts had been made to relieve it. The last chance went when a supply ship ran aground in the shallows of the Tigris only four miles from Kut. This was the last chance and when that failed, it was all up with General Townshend's force. Every supply being exhausted, and the garrison terribly reduced by casualties and sickness (from an original 14,000 men, only 6,000 Indian and 2,000 British troops remained) Townshend capitulated. This is a great blow to our prestige in the East.

The rebellion in Ireland is being crushed now that heavy artillery has been called up and the rebel strongholds in Dublin have been shelled. But there have been a great many casualties, including innocent civilians.

MONDAY MAY 1

The Irish rebellion is over. It has ended in the surrender of all the rebel commanders, including James Connolly, who styled himself General Commandant.

WEDNESDAY MAY 3

Three Irish leaders of the rebellion, Pearse, MacDonagh and Clarke, were shot this morning after being tried and found guilty. Three others were sentenced to three years penal servitude. Mr Birrell, Chief Secretary for Ireland has resigned and admitted in the House this afternoon that he made an 'untrue estimate of the Sinn Fein movement'. 'Sinn Fein' is the Gaelic for 'Ourselves Alone' and has been adopted as the motto of the Irish Nationalist extremists.

There is so much going on just now. Today Asquith's Bill for Compulsion was introduced to the House. It applies to all men, married or not, between ages of 18 and 41. Daddy is not yet touched, being over 43, but if the age limit is raised to 45, as may happen if the drain on men is very much greater, he will have to serve in some capacity – though his strength and health would not permit him to go in the trenches.

FRIDAY MAY 5

Four more Irish Rebels have been shot, while fifteen others sentenced to death had the sentence commuted to 10 years' penal servitude by General Maxwell, Commander in Chief in Ireland.*

Today we heard that dear little Sybil Wynne-Jones, who had such happy expectations of being a mother and was happily living at the Curragh with her husband, doing

* Eamon de Valera was spared, perhaps because of American intervention.

home duty after coming home wounded from France has just been very ill from the shock of the Irish rebellion. Her husband was suddenly called up from the Curragh and put in charge of the defence of the Castle at Dublin.

SUNDAY MAY 7

This morning I went early by Tube to Highgate to see Aunt Louisa who is ill. A number of soldiers just back for a few days leave came into the train with all the dust and dirt of the trenches thick on their boots and full accoutrements. It is so strange to think that in a few hours they are in our midst, fresh from the firing line. They look very strong and hard and so young, many of them.

THURSDAY MAY 18

The trial of Sir Richard Casement for attempting to land in Ireland and raising a rebellion against England has been going on for three days at Great Bow Street. He is remanded for trial in the High Court in 3 weeks time. It is creating enormous interest and is a romantic adventure. Evidence was given as to the way the prisoner tried to bribe the Irish prisoners of war at Limburg-Lahn camp in Germany to join an Irish Brigade which was to support the Irish uprising.

The few, who allowed themselves to be tempted, were treated with great consideration by the Germans. They were allowed a certain amount of liberty and better food. But the great majority repelled Casement's advances with indignation. He was hissed and booed, by the Munster Fusiliers especially, who showed their contempt so forcibly that one man struck him. The men who refused to be bribed were treated very badly and, at Sir Roger's own instigation, their rations were cut down to hunger point.

SATURDAY MAY 20

I have just been fulfilling the new Daylight Saving Law. Tonight is the night that everybody in the British Isles has to advance their clocks by one hour, to save daylight, electric or gas-light, and also coal. This has already been done in Germany, France, Holland and other countries.

I performed this ceremony because Daddy has gone off unexpectedly to Wales with Uncle Guy. He came home on leave for a few days and was longing to see Gelligemlyn. He arranged to spend four or five days there and urged Daddy to go with him and I urged him too.

SUNDAY MAY 21

Our first experience of the daylight saving is very pleasant. A much cooler morning, breakfast in a cool room before the sun has had time to heat it; and now, after dinner broad daylight at 9.15!

THURSDAY MAY 25

At present the family is preoccupied with the departure on Monday of Gerry and Brenda for Jamaica. Gerry is due to take up his official and secret post for the duration of the war, a vague term which makes their departure an adventure of uncertainty. Then the journey, what with mines and submarines, is anything but safe.

Gerry has to give up all his business on the Stock Exchange. Yet he is lucky to get a post with rank of Lieutenant in the Royal Naval Reserve, instead of being taken as a Tommy to serve in the trenches.

SATURDAY MAY 27

Today is Gerry and Brenda's last day with us. Tonight there is a family gathering in Muz's new house at Ovington Gardens, to say goodbye. Eugene and Nell Wason, Rigby, Nina, Guy who returns to the Front Tuesday, ourselves and the departing couple. Gerry, the expert in house arranging of the family, has just been able to finish arranging Muz's house before his departure. All the china has been put away, pictures are hung, furniture in the right positions etc. So now Muz, who hangs on G's every word, will feel that her house is just as he wished it to be.

TUESDAY MAY 30

Back again in London in time for lunch, after seeing Gerry and Brenda as far as Bristol. It was a sad leave-taking at Paddington. The two mothers and Eugene, whose health is very uncertain, were very affected and so were the dear departing couple, starting off on such an unknown adventure. When we had all recovered our composure, we three went into the restaurant car for lunch.

As our train steamed up the platform at Bristol, we found Edie and Lionel waiting there with little Winnie holding a box of chocolates for the two travellers. We only had about twelve minutes together and then their train carried them off to the docks at Avonmouth, where we were not allowed to accompany them.

FRIDAY JUNE 2

Tomorrow I am taking you to Brighton for a fortnight. Daddy is coming down for Sunday.

SATURDAY JUNE 3

Brighton
We have arrived on a lovely day at our comfortable rooms facing the sea, 139 Marine Parade, not at all the fashionable part of Brighton, but spacious, clean and quiet.

You were so impatient to get down to the sea, but as at Folkestone, there are only two or three places at long distances apart that one can get down to the beach, at least with a pram, so we walked a long way before finding we could get down by a lift.

There has been a great naval battle in the North Sea, and it was very serious in our losses. With a naval force which included 28 battleships and 5 battle cruisers we attacked a powerful German fleet of 34, off the coast of Jutland, with the result that we have lost 3 battleships *Queen Mary*, *Indefatigable* and *Invincible* and several other warships. Over 2,000 men on the *Invincible* died: there were only 6 survivors.

SUNDAY JUNE 4

The naval battle was a far bigger affair than anything we dreamt of. In their endeavour to get through our blockade the German High Seas Fleet were frustrated, for they fled back to their ports when they found Sir John Jellicoe with the main fleet coming to the rescue of Admiral Beatty's cruiser-fleet.

By their hasty retreat, when confronted with our Dreadnoughts, they robbed us of the opportunity of another Trafalgar. The King in his message to Admiral Jellicoe puts the situation in a nutshell. But there is an outcry in the papers against the policy of the First Lord of the Admiralty, Balfour. He may be responsible for the movements of the Fleet and for the fact that Admiral Beatty's Squadrons were too far from the giant ship support. Nor were they powerful enough to withstand the battering of the whole German Fleet. This battle was 'the most terrible ever dreamt of' said the rescued German captain of one of the cruisers sunk by us.

There has been a fierce gale all day with such rain that we had to take refuge in our sitting room all of us, and light the fire. You are thoroughly enjoying Brighton, you love the sea, the big waves which fascinate you and you have an enormous appetite. You are full of mischief and high spirits.

MONDAY JUNE 5

Brighton is full of maimed and crippled soldiers. They are here, recovering their health, but one sees numbers of them with only one leg or one foot. These men excite your warmest sympathy, you follow them wistfully with your eyes, murmuring 'poor wounded soldier'. We see them stroll about on crutches in front of our window. Often one, more sound in limbs, is wheeling a disabled comrade in a bath chair.

Aunt Edie came to us today, to spend three days with us.

The Battle of Jutland is now being viewed in the light of a British victory, as news comes into the Admiralty of fresh German losses. It is now stated that the Germans lost 18 ships to our 14.* This, taken with the fact that the Germans fled back to their harbours and that Jellicoe remained in possession of the high seas, goes to show that our Fleet got the best of the encounter.

---

*   This was a premature report. In fact the Germans lost four warships fewer than the British. The outcome of Jutland remains debatable to this day. It is true that the German High Seas Fleet did not emerge again until the end of the war. But not only were more British warships lost: in terms of casualties the Germans lost 2,551 men, while the Royal Navy lost 6,097.

TUESDAY JUNE 6

While Aunt Edie and I were out, enjoying ourselves very happily, taking a stroll on the big pier, we had the worst shock we have sustained since the war started. We had only just been saying that, for the first time for two years, we were experiencing some real enjoyment in a quiet way.

Then my heart stopped beating. I saw news-girls displaying posters and calling out the latest: **Kitchener and his Staff Drowned**. Aunt Edie clutched wildly at the newspaper, and there it was: Lord Kitchener and his staff had been aboard HMS *Hampshire*, bound for Russia on an important mission. The ship had been torpedoed off the Orkneys. Though four boats were seen by people ashore to leave the ship, rough seas were running and no trace of any survivors was found.

Only an upturned boat and a few bodies have been washed up. So this is the end of the man who saved England in the great crisis at the outset of the war; of the man who has raised and equipped in two years an Army of 5 million men. The shock of this announcement was so unexpected that we were dazed, and couldn't believe what we read.

WEDNESDAY JUNE 7

I think everyone hoped against hope that our Kitchener might yet be saved; that he might have reached the shore in a boat. It is unthinkable that the body of this unconquerable Englishman should be floating, unrecovered, among the waves about our shores. Yet this must be his fate. Not a word has been said so far of any survivors. Whether the *Hampshire* was torpedoed or sunk by a mine will probably never be known. The nation will not even have the solace of paying the highest tribute to his remains by burying him in the Abbey or St Paul's.

THURSDAY JUNE 8

There is news of two survivors of HMS *Hampshire*. Two telegrams, no post-office name given, have been received by the wife and the mother of two men on board, saying, 'Don't worry, safe and well'. This is in tonight's paper, so we may hear more.

Meanwhile, the death of Kitchener and the excitement caused by the Battle of Jutland, have turned our thoughts away from the critical fighting, which is going on at Ypres and at Verdun. The Kaiser is making himself ridiculous by his extravagant speeches of praise to his Fleet. He is showering decorations on them for their 'victory' at Jutland and for 'opening a new era for the German Navy'.

In Brighton one can't forget the war. The number of men with one leg or one foot off is immense. I saw one man wheeled along in a chair with only two short stumps from the hip. This morning three others were standing together on their crutches, with only one leg apiece.

WEDNESDAY JUNE 14

Lord Kitchener's body was never recovered from the sea. Only twelve men out of more than 600 were saved and reached the shore on a raft. But the body of Col Fitzgerald,

ST. PAUL'S CATHEDRAL.

Memorial Service

FOR

THE LATE

Field-Marshal Earl Kitchener of Khartum,

K.G., K.P., G.C.B., O.M., G.C.S.I., G.C.M.G., G.C.I.E.

TUESDAY, 13TH JUNE, 1916,

AT 12 NOON.

Memorial Service at St Paul's.

Kitchener's Private Secretary, was recovered, and buried with full military honours at Eastbourne. A Memorial Service, at which the King and Queen were present, was held at St Paul's in homage to Lord Kitchener. But his grave which was ready for him, near Lord Roberts and Wolseley, in the Cathedral, will remain empty.

SATURDAY JUNE 17

I came back to London to rejoin Daddy, leaving you behind for an extra week with Nannie. Mrs Tichborne Hinckes has asked you to stay a week with her two children. They have a large house in Sussex Square.

It will do you good to see other children under discipline; John and Diana, aged 5 and 3, are very well-behaved. I have enjoyed this Brighton trip greatly. At least we have all got rosy cheeks, you, Nannie and I, even if we have not acquired any other special beauty. Gertie Wykeham Musgrave enjoyed her few days with us, I think. She was very amused with you, but warned me that I should have to be careful not to spoil you.

News has been received at last of the manner in which Lord Kitchener died. It is exactly what one imagined, brave and collected to the last moment, without showing any signs of the strain such as all must have felt in the short awful moments before the vessel took her fatal plunge into the depths. The story told by two of the survivors is so dramatic that it will become classic and people will ponder over the scene as generations have done over Nelson's death at Trafalgar.

TUESDAY JUNE 20

On the Eastern Front, the Russians have taken Czernowitz once more, the most easterly Austro-Hungarian city. It seems so strange going through the same excitements as a year ago, when the Russians beat the Austrians out of this important place, only to have it wrested from them some months later. The battles rage over the same ground. Now all eyes are turned to the present Russian objective, Kowel, north of Lemberg. If they succeed in gaining Kowel, the Austrian-German line will have to fall back bodily.*

---

*   This campaign was part of the major offensive launched earlier in June by General Brusilov. On 12 June, he announced that his men had captured 2,992 Austrian officers, 190,000 Austrian soldiers, 216 heavy guns and 645 machine guns. This news provided much-needed solace to the Western Allies. Martin Gilbert, *First World War*, p. 254.

The Russians took the fortresses of Lutsk and Dubno a week or more ago and it is in this big drive that they have taken thousands of Austrian prisoners in less than 3 weeks.

WEDNESDAY JUNE 21

Today is Queen Alexandra's Rose Day, and there are millions of roses sold in her name for the hospitals by pretty girls and women dressed in white and decked out with roses. Although we have had Rose Day now for several years, it retains its popularity despite the fact that London has been overdone with flag-days for Belgians, Serbians, French, Russians, Canteens and other more obscure causes which I cannot even remember! Nobody can resist a rose, and the hospitals retain their claim on us whatever other calls are made.

FRIDAY JUNE 23

There is general feeling of suspense among us all, for there are unmistakable signs and rumours too, that the long-expected move forward is to take place next week. Romer told Daddy last night that his Command had been instructed to prepare beds for 250,000 wounded. Another man in the know told us today that in a fortnight's time there would be wounded from John O'Groats to Land's End.

This morning, I was quite glad to be all alone in the packing-room at Mulberry Walk Depot, so as not to have to talk. In the big workroom on the other hand, it was like a hive of bees, so busy were the workers. They had responded in large numbers to the Secretary's appeal, making the several thousand big shell-dressings which the Depot has been asked to furnish within three or four days. We are also asked to work there on Sunday.

I was packing these items in bundles of ten, dressings about a foot square, with double folds of absorbent wool, shell dressings! Words horribly suggestive of the gaping wounds caused by splinters of shell. I worked and worked, never looking up, to keep pace with the bundles that accumulated faster than I could wrap and stow them away on shelves.

How devastating to be making preparations for the appalling bloodshed we know is to begin in a few days. Now I suppose the Verdun records of men lost will pale in this new offensive when Sir Douglas Haig means to push the Germans home.

This afternoon I was present for the first time at the Committee meeting of the Chelsea War Refugees Fund. It took place in the Governor's House at Chelsea Hospital and we met in Lady Lyttelton's superb drawing-room which is hung round with Sir Peter Lelys and Van Dycks and wainscoted in old oak with carvings by Grinling Gibbons. I had to give my report on my little Belgian Surgical Depot which is doing so wonderfully. I am glad they have put me on the Committee.

SUNDAY JUNE 25

This morning, owing to the stress of work and packing to get off the large order for shell dressings, I took you to the Depot in Mulberry Walk to help me 'carrying parcels for wounded soldiers'. I would have given a great deal to have a camera to snapshot you walking to and fro with your arms full of dressings, bringing them to my table from the cupboard.

Your distant cousin, Sir George Younghusband has been invalided home on a hospital ship. He is one of the four generals commanding the relief force in Mesopotamia.

WEDNESDAY JUNE 28

Tomorrow is the big Chelsea Fair organised by my Mulberry Walk Depot for funds to carry on the surgical requisites work. I am to take the packing stall, and have asked Aunt Beatrice and Aunt Minna to help me.

THURSDAY JUNE 29

We had a fine afternoon at the Chelsea Fair. But it began to rain hard at 6.30, just after a swarm of people paying 1/- entrance had invaded the gardens. As it poured for the rest of the evening, a good deal of money was thereby lost, as people took refuge under trees for a while, then made their escape from the deluge. But from what I hear we shall clear about £1000.

Sir Roger Casement's trial has ended. He has been found guilty of treason and was condemned to death. His trial was a fine example of the fairness of British justice. Every chance was given to him. Though there is not the slightest doubt of his guilt, I can't help hoping that he may get a reprieve. He was evidently under the impression that here was his chance of liberating Ireland from her wrongs.*

SUNDAY JULY 2

Yesterday at last the big British offensive was launched and the Fourth Army attacked along a front of 20 miles. A continuous bombardment for a whole week, culminating in a concentrated firing of shells for 2 hours, had prepared the way for our Infantry, who penetrated the first line of enemy trenches.

We have at last heard from Uncle Gerry and Aunt Brenda from Jamaica. He is working in Intelligence out there, in Kingston. So far Brenda hates it because of the great heat.

I had also a letter from Audrey from Alexandria. She writes that Uncle Arthur arranged a beautiful Memorial Service for Lord Kitchener. It took place at sundown, on the edge of the sea. The troops, all Kitchener's Army, or nearly all, were formed in a

---

*　Sir Roger Casement's Diaries are now held in the National Archives at Kew (formerly the Public Records Office).

Handwritten extract and photo of John
Cornwell, VC.

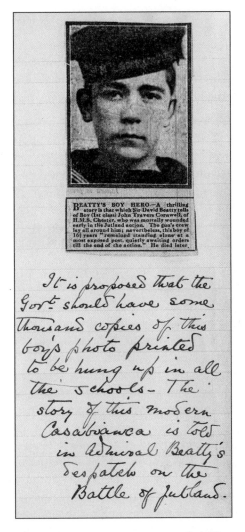

BEATTY'S BOY HERO.—A thrilling
story is that which Sir David Beatty tells
of Boy (1st class) John Travers Cornwell, of
H.M.S. Chester, who was mortally wounded
early in the Jutland action. The gun's crew
lay all around him; nevertheless, this boy of
16½ years "remained standing alone at a
most exposed post, quietly awaiting orders
till the end of the action." He died later.

It is proposed that the Govt. should have some thousand copies of this boy's photo printed to be hung up in all the schools — The story of this modern Casabianca is told in Admiral Beatty's despatch on the Battle of Jutland.

huge square. All through the Service the guns fired real shells out over the sea, the Field Marshal's Salute. *It did sound so splendid and angry as though we meant to avenge him.*

Early in the battle of Jutland, John Cornwell's gun crew on HMS *Chester* was wiped out. But this 16 year old boy 'remained standing alone at a most exposed post, quietly awaiting orders till the end of the action'. He was mortally wounded in the action, but became Great Britain's youngest VC.

WEDNESDAY JULY 12

Questions were asked in the House today as to why two trainfuls of German prisoners just arrived in England at Southampton were placed in first class carriages for the journey North. By contrast, our British prisoners in Germany have been made to travel in cattle-trucks, with every filth and indignity imaginable, as described for instance by Major Vandeleur after he escaped from Germany to England.

The reason given in the House for this handsome travelling accommodation was that there was no time to muster 3rd class carriages and the men were put into every available carriage.

Daddy was at Farnham Castle today, on official duty with the Bishop of Winchester. The Bishop told him that, for four hours without a break, the hospital ships at Southampton were yesterday unloading and despatching the wounded in hospital trains to all parts of England. And this is now going on every day.

On Saturday last Daddy and I went down to Richmond to see the splendid South African Hospital, to which our Cousin Roland Lightfoot (who volunteered at Cape Town) is attached as Paymaster. When we arrived, the King and Queen were expected, having announced their intention of visiting. We saw them come, and had to wait 1½ hours until they had been all over it. It is a splendid hospital, built of wood and erected in Richmond Park. Subscribed for by South Africa, it is intended for all the South Africans wounded in this war.

THURSDAY JULY 13

Today it was decided in the Commons to cancel the double Bank Holiday on August 7 and 8, as the munitions work must be kept going at highest pressure. Last Whitsun, the Bank Holiday was cancelled, with a view to combining it with the first Monday in August Bank Holiday. But now the country's need makes it necessary to put it off once more.

FRIDAY JULY 14

Bastille Day. This afternoon I was present at a fête given at the Automobile Club for the French Red Cross. A tea was given in the Concert room, and there was an entertainment by French artistes. A lady of our party had to go off at the beginning in order to meet her son who was arriving at four. She joined us again at 5.30, saying there was 'excellent news from the Front'.

TUESDAY JULY 18

I have just come back from tea on the Terrace of the House of Commons, a tea party for wounded Canadians, given by Uncle Eugene Wason and Aunt Nell. They asked me to help, and I sat at the head of one table and poured out tea. There were 20 men there and a most pleasant afternoon was had by all. I had two charming Scotsmen sitting by me and they told me far more about their experiences than I meant to let them do. For though one is dying to hear them speak about the war, one ought to try and talk of other things, to take their mind off it.

They both spoke so softly that it was hard to hear them. It seemed as though they were hushed and awed by the solemn days they have lived through. One told me that many men go out of their senses for a while from the strain of a long bombardment. Another thing that struck me was the <u>silence</u> in which the infantry attacks were carried out. The men go about their business of killing without speaking. When they get into the enemy trenches or hunt about for enemy in hiding, hardly a word is uttered.

Sir Douglas Haig has sent a letter from his Headquarters in France to the Conference of Munitions Workers held today. He is appealing to them to keep up the supply of munitions for the Army. Unless the supply is guaranteed, the great offensive will be hampered.

A Resolution was passed and telegraphed to Sir Douglas Haig, assuring him that he shall have all the munitions he needs. It was agreed at the Conference that all holidays should be postponed until the end of the war.

SATURDAY JULY 22

Last night we went to a dinner party, for the first time for months, to the Birkmyres. I sat near a cosmopolitan fellow, who spoke French and German like a native, and who, an archaeologist by profession (he has excavated in Egypt), is now instructing young officers of the New Army, in German tactics.

He amused me by telling me a story about a Belgian, who should be fighting, to illustrate his opinion that the Belgian race produces such contrasts – heroes of such uncomplaining firmness and milksops or cravens. This young man of about 25 was taken in as a refugee by one of my friend's acquaintances. After lunching happily and well, this young fellow's usual complacent remark was given daily with a smile 'Eh bien, je vais faire mon petit dodo'.*

TUESDAY JULY 25

It is fine and hot today and I got very tired taking a big sheaf of flowers all the way to Chester Square, walking most of the way to the house of a young Belgian bride of tomorrow. In these days we have to carry our own parcels! The bride is Mlle de Brunel de Montpelier, daughter of the couple that Uncle Hugh Lee took into his house until his marriage to Hilda. This was at the beginning of the war, when homeless Belgians of all classes came flocking to England to take refuge. The bride is marrying a Belgian of her own world, and I have been asked to the wedding.

WEDNESDAY JULY 26

At the wedding, there was a large gathering of Belgians and some English. A pathetic gathering of Belgians, I thought, so simply, even shabbily dressed, in well-worn blue serge coat and skirts or plain linen frocks. Only the two mothers wore sober dark silk dresses, and there was not one single smart wedding-function gown.

But the bride wore a graceful white satin gown, very simple, but with lovely old lace.

This marriage, in exile, of refugee Belgians, and their big gathering of refugee friends was really affecting. The bridegroom dressed in khaki, just like a British officer, was a smart, good-looking man, M. de Chaussée, belonging to one of the *premières familles* of his country. Meanwhile he is home for 12 days on leave. We all went to Hyde Park Hotel to congratulate the happy pair, but only the family attended the breakfast.

In the afternoon Aunt Ethel, Patience and I went to my Mulberry Walk Depot for the visit of the Princess Louise. Aunt Ethel helped me in the packing room, to demonstrate packing, and the Princess recognised Aunt Ethel, and shook hands with us both. She stayed, chatted and laughed with us.

She stayed altogether about two hours in the house, looking into every detail of the work. She had tea in the garden, with all the workers, a laughing merry throng of white-robed women standing in groups under the trees and enjoying the cakes and tea.

SATURDAY JULY 29

The Germans have committed another horrible act of brutal spite which has aroused the indignation of the world, just as the murder of Edith Cavell did. They have tried

---

*   'Well, I'm off to have my nap.'

and shot Captain Charles Fryatt, the British skipper of the steamship *Brussels* which was captured, after being surrounded by four German submarines. She carried a number of passengers, mostly Belgian women, who were returning to Belgium.

Now this Captain Fryatt had had various adventures with submarines, and was known as the 'Pirates Terror' because he had caused them much trouble. In March 1915 he had gone straight for a submarine in an attempt to ram her, only missing her by a few feet, as the submarine dived suddenly to escape destruction. For this gallant attempt Captain Fryatt and his First Officer had been awarded gold watches by the Admiralty.

When the Germans caught Captain Fryatt last month, they tried him before a Court Martial and condemned him to death as a *franc-tireur*.* At this time the submarines were sinking *on sight* every ship without warning, merchantmen, liners etc. of all nationalities, so the Germans affected to claim their legal right to do this. Well, the tribunal condemned him to death, then wired the sentence to the Kaiser and his Council, asking for confirmation. The Kaiser's sanction was wired back at once and the sentence was carried out next day.

Far from this act being a deterrent to English skippers, the indignation this aroused is making the whole nation more determined to bring Germany to her knees. The public feeling is that we will never make terms of peace with Germany's rulers who break every law of civilisation.

MONDAY JULY 31

A German submarine mine-layer of the latest type is now attracting all London to Temple Pier. Harmless and moored to the Pier, it is collecting thousands of shillings for Military Hospitals. Thus, a foolish prophecy of the Kaiser's has been fulfilled which boasted that his submarines would come up the Thames, exacting tribute from London.

This submarine is one we captured months ago at the mouth of the Thames, when it had got into difficulties. On being approached, she surrendered with one of the crew remaining behind to try to destroy her. No structural damage was done by the attempt to scuttle her, as she only sank on a sand bank to a few feet, whence she was raised by the Admiralty, repaired, and brought to London as a sight and a means to raise money for War Charities. There is such a crowd every day and such a queue of people waiting, that I haven't attempted yet to go and see it.

WEDNESDAY AUGUST 2

To gain an extra day's holiday in Wales, Daddy and I travelled down to Gelligemlyn last night. It also gave us a rather cooler journey, for the heat has been intense. So, at 11.15 pm after watching for a while the powerful searchlights crossing each other all over the sky in the nightly search for Zeppelins, we started out. We walked round to South

---

*   Irregular combatant. The controversy over Captain Fryatt featured in Ian Hislop's popular TV series, *Not Forgotten*.

Kensington to go by train to Paddington. This nocturnal walk, carrying our own bags, was also a result of the war, as there are very few taxis to be had by day and practically none by night. So I had taken the precaution to convey our luggage earlier in the day to Paddington and leave it in the cloakroom.

The petrol is now given out, doled out, by licence and on strict and very short allowances, for two reasons: first the lack of oil-ships to bring the petrol to England, secondly the 'staggering amount' to use the expression used in Parliament required at the Front.

My especial joy on arriving this morning at Dolgelly was fetching you from Hengwrt. We placed you between us in the car, Nannie in front and bore off a very happy, talkative little fellow to Gelligemlyn. Your conversation has been delighting me all day.

FRIDAY AUGUST 4

Today is the second anniversary of the outbreak of the war. What a two years it has been! To think that, shocked as we all were at the bloodshed of the first collisions between the armies and at havoc caused by the German heavy artillery, this bloodshed was a mere trickle compared to the wholesale slaughter that goes on now. Today too is published by the French Government a Yellow Book on the awful slave-driving raids at Liège by the Germans. They have systematically abducted members of every family in Lille, and then sent them off to unknown destinations.

Only mothers and children under fourteen were exempt. Young girls, boys, husbands and older people still able to work, were removed and the most heartrending scenes occurred. People of all classes were taken, high and low; young girls of good family packed into overcrowded trains next to men of the lowest type and nobody knew whither they were going.

They have been employed by the Germans for munitions, making barbed wire, harvesting and the women in many cases to be servants to German officers. Isn't it too revolting? This tragedy of Lille will live on like the Spanish Inquisition in the Netherlands.

SATURDAY AUGUST 5

Aunt Clara* writes from Norwich that the Zeppelins have been over the East Coast in fleets of 6 or more the last few nights. One night she counted 52 bombs dropping between 1 and 2 am, but as the houses (Norwich) were all in darkness the bombs all fell in the fields and nobody was hurt. The concussions shook her house. Next day she, Charlie and Knyvett all went to see the craters made by the bombs. The two boys were highly excited at climbing down into those they found.

---

* Aunt Clara was married to Georgina Lee's brother-in-law, Lt Col Harry Romer Lee, and Charlie and Knyvett are their sons.

TUESDAY AUGUST 8

Today I came up to town, leaving you behind at Gelligemlyn under the care of your Granny. I simply hated leaving you behind.

We had been doing much gardening together you and I, cutting off the dead roses and gathering up the grass which Uncle Romer Williams had trimmed away from the lawn-edges. 'Johnson' is your name when you are gardening and under that name you zealously do any work required of you. Romer amuses himself, shouting for Johnson in a stentorian voice, and you run up to him, laughing, touching your forehead and saying 'Yes, sir'. They all love you. It was so lovely at Gelli that it seemed a sin to come away; yet as poor Daddy had to come up, I couldn't leave him alone.

SATURDAY AUGUST 12

My Belgian Surgical Depot in Roland Gardens is worrying me with its *potins*.* The Depot has grown a good deal and we sometimes have as many as 21 at work in the room, too many, although the room is so spacious. And now they quarrel amongst themselves.

There has been a feud between the two heads of tables, the woman who leads the bandage-workers and the head shirt-maker! I had to send the latter away yesterday, partly because of her sharp tongue and partly because her dismissal was desired on moral grounds by the Aldwych Committee.

The woman departed with loud protests of her innocence convulsed with sobs, as she left me to put on her hat. If only she had gone away quietly, her work companions need have known nothing more of my reasons for calling her to a secret *tête à tête*.

These women are fine workers, but their bickerings and jealousies are a perfect nuisance. They all come and tell tales on each other and are full of crooked little 'adjustments' in their dealings, which are disconcerting. One can hardly call them dishonest, only not straight. Yet in other ways I immensely admire their patience, endurance and indefatigable work power.

SUNDAY AUGUST 13

This morning Daddy and I went on the top of a bus to get a little fresh air, to Temple Pier to see the German mine-laying submarine, which enables us to collect so much money for the War Charities. Up to a few days ago £3000 had already been collected. It looked much smaller than I expected and so narrow! She was flying the Union Jack and the German flag with the Iron Cross immediately below.

WEDNESDAY AUGUST 16

Last night we dined with the Danas. I sat near a Major McLeod, a splendid type of Scotsman of 52 who, when the war broke out, was a big merchant in Calcutta.

*   Gossip.

At the call of war, he threw up his work and though 50, joined the Cameronians. He has served two years in France and has just come home for good because his health was giving way. He lately married in France, while still on duty, a charming American girl who was nursing in an American hospital for French soldiers just outside Paris.

She entertained me a good deal after dinner with an account of her work, but she couldn't get over the apathy and indifference of the French ladies living in the châteaux around, in a very wealthy district. They never once came forward to help the work of the hospital, although the voluntary staff was terribly overworked, and could not cope with the making of the bandages and surgical requisites.

I have always felt that French people are selfish and afraid of acting or spending, in the public interest. They might give pennies, perhaps, where pounds would be quickly raised here.

THURSDAY AUGUST 17

Uncle Guy wrote a most interesting account of a tour he has just made all round the fighting front of the Battle of the Somme which still rages with unabated violence. He speaks of the extraordinary effect of our artillery bombardment. Villages, which lately were important enemy strongholds, are now 'heaps of dust and ashes'. He describes going down into some of the now famous 'dug-outs' where the enemy, safe from bombardment under 30ft of earth, were finally trapped by our infantry throwing hand-grenades down these luxurious cave dwellings.

They were lit by electric light and had every comfort and were approached by flights of wooden stairs. He describes the nauseating odours permeating from these caves. But he persisted in entering one and found a heap of corpses near the entrance. In one place he found a bit of German trouser still wrapped round the charred remnants of a leg.

TUESDAY AUGUST 22

My birthday today. When I awoke this morning Daddy pulled out from under his pillow two parcels for me, one an old French paste cross on dark green enamel, of beautiful design. The other was a big Spanish comb from dear Granny, so I had a very happy awakening.

MONDAY AUGUST 28

Today has been a day of great news. First, Italy declared war upon Germany, after being at war with Austria for a year or so. But more important, Rumania has at last thrown in her lot with the Allies and yesterday declared war on Austria-Hungary. She has done this because she wants Transylvania (now an Austrian province), where 1,000,000 Rumanians live under the tyranny of the Magyar race.

Two years ago, when war broke out, Rumania was governed by old King Carol, a Hohenzollern prince. He had reigned for about 50 years, and had created out of this old Turkish province, the most efficient state in the Balkans.* His people, seeing an opportunity of acquiring Transylvania, agitated to enter into the lists. But the King, declaring that he was a Hohenzollern, added that he would never fight against Germany.

Soon after this he died and his nephew Ferdinand succeeded him. He said he would always put the interests of his country before those of his kinship, being a Constitutional Monarch. Yesterday he gave his sanction to declare war on the Central Powers. The humorous side is that months ago the Germans made a deal with Rumania to receive large supplies of grain. It now appears that the supplies of shells and ammunition which they gave Rumania in exchange have given her the means to wage war against Germany.

THURSDAY AUGUST 31

The Kaiser has dismissed von Falkenhayn who was responsible for the attack on Verdun and its failure. He has replaced him by old Hindenburg, who now takes supreme command of the Army and becomes Chief of Staff. Hindenburg was always openly opposed to the Verdun attack and was furious that the legions he needed so badly on his Eastern Front, were frittered away in the futile attacks on Verdun

SATURDAY SEPTEMBER 2

This morning I had occasion to walk from St James's Square to Westminster, and I took the way down the steps of Duke of York's Column, past the ex-German Embassy. I never can go through there without a strong feeling of emotion that grips very close, a feeling of pride and deepest reverence for our country.

That view from the top of the steps, whichever way one looks, up sombre and busy Regent Street, or the quiet dignity of the great clubs, and in the distance, beyond the Government buildings, the beautiful Tower of Westminster, and Big Ben of the beloved solemn tones – it is all so typical of the solid seriousness of England.

Looking round at the vast number of temporary Government buildings that have sprung up for carrying on the war-work, on every open space, and thinking over the activity in the labyrinths of the Admiralty and War Office, it struck me for the first time irresistibly; *how* did we manage to stem the German invasion of France in the first months of the war?

Some day we can tell you how, in 1914, we saw the Green Park turned into a camping ground for the hastily mobilised cavalry and artillery; how we passed down the rows of horses tethered to the palings; how, on a memorable Sunday morning in August we stood on the fringe of the crowd by Buckingham Palace watching the 2nd Grenadier Guards file past the King and Queen to say goodbye, and how the crowd stood silent

* But his neglect of festering rural problems triggered the bloody peasant rebellion of 1907, which claimed thousands of Rumanian lives.

and motionless, too awed even to raise a cheer. I don't suppose one of those men remains now.

This was in the days when the lake of the Green Park was still undisturbed, before the Zeppelin days. For a long time now the lake has been drained, so that the tell-tale glimmer of the water at night shall not serve as a landmark to hostile aircraft.

SUNDAY SEPTEMBER 3

Last night, or early this morning at about 2.15, I was awakened suddenly. Through the open window, as soon as I gathered my wits, I heard the distant booming of many guns. I flew to the window to look out, but Daddy called out 'mind the light, keep the blind down and come downstairs quickly'. Of course as there were Zeppelins about, it was the best thing to do.

I groped feverishly for my slippers, but at last I found them and tumbled downstairs to get outside the hall door so as not to lose sight of anything. Daddy lingered behind to rouse the servants. Mrs Marsh, our elderly Scottish cook was in a big black velvet cloak and perfectly composed, having been through two raids already.

Outside, the night was dark and misty. I wanted to go out into the street to see a Zeppelin, as from this house we have a very small field of vision. But Daddy, obsessed with the risk of my being laid out by shrapnel from our own guns, hauled me back from the pavement and made me keep under the portico. I cannot forgive this because in the end we never witnessed the supreme event of this great raid. We only heard about it this morning.

Suddenly terrible retribution fell upon the raiders. A Zeppelin was seen to burst into flame at a height of 12,000 feet. Slowly it came down, down, down, amid the cheering of literally millions of people who were watching it, till it crashed to the ground a heap of ruins. The scene was witnessed from a very wide area, places 65 miles apart. She fell at Cuffley.

When I heard this, on coming down to breakfast, I wanted to start off immediately to go and see it. But Daddy said the military would never let people get within a couple of miles. When Ethel and I made an attempt to start for the scene, the policeman told me that thousands had come from London and were being turned back. However this morning at my work depot, a friend told me that she *had* gone, at 10 o'clock. After walking for miles, in the rain and mud, she stood within 30 feet of the remains.

They were steaming still, and she saw the half-charred bodies of the wretched crew. Some had limbs missing and it was a terrible sight.* The Commander of the airship was lying there, with the Iron Cross still visible on his breast.

Ethel and I went up to see Aunt Louisa who, from her house at Highgate, must have had a good view. We found her taking it all as a matter of course; she had not even

---

*   This airship was the SL (Schutte Lanz) 11. 'Being a wooden ship, she burned for nearly two hours after she reached the ground.' Joseph Morris, *The German Air Raids on Great Britain, 1914–1918*, pp. 126–7.

taken the trouble to get out of bed to look (she is about 75), leaving it to her faithful servant and companion Lizzie to report back to her. Lizzie was not so calm; she was frankly terrified, when the Zeppelin passed over the house. But she was also fascinated and stood watching the shrapnel from our guns burst in the sky.

Suddenly the houses about her were lit up in a bright red glare. She could see all the people craning their heads out of their windows. Then a tremendous cheering and clapping of hands arose from everywhere. Dazed and bewildered, not knowing what the clamour meant, nor the brilliant red glow, she dashed to a window at the back of the house and there she saw a mass of glowing fire drop slowly down from the stars towards earth.

TUESDAY SEPTEMBER 5

Yes, the Zeppelin was shot down by a young airman 21 years old and this afternoon he is announced as having been awarded the V.C. It seems he was up for two hours, awaiting the Zeppelins and chasing over one which escaped and then this one. I heard that when he came to earth again he was like one out of his real senses; the strain of it all, and then the extraordinary triumph of the end. But he soon came round to his normal state and now all London is talking only of him.

This is only the second time that a Zeppelin has fallen to an airman and in each case it is an Englishman, first Warneford, now Leefe-Robinson.* No wonder the Germans are amazed at the feats performed by our aviation service.

I must not forget to mention the conquering of German South East Africa,** which has been going on for months under General Smuts. This will be a valuable addition to the Empire. Following the conquest of German South West Africa, the Germans see the shattering of all their dreams of colonies in Africa.

To all of us, to whom our South African War is still such recent history, it is astonishing that those two great Imperial leaders, Botha and Smuts, were fighting *against* us, only 15 years ago. But this is what the British Empire does, it turns its conquered foes into loyal helpers of the mother country, so just and liberal is its rule.

SUNDAY SEPTEMBER 17

Gelligemlyn
As always happens when I get down to Gelligemlyn, my diary becomes an effort and the days slide by, with no writing.

We have had Uncle Tich here for a very short visit, brought to a sudden end this morning. A telegram has recalled him at once to the Headquarters at Norwich,

---

* Ironically, Captain W. Leefe-Robinson VC, the hero of the hour, died of 'flu a few days after being demobbed at the end of the war.
** It was allocated to Britain (along with other German colonies in Africa) under the terms of the Treaty of Versailles; then called Tanganyika until, in 1964, it merged with Zanzibar to form the independent republic of Tanzania.

en route for France where he has been given a staff appointment. He has been trying for months to get out to France and has at last got his chance. He only arrived yesterday morning. He was longing for some night fishing so after dinner, it being very dark, warm and still, he, Daddy and I went out to the Break-neck Pool and Bathing Pool, and were out till after midnight. He caught three sewin (Welsh sea-trout), one just 3lbs, a beauty.

The British have renewed the Push on the Somme and have advanced 3,000 yards. For the first time we made use of a new weapon which gave us considerable advantage over the surprised Germans: great armoured cars* heavily armed with machine guns attacked the German trenches, while many armed aeroplanes swooped down like hawks low over the enemy trenches, discharging a hail of bullets.

THURSDAY SEPTEMBER 21

One of my childhood friends, Hal Bromfield,** has been killed in the recent great dash of the Guards' Brigade. Hal, as we all knew him, was as brave as a lion, in his quiet way. I can well imagine how he would lead his men fearlessly into the hottest of the fire. It is so cruel to think of a man like him being taken away from his wife and child and an adoring family.

They say this charge of the Guards was extraordinary. The men went forward in an outburst of shouting which was heard above the roar of the guns. While the enemy trenches were being stormed officers were addressing each other as coolly as though they were in Piccadilly while the men encouraged each other and cheered each exploit by shouts of 'Go it Ribs', 'Stick to it Lillywhites', as though they were cheering at a football match.

SUNDAY SEPTEMBER 24

Glanrhos
Yesterday I came to Glanrhos, to stay with dear Mrs Graham-Clarke, who was like a mother to me, in the years of my girlhood.† Glanrhos, being only ten minutes from Glaslyn, by the river path, I was here almost daily. It was a hard tussle to leave Daddy and you even for three days. But Mrs Clarke wished so much to have me stay and I was so anxious to be here again and see Uncle Henry, Uncle Arthur and Aunt Audrey who are all at Glaslyn, that Daddy let me come. I have not been in my old haunts for 1½ years. The weather is lovely, like summer again.

---

*   A new weapon, certainly, but they were not armoured cars. This is the first appearance of the tank. Only 45 were used, with limited results, as many of them broke down. The first major success achieved by a tank offensive was at Cambrai, in November 1917. See diary for 30 September.

** Major Harry Bromfield DSO had served in the South African War with the South Wales Borderers. He was appointed Chief Constable of Radnorshire in 1909. He rejoined his regiment in February 1915. But on the formation of the Welsh Guards, he was transferred and had been at the Front for only six weeks when he was killed.

†   Georgina's own mother had died after the birth of her youngest brother, Arthur, in 1879.

MONDAY SEPTEMBER 25

There was another great Zeppelin raid on London and Eastern Counties on Saturday night, in which two Zeppelins were brought down. One met with the same terrible flaming death as the one at Cuffley 3 weeks ago. The other came down to earth unburnt and the crew of 22 officers and men were made prisoners. But our casualties were very numerous, 40 killed and 130 injured.

WEDNESDAY SEPTEMBER 27

Those wretched Zeppelins are coming over to kill as many civilians as possible. Seven of them were over the East coast and Midlands on Monday night and 43 more people were killed.

I have copied out of Gerald G. Clarke's diary from his time in the trenches these letters about separation allowances. They were received by a paymaster from the wives of some of the soldiers and are typical.

THURSDAY SEPTEMBER 28

Uncle Arthur has been mentioned in despatches by Sir Archibald Murray, Commander in Chief in Egypt. Arthur has done very good work at Alexandria as DAAG. But he is dying to get to France. He envies Uncle Romer who has just gone out there on a Staff job.

SATURDAY SEPTEMBER 30

Guy arrived this morning from France on a week's leave. We always hear so much from him about the war, for, like Arthur, he has a great gift for describing his experiences. He told us about the 'Tanks', the new armoured cars which go over trenches and through houses, and are quite impervious to machine-gun bullets. He described how one waddled up to a strong German redoubt, a fortress of dug-outs, which had defied our infantry successfully and how it clambered right onto the redoubt and crushed it!

They will not make a permanent effect on the fighting,* because high explosive shells knock them out and of course the Germans won't be slow to attack them in this way. They carry two officers and six men who have a very bad time of it inside. Their heads have to be protected with helmets or caps fitted with springs to break the knocks they get. They are banged up and down as the machine jolts over walls, down trenches and up again. They have no wheels, only a revolving endless chain.

Your new Nannie arrived today, to learn all about your little ways, before your old Nannie leaves you on Monday.

---

*   Georgina was right in relation to the Great War, but understandably did not appreciate the potential, long-term, of tracked vehicles!

Letters from wives of soldiers about separation allowances.

Copies of actual Letters received by a Regimental Paymaster from Wives of Soldiers relative to Separation Allowance.

Dear Sir, according to instructions on Ring Paper I have given birth to a Daughter on April 21ˢᵗ
                                        Yours truly.

Dear Sir, I write these few lines for Mrs Haynes who can't write herself being expecting and can do with it.
                                        Yours truly.

Dear Sir, I have received no pay since my husban went away from now here. Yours truly.

Dear Sir,
        Mrs Haynes has been put to bed with a little lad — Wife of Peter Haynes.

Dear Sir,
        We received your letter and I am his grand-father and grandmother he was born and brought up in the house in answer to your letter.

Dear Sir, You have changed my little boy into a little girl will it make any difference.
                                        Yours truly.

Dear Sir, I am expecting to be confined next month what am I to do about it ?   Yours truly.

Respected Sir, Dear Sir,
        Though I take this liberty as it leaves me at present I beg to ask if you will kindly be kind enough to let me

know where my husbin is though he is not my legible husbin as he as a wife tho she says shes ded I do not think he nos for sure but we are not married tho I am getting my allotment regler which is no fault of Mr Loy Georger who would stop it if he could and Mr Mc Kena, but if you could know where he is as he belong the Naval Royal Fling Corpse for ever since he joined in the January when he was sacked from his work for talking back at his boss which was woman at the landry where he worked I have not had any money from him since joined tho he told Mrs Harris what lives on the ground floor as he was a Pretty Officer for 6/ a day and lots of warm underclothes for the winter & cold weather and I have three children what he is the father of tho he says it was all my fault, hoping you are quite well as this leaves me at present I must now close hoping you are quite well.
                                        Mrs Jane Jenkins.

TUESDAY OCTOBER 3

There was another raid by 7 Zeppelins over the Eastern Counties and London and yet another Zeppelin was brought down in flames to the north of London at Potters Bar, making the fourth destroyed in the three big raids. This time only one civilian was killed by the bombs. The Commander was found still alive, but terribly injured and he died 1½ hours later. The bodies of the crew were found in the wreckage.

WEDNESDAY OCTOBER 4

This evening we had a good time on the shingle at Gelligemlyn Pool. This time Uncle Guy gave us all the fun. He hooked a lovely 3lb sewin, which gave him a good play. This time you found your tongue; you ran along the bank shouting 'a salmon! A salmon, Uncle Guy got a salmon', and when it was landed at your feet, you couldn't take your eyes off it.

Presently I looked at my watch and said 'Now, children, its 6 o'clock, time to go to bed!' You pulled up your sleeve, looked at your wrist and said 'This is my watch and it says time to stay down here!' Not bad for an under three year old!

MONDAY OCTOBER 9

I am haunted by something Aunt Beatrice told me yesterday. She went down to Eton last week to see Henry (Dunsmure) and had a long chat with his housemaster Mr Hare.* He told her that 27 of his own boys have been killed up to now. He went on to say he had been staying lately with the parents of three brothers, old boys of his, who had all been killed.

The poor mother, he said, was a broken woman. He heard her screaming at night, when her anguish was past bearing. She wandered into her boys' rooms when all the house was quiet. The parents are wealthy and having lost their three sons, are giving away all their money in war charities. But the thought of that mother quite haunts me.

TUESDAY OCTOBER 17

Neville Street

We have been back in Neville Street since last Saturday evening and I have not yet had a moment in which to write my diary. There is always so much to settle on first coming home, housekeeping arrangements and now my additional war-work, the Belgian Depot which depends upon me.

This morning I insisted on attending to your little necessities, Depot or no Depot. So we spent most of the morning at Harrods. We did very little in the end, because shopping has become so difficult and slow. I suppose the girls employed everywhere are not the sharpest ones, as most of these women have gone to work in the munitions

---

*   J.M.H. Hare was a housemaster at Eton from 1893 to 1920. Every Sunday the names of Old Etonians who had been killed were read out in Chapel.

factories where the pay is higher. Also one can rarely get just the thing one wants and it takes so long to get substitutes.

THURSDAY OCTOBER 19

Today is 'Our Day', Red Cross Day, and the flag-sellers must have made very large sums of money, selling little silken flags for the Hospital funds, *and* pieces of wire from the first Zeppelin to be brought down by our airmen. This is the cover of the tiny envelope containing a little bit I bought.

+ GUARANTEE

This is a piece of wire of the first Zeppelin brought down at **CUFFLEY, HERTS. September 3rd, 1916.**

The wire having been given to the British Red Cross Society by H.M. War Office, it is being sold to help the wounded at the Front. **Price 1/-**

Today I went to the first of a series of lectures on the Montessori System. I am so taken with the principles and I want my boy to grow up with full scope for his individual characteristics. I want to learn all I can so as to help him to develop to the best of his ability.

SUNDAY OCTOBER 22

Our losses lately have been enormous. They are not released to the public, but one can judge from certain scraps of information that reach one, such as we received last Saturday, on our arrival at Paddington at 5.15 pm. By that hour it was dark, and the station badly lit. But on a distant platform we saw the unloading of a hospital train, arrived from Portsmouth.

The platform was covered with stretchers. As the wounded were removed in their stretchers from the train into the great Red Cross ambulance motors, the stretchers on the platform were put into the train to replace those put into the ambulances. Our porter told Daddy that, during *that day alone*, 4000 wounded had arrived at Paddington. Not to mention those arriving at Charing Cross and Victoria on the same day.

I had a note from Mrs Talbot, telling me she had just been on the East Coast for a week-end to see her husband, 'taking advantage of a full moon' to do this. This sentence is an indication of the times we live in! London is supposed to be safe from Zeppelins during the moonlight nights, so she left her boy behind in comparative safety.

WEDNESDAY OCTOBER 25

The aeroplanes are busy overhead tonight; it is close on 10 pm. They are now our great safeguards against Zeppelins. All four that were brought down in flames were destroyed by our aviators and not by the guns.

FRIDAY OCTOBER 27

Tomorrow is your third birthday. You are so excited about it, and tomorrow morning, when you come into my room, there will be your parcels on the sofa according to the little story of 'Harry's birthday' which you are never tired of hearing. When I look back on this evening, three years ago, just before you arrived, how excited I was at the first warning I had of your approach!

I had walked all the way to the Park and back up Queen's Gate in the morning. I remember every detail of that last day before you were really there. How Aunt Amy came to tea and I got so tired and how after dinner I played patience, until the first dear little summons came.

I went off to my room saying goodnight to Daddy and never a word else for fear of spoiling his night. And how he slept happily all night in his room at the top of the house, never dreaming that there was anything unusual happening, or that his precious little son would be there by eleven next morning!

SATURDAY OCTOBER 28

Your birthday has been a very happy day for us all my pet and it was a very tired little fellow who went off to bed at half past six. In the midst of it all, Sybil and Charlie Wynne-Jones came in unexpectedly. They were delighted to drop in on the birthday party. They have come up from Ireland before his departure on Monday for the Front. He goes now as ADC to General John Vaughan, who is commanding a Cavalry Division out there.

We saw in yesterday's paper that Cathcart Wason has been given the CMG for his services in the Persian Gulf.

TUESDAY NOVEMBER 7

Eugene Crombie went back to the fighting line this morning at 6 am after being invalided for nearly a year. He dined here with his mother, sister and fiancée two nights and now he is back in the danger zone, God keep him! These young lieutenants have a very small chance of returning safe home. God bless them all.

On 31 October Colonel Scott, the father of Sybil Wynne-Jones, died at Penmaenucha. He died on the very day that Sybil, after being here on your birthday, went up to Yorkshire after seeing her husband off to the Front. He died suddenly and painlessly in his armchair after his dinner on the evening of the 31st. Poor Sybil, having just bidden her husband farewell, is now left to see all the sad business through, alone.

SATURDAY NOVEMBER 18

Marshal von Hindenburg has written an open letter to the German Chancellor, Bethmann-Hollweg, calling upon him to arouse Germany to the terrible crisis she is faced with and to warn the people that Germany will lose the war unless every possible effort is made.

SUNDAY NOVEMBER 19

In today's paper is published a letter by Emile Cammaerts the Belgian patriot and poet,* expressing the indignation of Belgium at this latest German outrage. I have heard Cammaerts recite some of his patriotic verses and very inspiring they are. He writes as follows about the deportations:

BY THE WATERS OF BABYLON

As I write these lines the slave raids are going on; the tramp of soldiers is heard through many towns and villages by anxious women and children; men are kidnapped right and left, and these terrible trains roll towards Germany packed with human cattle to the strains of the 'Brabançonne'. Ten days ago, in Flanders alone, 15,000 had been taken. The Germans pretend to requisition only the able-bodied unemployed of military age. As a fact all those in certain zones who can render any service are seized, whether employed or unemployed. If things are allowed to go on at this rate we shall witness the wholesale deportation of an entire people, reduced to slavery. All the country's best blood will be used up in the German workshops and mines, or, worse still, in the trenches. Our preachers have frequently chosen as a text the well-known Psalm: 'By the waters of Babylon we sat down and wept'. Did they guess that Belgium should not only suffer from exile and oppression, but that her sons should be carried away captive in the land of her conquerors?

The *Observer*, November 19, 1916

I repeat all these things, that you may realise, in happier years, what the German Government of the early 20th century was capable of.

TUESDAY NOVEMBER 28

There has been much excitement in our South West London today. A German aeroplane flew over us at midday and dropped 6 bombs. I was shopping in Oxford Street and was quite ignorant of it all. But at lunchtime Daddy rang up to ask if we were all safe. He had just heard that bombs had been dropped on South Kensington. The nearest to us was one that fell in Basil Street in the mews, opposite Knightsbridge tube station.

---

*   In World War II, Francis Cammaerts, son of Emile, joined the wartime Special Operations Executive, and served with distinction alongside the Maquis.

Another fell through the roof of Spiking's shop, the confectioner opposite Harrods in Brompton Road. Another fell into a house in Lowndes Square, wrecking a billiard room and another in a mews off Belgrave Square. After lunch I went out with Miss Green and saw the mews off Belgrave Square and the Basil Street mews, but the police would allow nobody anywhere near. This is the first time a hostile aeroplane has visited London in broad daylight.

The old Austrian Emperor, Franz Josef died at Schönbrunn some days ago, on the 21st November.* His death makes no difference to the War, as Germany has her claws well into Austria. The new Emperor, the young and weak Archduke Charles, is entirely under the Kaiser's thumb.

---

* The Austro-Hungarian Emperor Franz Josef had reigned for sixty-eight years. His government's disastrous decision to declare war on Serbia in July 1914 hastened the disintegration of his Empire.

Book IX

November 29, 1916 – November 30, 1917

WEDNESDAY NOVEMBER 29

Today at my work depot in Mulberry Walk, there was some amused excitement. One of our workers, Mrs Bruce Williams (the American wife of one of the Generals at the Front), came in, looking very earnest and said 'There is a big air raid going on now at this moment, all over London, I have already counted 20 bomb explosions'. Everyone ran outside and jokes were freely bandied, – 'Go in, go in, Mrs Dana, else you will be found dead and not at your post' etc. etc.

Hearing and seeing nothing at all, we all went back to our different works. Soon the whirr of sewing machines and hammering of splint making was as loud as before. Nobody thought any more about it. Well, the good lady's lively imagination had been too much for her, for nobody else in London seems to have heard explosions, nor has there been anything in the nature of an air raid!

Tonight welcome changes are announced at the Admiralty: Sir John Jellicoe, hitherto in Command of the Grand Fleet goes to the Admiralty as First Sea Lord. Sir David Beatty, only 45 and the hero of all the sea-fights in the North Sea, becomes Admiral of the Grand Fleet in Jellicoe's place.

Beatty is the youngest of our Admirals, but his skills, audacity and pluck have won him this distinction at this critical period in our history.

THURSDAY NOVEMBER 30

Mrs Gerald Paget lunched with me today. I had asked Mrs de la Rue, who is always so cheerful and a great friend of Mrs Paget's, but she fell through so we had a *tête-à-tête* and nobody could be more amusing company than Mrs Paget. She takes interest in *everything* except gossip and this she never indulges in, she abhors it. She was very despondent about the situation, asserting repeatedly that this war will see the end of our present civilisation.

Things are looking black in Rumania, where the German flood of invasion cannot be stemmed, and the fall of Bucharest is imminent.

There has been a great revolt in Antwerp against the Germans over the deportations. The Belgians are refusing to be carried off to work in Germany. Many people have been killed, both Belgians and Germans.

WEDNESDAY DECEMBER 6

We are in a state of political upheaval. Asquith has resigned, pushed to it by Lloyd George who refused to act as War Minister unless the Council was reduced to 4, *minus* the Prime Minister as Chairman. That is, Lloyd George and his adherents Bonar Law and Carson are agreeable to the Prime Minister joining the Council ex officio for *consultation*, but not as Chairman. Asquith held out firmly, but his resignation was suddenly announced this morning. Bonar Law was summoned to the Palace today, so the Press jumped to the conclusion that he would be Prime Minister. But he has declined.

All the leading Ministers have been summoned by the King in turn. The general feeling is very strong against Asquith and poor Viscount Grey. The latter is deemed responsible for the chaotic situation in Greece and for the lamentable failure in the Balkans.*

THURSDAY DECEMBER 7

The Germans have entered Bucharest and have also captured Ploesti, the important station on the railway line to Russia.**

The Kaiser is boisterously triumphant over this fresh capital added to his crown. Brussels, Warsaw, Belgrade, Cetinje,† and Bucharest make a wreath of which he may well be proud. It is true Paris, London and Petrograd are not likely to fall to his share. But the grain and oil of Rumania will give Germany a fresh life for the struggle. It's terrible.

The new Government formed today, may change all this. Lloyd George is a man of rapid action, and as Prime Minister he may change the whole aspect of affairs.

Lord Derby in a big speech at the Guildhall yesterday stated that, unless the country had a War Council of a very few, who could give the necessary power quickly to the military authorities 'the plans of the General Staff for the Campaign of 1917 might very possibly fail'. There is not a moment to lose, he urged. Altogether one feels that the Government is on the verge of a panic or something not far short of it.

SATURDAY DECEMBER 9

The Allies have started the total blockade of Greece. Empty granaries and storehouses ought to make Royalist Greece realise where King Constantine's folly has led them.

---

*   In October 1915, British and French troops under General Sarrail had landed in Salonika, southern Greece. Their intention was to rescue the Serbs. The Allied Forces could not save either the Serbs or the Rumanians, hence the 'lamentable failure'. Colin Nicolson, *The First World War, Europe, 1914–1918*, p. 118.

**   In 1856, one of the first oil refineries in the world was opened near Ploesti.

†   From 1878 to 1918, Cetinje was the capital of independent Montenegro, which became a republic within the newly formed Yugoslavia.

Meanwhile there is great danger that our forces under General Sarrail* in Macedonia will be confronted with far more powerful enemy forces, since the Germans will now be able to spare troops from Rumania.

I went to Eton today with Aunt Beatrice and Uncle Alex for Henry's confirmation. It was very impressive seeing all those boys just verging on manhood when they too will be called upon to fight for their country. They are taken at 17 now to train and are packed off in 6 months to the fighting line. It is terrible.**

I look forward to the day when, in happier times, Daddy and I shall again be in the beautiful Chapel witnessing your Confirmation, please God.

MONDAY DECEMBER 11

The new Ministry is announced. Congratulations are pouring in from the friendly neutrals such as America and Holland and from all our Allies on the selection of England's strongest men. Lloyd George is Prime Minister and the War Council of 4 consists of: Lord Curzon, Lord Milner, Henderson (Labour Member) and Lloyd George himself. Sir Edward Carson, the dauntless, energetic Irishman is First Lord of the Admiralty.

The only disappointment is that Mr Balfour remains in office as Foreign Minister. He is not thought strong enough to deal with the Greek situation. All the minor Offices are filled with new men, who are businessmen. For instance the Office of Food Controller is taken by Lord Devonport who rose to his position by success in commerce.

This whole crisis arose and was settled within 8 days. It has taken place quietly with no more apparent effect than the excitement of the newspapers. Yet these changes may mark the turning point in the world's history.

Lloyd George is laid up with influenza tonight and is confined to his room. It is said that while resting his body, his restless brain is devoted to energetic prosecution of the war. Bonar Law, now Leader of the House appeared in Parliament today for the first time in his new capacity. He announced on behalf of Lloyd George that the Prime Minister would be unable to announce his policy before Thursday.

TUESDAY DECEMBER 12

Tonight we are all amused at the German Chancellor's announcement in the Reichstag that Germany had, in concert with her allies, proposed entering into negotiations for peace. He then went on to boast of all their victories and of the triumph of the fall of Bucharest and conquest of half Rumania.

---

*   As French Commander-in-Chief, Sarrail had already been at odds with the Greek royal
      family, who favoured the Central Powers. Through 1917, he was overall commander of all
      the Allied troops in Salonika.
**   1,157 Old Etonians were killed in the war.

THURSDAY DECEMBER 14

It seems that the most feverish excitement has reigned in Germany and Austria since the Kaiser's proposals for peace were made. In Berlin people spent hours all night through a snow storm outside the offices of the big papers, in the hope of getting news of the reply from the hostile Powers. In the Press, England, France and Russia have scornfully set aside these proposals though no official replies have yet been given. Although the tone of the Allied Press is so unpromising, the Germans still delude themselves that we shall all jump at their offer!

Meanwhile Government work is in abeyance, owing to the most unfortunate illness of Lloyd George. Influenza is rampant and numbers of distinguished people are down with it. It is hoped that he will be well enough to attend at the House on Tuesday next.

TUESDAY DECEMBER 19

We are at **Brighton** again for a few days, you, Nannie and I and Daddy joins us in a few days. We came back to our same comfortable rooms with Mrs Brown, 139 Marine Parade. We have been having detestable weather in London, nothing but dark, damp, foggy days for several weeks. We have all had such bad colds that we felt 10 days at Brighton would cure us. Today we have had lovely sunshine for some hours, and a beautiful heavy sea, with wild waves. It is delightful to breathe pure air after what we have been having.

WEDNESDAY DECEMBER 20

At last today we know a little of Lloyd George's policy as new Prime Minister. Last evening in a long speech of 2 hours' duration, he stated to the House his plans for the most vigorous prosecution of the War. It was thrilling and we shall eagerly watch the unfolding of these vast schemes. One thing is certain – every civilian will be mobilised for state work. This is to release men fit for military work who are at present employed in civil work.

Another important step is the taking over by the Government of *all* the mining industry, in addition to the coal fields of Wales which they annexed some time ago. Shipping too is to be entirely under Government control, so as to enable our food supplies to be on a better balanced footing.

The Food Controller* is going to make drastic regulations. Our food supplies are causing grave concern, owing to the failure of the harvest in America, and the submarine menace.

---

*   Not as drastic as she feared. Lord Devonport (1856–1934), formerly H.E. Kearley, introduced voluntary rationing of bread, meat and sugar in February 1917.

Christmas Day

I haven't written for some days. Since I last wrote, President Wilson has caused a sensation and a great deal of vexed comment by sending a note urging the Allies to consider the German peace overtures, 'since', he adds, 'the aims of both belligerent parties seem virtually the same, viz: the recognition and protection of neutral and small nations, the recognition that they must be respected as well as the powers now at war'.

This last clause has amazed and angered the British and French who cannot understand Wilson's naiveté and misunderstanding of the aims for which we entered the war.

Many press comments are indignant. But on the whole the Press observes a great deal of self-control, believing the President to be prompted by humanitarian motives and not by pro-German ones, as would appear initially to be the case.

THURSDAY DECEMBER 28

We moved today from 139 Marine Parade to 81, so as to give Muz a full week to be out again in the sea air after six days illness with an influenza cold. Daddy went back alone to London this morning and you, Nannie and I came to these rooms, as our rooms at Mrs Brown's were engaged from today.

The Tsar has given a resolute reply to the German peace overture by exhorting his soldiers to fight on until Germany is defeated. He stated openly that the only terms on which Russia would make peace would be the restoration of German, Austrian and Russian Poland to a free kingdom and Russia to be mistress at Constantinople and the Dardanelles.

SUNDAY DECEMBER 31

The last day of the Old Year! What is 1917 going to bring? The Nation is agog with expectation! In a week or two we men and women, without limitation of age, will be told what the Country needs us to do to help win the War. The mobilisation of the Nation at large is essential to meet the great demands made on us all.

We are promised all sorts of drastic measures, beginning with a great restriction in railway traffic, and an increase of 50% on fares. Rather awkward for going to Wales! Then a meatless day per week is to be *de rigueur*. But who cares what we have to put up with if the war is won in this year of 1917, as predicted by Kitchener? For it was he who foretold a war lasting three years.

I am writing this at 10 pm in our sitting room at Brighton. Granny and I are sitting up to see the New Year in. Whether we can last out till midnight depends upon our fire! No more coals in the scuttle.

1917

1917 had a black dawn; it will have a darker night
The Nation, February 24, 1917

THURSDAY JANUARY 4

Uncle Tich is home on leave from the Front. His impression is that the Germans cannot hold out more than another six months or so, because they are starving. Our blockade is working thoroughly now and, as evidence of the food crisis in Germany, a friend of Daddy's, Axel Berg, half Russian and now in the Russian Government's employ in London, told him that he had just seen two Russian Officers who had recently escaped from a German internment camp at Wesel.

These men, unable to eat the dreadful loaf served for rations, handed it over regularly to the German officer in charge, for his young wife. This woman, overcome with gratitude at the Russian prisoners' generosity, came to thank them with tears in her eyes for this unexpected and priceless addition to her household fare. This shows to what extremity the German population is reduced.*

WEDNESDAY JANUARY 10

This morning I went with Daddy to see Uncle Tich off at Charing Cross on his way back after a week's leave. Aunt Clara was with him, and Granny. It is a most impressive sight to see one of these huge continental trains filled with officers and some nurses, going back to France.

The platform is thronged with wives and mothers, mostly silent and calm, and the men, many with the scarlet and gold tabs showing staff-rank, look so clean-cut and smart. It is incredible to think that we are so near to the fighting, even on this side of the Channel. Uncle Tich, starting at 12.30 today, expects to be at his quarters at Ypres by seven this evening.

Lloyd George has just returned from a Conference of Allied Ministers in Rome. He seems to have won the confidence and admiration of the French and Italians, the latter welcoming him with open arms in their Country. He is called in the Italian newspapers 'the Prime Minister of Europe'; his energy and personal magnetism seem to have kindled fresh confidence in all the Statesmen, and the results of the Conference are said to be most satisfactory.**

---

*   Food riots had been severe in thirty German cities and the deaths of 121,114 civilians in 1916 were attributed to starvation caused by the blockade. Martin Gilbert, *The Routledge Atlas of the First World War*, p. 77.

**   Not entirely for Lloyd George, who was unable to persuade his colleagues to agree to a concerted Allied offensive on the Italian Front.

THURSDAY JANUARY 11

The mud at the Front is unbelievable and men are sinking in it. Eugene Crombie has written a description of it to his mother. Frequently when a man is so engulfed in the mud, nothing can save him except this sort of rescue. Help is sent with several stretchers which are lowered on each side of the imprisoned victim. The rescuers then stand on the stretchers and pass a rifle under each arm of the victim (if the armpits are still free). The man is then hauled up by means of the rifles.

Eugene says that, added to wading through unknown depths of mud, there is the horrid sensation of treading on something soft and yielding which you know to be a corpse, or part of one, buried in the slush. Still, he adds, even this is nothing to seeing corpses half-gnawed by rats.

FRIDAY JANUARY 12

I am waiting to hear from Uncle Guy* whether the large consignment of toys I chose for him at Gamages' have reached the 2nd Army Headquarters yet. He runs a wonderful Canteen in connection with his Grenade School at Terdinghem and is going to give the schoolchildren of the village, whose fathers are all fighting in the French Army, a real English Christmas Tree. I spent £9 for him on presents ranging from 1/- to 2/6 for 135 boys and girls. The presents are splendid, and of course I included many models of guns, the celebrated French 75's** especially. As French schoolchildren don't get these sorts of treats as our English village children do, I think their delight will be voluble!

Today the great Victory Loan is issued, the loan that is to help us to win peace. By this evening already a hundred million bonds have been subscribed! I am buying £100 for £95, mostly the produce of the sale of the old Persian carpet my Father gave me when I married. I would never have parted with it had we had a house to show it in, but here it was getting very threadbare and it seemed a sin to keep it in such a bad condition.

Today the Allies' reply to the American Peace Note is published. It states in a dignified way what our aims are in this War and on what terms we will make peace when the time comes. It is a historical document of the greatest importance, along with Lloyd George's stirring speech. You can imagine, the effect his burning eloquence has upon us all, and upon our Allies who look to him as their main pillar and support. He has the gift of saying just the very thing which appeals most to the emotions of the moment.

---

*   Captain Guy Lee MC, 1st East Kents (the Buffs), was Commandant of a Grenade School behind the lines and had recently received the Order of Leopold from the Belgian Government.

**   Celebrated, because the highly effective 75mm gun, known as the 'Soixante Quinze', was the first effective quick firer in Europe and could fire 20 rounds a minute.

WEDNESDAY JANUARY 17

This afternoon I was at Mrs Gerald Paget's at one of her teas, and met Verena Barneby.
I lunched there yesterday alone with Mrs Paget, who likes discussing things with me.
We discussed *Raymond*, Sir Oliver Lodge's book on the revelations of his son Raymond
killed in the war and with whom Sir Oliver thinks he has established direct
communication, through a spiritualist medium. The book has created enormous
interest, because of Sir Oliver's position in the scientific world.

*Sir Oliver Lodge (1851–1940), a distinguished physicist and a leader in psychic research, was
elected a Fellow of the Royal Society at the age of 26. The recipient of honorary degrees from
thirteen universities, he was knighted in 1902. He became prominent in psychical research and
investigated the famous mediums, Mrs Piper and Eusapia Palladino. On the basis of evidence
he had observed, he concluded that the mind survives the dissolution of the body.*

*Lodge and his wife had six daughters and six sons. Their youngest son, Raymond, was killed
in action. After this, Lodge wrote* Raymond or Life after Death *(1916). In this he describes
the successful attempts of his family to contact his son via a medium. He devotes the third
section to his beliefs about the afterlife.*

*The diarist remains sceptical. Yet spiritualism did provide a possible lifeline and a flicker of
hope for some of the sorely bereaved. Another strong devotee of spiritualism was Sir Arthur
Conan Doyle, whose nephew was killed at the Ypres Salient.*

All those with leanings towards spiritualistic belief think that this book is going to
raise the science of communicating with the dead into general use. Spiritualism is to be
the general 'religion' in ten years or so. You, my son, will see whether this is verified.
I personally do not think so. I simply cannot believe that these communications are
anything more than the medium's imagination and good luck. I may be wrong in my
scepticism.

Just had a telephone message from Aunt Audrey whom we were expecting to dinner.
She's had a cable from Marseilles from Uncle Arthur* saying he's on his way home from
Alexandria. He has invented 'something splendid', a bomb or bullet proof item, and is
being sent home to the War Office to see about it, as the military authorities in Egypt
are 'frightfully keen on it'.

There is nasty news tonight in the report that ten British ships have been sunk by a
German Raider in the Atlantic. This recalls the feats performed by the *Emden*.

FRIDAY JANUARY 19

I am still trembling from the shock of a terrible concussion and distant roar which
occurred ten minutes ago. It seemed to me as if our roof were giving way, but it was only

---

*   Col Arthur Clive-Davis had been stationed in Alexandria since June 1915. He was the
     youngest of Georgina Lee's three brothers. See diary entry for 10 June 1915.

one explosion, over in a few seconds, so it can't be a Zeppelin blowing up munition works. Daddy went out into the street and spoke to two ladies who said that the whole sky was lit up like a red sunset and then came the roar.

I was alone writing in the drawing room and rushed to the Nursery to be ready for emergencies! Daddy had been sitting by your cot saying goodnight, when the window curtain was blown right into the room. The bathroom window flew open, while Nannie was in there and everyone's thought was Zeppelins! It may be a big gasometer blown up. It sounded more like that than a munitions factory.

SATURDAY JANUARY 20

It *was* a munitions factory, and a terrible disaster. The chemical factory at Silvertown, near Blackheath and Woolwich caught fire. A few minutes later all the explosives went off and the whole factory blew up, dragging in its ruin other neighbouring factories and whole rows of small houses close by. The death roll is very high though not as high as at first feared owing to the few minutes warning between the outbreak of fire and the explosion which enabled many of the workers to escape. Most of the casualties were local, but the effects of the explosion were felt all over London.

This shattering explosion took place at 6.40 pm, after fire had broken out in the melt-pot room of the Brunner, Mond & Co. factory at Crescent Wharf, on the Thames at West Silvertown, east London. Flanked to the east by an oil depot, with a residential area a quarter of a mile to the north, it was hardly an ideal site for the hazardous process of purifying TNT.

The afternoon shift of twenty, of whom nine were women, had come on at 2 pm. Two of them escaped, being in the ladies' lavatory, 120yd away from the TNT building, at the critical moment. The fire station was just opposite, but there was barely time for the firemen to start quenching the flames before the fire reached crude bags of TNT.

In faraway Hampstead, Caroline Playne heard 'the most uncanny loud noise that I ever heard . . . I turned to look and the whole sky to the east was lit up with glowing blood-red light'. The explosion was heard 50 miles away in Cambridge.* There were 73 fatalities, including two firemen. The fires raged throughout Saturday, when the scene was guarded by troops with fixed bayonets. All buildings within 400 yards were completely demolished, including the fire station and two schools. SS Italia, a ship in dock, was set on fire.**

The other day you called me to a shop window, Stewarts', where, in spite of the sugar difficulties, there was a gorgeous display of chocolates and sweets. 'Look at those lovely

* Dr Edwin Robertson, whose school had been destroyed by a direct hit, lived at West Ham. He recalls the explosion: 'Our house was lit by gas-mantles . . . the house shook and there was a terrific noise. Our gas-mantle shattered and we hurried to turn off the gas. A neighbour said "It's the Kaiser's birthday present!" We were not told it was an ammunition dump. As a little boy, I was excited.' Letter to the editor dated 22 February 2006.
** Frank Salisbury, former Borough Librarian for West Ham, describes this disaster in *After the Battle*, No. 18, 1977, Plaistow Press, London.

sweets, Mummy, will you get me some?' I replied that we had some barley sugar at home, and that we mustn't have expensive chocolates in war-time. 'When will war-time be over?' said you promptly, jumping to the crux of the question that is in all our hearts!

You hit upon another vexed question with your acute little reasoning powers.

- Mummy what does your newspaper say?
- It tells me how a horrible German submarine has just sunk ten of our British merchant ships.
- Why did the German submarine sink our English ships?
- Because the German submarine had torpedoes to fire and our ship had only passengers and cargo. (I explained what cargo meant.)
- Mummy, why hadn't the English ships any guns?

This is just one of the questions occupying the Admiralty.

The *Daily Mail* has started a campaign against Spiritualism. This movement is flourishing and gaining much wealth out of the sorrows of the bereaved. Though I have often criticised the *Daily Mail*, I will give it full credit for showing up the imposture of the professed spiritualists. Poor Sir Oliver Lodge, who at least is sincere, is blamed for supporting these impostors. His Book *Raymond* is dubbed 'half-a-guinea's worth of rubbish'.

MONDAY JANUARY 29

The submarine menace is now acute. These islands are faced with a real shortage of food. When Uncle Arthur arrived from Alexandria the other day he described having seen 17 German periscopes before landing at Marseilles and said 'I think England will be hungry soon'. The daily toll of ships is growing heavier,[*] and the Germans are seizing upon the U-boat as their last chance.

This submarine menace is now what we fear most. It really marks the death grapple between Britain and Germany.

This week there has been a great naval conference in London. As a result, the sea-campaign will be greatly intensified. Merchant ships will be armed, to give them a chance of defending themselves, as the Germans sink unarmed ships without the slightest compunction. The last Government is blamed for going to sleep after the successful war waged by Lord Fisher against the first submarine campaign in the Channel.

Today my little Belgian Depot moved from Roland Gardens to the 2nd floor of 115 Queen's Gate, much larger and more convenient premises. The women were very pleased and all helped to clean the three 'new' rooms. I shall feel much more the mistress there. At Roland Gardens we had to consider the authorities of the hostel, and our interests often clashed.

---

[*]   It would grow far worse. In the month of April alone, 168 merchant vessels were sunk or captured. The beneficial impact of the convoy system was not felt until May. R.H. Gibson, *The German Submarine War 1914–1918*.

WEDNESDAY JANUARY 31

The war is reaching a terribly acute stage. One feels strung up to expect anything dreadful at any moment. The Germans, maddened and desperate by their internal situation and the prospect of starvation, intend to wage a war with their submarines beside which their infamous exploits so far will pale into insignificance. They will sink every ship on sight, neutral as well as enemy, which enters the War Zone.

THURSDAY FEBRUARY 1

The German Government has announced two things today which stun us all. First they state that Britain has used her hospital ships frequently as transports, for men, munitions and supplies (lie no. 1). Second, as Germany has frequently drawn the attention of the British Government to this breach of Conventions (lie no. 2), her submarine commanders have orders to sink on sight all hospital ships. This new campaign starts today. If anything can surpass this in ignominy, I should like to hear.

I have an intense feeling that we are in the death-throes with Germany. If she fails in this, she has played her last card. Will you ever be able to realise what the strain of these days is? Yet what an intense exultation we feel, silent and unspoken that things have come to this last great struggle. The whole of civilised Europe depends for its salvation upon our English ships and our sailors, God bless them.

Yesterday as 6 o'clock struck, I, wishing to introduce the vexed subject of bedtime as pleasantly as I could, said 'Harry, what do you think about bed?' 'I don't think about it', was your reply.

FRIDAY FEBRUARY 2

Today the German Government has declared war upon all neutral shipping. U Boats have orders to sink on sight any and every ship of whatsoever nationality in these zones. The German statement declares that no ships will be allowed to ply between England and America save one passenger liner per week, with these restrictions:

1. *The port for this one liner is to be Falmouth.*
2. *The liner must leave New York on Sundays only and leave Falmouth again on one specified day.*
3. *The ship must carry passengers only.*
4. *She must fly a special flag, as detailed by the Germans.*

This impudent declaration has aroused great anger and stupor in America. It is thought very probable that Count Bernstorf, German Ambassador at Washington, will be given his passport.

The impudence of it all is aggravated by the German statement that the new marine war will begin 5 days from today. There is no time for Americans to get home from Europe. Holland seems to be terribly upset and has at once cancelled all the sailings for her liners.

The war zones of German submarines.

SATURDAY FEBRUARY 3

Today we are rationed for the first time! The rationing will affect only 3 comestibles so far:

Meat	2½ lbs weekly per head
Bread	4 lbs weekly per head
Sugar	¾ lb weekly per head

We do not exceed this liberal allowance already, at least we have not lately. As we are seven in the house, I reckon we can have weekly:

13 Loaves of 2 lbs each, with
1½ lb Flour for puddings etc.
½ lb Flour for Cake

As for sugar, for weeks past I had imposed a limit of 5lbs for the household. Now I see I can use another ¼ lb, *if I can get it!* It has been very difficult to procure sugar at all, most grocers absolutely refusing to supply any. But my dear Army and Navy Stores allow a certain fixed proportion on grocery orders.*

The meat will be more difficult as the 2½lbs include bone. It includes bacon for breakfast and ham so it will mean a great deal of goodwill and patriotic loyalty on the part of women, because these rations are at present left to our honour to enforce. There is to be no system of tickets yet, as in Germany. But the Government will resort to compulsion if the country does not respond.

This afternoon Daddy and I had a delightful time with you in the Park on the Serpentine, which is hard as a rock. Saturday afternoons are Daddy's one chance of being out with you. So we all marched up, Nannie wheeling the pram, and had a most healthy, amusing afternoon on the ice, making you slide and run and you were 'so incited' you kept saying, and laughing all the time. The Serpentine has not been frozen over for 20 years.

SUNDAY FEBRUARY 4

The clash of great events becomes louder every day. Today President Wilson has broken off diplomatic relations with Germany. Count Bernstorf has been given his passports, and W. Gerard, U.S. Ambassador in Berlin, has been recalled. Bernstorf's remarks on receiving his passport were tearful – 'I expected as much; I do not see what else America could do. How am I going to get home?' With the Atlantic and Channel guarded by our patrols, and our new minefield area, I don't see how he **is** to get home except by our courtesy!

Every American Consul in Germany, Austria, Bulgaria and Turkey has been instructed to shut up shop and suspend all work connected with enemy interests. These are to be taken over by the Spanish Government.

MONDAY FEBRUARY 5

President Wilson has made a firm stand at last and a spirited speech to Congress. If Germany carries into effect her threat of indiscriminate submarine warfare, Congress

---

*   The sugar crisis grew worse. On one day in April, stocks of sugar were sufficient for only four days' consumption. Llewellyn Woodward, *Great Britain and the War of 1914–1918*, p. 510.

will be asked to confer on the President all powers necessary to protect American interests.

The cold is more intense than ever and last evening we had a heavy fall of snow. But it did not deter Daddy and me from walking to Ovington Gardens for supper with Muz. Everyone walks nowadays and scarcely anyone contemplates getting a cab at night. What an extraordinary change from the first 2 or 3 years of my married life, when I was so spoilt by having a car lent me very often, for afternoon or evening use! But it is strange how easily one slips from one curtailment of comfort and ease to another without a regret.

I have already organised the household supplies according to the War Rationing which starts today. I have a book which I shall take down each morning to the kitchen when giving orders and shall inscribe the net weight of bread and meat consumed each day. The allowance of sugar must be weighed out for the week and must suffice.

SUNDAY FEBRUARY 11

We are doing very well on our rations and I don't think we need pinch ourselves too much yet. Cakes must vanish from the tea-table, except very occasionally. America has not yet declared war, but is calling for a million recruits. The Ambassadors are on their way home.

Meanwhile the daily toll of ships sunk, neutral and British, is very high. 12, 14, 16 ships a day, i.e. up to 32,000 tons daily, are being lost. Measures are being taken to fight down the submarine peril. Destroyers are being greatly increased in number to act as convoys and 'sea-lanes' are to be established.

For sheer courage and resource, nothing can beat the British Merchant Navy. Starting on a voyage, say to America or Cape Town and never knowing at what instant death may pounce upon them without warning, by mine or torpedo. Yet no sailings are cancelled. Business goes on as usual. The tradition of the sea is so ingrained in the breed, that these new perils do not turn our sailors from their purpose. As a contrast, I could not help noticing the advertisements of the Dutch shipping companies, cancelling sailings of liners etc.

Today, Charlie Finnis, Daddy's old friend, came to lunch with his bride of one month's standing, to say goodbye before leaving for France this week. He only got his Commission a month ago and he is already being sent over. This shows you the times we live in. A subaltern of 44 with one month's experience of the Army!

TUESDAY FEBRUARY 13

The Game Laws of England! They too have had to make way for the necessities of England at war. Not only is it illegal to feed game birds on corn or maize, but game is no longer protected. Anybody can shoot down the pheasants and any other game on the land of which he is tenant. This is partly to use all available food, and also to prevent these birds eating the precious crops. Some few weeks ago it was the shooting of all hunting packs, to save their food; and naturally too of foxes to prevent them eating poultry.

I have just finished my frugal tea all alone in the drawing-room. Formerly I should have felt disgracefully mean – a small rack of toast, the loaf (no cut bread and butter), a little butter and jam, no vestige of cake, scone or buns to offer the casual visitor. The meanness now lies in purchasing these luxuries. I feel dishonest at going into the cake shops, unless I am expecting someone for certain. The funny thing is that this economy is not for the sake of saving one's pocket. We have no longer to think in pennies or shillings, but in ounces and pounds. Whatever I can save in terms of bread and flour in my household, leaves the more for those who mainly live on these two essentials. Shall we ever outlive this urgency of economising the food stuffs for the sake of everybody?

WEDNESDAY FEBRUARY 14

There is a first indescribable little feeling of Spring in the air today. Though the wind is still bitterly east, the sun shone and the atmosphere was clear. Have we ever longed for Spring all of us, as we have this winter? This tense expectation of great decisions to come keeps all our minds fixed on the moment when the great advance will begin on all fronts.

Sir Edward Carson,* First Lord of the Admiralty, in an interview with a French correspondent stated that every brain in the British Navy is devoting himself night and day to solving the submarine menace.

MONDAY FEBRUARY 19

Last week we overstepped our meat ration by 3lbs. I found this out this morning by weighing what was left in the larder from the stock that came into the house last week. But it was all on account of a piece of ham and of a chicken of which weighed a good deal – and all bone compared to the solid meat on them! So this won't occur again. But I felt like a criminal, on balancing my ration book accounts.

FRIDAY FEBRUARY 23

Today the new food restrictions have burst upon us like a bombshell! As I walked into Mrs Byrne's drawing-room to tea this afternoon, I found her and 3 astounded ladies poring over the evening paper announcing the drastic measures which Lloyd George's Government have imposed, 'to avoid disaster', says Lloyd George in his speech.

These measures should have been taken 2 years ago. They are now absolutely essential. We are to give up importing tea, coffee and cocoa. Whether this applies to Indian and Ceylon teas is not yet clear. The supply of food in the country is lower than it has ever been. Any available ships are now required to transport munitions to Russia, unless the Allies are to suffer a breakdown in that quarter also.

---

* From 1910 Carson had been leader of the Irish Unionists in the House of Commons. As First Lord of the Admiralty he did not see the value of the convoy strategy. Sir Eric Geddes succeeded him in July 1917.

All this I learn in a few moments at Mrs Byrne's sitting disconsolately behind the tea, now a prohibited luxury. There are other restrictions, but these hit the housewife hardest. For a long time past, since the war started in fact, I have kept no stores in the house except for a week's requirements; and if everybody did the same it would be much fairer. But there is a great deal of hoarding going on. Lily who does my weekly shopping at the Army and Navy, tells me that the grocery department has been besieged, for weeks past, with women ordering in large stocks of goods.

I came home and found you unconscious of the seriousness of the situation, but your sharp little eyes were riveted on me as I was telling Nannie the news. Later, when we were having a game, I asked you to be porter and carry a sack of tea into my house. You shook your head and said 'I can't do that; there's no tea in England, the Germans have sunk our ships'.

Well, these hardships are a pinprick compared to the sufferings of France and Belgium.

SUNDAY FEBRUARY 25

The tea scare is not so pressing as we thought at first. A certain amount of Indian and Ceylon Tea is still allowed in, but none from China or Java as there are still large stocks in the country, as there are also of coffee.

The worst announcement from submarine warfare came last night; the Germans have sunk seven Dutch liners which were proceeding all together on their way from America filled with cargoes for Holland. They had been taken into Falmouth to be examined by us but were allowed to proceed on an appeal being made by the Dutch Government. Soon after leaving Falmouth they were all attacked and sunk without warning. 200 of the seamen were landed at Portsmouth. These 7 ships, with 2 British vessels also sunk, make a total of 40,000 tons of shipping lost *in one day*.

MONDAY FEBRUARY 26

Broadstairs and Margate were shelled at midnight last night by enemy destroyers. They bombarded the towns for about ten minutes, doing very little damage but killing one woman and one child and seriously wounding two children.

We are retrieving our disaster in Mesopotamia by degrees. We have just retaken Kut, where General Townshend and his force surrendered last year, after ¾ of his troops had died from starvation and sickness.

At last the official figures of the Great War Loan have been stated by Bonar Law* in the House today, and they far exceed the first rough estimates. A thousand million pounds of new money have been subscribed and there are 8 million subscribers.

---

*   Andrew Bonar Law (1858–1923), Chancellor of the Exchequer, might have succeeded Asquith as Prime Minister. On the same day as the latter had resigned (5 December), George V invited him to form an administration. Unable to gain sufficient support, Bonar Law advised the King to call on Lloyd George.

MONDAY MARCH 5

In a fortnight's time we are leaving this dear little house in which we have spent the first 7 years of our married life. But I can't help loving the new house we are going to, nor taking delight in its doing-up, with its fresh paint and paper, new baths etc. Until the house is ready, you are going with Nannie to spend a month with Pat Talbot at Treholford, near Brecon.

You are getting a funny little creature. This morning at breakfast, you came into the dining room carrying a big box of bricks. Daddy said 'Shut the door, Harry'. Whereupon you answered jovially 'Give me a chance, Daddy', and deposited your load on the table before complying. I don't know where you learn the grown-up expressions you come out with so aptly.

THURSDAY MARCH 8

We have plunged into winter again! 9 degrees of frost and a biting east wind. The wind has been east for months now and we don't seem able to shake off this worst of all winters.

The photos of my Belgian Surgical Depot have just arrived. I had them taken at the request of M. de Vigneron, Secretary of the Belgian Red Cross. He wished to insert one in the big printed report for 1916, but they gave up the idea as it would have meant doing the same for all organisations working for the Red Cross. However, all the workers were delighted. These photos are to be scattered broadcast among the Belgians fighting and the relations of my women.

FRIDAY MARCH 9

The results of the Commission on the Dardanelles Expedition are published today. The document holds 3 people mainly responsible for the defeat: Mr Asquith, Lord Kitchener and Winston Churchill. The Prime Minister, because he was too weak. Kitchener, because he consulted none of his Staff and took upon himself labours that were beyond one man. Thirdly, Churchill because he overrode the scruples of his naval advisers, or ignored them. Fisher is also blamed for having held his tongue when he should have spoken, and for having given only half-hearted assent to the measures taken. The findings of the Commission are signed by Lord Cromer, lately dead, and among others Lord Justice Pickford.

This chapter is one of the most disastrous in our history. In spite of the unrivalled heroism of the Anzacs and other British Forces, the expedition was a complete failure and a great blow to our prestige. The estimated Allied dead were 46,000.

MONDAY MARCH 12

Baghdad has fallen into our hands! This is the first decisive success we have won in the East since the war began. It will go some way to re-establishing our military prestige after the Gallipoli disaster.

Only last week the Hungarian Premier, Count Andrassy, was boasting of the new line which would be Germany's railway by the end of the war, the 'Antwerp–Baghdad Railway'!

FRIDAY MARCH 16

Astounding news from Russia today. The Tsar has abdicated. The Duma has asserted itself, carrying with it the Army and most of the aristocracy. The Tsar's brother the Grand Duke Michael, a reformer, has been made Regent for his young nephew, the Tsarewitch. Axel Berg, a half Russian friend of Daddy's, told him today that when the news came through yesterday to the Russian Embassy in London, the staff shouted Hurrah! – for joy and relief.

Now the War will be vigorously prosecuted, as the Provisional Government is entirely at one with the Allies. So, in 2 or 3 days, the Revolution which has been so long coming has at last come swiftly, and the nation has taken a leap forward of two centuries.

This is our last night in this little house and so the first 7 years of our married life ends tomorrow. We are going to Granny for a few weeks till the new house is ready.

MONDAY MARCH 19

The Russian Revolution is calming down. Meanwhile the Provisional Government of moderates is doing its utmost to preserve order. But there is much anxiety owing to a small violent section of extremists. They are preaching anarchy and seem to be gaining ground among the people.

MONDAY MARCH 26

At 12 o'clock Granny and I were at our post at Brunswick Gardens, waiting for the first vanload of our furniture to arrive. But it never turned up till 3.30, and in a snow blizzard. We were frozen with our long wait in the cold house and angry at the extraordinary dilatoriness of the removal men. But my anger was quickly disarmed at the sight of the 4 decrepit old fellows, knock-kneed and splay-footed. They could barely struggle under the chests and chairs they had to carry.

These men are all that the National Service Call has left available for private citizens, indeed we are lucky to have *them*! We shouldn't have, had we not made a contract with Shoolbred's last December.* Now we hear that the Government is going to stop all house removals. The same also with house painting and decorating. The Government requires for national work all men up to 60. It takes these poor fellows a

---

* James Shoolbred of Tottenham Court Road was one of the finest cabinet makers in London. In 1914, Col A. Shoolbred mobilised the Queens Westminster Rifles – one of the first TA Regiments to go to France – using horses and furniture vans belonging to his own depository.

whole day to move just one van load and this only a very modest sized one! I gave them each some money for a good tea, for it was snowing and bitterly cold.

Daddy has brought back word that the whole East coast is strongly guarded, men thick in every trench, so evidently an invasion is expected. I am glad you are off to Breconshire! I think the West of England is safer for babes. But how exciting it all is.

TUESDAY MARCH 27

The meaning of all this was nothing but a great test for mobilising in case of invasion. It all worked perfectly, as the secret was well-kept, and everyone believed in the reality of the event.

I have spent all the afternoon at Brunswick Gardens superintending the unloading of one more van. It is interminable and it isn't over yet. Tomorrow it will still be going on.

I retire to tea, late in the afternoon, exhausted, to Derry and Toms. But I can hardly enjoy the refreshment, feeling strongly that all afternoon tea ought to be done away with. One really does feel the food restrictions very much now. Voluntary though they are, we all endeavour to eat as little as we possibly can. Any cakes or luxuries containing the barest pinch of sugar are strictly taboo.

TUESDAY MARCH 28

Today Muz received a present of 2lbs potatoes from Sybil Wynne-Jones, who is the fortunate possessor of a small supply from her own garden. As Muz hasn't had potatoes in the house for some weeks, we valued enormously our one baked potato each at dinner. As potatoes are a necessity to the poor, we do not attempt to buy them now, much to the disappointment of the servants who can't understand dinner without potatoes!

SUNDAY APRIL 1

Winter has set in again. For the last 3 mornings we have awakened to find the roofs all white, though the snow disappears again by midday

This evening we hear that fires have been seen in St Quentin, and that the Germans are destroying the town before evacuating it. These ruthless barbarians are systematically devastating every village, town and area of cultivated land as they retire. The whole of the invaded part of France is a heap of ruins. Trees, fruit-trees especially, have been hacked through, just to kill them.

There is a campaign started by the Press* and by public opinion to get the Allied countries to declare officially that they will never treat for Peace with the Hohenzollerns. Now that Tsardom has gone for ever, every obstacle has vanished. The German people must be made to understand that war will be carried on until the Hohenzollerns are routed and overthrown.

* Especially by the Northcliffe Press.

MONDAY APRIL 2

Heavy, heavy snow has been falling all the morning and the streets are thick. No sound of traffic is to be heard. What a winter! It has been relentless since last October, always damp and bitterly cold.

THURSDAY APRIL 5

America has at last declared a State of War between herself and Germany. After months of repeated provocation, Mr. Wilson, the President, has stated in a fine speech to Congress, the principles for which America as the champion of liberty must draw the sword:

> *We are not entering this war for selfish motives. We seek no increase of territory, no indemnity to compensate us for the heavy sacrifices we shall have to make.*

It is a wonderful time in which we live, and I am thankful I was born to see the dawn of the new era of universal freedom. President Wilson has set this entry into War on very high ideals.[*]

As a start, America is about to seize all the German shipping in her ports, which includes 80 large vessels and liners. One of these, the *Vaterland*, is the largest liner afloat, 55,000 tons.

Uncle Romer came back from the Front last night on 10 days leave. He slept here. He has given Muz and me each a glazed tile, unbroken, which he picked up among the ruins at Ypres. It is a brand new one, highly-glazed, out of a new house only just completed when war broke out, and now a mass of debris. I am going to have it encircled in a piece of ebony, to prevent it being broken, and shall just have the word **Ypres** engraved on it.

EASTER SUNDAY APRIL 8

A bright but very cold day. We have had snow every morning on awaking this last week. Yet, as we advanced our clocks one hour, 'Summer Time' begins today. With this new setting of clocks, it is still bright daylight when we dress for dinner.

TUESDAY APRIL 10

Splendid news today of our British advance. This time the advance has been North of Arras and towards Lens, the coal district. If only we regain the coal-mines for France, that will be an immense gain, provided the barbarians don't destroy them first.

---

[*]   Earlier, there was a joke going the rounds about President Wilson. It was said that, if he ever went to war with Germany, he would probably go to war with Great Britain as well – to preserve his declared policy of strict impartiality!

THURSDAY APRIL 12

Today was Angela Monier-Williams' wedding to Major Wolley. Muz and I drove down to Chessington in Minna's car, our last drive for many a day. All private cars are to be stopped from this month, no petrol being allowed for civilians.

Also, the scant food rations we now live upon were set aside for this occasion. There was a display of bread and butter, sandwiches and cakes such as we have not seen for many a day. No sugar-iced cakes though, and the wedding cake of the simplest description. It was procured by licence, I suppose, as one must now have a special licence to obtain a wedding-cake.

Talking of food conditions, what do you think of this? Minna and her little family received on Easter Monday, as an Easter Egg offering from Kathleen Wason, 4 large potatoes from her garden, one for each of the family! We have not eaten potatoes for weeks.

SATURDAY APRIL 14

Hengwrt

Daddy, Granny and I travelled down to Hengwrt today for ten days' holiday. Cader Idris covered with snow, but bright sun from Shrewsbury onwards. Train crowded, and fares increased 50% to discourage travelling. Our fares cost us each £2. 16. 0 instead of 37/-. The rolling-stock has been sent to France in great quantities. We passed some trains laden with rails and timber-props for France for strategic railroads, trench supports and dug-outs.

I had a shock in the train! When we reach Bala, I found one of my pearl and diamond earrings had dropped off. As Daddy had given them to me when you were born, I loved them more than anything else. We ransacked the carriage to no avail. Then remembering I had jumped out of the train to stretch myself at Ruabon, I knew I must have dropped it there. Daddy got hold of the station master and bribed him to telephone to Ruabon and send any message on to the Dolgelly stationmaster. I arrived at Dolgelly with fear and misgiving, but the first person we saw was one of the friendly porters carrying a telegram to say the earring had been found, slightly damaged, on the platform. Imagine my delight!

Yesterday I had a most interesting little interview at the HQ of the Belgian Red Cross. I had previously had a letter asking me to go there, as a certain decoration was to be instituted by the Belgian King, for those ladies who have given their services voluntarily to the Belgian Red Cross. I, as head of the Surgical Depot was *toute désignée* (specially marked out) for this honour, and I was begged to go to the Headquarters to suggest any other deserving individuals working with me.

At 4 pm I was ushered into the office of the Chief Secretary, W. Maeterlinck, cousin of the writer.* He received me courteously and explained that the Belgian Government

---

*   Maurice Maeterlinck (1862–1949), sometimes called 'the Belgian Shakespeare', wrote a number of highly successful plays, of which *Pelleas and Mélisande* is perhaps the best known. In 1911, Maeterlinck was awarded the Nobel Prize for Literature.

wished to express their gratitude, first to *ladies* (adding that Belgians are always occupied with ladies first and foremost. I replied that this amiable little weakness was well-known to us!). The men would be attended to later, for the devotion with which they had worked for the wounded and suffering of Belgium.

The Government wished specially to distinguish us English women who had worked as whole-heartedly as the Belgian ladies. But they were anxious to keep the Order as select as possible. It would be called after their Queen, *Ordre Elisabeth*, for the women recipients of the order, and would be *un souvenir de la Grande Guerre*. I replied suitably, expressing my appreciation of the honour conferred and the great happiness it had been for me to do the little I had done for Belgium!

The only other person there entitled to the distinction was Miss Simes. She is the lady in Boston who collected the £1,000 from American people, who have kept our industry going for fully another 12 months. I don't know whether there will be an official investiture of the Order. If there is, what fun it will be.

TUESDAY APRIL 17

We have at last started reprisals for the German outrages against our hospital ships, two of which were sunk this last fortnight. One was empty of wounded, but 9 nurses and 36 of the medical staff were drowned, while the other one, sunk in the Channel, was laden with wounded. They were safely transferred on stretchers to rescue ships. But imagine the horror of this for helpless men.

Having given the German Government ample warning about the consequences of repeating any such outrages, we have started reprisals. A big squadron of air-machines, French and English, flew over Freiburg and dropped a number of bombs.

WEDNESDAY APRIL 18

President Wilson is exhorting every community in America to do its duty to the great Allied cause. First, all the resources of the Country are to be employed to produce food for the Allies. 'Hundreds and hundreds of food ships must be sent to Europe, submarines or no submarines. If they are sent to the bottom, others must take their place. The supply of food is of supreme importance. Every acre of land must produce *and not only during the war, but for some time after peace is declared, the world must look to America for its food supplies.*'

In solemn, calm words he addresses all munitions makers and railway suppliers, to take their place in the great Army of 'International Service'. He adjures them all not to seek great profits, but to work only for fair remuneration.

The bread question is getting more and more serious. We are all begged now to save one more pound of flour per week, making 2lbs flour our ration. We can eat one slice of bread at breakfast, but generally have a half-slice. We make up with oatcake and barley scones. Yesterday we went into Dolgelly for an entertainment. On the way Mrs Holland passed us in her car (she is finishing up her remaining slender stock of petrol). As she picked up two of our party to give them a lift, Aunt Beatrice asked her and her two friends to come in to tea.

They were so apologetic in accepting, because of course it means that, if more people drop in, there is less food to go round! Nobody ever eats as much as they would have done in former days and food is now the main topic of conversation. How can we find substitutes for the sugar craving most of us have?

FRIDAY APRIL 20

Today is the first spring day we have had, bright blue sky, hot sun, though cold wind. The first time we have felt the warmth of sunshine for 6 interminable months. I spent the day at Glyn, helping Aunt Ethel to dig her flower beds, as gardeners are scarce. Immediately on arriving I had to go into the kitchen to show Aunt Ethel's cook how to make a particular kind of oatcake I have just learnt to make. We are so dependent now on oatcake, to replace bread.

MONDAY APRIL 23

The Germans have torpedoed two more full hospital ships in the Channel, the *Lanfranc* and the *Donegal*, with a loss of 80 lives. They were escorted too, and this fact makes it more serious than ever. Up to the present our escorted ships have gone safely across for nearly 3 years. On the *Lanfranc* were 167 German wounded prisoners. Of these 152 were saved. Those who were drowned lost their lives because in their frenzy and fright they tried to jump from the doomed ship to the rescue ships that came hurrying into the scene.

There were two or three Germans only whose conduct stands out in a better light. One prisoner, a brigadier general, said to a British officer sadly and quietly after the explosion 'I like not my country for this'. If he returns to Germany, he will bear witness that we do not use our hospital ships for transporting military material.

TUESDAY APRIL 24

It is curious to see this country, hitherto given up to sheep-pasture, now ploughed over everywhere, for potatoes, oats and, wherever possible, wheat. They have even started a womens' plot on the Jelf-Reveleys property, where the ladies of Dolgelly, even Nelly Enthoven and Aunt Ethel, go, dig and raise vegetables to supply Mary Richards' hospital up at Caerynwch.

WEDNESDAY APRIL 25

Aunt Beatrice and I are just going to Caerynwch to see the house transformed into a hospital, with Mary Richards as Commandant. She has 14 wounded there. But all these private hospitals may now be interfered with, since the wounded from France are to be mostly tended in new hospitals in France.

The submarine peril having become grave in the Channel, hitherto quite immune, the hospital ships are being singled out for outrage. A great appeal has been made to all doctors of military age in Great Britain to go out for medical service. Those doctors who are beyond military age are asked to replace in England the younger doctors who will leave the country.

THURSDAY APRIL 26

3 Ovington Gardens

Have just returned from Hengwrt with Daddy to Magna's house. She told us the dreadful news that dear young Eugene Crombie died of wounds on April 23. It is too terrible. I am stunned. His mother adored him and is distracted. When I think of her sweetness to you and to all the children she has befriended and loves having about her, and now she is robbed of her own son.

John Eugene Crombie
CAPTAIN
4th Battn. Gordon Highlanders.

BORN APRIL 30, 1896

FELL IN BATTLE APRIL 23, 1917.
'Took his fill of music, joy of thought, and seeing, Came,
and stayed, and went, nor ever ceased to smile.'

R.L.S.

Today in the train, reading the terrible fighting going on now, on the Arras front, I thought of Eugene and wondered how he could escape. His tunic had just been sent home to have the Captain's 3 pips sewn on. He had just been promoted and would have been 21 on 30th April.

FRIDAY APRIL 27

Saw poor Minna this evening. It was piteous. She read me Eugene's last letter written 2 days before he was killed, giving a description of 'a bit of real hell' which he had experienced the night before. 300 men under him, in a deep railway cutting, 150 mules bringing ammunition; the men tripping up in the dark over bits of wire, over broken sleepers, the mules lashing out in their terror and the continuous roar of shells bursting all round, the ground whipped by a rain of shrapnel fragments. High explosive shells dropping about, one of them blew 15 of his men to bits etc. . . .

The whole picture was terrible in its intensity. This is the life our men are living now during the Arras battle, and, two days after this particular episode, he received his own death-wounds.

SUNDAY MAY 6

38 Brunswick Gardens

These last 8 or 10 days have been such busy ones getting into the house, that I have lost all count of time. A quick glance through the papers is all I have had time for, and yet the news is serious enough to keep one's mind busy with nothing else.

The food question becomes daily more acute. More and more shipping is being destroyed by the German U Boats.* It seems really to be a race now as to whether we can bring Germany to her knees before we get starved out. When one asks for any particular item in the shops, one is told 'none to be had'. Cereals of all sorts, macaroni, raisins etc. are 3 or 4 times the old price.

WEDNESDAY MAY 16

There has been a strike of motor buses for 3 days now, and any travelling is done by underground. Imagine the crush there. Not a bus to be seen. The omnibus men, striking for higher pay, are defiant, and care nothing for the terrible dislocation of traffic, or the interference to the munition-makers who can't get to their work.

Then there is a huge strike going on among engineers for war work. 250,000 men out. In fact the state of unrest in the country is very great. The Government dare not raise their hand, for fear of provoking riots. There will be an awful upheaval after the war among the working classes. They are very unsettled now, and one constantly hears rude remarks as to what 'they' mean to do, and how 'they will be on top then' etc.

*This strike, which lasted from 30 April to 19 May, started at the textile machinery works of Messrs Tweedale and Smalley, Castleton, a firm which had introduced a large number of women for shell work. Several men refused to instruct the women in the use of grinding machines. They were at once discharged. By 5 May, 60,000 men were idle in Lancashire. Though press censorship kept the news of the strike out of the papers, by the end of the week the strike was general in London and thousands of men were out at Sheffield, Rotherham, Coventry and Derby. It was estimated that 1,500,000 working days were lost through this disastrous strike and on 18 July, Dr Addison, the Minister of Munitions, resigned.** He was succeeded by Winston Churchill.*

---

*   In the single month of April 1917, 373 British and neutral ships were sunk.

**   For a full account of the industrial strife caused by the Dilution Bill and the introduction of 'munitionnettes', see *History of the Ministry of Munitions*, vol. VI, Part I, *Manpower and Dilution, 1916–1918*, published in 1922.

THURSDAY MAY 24

The Americans have sent their first direct aid to us in the shape of a fleet of destroyers to help protect our shipping. The enemy are at last beginning to lose a good many U Boats.

Nevertheless there is no loosening of the strain on our food supplies. Articles become more and more limited and another British troopship has been sunk, with a loss of 413 lives.* Think of the sensation such an event would cause in ordinary times! Now we only murmur 'How dreadful! Yet so accustomed are we to hearing of horrors in one form or another that we grow quite indifferent. There is a limit to one's expressions of horror, but no limit to the horrors themselves, for what can be worse that the daily slaughter at the Front?

But the consciousness of it all is never absent, all the same, and it makes us extraordinarily lacking in vivacity or spontaneity and curiously silent. I am conscious now of not wanting to go out to see friends, or to have them here. I have suddenly nothing to say to them, and I find myself uncomfortable, realising that I am being dull and uncompanionable.

There is so much on one's mind nowadays. The housekeeping has become such a formidable, lengthy business. I go out and do my household shopping every morning myself, pay cash for everything, as this is a great check on expenditure. Bananas have become unprocurable, and with oranges at 3d each and small apples 4d, it is difficult to obtain fruit. The import of all these foreign items has practically ceased. We never realised till now how England's market supplies were so dependent on foreign lands.

THURSDAY MAY 31

Just a week ago since last I wrote, and again my chief preoccupation is how to make my housekeeping allowance last the week! I've had £6 this week, with still 2 days expenses to incur and my purse is empty! The money simply flies and yet I get only the barest necessity. I now buy each day the needs of the day only, with nothing left over so that no waste is possible.

The price of meat is awful. Mutton 2/- lb and Beef nearly as much. If only the prices of everything were not double and treble what they were, and our household so much increased from what it was when we first married – 4 servants instead of 2, and you, my son, a most substantial source of expenditure.

On Sunday we went to Church to hear the King's Proclamation. He exhorted his people to economise on flour and other supplies from the country. We are only to use flour for bread, so as to defeat the enemy's intention of starving us out.

There has been a dreadful air-raid over Folkestone. 16 German aeroplanes invaded the town on Saturday last, when the people were at their busiest, between 5 and 6 o'clock doing their shopping for the Whitsun week-end. Bombs were dropped on

---

*   The *Transylvania* sank in the Gulf of Genoa on 4 May.

Tontine Street, the narrow part of the old town. About 80 people were killed, mostly women, but also 26 children.

Muz had a letter from Mrs Latham Brown. Her husband had just gone to post letters when the bombs began to drop. She rushed out to get him and saw him coming towards her. Then a bomb crashed through the house next but one to theirs, wrecking it and burying the cook in the debris. Another bomb fell near them in the street, so they ran for shelter into the nearest house. It seems blood was flowing in Tontine Street in the most dreadful way, horses and people being blown to bits.

SUNDAY JUNE 3

Yesterday I took Harry to Hyde Park, Nannie having taken Patience to the Zoo.* There was a great crowd gathered there. The King was holding an Investiture in the open, awarding VC's to war heroes. There were 5 aeroplanes circling over the Park all the afternoon.

Last night, when both you and Patience were in bed in the night nursery, Nannie heard Patience reproving you for something. 'I'll kill you Patience if you say that', said you. 'Then you'll be hanged for murder', said P. 'What does that mean, hanged for murder?' asked you. Then Patience explains 'You see those pictures on the wall? well, you'd hang just like that'. You said no more.

FRIDAY JUNE 8

There is a tremendous fresh offensive just started by Haig south of Ypres, which has resulted in the British capturing the great ridge, Messines. The attack began yesterday at dawn, and opened with the explosion of gigantic mines under the German positions, which we had tunnelled and laid a year ago.

The explosion was timed for just after 3 am. At 3 o'clock, Lloyd George, staying at Walton Heath, was awakened by his order, to hear the battle begin. At 3.10 am the earth shook and the dull roar was distinctly heard all over the South-East of England.

The explosions were followed by a hurricane bombardment, and the positions were all taken. Sir D. Haig says in his despatch that the enemy aircraft were prevented from taking part in the subsequent action by our airmen.

SATURDAY JUNE 9

The war would probably be over this year if those wretched Russians hadn't let us down. Not only are they doing nothing on their Front, but their Socialists and workmen's delegates, and a large part of the Russian Army are in favour of immediate peace with Germany.

---

*   Patience was the daughter of Baynes and Ethel Badcock, Georgina's youngest sister.

WEDNESDAY JUNE 13

Nannie has just brought you back from the Park at 12.30 looking white and scared. She asked whether I hadn't heard the raid? 'What raid?' I replied, 'Didn't you hear the bombs, Madam, and the guns?' Well, I had heard two faint booms and one aeroplane droning, but as they are always practising the guns, I hadn't paid the slightest attention, but went on with the blinds I was making. It shows how little one can be aware in London of what goes on only a mile or two away. There has been a very bad raid; 10 children killed and 50 injured in one school, altogether 145 killed and injured in the City alone.

Nannie was sitting sewing under the trees in the Park with you asleep in the pram, when the guns began. Soon the reports grew louder and more rapid, then came sharp cracks overhead and the droning of engines. Other nurses took the alarm and scurried off in all directions with their children, but Nannie, very frightened, crept under the thickest tree with you, still fast asleep. A park keeper came by, and Nannie asked what the guns were firing at. He replied 'The Germans have come over and are dropping bombs.' In 10 minutes the battle subsided and she came home.

Then Daddy rang me up at 2 to ask if we were safe. At Westminster they could see the shrapnel bursting in the sky beneath the aeroplanes. At 12.30 he went to the Registry at St Paul's and found that one bomb had fallen only 200 yards from his office. He saw the roadway broken up and the police clearing the debris.

Our aeroplanes were hot in pursuit and I expect tomorrow we shall hear that some of the Taubes have been brought down. Everybody is very calm about the raid, nobody here takes much notice and the streets were black with sightseers during the raid.

A big piece of news today: King Tino of Greece* has at last been made to abdicate by the Allied Powers. The masterstroke which has forced the abdication was the seizure by France of the Thessaly crops, to be distributed throughout Greece impartially, instead of Tino seizing them for the use of his partisans alone.

Now he is helpless. Greece won't have the Crown Prince either, as he is the tool of the Kaiser like Tino. The Venizelos** Government will now be in power.

FRIDAY JUNE 15

The air raid on London was far worse than we first heard. There were 108 deaths and over 500 people injured besides.

The letter I have just received will be interesting in future time of plenty:

---

*   King Constantine of Greece was mockingly known as Tino, because of his refusal to authorise Greek military aid to the Allies.

**   Eleutherios Venizelos (1864–1936) first became prime minister in 1910 and led Greece during the Balkan Wars. He was ousted by the King because of his pro-Allied policy. When Constantine abdicated, he returned to power as legitimate prime minister and declared war on the Central Powers. Later, he represented Greece at the Peace Conference in Paris.

Letter from Lord
Devonport, Food
Controller to
The Head of the
Household.

No. 67.

Ministry of Food,
Grosvenor House, W.1.

ON HIS MAJESTY'S SERVICE.

I wish to appeal for the immediate help of every man,
woman and child in my effort to reduce the consumption of
bread.

We must all eat less food; especially we must all eat
less bread and none of it must be wasted. The enemy is
trying to take away our daily bread. He is sinking our
wheat ships. If he succeeds in starving us our soldiers
will have died in vain.

In the interests of the country, I call upon you all
to deny yourselves, and so loyally to bridge over the anxious
days between now and the harvest. Every man must deny himself, every mother, for she is the mistress of the home,
must see that her family makes its own sacrifice and that
not a crust or crumb is wasted.

By a strict care of our daily bread we can best help
the men who are gallantly fighting on sea and land to
achieve victory, and so share with them the joys of the
peace which will follow.

No true citizen, no patriotic man or woman will fail
the country in this hour of need.

I ask all the members of your household to pledge
themselves to respond to the King's recent Appeal for
economy and frugality and to wear the purple ribbon as a
token.

29th May, 1917.

Food Controller.

THURSDAY JUNE 28

The first contingent of American troops has landed in France. They were received with
great enthusiasm by the crowds which rapidly assembled near the quays, when their
arrival was announced. Their disembarkation was witnessed by a number of German
prisoners, who stared open-mouthed. Their Commander-in-Chief, General Pershing,
had already landed in England with his staff 2 weeks ago and is now in France.

FRIDAY JUNE 29

Verena Barneby has sent me Mrs Paget's letter describing the Zeppelin raid, and as it is
remarkable, I copy it:

Last night a Zeppelin was precisely over the Crossways for three quarters of an hour. At 2.45 am Mrs Brown (her faithful maid), to whom I am communicated by a speaking tube, spoke thus: 'Madam, I hope you have not a light. There is a Zeppelin hovering over us.' I said: 'Nonsense, Mrs Brown, these things are on your nerves, do go to bed'. At the same time I heard a most extraordinary and stationary noise. This had awakened me and I **had** had a light on for some time.*

However I told Mrs Brown she had better come down; and, quite certain that there was no Zeppelin here, I opened the French window on to the roof of the Loggia and Ham! Dam! Yam! there I saw it immediately above me, so that I had to rick my neck. A fat, long Havana, very high, looked to be about a foot from the roof's cornice and there the creature hovered, emitting crackles of what looked like the fairest of constellations into an indigo sky just dawning in the east. It was at times just keeping its engines going, but never far from any part of the roof.

I now know that it was being attacked by one of our air machines. But for three quarters of an hour I expected bombs, especially as every moment it was getting lighter and I supposed they would see us and drop one for practice. Just at 3.30 there came a perfect shower of these constellations and fireworks and I said: 'Mrs Brown, perhaps we should be a little safer on the ground floor'.

*Slowly and with dignity (please believe I did **not** run) I descended the grand staircase. Never have I admired it less. It now looked to be made of paper. It was quite hopeless anywhere had a bomb dropped; but I think I had an idea of lying down flat on the drawing room floor, together with Mrs Brown, the kitchen maid, the under house maid and between-maid, who had by now joined us without a sound, and all in nightgowns of various hues.*

Lettice had only left me two days before, talking all the time of bombs and air raids which never came. What a pity she just missed the real thing. As I got into the drawing-room, the east side suddenly became illuminated with a violent red glow. I said sourly 'Now what is this?' and this time tore (I regret to say) to the east window and flung open the shutters. There, just disappearing over the copper-beech was a huge bolster of roaring red flame.

We then all realized that we were saved; all but one flew to the attic. By the time I arrived, the glowing mass was steadily floating to the earth. Just as it fell, a plane from the blue shot down upon it like a hawk.

Ten minutes afterwards Mrs Brown and the kitchen-maid were on their bicycles in hot pursuit. Presently every road of the Crossways was filled with dust and cars and carts and pedestrians and donkeys and infants in arms all tearing after, closely followed by what appeared to be the whole of the East Coast troops – all this just at daylight.

The Zeppelin fell just outside Theberton Church, three miles away.** When the servants got there it was still burning. One German escaped, two were wounded, and the rest nowhere. A grim and beastly experience. So glad I am not a man so that in no way I have these outrageous murders on my conscience. Not that one could make peace where no peace would be. But that is just it. Evil breeds evil, crime crime, outrage outrage, and no man who has conceived and started it can bind the demon of his handiwork.

Your still living old friend

Lucy Paget

SUNDAY JULY 1

Uncle Guy is home on leave from his Grenade School at Terdinghem and went first to Cambridge to give two lectures on bombing to officers training there. He came to this house today and we were quite a family gathering at tea. He duly admired the house and its contents, but you, my chief treasure, are still at Bazzleways with Clara. She writes that you are so happy with Charlie and Knyvett that she wants you to stay an extra week. You three little boys sold Alexandra Day roses in the main street of the village of Milborn Port, and collected £29/5/2 in the afternoon.

The Greek Government has now openly declared itself for the Allies and a state of war exists now between Greece and Germany.

MONDAY JULY 2

This morning I found myself accidentally on the route the King and Queen were to take on their way to a service at Westminster in commemoration of the Anzacs intervention in the war. The Queen was also due to open the National Baby Welfare Exhibition at the Central Hall. There is a universal movement on foot to promote the welfare of babies now so precious to the nation.

As the crowd was not too alarming, I waited to see the Sovereigns, and was very interested to see that the whole route was policed by our Special Constables, men of anything up to 70 and more and a fine show they made. The Queen looked very calm and suave, and pretty Princess Mary, with her dazzling complexion, sat opposite. Quite a simple little affair, just the Sovereign's carriage, with outriders in scarlet, and one carriage behind, with one lady and two equerries in attendance. The sight of the King going by so quietly, with no show of military or other display is affecting in these times, so precarious for royalties on Continental thrones. Our Royal Family seems secure enough, no one can doubt it, when one sees the King and Queen. I am glad I stayed.

SATURDAY JULY 7

My first really big air-raid experience today. I was in Church Street, shopping, just coming home with a basket full of provisions (we have to carry our parcels nowadays). Then, as I turned into Berkeley Gardens the report of a gun rattled through the air,

---

*   This was the L48, the flagship of the raiding squadron, commanded by Kapitänleutnant Eichler, which raided East Anglia on 17 June. After circling over Suffolk, he headed for Harwich but was diverted by accurate gunfire in the direction of Saxmundham. It is at this moment that Mrs Paget's faithful maid, Mrs Brown, tells her mistress via the 'speaking tube' that a Zeppelin is hovering directly above their house.

**   Official records confirm that the L48 was attacked and set on fire over Theberton by Capt R.H. Saundby, Royal Flying Corps, in a DH2 and by Lt L.P. Watkins, Canadian Army, in a BE12. Eichler and four of his crew were killed instantly, after jumping from the airship. Lt Meith and two other crew-members were rescued from the blazing wreckage by a local constable. H.A. Jones gives a detailed account in *The War in the Air*, vol. 5, pp. 33–4.

followed by another and another. Looking skywards I saw a sight I shall never forget. Coming towards me from the north east, like huge brown birds, was a flock of aeroplanes.

Michael MacDonagh* was crossing Blackfriars Bridge in a tram when a fellow passenger asked him about the twenty large aeroplanes overhead: 'Are they Germans?' 'Oh, no,' I replied, 'If they were Germans, we should hear our guns firing at them. I feel sure they are our own airmen, carrying out manoeuvres' . . . It was not until he was walking towards his office at The Times *on the north side of Blackfriars Bridge that he heard the swish of the first bomb – and its explosion. He relates how the scene in the streets was instantly transformed as everyone rushed for Blackfriars Underground station. Seventy-six bombs were dropped in all: one scored a direct hit on the General Post Office, another narrowly missed St Bartholomew's Hospital. Fifty-seven people were killed and 193 injured.*

    The first daylight bombing raids of the war had the same traumatising impact on unsuspecting Londoners as a terrorist attack has today. This raid was the most daring air attack which the Germans had yet made – and the first in broad daylight. So low were the planes that they were seen by millions of people – including Georgina Lee – all over London.

    Not waiting to fumble for the latch key I went down into the basement, no one there. I went up into the hall and found all the maids, Beatrice Dunsmure and Daddy. Daddy telling them all to go down at once. So down we went. For ten minutes there was an incessant bombardment of guns going in all directions. Through the kitchen window we could see the planes circling almost overhead.

    Beatrice and I then insisted on going up and outside to see more, and for another ten minutes we watched the turns and twists of one aeroplane detached from the rest and three others in a clump further off. The battle lasted 20 minutes and the roar of the guns was incessant. How I thanked my stars you were away.

    When it was all over, I went off to my Belgian workroom, where I found the women highly excited, all talking at once. Some had been in the basement, others in the street. There were about 20 aeroplanes altogether. Daddy saw a gentleman get into the omnibus he was in, with a nurse and his 2 children whom he had been to rescue in Kensington Gardens. The little girl carried a piece of shrapnel still warm which they had picked up in the Broad Walk. The danger is not only from the bombs, but from splinters of our own shells.

SUNDAY JULY 8

This morning Beatrice and I went to the City to see the damage. One house had poured itself into the street, literally. A bomb had fallen on the roof of the GPO and set fire to part of the building. Bee herself picked up a fragment of bomb, and I bought some bits from little boys who were picking them out of the gutter.

---

*   Michael MacDonagh, then a correspondent for *The Times*, gives an eye-witness account of this audacious raid. *In London During the Great War*, 1935, pp. 198–9.

THURSDAY JULY 12

This morning, while on duty at my Belgian workroom, old Mrs Cottle, the caretaker, told me that enemy aircraft had passed Sydenham on the way to London. It shot into my mind that you were out in the Park, not with Nannie, but with Gwen the housemaid.

So I went to the nearest telephone, rang up the parlour maid and asked her to beg Lily, our very sharp little cook, to go to the Park at once to tell Gwen to take cover in good time. Guns were heard to the south of London, but nothing more happened. Lily found you at once, but there was no need to bring you in. Still, this is the state of things hanging over us daily, and for parents with young children, it is anxious work.

Today the Secretary of the Belgian Red Cross, M. Demeure, his wife, and Mme Maeterlinck came and visited the Belgian workroom. They were enchanted with the work. We had a big display as it was the end of the month's work before it is sent to the Red Cross on the 15th.

SUNDAY JULY 15

Things are becoming very unsettled internally in Germany. After much dissension the Chancellor, von Bethmann Hollweg,* has resigned. He has always been the Kaiser's chief support and his policy has not been so blind and fanatical as the ultra Prussian clique. The Socialists too have been growing more insistent on reforms being introduced in the Reichstag.

Finally the Crown Prince, at the head of the Prussian reactionaries, has called Hindenburg and Ludendorff to Berlin, to quell the socialists and depose Bethmann, whose policy is too liberal for them. Whereas Hindenburg still prates about victory and the annexations Germany 'must' claim.

Bethmann is also the one who, at the beginning of the war admitted in the Reichstag that 'a great wrong had been done to Belgium which must be repaired, but it was a military necessity, and necessity knows no law'.

As the war drags on and German hopes are no nearer realisation, the people are bound to break out, with Russia's example before them.

MONDAY JULY 23

The raiders bombed Felixstowe, Colchester and Harwich yesterday killing 9 people and injuring about 30. 22 aeroplanes came over, but were dispersed by our aircraft, and had to return after hovering over the coast.

The newspapers make bad reading. The news from Russia is grave. The mutiny among the armies on the Galician front is so serious that Russian troops have retreated

---

*   Theobald von Bethmann Hollweg had been Chancellor since 1909. Not a militarist, he
     favoured a negotiated peace and tried perhaps to clear the way for mediating with the USA
     in 1916. But he lost the confidence of the Higher Command and also lost control of the
     Reichstag.

on a front of 23 miles thus giving up the ground won by Brusilov. Just a year ago. It is perfectly horrible.

They have tried to murder Kerensky, the brilliant young statesman who is burning his life out to save Russia. As War Minister he journeyed from one army to another, to keep up the spirits of the disaffected soldiers. But he cannot cope with the spreading revolt. He has just been made Head of the Provisional Government.

I am sure the Russian people will never calm down until they have had their full fling of revolt, with all its terrors and excesses. Then the reaction will take place – as it did in France. I get so sick of the papers which represent so many deferred hopes, so many increasing anxieties for us all. We were all so confident that the war would be over before the winter. Now July is witnessing deadlock in the West while the Eastern Front is collapsing.

I went to Christie's today to see the *Hope Heirlooms*, priceless old Greek statuary, to be sold today. There was the magnificent *Athene*, attributed to Phidias, which is expected to reach five figures. The other day a Raeburn, *The Macnab*, fetched 24,500 guineas, and a van Goyen* 17,000, so there is no lack of money in the country. Yet, when we offered our beautiful van Goyen to Tooth, the art dealer, he only offered us £600, an offer we declined.

TUESDAY JULY 24

Heavy cannonading has been heard in London today. Lily, our cook, whose big window at the top of the house faces east, tells me that when she sits at night on the sill watching the wonderful play of searchlights in the sky, she often hears the distant thuds of heavy guns, from the artillery on the Belgian Coast.

THURSDAY JULY 26

I am now, for the first time, in sole charge of you, my son. Nannie has gone away today for 10 days, to marry her soldier. He came home wounded from the Front, but is just discharged from hospital. As the weather is still frightfully hot, I don't relish the long pram outings which are your daily routine. We go to the park all the morning and afternoon and the journey to and fro in the shadeless street rather does for me!

MONDAY JULY 30

There are gigantic preparations in Flanders. The great artillery storm gains every day in strength. If only that wretched Russia hadn't let her Allies down in this lamentable way.

---

*   Jan van Goyen (1596–1656) was one of the most gifted landscapists in the Netherlands in the seventeenth century.

MONDAY AUGUST 13

It is a fortnight since I wrote last. In the interval your Nannie came home from her wedding, and we packed up and travelled down here to Gelligemlyn on the 8th.

Travelling is now very difficult and uncomfortable, fares almost doubled since pre-war days, luggage allowance limited to 100 lbs per ticket, and great restrictions on the number of trains. Every carriage is full to bursting, and people unable to find a seat have to line the corridors. The journey is now taking just under 8 hours.

Events in Flanders have been held up owing to the heavy rains. They came just at the wrong moment for the offensive.* Uncle Tich, who organises supplies for his Welsh Division, wrote that everything had to go up to the firing line on pack horses. Anything in the nature of a wheel was hopeless. If any horse got off the track and stepped into a shell-hole, a pool of mud, he disappeared and was seen no more.

WEDNESDAY AUGUST 22

My Birthday. Beatrice and her 2 children, Aunt Ethel, Isobel Badcock and I, all walked to the Pistyll Cain Waterfall and had lunch there.

The fighting is raging fiercely round Lens. We seem to gain ground inch by inch. Uncle Tich writes depressed letters from the thick of the fighting zone. Also it is demoralising to keep hearing of the Russians 'retiring a little', as they are doing again today in the new battle of Riga. They are hopelessly disorganised and demoralised.

WEDNESDAY AUGUST 29

Today Muz had invited 16 of the wounded soldiers from Caerynwch to tea. We had made great preparations for their amusement in the form of 3 life-size figures of the Kaiser, Crown Prince and Hindenburg, for the Tommies to knock clay pipes out of their mouths, and win prizes of knives and India rubber pouches. But the rain is pouring down, so the men will probably be put off, and come tomorrow.

SATURDAY SEPTEMBER 1

Back in London again and I feel quite *désoeuvrée*.** The weather is still awful, and our main preoccupation and everyone else's is the ruin of the crops. Floods and gales have been incessant all through August, and the reports are very serious from all over England. It is too awful to think that this harvest upon which we depend to make us safe from shortage and starvation should be ruined.

Immense efforts were made all over the country to cultivate thousands of acres of land never before used for corn or potatoes. The prospects of a plentiful return for all this trouble were favourable until 3 weeks ago, and now we hardly dare speak of it. On our way across country from Wales the fields were full of corn either uncut or in ragged

---

*   Passchendaele.
**   At a loose end.

stooks, much blown about by the gales. Much of the corn is already sprouting where it stands. Perhaps September is going to improve matters.

We must be up early tomorrow even though it is Sunday. Ruth Marshall is to be hurriedly married to her fiancé who is ordered out to India. The parents had hitherto prevented this war match being consummated because of their youth and his inability to keep a wife yet. But they have given way now that he is ordered off and they may be separated for some years if the war drags on.

So the ceremony takes place at 8.30 am, the only time they could get the Church on a Sunday. Ruth only knew of her approaching marriage last night, so she hasn't had much time for preparations, but this is quite in the order of things nowadays.

TUESDAY SEPTEMBER 4

The war-wedding went off very simply on Sunday. Punctually at 8.30 we arrived at St Cuthbert's, Philbeach Gardens, having had to walk all the way. We met a little group of guests and walked into the church going straight to the little side Chapel where the Ceremony took place. Early Service was still going on, so we had to wait till the Vicar had given the benediction, when he came over to the Chapel. The bride was sitting with us, waiting.

The Service only lasted 10 to 15 minutes. There were no hymns and no address. We then walked across the road to Aunt Amy's house and had a hot breakfast, 16 of us sitting down. The little bride was unnerved and cried a good deal. But she has had a long and trying engagement of 2 years and she knows she has to be separated from him in ten days.

Also she has had her nerves upset since the last big air raid. She was working in the City in her office (as most women are doing nowadays), when the raid began and bombs began falling all round. She and others were hustled to the basement and later a large piece of shrapnel was found under the desk at which she had been sitting.

Afterwards we went to the Tower to call on General Sir George and Lady Younghusband. He has been made Keeper of the Crown Jewels, as he was invalided home from the Mesopotamia Expedition, when he commanded a division which made a gallant, but vain attempt to relieve Kut. The Younghusbands have a lovely residence in the oldest part of the Tower and look down upon Traitors' Gate and Bloody Tower. He is a charming man, very chatty and full of information.

A serious air-raid by moonlight last night, in which Chatham suffered severely. 107 sailors are killed and over 80 wounded.

WEDNESDAY SEPTEMBER 5

Last night at one in the morning Daddy and I shot out of bed in the midst of our slumbers, at the sound of two loud reports. We groped for our dressing gowns, and mechanically walked downstairs, as by force of habit. Lily, the cook was on the stairs, on her way to awaken us (she is sharing a room with another maid on the first floor) and she said 'There's a raid, and we've been hearing explosions off and on for an hour'.

Sure enough there was the deep organ-like drone of some aircraft overhead. We could see nothing – the bright moonlight completely dimmed the searchlights. We were craning our heads out of the window, all in dressing gowns, Daddy and I, Lily and Florence and again I thanked my stars that you were away and the household reduced by 3 inmates.

Nothing more happened except some distant thuds. We went to bed again in about 15 minutes and I was soon asleep. It is an eerie experience, so little is manifest in these night raids, yet the results, when known, are startling.

Today we found that 5 bombs fell on Edgware Road. All these bombs fell near Uncle Henry's house in Portman Street, while Bourne and Hollingsworth's in Oxford Street was much damaged. Bombs fell opposite Charing Cross Station, just missing the hospital roof by a few feet and smashing the Little Theatre like a pack of cards. Altogether 40 bombs fell on London.

The Germans have taken Riga, the Russians simply retiring everywhere along the Front. The officers are powerless to control their men.* The state of affairs is deplorable.

FRIDAY SEPTEMBER 7

I went to see the damage done in Edgware Road. The glass frontages to the shops on both sides were smashed. It was a bizarre sight, for some of the shops had not put boards up, but were carrying on their trade with open fronts, like booths at a fair. In one shop coats and skirts hanging on pegs were to be had, apparently, by merely stretching out a hand from the pavement.

Miles the Chemist, Uncle Henry's dispenser, was badly damaged – at least his premises were. Uncle Henry went round and on his saying he was a doctor, the police let him pass through the cordon. Uncle Henry found poor old Miles distractedly clearing up the debris of his bottles on the floor, where the magnesia was mixing freely with the castor oil.

Close by in Norfolk Crescent, a house was struck by a bomb and two servants were killed. Yet there was nothing apparent from the front of the house which was intact.

SATURDAY SEPTEMBER 8

This morning, waiting for a bus at Notting Hill Gate, I saw old Mrs Major standing by. I went and spoke to her, for since her only son went to the war, she needs cheering up whenever possible. Mrs Major is the widow of an old character, a very old acquaintance of the Lee family ever since they lived at Charterhouse, when Old Major had a tumble-down second-hand furniture shop at Islington.

---

*   Mutiny among the Russian troops was now rife. They were throwing down their arms and refusing to go forward while, in the words of Sir John Wheeler-Bennett, 'their officers, threats and prayers alike proving useless, spat at the silent men and went towards the enemy alone'. Martin Gilbert, *First World War*, p. 343.

He was a most honest, straightforward old dealer, devoted to the family through whom he got many clients. Then he set up in a much smarter shop in Church Street, quite near here. Daddy and I bought all our old furniture from him when we married. Well, the move was a great success, and they began to make quite a good business, when poor old Major died a year ago.

The only child, Harry, replaced his father and carried on wonderfully till he was swallowed up in the Army, leaving the poor old mother to carry on alone as best she could. I often go in and see her, but this morning she said 'Oh Mrs Lee, I've just come from Clapham (it was 9.30 am). Ever since the last raid, I'm so frightened of being in my house that I've had to go away each night to sleep with my relations'.

She has one elderly woman with her as a servant, but this woman is more frightened than herself. It's very hard on old people, because these things make a real impression on them, and they don't realise how small the risk is for the individual in London.

Today Daddy and I had to go to Charing Cross, so we saw the damage done by the bomb that fell by the entrance to Charing Cross Hospital. A huge hole was made in the road, and chunks of stone had been hacked out of the frontage and the pillars. Every single window had been shattered and the sash-frames blown in, so that all the wards were unprotected from the elements.

Can you imagine the horrible scene in this hospital, the busiest in London, when together with the terrible crash of the explosion, thousands of panes of glass were blown into every ward? Two or three casualties who were actually being carried into the hospital were killed outright by this particular bomb. Also a little cafeteria just opposite was partly wrecked and several soldiers standing in the doorway were killed.

WEDNESDAY SEPTEMBER 12

We have had no more raids, though we expected a whole series during the week of big moon. Fortunately the nights were overcast and wet, so the raiders haven't reappeared. Now I suppose we shall have peace till the next full moon. Tich and Clara came up for the night to the Carlton, and we went to dine with them. He is on his way back to France.

He was quiet and rather depressed. He hates the whole thing out there, and told Daddy that the conditions at the Front defy description, so terrible are they and so haunting are the sights. He is so calm, self-possessed and lion-hearted by nature, that it is dreadful to think that even men like him are affected.

SUNDAY SEPTEMBER 16

Kornilov's rebellion has failed, Kerensky has proved the stronger man. Kornilov, therefore, has been forced to surrender and has been placed under arrest. We all hope that Kerensky will treat him generously and not make a martyr of him. There is a very strong feeling for Kornilov in England, although he fought against us with the Boers in the South African War.

THURSDAY SEPTEMBER 27

A house in Ovington Gardens has been struck by our own shells! We have just heard this from the builder who is left in charge of it. It must have happened on Monday night. The shell fragment struck the roof, glanced off on to the glass-house lounge on the first landing, smashed the glass and timber, besides causing a fall of soot down the drawing room chimney all over the carpet. Fortunately, like the rest of us, the owner is insured against air-raid damage.

SATURDAY OCTOBER 6

We are at last in possession of Gheluvelt, the scene of such desperate fighting in 1914. Haig makes moves with the limited objectives which are now his tactics, but these objectives are usually gained. The French seem delighted at the strides we are making, as slow and methodical as the motion of gigantic machinery.

SATURDAY OCTOBER 13

Daddy and I return to Brunswick Gardens today, leaving you behind at Gelligemlyn for another three weeks. I am not afraid of the danger from bombs or shrapnel, the risk being very small, but I object to taking you downstairs out of your bed for two or three hours, in cold weather. I also object to the injurious effect on your little mind from the deafening roar of guns and explosions. This is the only part I mind.

Several timber merchants have been over to see the larch wood at Gelligemlyn. Their offers for purchasing it start at £2,000. No timber is being imported from Norway or anywhere, so the Government is buying up woods all over the country. Larches are used for pit-props, and timber is required also for sleepers etc. for the railways in France, so all landowners are putting their woods to use and profit, not entirely of their own will. But they resign themselves cheerfully enough on the whole, as the loss of their woods means substantial increase of their capital.

Think what this wholesale cutting down of coverts will mean to sporting England. There will be no covert shooting for years to come. I don't know with what feelings poor Owen, Dad's old keeper, views this sacrifice of the Gelligemlyn Wood. The prospects of shooting on dear little Gelligemlyn are dim indeed for this generation, even if they could begin planting at once. They can't do this, because no wire or fencing can be bought now! You will know, my son, *a very different England* in your generation to the country we knew up till three years ago!

SUNDAY OCTOBER 14

We have been to see four different sets of friends this afternoon, and everyone talked of the air-raid week which we just missed. I am quite sorry we did miss it. Romer Wynn and his lovely young wife and tiny baby have come to live in a house just opposite so as to be near us, for about 6 months.

WEDNESDAY OCTOBER 17

This evening Mrs Labertouche, a young widow who lives a few doors off, came to see me. We hadn't met since August. She came to talk over what is best to do with you children in case of air-raids. Not that she is in much doubt, for she means to carry Peter off to the country next week for the ten days of the moon period.

Soon there will scarcely be a house in London without shrapnel or unexploded shell in or through it. Why, four houses in our Brunswick Gardens had shrapnel through them, while at the Grahams' house, No. 26, an unexploded shell went slap through five storeys and rolled into the basement. All this to the horror of the servants, who did not know that it couldn't explode. A bomb fell into the Royal Academy, Burlington House and wrecked Room IX, I think the Gem Room. It penetrated the underground premises, wrecking the art students' room, and some of the statuary presented by King George IV.

SATURDAY OCTOBER 27

Tomorrow is your birthday, my precious little son, and for the first time you are spending it away from us. We are still keeping you out of London, until we can hope to be tolerably safe from raids for awhile. Just now we are expecting them every night, full moon being on 30th and all shops and offices close at 5 pm for the next 10 days, to give people time to get home after work. Every night we have by our bedside warm clothing and fur coats for a possible alarm, and we have some Oxo to make hot soup on our gas stoves.

It is quite exciting, but a funny state of affairs. The only people who seem to mind are the mothers of young children and they are keeping the children away, as we are doing with regard to you. Meanwhile you are being happy and unconscious of it all, at Gelligemlyn. I write to you nearly every day . . . at this very moment as I write, 6.30 pm, the warning car has rushed past our house, ringing its bell like a fire bell. Daddy who was just going out for an evening paper has gone out all the same, as one always has a short respite before the guns begin.

Later: It was a false alarm, after all.

SUNDAY OCTOBER 28

There is a horrible development on the Italian Front. The Germans have been massing a whole Army, troops withdrawn from the Russian Front where nothing is going on, and have simply broken through the Italians. Not only is Gorizia* lost, which cost Italy so much sacrifice to win from the Austrians, but the Germans are pouring down in the Venetian plain, towards the sea.

---

*   Gorizia is the capital of Gorizia province on the Isonzo river, north of Trieste.

TUESDAY OCTOBER 30

We had a ridiculous situation last night during a raid. I had retired to bed very early at 9 o'clock feeling rather a worm, having been thoroughly chilled during the day. My bones were aching all over and I felt sea-sick! I got into bed, flanked with a couple of hot water bottles and tried to go to sleep, thanking Providence that we were not likely to be raided. At 11 o'clock Daddy had just put out the light when there was a loud prolonged policeman's whistle, and a hoarse shout of *Take Cover!*

'Leave me where I am', said I, not caring what happened. I simply couldn't lift my head from my pillow. So Daddy made me stay where I was till the guns began and he went down to make me a snug haven in the safest place on the house, against the party wall at the front of the stairs. He dragged a small sofa there out of the hall, lit an oil-stove, and then went across the street to the Wynns to be sure they had heard the warning.

There he found the household assembled in the kitchen before a fire, eating biscuits and hot cocoa; Gladys, lately so ill, wrapped in her fur coat, and the dear little baby crying piteously. The poor mite had had a little operation performed a few hours before and was very miserable. This is a glimpse of two households out of the millions in London all disturbed by the raid.

However, I stuck tight to my bed, and to our relief we suddenly heard the blessed notes of the All Clear bugle, ¾ hour after the warning, and not a gun had been fired! Now we are all determined not to move from our beds until the guns begin to bark.

THURSDAY NOVEMBER 1

We had a proper raid last night! Full moon, but plenty of small clouds and perfectly calm. Roused from our sleep at 11.45 pm by prolonged whistles and hoarse shouts of *Take Cover!* We dressed with warm wraps, went down and waited with the servants. ¾ hour passed with practically no gun-fire so we determined to go back to bed thinking it was an abortive raid.

We had hardly got to our rooms, when the guns suddenly burst forth, and continued booming for 1½ hours. The raiders came in 3 relays. At one moment, above the din of our guns, we heard the deep drone of a raider, so loud that it pervaded the house in spite of closed windows and drowned our guns. This was a creepy five minutes, for it must have been very near.

The sighing of the shells was just like the moan of a dog. I couldn't believe it wasn't a dog. We were up 3 hours, going back to bed at 2.45 and the All Clear bugles sounded at 3 am. I have put back your return till 9th and I was thankful you were not here.

News of brilliant victory at Beersheba and Gaza in Palestine, by General Allenby. I had just had a letter from Uncle Arthur who is with GHQ in the desert, '2 miles away from Delilah's Village'. He tells me things are working up for a grand finale there. He is now a Colonel.

SATURDAY NOVEMBER 3

Two days of dark, damp, dripping days, days to make the spirit rebel and clamour for relief from the oppression of leaden skies. Yet, on my shopping round this morning, I saw nothing but cheerful faces and was greeted by all the tradesmen with 'this weather will keep them away', and similar expressions of defiant resolve.

I went to see old Aunt Fanny today, an old lady of 85, living at Wandsworth. For the first time I found her shaken by the last raid, but bombs had fallen very near her house, 5 people being killed in a neighbouring street.

The Italian Armies seem to be making a stand after their débâcle. The cruel thing is that 3 weeks ago, they were quite confident and strongly established. Lloyd George and Painlevé, the French Premier have met and conferred hurriedly. They are in complete agreement over the Allied help to be given to Italy. The policy of co-ordinating the English, French and Italian Fronts is now to be followed.

From day to day one sees the rapid development of aerial warfare. Next year the Air Services will be of paramount importance. Today, for instance, the American Government appeals 'to all young men in the country to join the Air Service' – as though that, and not military service, were the more necessary.

THURSDAY NOVEMBER 8

The Russian news is pretty bad. The Extremists have got the upper hand at last and declare they are going to make 'an immediate peace'. Kerensky and his Ministers have been deposed. That's a fine situation.

Elsewhere the news is good. Passchendaele Ridge has been taken on the Western Front and we have taken Gaza at last.

FRIDAY NOVEMBER 9

I met you at Paddington this evening, and found a boy with strong thick legs planted firmly on the platform and a bright alert little face peering everywhere for Mummy. Great joy and exclamations on catching sight of her. The dear old family 'growler' which I had ordered because taxis are almost impossible to get hold of, brought us home and all the way you kept spotting familiar landmarks, not seen for three months. We asked you which you liked best, Gelligemlyn or Brunswick Gardens? You thought a bit and then said 'Gelligemlyn . . . but I like to be with Daddy and Mummy, that's all I care about!'

WEDNESDAY NOVEMBER 14

The war is entering a very critical stage. The invasion of Italy has not yet been stopped and the Italians have had to retire several times again. The British and French have poured in a great many troops and these regiments have been received with great outbursts of enthusiasm.

Meanwhile Lloyd George has been very busy in Paris, organising a Supreme War Council of Allies which is to sit permanently at Versailles. This War Council will direct the policy of the war as a whole. In a historic speech, he put all our failures since the war began down to the lack of cohesion among the Allies.

Each Country tried to pursue its own plan, instead of subordinating their private interests to the good of the Allies. For instance he declared that at one time it would have been quite possible to knock Austria out if we had joined the Italians in making a thrust right into the heart of Austrian territory, where she was weakest.

Meanwhile in Palestine we are doing splendidly. The Turks are now being driven back to Joppa, after their boast that the British would never move them from their line once they came in contact with the main Turkish forces. Allenby's next objective is Jerusalem.

FRIDAY NOVEMBER 15

Thanks to the convoy system the submarine war has been countered at last, and we have just had the lowest week of losses, only one large vessel being reported sunk.

No news from Russia today. Last night it was reported that Kerensky, joined by his old opponent Kornilov, and Kaledin, Chief of all the Cossacks, were marching together on Petrograd. At all events there is some hope now if these three men are united in their endeavour to squash the anarchist portion of Russia and to restore order.[*]

TUESDAY NOVEMBER 20

I have been all day at the Grafton Galleries, helping to sell items at Mrs Dana's art-stall during the big 5 days' sale for my old Mulberry Walk Depot. We had the popular Silhouette Artist, doing silhouettes as fast as he could all day, and this is what he did of me!

WEDNESDAY NOVEMBER 21

When I came home from my bazaar this evening, the news was spreading like wildfire of a big British victory near Cambrai. The Hindenburg Line is pierced, it is said, to a depth of 4–5 miles.

Georgina Lee in profile.

FRIDAY NOVEMBER 23

Today I had my Union Jack flying for the first time to celebrate this Cambrai victory. This is the dear Peace Flag I made months ago. For the first time, too, since the war

---

[*]   It was a vain hope. General Kornilov had remained loyal to the Tsar, but both his rebellion against the Provisional Government and the Cossack uprising that he led against the Bolsheviks were crushed.

began, the bells of St Paul's and some other big churches rang a joyful carillon at midday, in honour of this first victory. The steps of St Paul's were thronged with hundreds of people who sang the National Anthem at midday.

SATURDAY NOVEMBER 24

I had a very successful little At Home this afternoon of between 40 and 50 people and, to help my Belgians, I had a little exhibition of their beautiful needlework, to get them orders. It was most successful too. You were there to help me to entertain my friends, taking them down to tea and attending to their wishes. You amused all the men very much, especially Uncle Henry, whom you asked if he would have a smoke and offered him cigarettes.

TUESDAY NOVEMBER 27

I had a blow this morning. Our cook, who has been in the family 10 years, including 4 with me, announced this morning that she felt it her duty to join the Women's Army. Her brothers and cousins, whenever they come home from the Front, chide her for not joining, while all the girls in her village are either munitions makers or serving in the Women's Army. She feels acutely she is being sneered at for not doing her duty. I could only commend her, of course, for her proper feeling, but it is a break up of the happy home here! I expect the others will follow suit.

This afternoon I sent you and your mate Peter with your nurses to Trafalgar Square to see the display of captured German guns. Also the 'Tank' which is there in support of the appeal for subscriptions to the new War Loan. You were very keen and eager when I explained to you what the Tank was and the achievements of its comrades at Cambrai.

FRIDAY NOVEMBER 30

The treacherous Extremist party now in power in Russia is proposing an immediate peace to Germany. An armistice has been agreed. If peace really is concluded, one of the first results will be the liberating of nearly 2 million prisoners, German and Austrian whom the Russians hold. The likelihood of this army of prisoners being freed to fight us in the West, to say nothing of the German armies hitherto employed on the 1000 mile Russian Front, is not a cheering prospect.

Previous to this, all seemed in our favour. It is unthinkable that the ignorant madmen, now at the head of affairs in Russia, *can* remain in power for long, but they may do incalculable damage to the Allied cause. It is extraordinary that the saner elements have not the strength to rise to the emergency and put an end to this terrible confusion.

The Commander-in-Chief of the Russian Army is now a mere private, or an ensign. A peasant, a private and a doctor were chosen as plenipotentiaries to go into the German lines and negotiate an Armistice.

BOOK X

DECEMBER 2, 1917 – SEPTEMBER 9, 1918

SUNDAY DECEMBER 2

Yet another book started, and the war seems farther from its end than it did three years ago. We have entered a very critical, fierce phase, for once again Germany's position is better than our own. We have had to evacuate again some of our hard-won terrain. The Germans are massing enormous forces behind Cambrai, either to break through again, or force us to call back troops from Italy once more.

But worse than anything is the hopeless chaos in Russia, or rather the reign of terror caused by the domination of the Bolsheviks. They are abolishing *everything*, Law Courts, Property, order – everything which means Government as we know it.

The Bolsheviks are involving Rumania in their treachery, and the Rumanian soldiers are half-won over by them already. So it really means that England and France must now bear the whole burden, until America is ready to strike – which we hope will be in the early Spring.

THURSDAY DECEMBER 6

Aunt Edie came to stay with us yesterday, and at 5 o'clock this morning we were roused from our beds by Lily, always the little watch-woman, calling out that the guns were going hard. We all began dressing, you were brought down to my room and carefully wrapped up in warm things, for it was bitterly cold, and with much laughter and chatter, we repaired to our cosy place on the ground floor landing. We lit the stove, settled ourselves on the sofa and arm chairs, and soon had some hot tea and biscuits to cheer us. It lasted an hour and a half, guns going hard, but there were no casualties in this neighbourhood. This time few explosive bombs fell, but many incendiaries, which don't make much noise and this is why the sounds did not alarm you, for you thought it all a great joke.

But had we been still in Neville Street, we should have been in the thick of it. Several bombs dropped on Onslow Square and Gardens. Also a house was set on fire by a bomb almost opposite Uncle Henry's house in Portman Street.

SUNDAY DECEMBER 9

The Germans are relaxing their efforts on Cambrai it seems. Their casualties in the battle since Nov 20 are estimated at 100,000, so no doubt the effort has exhausted them for the time being. The newspapers make such horrible reading just now, that one never picks one up without a feeling of distress.

TUESDAY DECEMBER 11

Jerusalem has been taken by General Allenby! This is a piece of inspiriting news after the depressing events of the last month.

WEDNESDAY DECEMBER 12

Allenby made his formal entry into Jerusalem yesterday, proceeding thither on foot and with ceremony, accompanied by representatives of France, Italy and Russia. All the Holy Places are being carefully guarded, by his orders and the usual custodians of these Holy Places, Turks mostly, were ordered to continue their watch and ward of the places entrusted to their keeping by their former Turkish Masters.

TUESDAY DECEMBER 18

There is a tremendous air-raid going on now, and has been for an hour and half, since 7 pm. I was waiting to go up to see you after your bath, when two great explosions, sounding quite near, made me fly upstairs. I met Nannie, looking white, with you in her arms. We wrapped you in my eiderdown quilt and laid you on the sofa on the ground floor landing.

For a while the bombardment of all our guns was very fierce, and dozens of people were hurrying through our street to get home. Now all is as silent as the grave – but it may start again for we have had 8 or 9 alternating periods of bombardment and calm tonight. Daddy had *just come* in when we heard the first two crashes, but a friend from Highgate had only left us a ¼ hour before, so I don't know what happened to her. Thank goodness you are not in the least alarmed. After telling you stories, I have been writing letters to while away the time.

The Russian Armistice with the Germans is now an accomplished fact, and they are going to negotiate a peace treaty now. Things are going from bad to worse there.

The All-Clear has just sounded at 10 pm – so the raid lasted 3 hours.

THURSDAY DECEMBER 20

Everyone seems to have taken the raid very philosophically except those who suffered, I suppose. Ten people were killed and over 70 injured. But there wasn't any great damage to property. It was of course a bad hour to start; just as streets, trains and buses were full of people going home.

Civil War has broken out in Russia. Ukraine, the land of the Cossacks, is in full revolt against the Bolsheviks and they are fighting fiercely. *Tant mieux*. The more they exterminate each other, the sooner they will turn with longing towards a firm, honest Government. I can't believe that a resuscitated, democratic Russia can make friends with the Prussians.

Tomorrow we go to Gelligemlyn for Christmas. I am thankful for a fortnight's respite from house-keeping. The difficulty of feeding my household of 7 is very great, or I should say, laborious, for it means going from one shop to another to obtain even a ¼lb butter!

SATURDAY DECEMBER 22

Gelligemlyn
We arrived here last night at 10 o'clock. We fully expected to be one hour late, but we didn't bargain for 4 hours! The engine broke down coming up the Llanuwchllyn hill, just before Drwsynant. We were stuck for 2 hours on the bleakest bit of the wild moors till an engine came to pull us back to Llanuwchllyn, where we were shunted about and finally hooked on to another train for Dolgelly!

Your spirits never flagged at all – and thanks to you we remained cheery to the end of our ordeal. We were very hungry, but fortunately I had provided plenty of food for a second meal. During the long drive home which took an hour, as we only had one horse, you were tucked up at the far end of the bus on Nannie's knee, among the handbags etc.

CHRISTMAS DAY

You three little boys have had a very happy Xmas, with your stockings and numerous presents. They were all 3 put up in the dining room and the pandemonium was complete. It was your first experience of stockings and I shall never forget your joy. Charlie and Knyvett are delightful boys – so well-mannered and full of fun.[*]

Otherwise our Christmas was overshadowed by anxiety on Ethel's behalf, because Baynes is so ill. When we arrived at church, Beatrice Dunsmure – the daughter – told me that Baynes had taken such a bad turn that the Doctor had telegraphed for a surgeon from Birmingham to come prepared for an operation, with anaesthetist and two nurses.

They motored at night and arrived early this morning, Christmas Day. They did not operate, because Baynes is too weak, but he must be built up and strengthened, for an operation later to remove the obstruction in the gall-duct, which they think is due to gall-stones.

THURSDAY DECEMBER 27

I have just returned from Glyn where I went yesterday to stay the night to help Ethel with the nursing. Fortunately a nurse turned up while I was there. She had been two days getting here, having got 'hung up' at Oswestry on Christmas Day and Boxing Day for lack of trains. Baynes is better, the acute attack is passing over.

---

[*]   Charles and Knyvett Lee are Harry Lee's first cousins.

Charlie and Knyvett performed a wonderful little play today with their clever signorina who has coached and inspired them.

FRIDAY DECEMBER 28

I've just had a letter from Uncle Arthur, written from Jerusalem.* He says the campaign has been a wonderful one all through.

1918

Eat slowly: you will need less food
New Year slogan of the Food Ministry

TUESDAY JANUARY 1

The first day of the New Year. What is 1918 going to bring? It is full of enormous possibilities for happiness or disaster, victory or humiliation. And yet our minds will not face the idea of humiliation, it is unthinkable. The food shortage is very real now, to us housewives. We need all our wits to solve it satisfactorily.

WEDNESDAY JANUARY 2

Uncle Tich and Uncle Guy have both got the DSO, announced in *The Times* of today.

FRIDAY JANUARY 4

Guy is off to India on the 7th to take up command of the bombing and trench warfare schools in India. He was personally requested by the Indian Government, as his bombing school in France was the first of its kind.

Baynes is recovering by degrees from his illness, but will be an invalid for some time.

We return to London tomorrow. I don't hanker after it very much, as there is the struggle for shopping and getting about by day, and the likelihood of being bombed at night. This is a topsy-turvy world, with the prospect of years of difficulty and reorganisation of our lives. There will be a great upheaval in all our old customs and habits. Fortunately for you, my son, it will be easy to adapt to the social changes as you are still so young.

---

*   The news of the capture of Jerusalem was a much-needed shot in the arm for a weary British public. It was also a personal triumph for General Allenby, who was promoted Field-Marshal in 1919 and fêted as one of the great victors of the war.

SUNDAY JANUARY 6

We returned to Brunswick Gardens last night. Today was the Day of Intercession appointed by the King for general supplication, throughout the Empire. Daddy and I went to Church to assist at the Service. Thanksgiving was offered for our safety in these islands or, at least, for our being preserved so far from the worst horrors of war in our land.

On arrival here last night, Lily the cook informed me that meat has been unobtainable in London these last 3 days. Hilda Lee told me that they have had no meat and no butter this weekend.

THURSDAY JANUARY 10

The Germans have sunk one of our hospital ships, the *Rewa*, with 300 wounded on board in the Bristol Channel, outside the war zone. She was fully marked according to German specification and brilliantly lit up. The Huns had promised, if these instructions were observed, to spare Red Cross ships.

All the wounded and crew except 3 Lascars, were saved by the extraordinary skill and promptness of patrol vessels. Everyone had been got off the sinking ship into the boats, and after an hour, the men and nurses were all taken aboard the patrol vessels that hurried to the scene.

I went today to call on the Hortons, at the Carlton. Their only son, a boy of 20, joined the British Army from Harrow, and was severely wounded at Cambrai. He was there today, out of hospital for the afternoon, both arms helpless, but very pleased with the Military Cross just awarded him. He behaved with great gallantry at Cambrai. Leading his men to the assault he had both arms badly shattered. But he ordered them to follow him and uphold the honour of the Scots Guards.

MONDAY JANUARY 14

I hear that domestic life in Germany is getting desperate, and the health of the nation is deteriorating for lack of proper food. Tuberculosis is rife and the birth rate is alarmingly low. The Government is encouraging strange measures for the increase of birth. Married and unmarried women are encouraged to have children by any means, as a patriotic duty!!

FRIDAY JANUARY 18

I am so shocked to see in *The Times* the death of Evan Lewis-Lloyd, son of my childhood friend, Elsie Evans-Williams. The poor boy was here only a month ago with his mother, looking such a smart young naval officer. He was on a destroyer, one of the 3 lost together six days ago.

LEWIS-LLOYD – Drowned at sea, on the 12th Jan. LIEUTENANT ROBERT EVAN Lewis-Lloyd, Royal Navy, of Bryntirion, Rhayader, and Otterhead, Devon, son of the late Robert Wharton Lewis-Lloyd, and of Mrs R.W. Lewis-Lloyd, of 45, Park Mansions, Knightsbridge, aged 22.

TUESDAY JANUARY 22

We've had news that Uncle Arthur is Military Commandant of all the unconquered part of Palestine, outside Jerusalem. Audrey told me on Saturday night, when we met at a family dinner given by Uncle Alex at his Club.

There is a distinct wave of pessimism going over us all caused mainly by the developments in Russia. The Bolsheviks are establishing themselves more firmly and no other party seems strong enough to overthrow them.

The worst of it is that they are genuinely admired in England by our Labour Party. They find warm partisans here, and at the Labour Congress at Nottingham, the Russian Ambassador, Litvinov,* exhorted our democrats to follow the Bolsheviks' example. Every reference to Lenin and Trotsky was vociferously applauded.

This does not augur very well for the future. The Labour Party is in favour of continuing the war until we win such a peace that will enable our Army to be disbanded. They do see that if we first make peace with Germany's armies there is not much prospect of a lasting peace. But after peace is declared, then *le déluge*.

The food shortage is acute. Meat, butter and margarine are practically unobtainable. The meat shortage has taken us all by surprise. My butcher has been closed for 4 days. Were it not for some pheasants and rabbits Muz sent me from the country, we should have had no meat of any sort.** To add to my troubles, the one joint I can reckon upon, as it is sent to me from Dolgelly, has not arrived this week. It must have been stolen in the post, an everyday occurrence now with butter and eatables.

MONDAY JANUARY 28

It is 10 pm and a raid has been going on for 2 hours already, having started just as we were finishing the soup. We have had our dinner, but the servants are waiting about supperless, very stupidly, saying they 'couldn't eat anything, thank you'. I must say, the bombardments have been continuous and very heavy.

---

* Litvinov was the Bolshevik diplomatic representative in London and it was feared he would spread Marxist ideas to the populace. In October 1918 he was arrested for 'propaganda activities', but returned to Russia three months later.
** 'The queues at the Smithfield Market around those butchers who do a retail trade were very large. At 11 o'clock, one queue consisted of 4,000 people.' *The Times*, 21 January 1918.

TUESDAY JANUARY 29

The raid lasted 5 hours till 1.15 am. Then the bugles sounded the All Clear. There was a peaceful interlude at midnight which misled us into thinking it was over, so we took you up to bed, but at 12.30 the guns began again and you were brought, still asleep, to the drawing room and left on the sofa where you finished the night, Nannie sleeping on a mattress by you.

You were awake again as usual at 5.30. When I heard this, I exclaimed 'Poor Nannie!' Whereupon you remarked 'Yes, I sometimes feel rather sorry for Nannie too', 'Why?' 'Because she hasn't got much money, but when I'm big I'll give her every penny I've got!'

There were a good many casualties last night, owing to a bomb falling in the midst of a large gathering of people taking refuge in one of the so-called 'shelters' provided by the district authorities in public buildings.

Later: The catastrophe occurred at the premises of *John Bull*, Bottomley's notorious paper. This building had 4 floors, with a basement of concrete, large enough to accommodate some hundreds. It was crowded with men, women and children who flocked there at 8.15 when the warning came.

At 12.15, when the people were thinking the All Clear would sound at any moment, there was a terrific crash and a blinding flash. A bomb burst through every floor and exploded among the people, bringing down all the interior walls of the building and the heavy machinery on top of them. Very few escaped without injury.*

WEDNESDAY JANUARY 30

Last night we were up again till 1.30, with another raid, starting soon after 9 pm. The raiders dropped bombs on Chiswick and Kew. The bombardment of our guns was deafening for about half an hour.

It is a strange scene in the dim light of the oil-stove, on the landing, you slumbering on a little sofa, hand thrown out and head thrown back, your Nannie crouching beside you, and the maids sitting around on the stairs near the stove. The six grown ups (including maids) move about whispering quietly so as not to awake you.

Daddy and I remain on first floor in the drawing room which is not so safe, as it is surrounded on two sides with large windows from top to bottom. But here we can have our lights and read to make the time go more quickly.

---

* Thirty-seven civilians (mainly women) were killed. They had taken refuge in the Odhams printing works, in Long Acre. Along with the collapsed ceilings and heavy machinery, the bomb brought down a huge water-tank, which crashed onto the hapless people in the basement. Among these casualties was the Vicar of St Paul's, Covent Garden, the Revd E.H. Mosse. See Plate 22.

WEDNESDAY FEBRUARY 6

Uncle Tich received his DSO from the King at Buckingham Palace today, and I lunched with him with Muz at the Cavalry Club afterwards. I had you brought to the Club so as to see the decoration, and then I took you to Christie's to see the Banks family portraits that are being sold on Friday.

FRIDAY FEBRUARY 15

We are all in the throes of filling in our registration cards for butter or margarine and meat. The meat allowance per head per week is very small, one shilling and 3 pence worth of butchers' meat, and 5 ounces of bacon (uncooked), or ham or poultry. You, poor lamb, and all children up to 10, are only allowed half that, seven pence half-penny and 2½ ozs! We can only have 4 ounces of butter or any kind of fat.

SATURDAY FEBRUARY 16

Lovely weather again – a wonderful February, mild and bright. But we do not like to see the days getting clearer than ever when the moon is getting older and in 2 days we can expect raids again. The preparations for the coming clash on the Western Front are colossal. All the world is waiting in a hush of suppressed anxiety for the opening of the conflict which must surpass all previous campaigns in horror.

SUNDAY FEBRUARY 17

Just as we were getting very sleepy and ready for bed last night the 'maroons'* went. In a jiffy I had everything ready on the landing by the drawing-room, for your bed. The sofa hastily dragged on the landing, blankets and pillows arranged, and before the bomb woke you, you were comfortably settled and asleep again. Only one bomb was dropped but it made a terrible bang, and shook our house. No guns were going at the time.

Today I heard it had fallen on one of the official residences at Chelsea Royal Hospital, killing a Captain, his wife and 3 children, one whole little family wiped out.

Later, 10.30 pm: I am writing this, again waiting for the bombardment to begin. The maroon signals were fired 20 minutes ago. Your camp bed is out on the landing away from the window, where there is a double wall protection between you and the street. You are so familiar with the sound of the guns that it does not occur to you to be frightened.

TUESDAY FEBRUARY 19

I saw today the results of Sunday night's awful bomb. The devastation is terrible. One of the lovely old residences in the grounds of the Royal Hospital Chelsea, to the left of

---

*   Used as a warning signal when air raids were imminent, maroons were fireworks which went off with a loud bang.

the beautiful Chapel facade, was sliced in half by a bomb of terrific force, and literally crumbled to dust.

Red bricks and splinters of wood littered the grounds where bits of carpet, tiny fragments of fur, wool out of mattresses hung on the shrubs along the outside railings, over the heads of the people watching in awestruck silence as the workmen cleared the mountains of débris. Two of the 5 children were found impaled on to the railings, dead. The bodies of the Father, Mother and lady guest were also found in the wreckage. The other 3 children were rescued unhurt.*

Every house in Leonard's Terrace and Burton Court beyond the great open military ground, had its windows blown out. All the buildings in the precincts of the Royal Hospital grounds were coated with yellow dust. Their windows were mostly broken, the latticed panes of the Chapel included. It gave them a sinister desolate appearance.

Winifred Monier-Williams who lives opposite had all the windows of her house blown out. The shutters were closed when I went this afternoon to enquire after her. I found she had left with the child an hour previously for the country.

THURSDAY FEBRUARY 21

Trotsky and Lenin have made negotiations for peace with Germany. They would agree none of Germany's terms, yet proclaimed war at an end and demobilised the Army and Navy. The Germans have resumed hostilities and are now marching, virtually unopposed, on Petrograd. The Russians are feverishly trying to arrest the demobilization. They have put in command of the Navy some former admirals in place of upstart sailors.

SATURDAY MARCH 2

There is a grave likelihood of raids multiplying with the coming of spring and, added to our anxiety about you, *les domestiques* are beginning to wobble. The chief one suggests going to the country for some months and coming back to us when things are quiet once more!

SUNDAY MARCH 3

Today we had a small sirloin of beef for lunch, having gambled with 15 out of our 18 meat coupons for the week on this one joint!

WEDNESDAY MARCH 6

Disappointing news from the Far East. Japan has so far not committed herself to landing at Vladivostock and occupying Siberia, to counteract the German invasion of Russia. The fact is, that though England, France and Italy are in favour of Japan's

---

*   The victims were: Captain-of-Invalids Ernest Ludlow, his wife Jessie, their two sons Ernest and Bernard, and niece Alice Copley. In 1945 the same wing was hit by a V2 rocket. Letter from Jon Nuttall, Curator, to the editor. See Plates 23 and 24.

intervention in Siberia, America is against it. This is not from suspicion of Japanese motives, but because she thinks it a bad precedent, and simply repeating Germany's brutal aggression in the West. So the danger of the stores and munitions accumulated for Russia's help at Valdivostock by Japan and America, falling into German hands grows greater every day.

The Russian Peace is signed, and several provinces are torn from Russia – including Courland, Estonia and Poland while the economic benefits to Germany are enormous.*

THURSDAY MARCH 7

Poor Rumania is the next to be forced to make peace, a knife at her throat. She loses most of her coast line on the Black Sea. But she is allowed a narrow strip of territory as a route to the port of Constanta. She must allow the free passage of enemy troops through Bessarabia, which leads to Persia. So Germany has done well in the East so far.

Today was Tank Day in Kensington. The open space near St Mary Abbott's was decorated with flags, and one of the Tanks was there for the Sale of War Bonds.

FRIDAY MARCH 8

Last night we went to bed in full security, we thought, as there was no moon. But we were just setting to sleep at 11.30 when boom! went those horrible maroons. It was the most noisy raid we have had yet, all the guns in this district were going, and we could hear the planes overhead. Nannie saw the great flash of one bomb through the window to the north and I saw the result today, appalling. One of these very big bombs fell in Warrington Crescent, Sutherland Avenue near the Regent's Canal, demolishing three large houses entirely and partly wrecking several others.

The havoc wrought in so many homes in the entire district is indescribable. Not merely panes of glass broken, but whole window frames and sashes wrenched away, curtain poles and hangings blown down in hundreds of large handsome houses.

Ambulances were still coming through the enclosure to take away the injured. The crowds in the streets were there in thousands.

SATURDAY MARCH 9

Just as we arrived on the scene in Warrington Crescent to see the destruction, cheering burst forth from the crowds, as a large motor car drove up and we saw the King, the Prince of Wales and two or three other men in khaki. Of course the crowd is railed off for some distance from the actual wreckage, but we saw the khaki figures stepping or jumping across the mountains of timber and stone. 'Come away' said Daddy after a while, 'you'll see plenty more in a few weeks!' So like his pessimism!

---

*   The Treaty of Brest-Litovsk ended hostilities between Soviet Russia and Germany. Russia
      also lost the Ukraine and Finland under the terms of this treaty. However, it was annulled
      eight months later, following the Armistice on 11 November.

The Queen came yesterday to see the scene of desolation, with General French, who commands the Air Defence. I suppose the King and Queen were interested in this because it is by far the worst damage so far caused by one bomb. The destruction spread over a radius of a quarter of a mile.

There is an exodus of children and servants from London. Many houses are closing down because servants won't stay for the raids (including ours!). It is too sickening to think of our charming home, which we installed only a year ago with so much joy, being closed down so soon. But I daren't keep you here and you are to be packed off next week to Aunt Edie at Clifton. I suppose we ought not to have taken on a new house last year.

FRIDAY MARCH 15

Thank goodness I have seen you safe out of London. You went off from Paddington this morning after spending the last two days here in the highest state of excitement at the thought of all the surprises awaiting you at Clifton. You have gone off with the pleasantest possible recollections of the raids. 'The guns are lovely and I like to listen to them!' you told me.

The disastrous and mad Russian peace is enabling the Germans to bring over the whole of their strength from the East to the West. They are now massing huge numbers of men and guns on the Western Front.

TUESDAY MARCH 19

This morning I met Mrs Frank Anson. She came up and spoke to me as I was waiting for a train at South Kensington. I told her I was going to the stores to buy woollen underwear, two years in advance, as I hear woollen goods are not to be made for civilians at all. From now not a cloth or woollen of any sort is to have more than 15%–30% wool.

Mrs Anson told me she and her husband have two boys in France (one badly wounded, one in Mesopotamia, and the fourth, a boy at school, has just developed tuberculosis).

I went to the Chelsea Committee this afternoon at Mrs Erskine Childers' flat,* with Lady Lyttelton in the chair. Contrary to custom we settled quite a number of points, several concerning my industry. I think committees are rather senseless, as the work is always carried on by two or three strong individuals.

FRIDAY MARCH 22

The great German offensive, so long expected, began yesterday on a 50 mile British Front. The enemy attacked with 19 divisions and penetrated some of the first line. All

---

*   Her husband, Robert Erskine Childers, was the author of the spy classic, *The Riddle of the Sands*. He became a leading figure in the struggle for Irish independence. His son was the fourth President of the Irish Republic (1973–4) and the second Protestant to hold the office.

the German Army, with the Austrian and Bulgarian Armies, are massed in the West. The battle just started is being watched with feverish interest by the whole German people, so say their papers.* It is looked upon as a single combat between Germany and Great Britain in which one or the other must go under.

SATURDAY MARCH 23

Bad news today. The Germans have broken through our defensive system and our reserves to the South-West of St Quentin, and stormed ahead for about 15 miles. It is described by us as a 'tactical, but not a strategical break-through'. The enemy claims 35,000 prisoners and 400 guns.

I was packing in my bedroom, waiting for Daddy to come home to lunch, when he came up looking worried and gave me the news. I felt so upset that I could scarcely eat any lunch, nor could he – knowing what our men are going through – and thinking of the anxiety that must be reigning out there. We *know* that our armies will never give way, but we haven't half enough men. America won't be ready to throw in her armies till next spring, though we hear there are 500,000 Americans already in France.

SUNDAY MARCH 24

For the first time since that terrible crisis at Mons in August 1914, Daddy and I have both felt that anxiety which makes one so restless and unable to feel the slightest pleasure in the exquisite beauty of the lovely Spring days we are having.

We are leaving this house on Tuesday to go to Muz at Ovington Gardens, feeling so uncertain about the future. Everything is packed up as though we were to be away at least a year, and who knows when we shall be back? I won't have you here, as long as raids are possible, and we can't be separated from you for an unlimited period. Every friend we have is in the same dilemma. Couples with children have to decide whether the mother will go with the children out of London, or stay with the husband, and what to do with the household, and where the husband is to live if he has to go back to bachelor life. Added to all this there is the increased expenses caused by the break-ups and the difficulty of food.

MONDAY MARCH 25

Thank Heaven, the news is better this afternoon. Our men have taken up their old line along the Somme, from which they began the advance in 1916. We have lost Péronne, at least the Germans claim this. Daddy brought the news he had heard from his partner Mr Dashwood, now in the Grenadiers, that the break-through at St Quentin was ill-luck. Under cover of a thick fog the enemy got on top of our men and formed a great wedge through which they poured.

---

*   Extracts from German newspapers were regularly reprinted in *The Times*.

Our men seem to have made a heroic defence, but were hopelessly outnumbered in some places by six to one. Now is the moment for our glorious race to show its grit and determination. As Emerson said of our country 'This aged England sees a little better on a cloudy day; in storm of battle and calamity she has a secret vigour and a pulse like a cannon'.*

TUESDAY MARCH 26

3 Ovington Gardens
Daddy and I arrived here this evening, leaving our dear house packed up and put away in curl papers. It is delightful being with Muz, and a great help to us for a time, as our cook has run away from raids for the time being, and the parlour-maid has gone to wait in a club at the rate of 30/- a week.

We are much more happy over the news tonight, for it is evident our heroic men have stemmed the rush, and are not to be overwhelmed. Thank God! I feel inclined to be on my knees all day – so unlike me!

THURSDAY MARCH 28

Daddy has just come in from Westminster. Mr Dashwood came into the office and told him that every available man was being pushed out to France. 800 men, including 25 officers of his own regiment are leaving tomorrow for the Front. This leaves scarcely a man to mount guard at Buckingham Palace. All the Yeomanry Territorials are going; all the divisions on the East Coast are to be replaced by volunteers and sent to France.

These volunteers are at last to be regularly employed for Home Defence, and there is a great call for the National Service to all men above military age. Daddy also saw Captain Dampier Palmer, working under Geddes in the National Service Ministry. He told him that the War Council has 'got the wind up' over the great emergency and the shortage of men. They are taking every measure they can think of to meet the gravity of the situation. Daddy asked him to give him a job, as the Doctors wouldn't pass him for military service. Besides he is over military age – so he will have to do whatever presents itself, and the office must go to pot!

Lloyd George has sent a message to the USA calling on them to speed up reinforcements, as the peril is great, and the Allies are in danger of being overwhelmed. The great battle, he says, is only beginning, and on its issue depends the fate of the world. It is not only necessary to hold the Germans at bay, but they must be defeated.

The USA, it seems, feels her unpreparedness deeply, and her inability to take her full share in the great battle. However American troops are now fighting shoulder to shoulder with British and French.

---

* From a speech he made in Manchester, in 1847. An influential American author, philosopher, poet and essayist, Ralph Waldo Emerson (1803–82) believed that not all life's answers are to be found in books. His two volumes of *Essays* (1841 and 1844) earned him an international reputation.

GOOD FRIDAY MARCH 29

In the midst of our newspapers at breakfast this Good Friday, comes your dear innocent little Easter card, your Easter surprise to us.

SATURDAY MARCH 30

Last night at 3.30 we jumped out of bed, startled from sleep by a great crash. Was it the big 75 mile range gun, the mystery gun which has been shelling Paris, pointed at London? Everybody seems to have thought the same, but our doubts were soon dispelled by the battering against our windows of a terrific hail storm. We realised, with much laughter, that the crash was only thunder.

MARCH 31 EASTER SUNDAY IN THE GREAT CRISIS

We have spent the morning in Church and heard Mr Gough's patriotic service at Holy Trinity, Brompton. The gist of this was that love of England will carry us through, even if we have begun to lose faith.

These people are always alluding, in print and in public utterances, to the pacifists and Doubting Thomases. Personally I never come across any, and cannot imagine how any English person can ever doubt that we won't pull through. How could our race ever be downed by those sneaking Huns, whose greatest aim is to hit their enemies below the belt by every foul means?

The enemy is 11 miles from Amiens. It will be a nuisance if they get command of the railway. However they were in Amiens for a week in 1914 before the battle of the Marne.

MONDAY APRIL 1

Never have we seen such a quiet Bank Holiday. I walked across the Park with Uncle Henry from Marble Arch to Hyde Park Gate at one o'clock and it was deserted. We passed half a dozen solitary people. It rained after lunch, so we did not go out again until 5, and at that time also we found the streets empty.

All the munition workers have given up the Easter holidays to churn out the munitions urgently needed in the great battle.

At Péronne, too, in the retreat from St Quentin, we had to abandon great stores of all kinds, as it was one of the depots. The people have realised at last that the war is battering at England's gates. A great seriousness and determination have fallen over the country.

The great French General Foch has been made Generalissimo of the French, English and American forces.

TUESDAY APRIL 2

In response to Lloyd George's message to the USA, more American troops are embarking rapidly for France.

I had the most delightful news of you this morning from Nannie and Aunt Edie. The former tells me you and Geoffrey have little fights. She doesn't interfere. But apparently things came to a crisis when you came to loggerheads and with clenched teeth you called Geoffrey a 'beastly spoof'. You and Geoffrey were looking at a photo of me and Geoffrey remarked that he didn't like that dress. Without a word you gave him a punch in the stomach, then walked up and down, speechless and furious. Aunt Edie asked you what was the matter and you replied 'Geoffrey said he didn't like my Mummy's photo'.

This is a thing I can never forget, that at 4½ you already dealt blows for your Mummy's defence!

SUNDAY APRIL 7

Our wedding day – married 8 years – and also the glorious anniversary of America's entry into the War a year ago. Eight years ago our wedding day was the happiest, brightest day of my life up till then. A day when my chief impression is the sea of faces upturned towards the staircase, as I made my way downstairs in my travelling dress to say goodbye to the friends of both our families. It was at Bailey's Hotel near the Church in Gloucester Rd where we were married. And then the delights of the trip to Switzerland and the Italian Lakes.

MONDAY APRIL 8

Many of our friends are in deadly anxiety about their men at the Front, as no letters have come through for a fortnight, since the beginning of the battle for Amiens. Everyone fears the worst. Aunt Kitty Berkeley has not heard from John.

The Germans are now only 8 miles from Amiens. They are attacking the crucial Boulogne to Paris railway with their guns, and the station at Amiens is guarded by our air squadrons. These battles are going on overhead above the trains, which so far are not interrupted. When you go to Paris for the first time from Boulogne or Calais, you must remember this when you go through Amiens as I have done so often in my girlhood.

TUESDAY APRIL 9

Uncle Tich and his whole division have been sent down south at an hour's notice from Armentières. I suppose to relieve the Armies where the thick of the fighting has been. But today there is a great gas-shell bombardment going on around Armentières and La Bassée, so the battle is spreading there also. Tich is AAG* for the 38th (Welsh) Division, and writes that he is exhausted from overwork and has not lain down to sleep for 3 nights.

New Manpower Bill
Lloyd George introduced his new Bill today, to meet the terrible demand for men to replace the losses at the Front, and to meet the great German effort. He announced that

---

*   Assistant Adjutant-General.

from now on there will be exceptions only for the medically unfit. The age limit is to be raised to 50. He said it was proposed to send to the fighting lines only those above the age of 42 who are particularly fit.

The older men will mostly be employed for Home Defence so as to release the younger men for the firing line. This measure will affect Daddy. Although he will never be strong enough for hard military duty, he will no doubt be taken for Home Defence.

WEDNESDAY APRIL 10

The news is not good today. The Germans are back again fighting us for Messines Ridge which we won in 1916 with such glorious bravery and skill. It is only about 4 or 5 miles from Ypres, and the new thrust is a push for Calais. So we shall go through all the torments of our old anxiety during the battles of Ypres.

We were unsuccessful yesterday in our attempt to get rooms for you at the charming little inn at Fair Mile, on the Oxford Road, half a mile out of Henley. I spent the day there trying to find you some other abode. But everywhere is crammed with people, who have left London.

SATURDAY APRIL 13

The crisis in the battle for Calais is acute. We are all holding our breath for the developments which each hour may bring. There seems to be a hush over London, and everyone in the streets is reading a newspaper as the fresh editions come out. The Germans are now 37 miles from Calais, and the tide of the invasion is only about 10 miles short of its high-water mark in the first months of the war. Every mile that the British are pressed back is doubly dangerous, every mile that separates us from Calais doubly precious.

Sir Douglas Haig has issued this soul-stirring Order of the Day, calling on every man to die where he stands rather than give way:

FIGHT IT OUT

SIR D. HAIG'S ORDER TO THE ARMY

The following Special Order of the Day by Field-Marshal Sir Douglas Haig is issued for the information of troops in France:

To all ranks of the British Army in France and Flanders
Three weeks ago to-day the enemy began his terrific attacks against us on a 50-mile front. His objects are to separate us from the French, to take the Channel Ports, and destroy the British Army.

Words fail me to express the admiration which I feel for the splendid resistance offered by all ranks of our Army under the most trying circumstances.

Many amongst us now are tired. To those I would say that victory will belong to the side which holds out the longest.

The French Army is moving rapidly and in great force to our support.

There is no other course open to us but to fight it out. Every position must be held to the last man: there must be no retirement. With our back to the wall, and believing in the justice of our cause, each one of us must fight on to the end.

The safety of our homes and the freedom of mankind depend alike upon the conduct of each one of us at this critical moment.

MONDAY APRIL 15

The strain is relaxing, and the German rush is stemmed for the time being. But what a time we've been through. The French reserves, hurried up to help the British, were not after all needed, thank goodness. Our men did their work unaided. We breathe again – but the attack will of course break out again elsewhere.

THURSDAY APRIL 18

The battle seems to be slackening again, and this last effort of the Germans is fruitless so far. Poor Nannie's husband has been gassed and is in hospital at Boulogne.

FRIDAY APRIL 19

We brought you back this afternoon to 3 Ovington Gardens, arriving in a black storm of snow, wind and hail. We have been having horrible weather for a fortnight, bitterly cold, with rain and snow.

TUESDAY APRIL 23

Tonight there is very cheering news of a most gallant Naval raid on Zeebrugge and Ostend. Five obsolete minelayers, laden with rubble and cement, were sunk so as to block the passage out of the Zeebrugge–Bruges Canal and bottle up the submarines in the pens at Bruges.

A contingent of 700 Marines were landed on the Mole. They stormed the defences and had a fierce hour's fighting; this party was used to distract the enemy's attention from the main operation, which was the blocking of the two exits from the submarine pens. The whole enterprise was perilous and hazardous in the extreme, for the navigation conditions were quite unknown, the mine-field unknown also. It was a most gallant affair, carried out by volunteers from the Navy and Marine Force.

The ships taking part were able to approach under a dense smoke-screen. It is too early yet to know the results because the weather was so bad that aerial investigation was impossible, and it only took place last night. But when the exhausted men were landed at Dover, they were too tired to say anything except that their objectives had been accomplished.*

SUNDAY APRIL 28

I have just come in from Holy Trinity, Brompton, where one passage in Mr Gough's fine fighting sermon impressed me very much. Denouncing the insidious pacifists in our midst, he referred to one member of Parliament who had the effrontery to say publicly that it would be far better to let the war end indecisively, because it would be a deterrent in the future, proving the futility of War. 'It would not prove the futility of War', he said, 'but it would prove the futility of Righteousness and the immunity of Sin.'

TUESDAY APRIL 30

I went yesterday with Muz to the House and heard an interesting debate on the resignation of General Trenchard as Chief of the Staff of the Air Service. His resignation has caused a storm of anger especially throughout the Air Forces and whole Army in France, where General Trenchard's 'incalculable services' had made him universally revered.

It was suggested by Lord Hugh Cecil who made a strong speech, that General Trenchard's decisive, prompt measures had ruffled the War Council and civilian members of the Government. To these allegations, Lloyd George gave an angry denial, provoked to an outburst by Lord Cecil's retort that 'The Prime Minister seems to think of nothing so much as his retention of office'.

In a long and characteristic speech Lloyd George explained that General Trenchard's brilliant and incalculable services to the Air Forces were more those of a leader than of a far-seeing, plodding Chief of Staff. After expert investigation it had been ascertained that his services could find better scope in another capacity.

WEDNESDAY MAY 1

The news of Uncle Baynes is dreadful. Poor, poor fellow! To be taken away in the prime of life, a man whose intellect and remarkable individuality ought to have left their mark on his generation. Yet a curiously warped outlook and a queer kink somewhere in his brain just prevented his achievement. Years ago he received an injury to his head in a railway accident in America and to this is attributed the satanic moods he occasionally indulged in. At other times he was the most amusing and fascinating

---

*   The Ostend raid failed as *Brilliant* and *Sirius* were scuttled 1 mile east of the harbour entrance. Despite a second attempt, Ostend Harbour was never blocked. But the Zeebrugge raid provided a welcome boost to British morale and the headlines on 24 April glowed with the whole daring exploit. Eight Victoria Crosses were awarded, and three more for the second attempt at Ostend. Julian Thompson, *The Book of the War at Sea, 1914–1918*, p. 400.

conversationalist one could meet anywhere. I say 'was', because for the last six months he has been an invalid.

His recent operation has disclosed a growth and he is given from 3 to 6 months to live. Poor Ethel! I want to be with her the whole time to help her through the dreadful ordeal of these coming months, but I am tied up with my own little family here.

THURSDAY MAY 2

The Germans have been fought to a standstill again. The furious fighting of the last week has not reaped the success they so desperately wanted. Clemenceau is cheerful and Sir Douglas Haig has addressed special Orders of the Day to various British divisions, praising them for their gallantly and steadfastness, which has foiled the German attempt to force their way to Calais.

WEDNESDAY MAY 8

I arrived at Cheltenham early this afternoon and was met by Ethel. Baynes was impatient to see me, poor fellow, so we went to the Home almost immediately, to have tea with him. His bed was drawn close to the open window, the view on to the trees and flowers in brilliant sunshine was peaceful enough for his eyes to rest upon. He is very, very altered. He was affectionate, but so weak.

Ethel and I never cease talking, and we are inseparable. It is a comfort to her to have me to discuss present and future arrangements.

WEDNESDAY MAY 15

I left Cheltenham today. Baynes looking stronger, but just as ill. I hated leaving Ethel alone in such circumstances. She will need all her pluck in the coming months.

SATURDAY MAY 18

A dramatic development in Ireland. Lord French, now Viceroy, has ordered the sudden arrest of all the Sinn Fein leaders, 100 or more, including de Valera and the rebel Countess Markiewicz.* They have been placed under arrest on a warship for deportation. The Irish Government has the details of a pro-German plot, and all those implicated are now caught.

---

*   Constance Gore-Booth, who was born in County Sligo, married Count Markiewicz in 1893. An ardent campaigner both for women's rights and Sinn Fein, she took an active part in the Easter Rising in April 1916. Sentenced to life imprisonment, she was released in the General Amnesty of 1917.

MONDAY MAY 20

Whitmonday
The Germans celebrated Pentecost yesterday by launching a very big air raid. I was just dozing off when those horrid whistles began! We left you undisturbed until the guns began in real earnest, then rolled you up in a blanket to carry you to the drawing-room sofa. I had to let Daddy carry you, you are too heavy for me now. We fondly hoped you might sleep through it – vain hope! At 1.30 the all clear bugles sounded.

We bundled you up but before I could put out the light, the warning whistles went loudly again and the wretched guns began again! This time you became unmanageable, but in ¾ hour this fresh attack was over. You finally got to bed at 2.30, a very demoralising experience for children. You were pale and fractious today. I am so worried not being able to send you away again with Nannie She is away for 10 days holiday with her husband on leave and doesn't want to leave London while he is here.

TUESDAY MAY 21

Three Rhine towns, Cologne, Mannheim and Düsseldorf have been mercilessly bombed by us. To retaliate, the Germans have committed an act of savagery by bombing our base hospitals well behind the fighting line and killing hundreds of wounded and nurses. This outrage was on Sunday night, the same day as our raid here.

MONDAY MAY 27

Tomorrow we are separating, you and I. I have been taking Nannie's place for 10 days and tomorrow, when Daddy and I go to Gelligemlyn, you go to Aunt Clara at Bazzleways for a fortnight, with Gwen our housemaid.

The long-delayed German offensive has begun again, on the Aisne, but our air-squadrons have interfered very much with their preparations.

TUESDAY JUNE 4

Gelligemlyn
We are having the most perfect holiday I ever remember here, such glorious weather, such freedom, such immunity from servants and no one to bother about except our four selves. No cooking, except boiling eggs, and water for tea and meals in the kitchen.

As for the war, we try to forget it, but that is impossible. The Germans were only 43 miles from Paris yesterday, and our lines are back on the Marne, as in September 1914.

SUNDAY JUNE 9

This last week has been a critical one in France. The German advance on Paris has again been checked for the time being, but Clemenceau has spoken out to his people, telling them that France will never yield nor surrender. He has warned them that they have 'cruel hours' before them.

SUNDAY JUNE 23

I am now back in London at 3 Ovington Gardens and I am awfully anxious; Daddy has been graded 2. He is nearly 46, and has delicate health. It is a mistake. He would never stand the physical labour of a Tommy in the ranks. There is a great outcry against grading these older men 2 instead of 3, and against the farce of a medical examination, lasting 2 minutes. What is the use of putting men into the ranks who are medically unfit, to destroy their health permanently and throw them back in a few weeks as useless? Daddy is to be re-examined.

Meanwhile the war news is getting better. The Germans have done little for 2 weeks now in the West, when they should have been entering Paris and Amiens and the Channel Ports. Either their losses have been so awful that they are obliged to wait for still more troops from Russia, or else it is possible their armies are being attacked by an epidemic.

Meanwhile the Austrian Empire is cracking, the people are rioting everywhere for food and peace. With the failure of their offensive, it is easy to see how discouraged and exhausted the people must be.

WEDNESDAY JUNE 26

This afternoon Muz and I had an amusing sight. Passing along Knightsbridge by the Embassy, there was a big crowd, and several policemen, military and civilian, standing in the roadway, were holding up every single motor car and asking to see the permit to use petrol. It is an open scandal that hundreds of people are still obtaining petrol under false pretences and it is high time the police intervened wholesale.

Heaps of cars gave unsatisfactory replies, and we were amused to see the policemen taking copious notes in pocket books. We stood quite half an hour, fascinated by the dismayed looks of delinquents and the relieved laughter of those who were all right.

FRIDAY JUNE 28

Sir Auckland Geddes, Minister of National Service,* is having a bad time over the failure of his recruiting of men up to 50 and the hopeless mistakes in grading men suffering from serious physical ill-health or disabilities. The whole system is to be revised, but Lloyd George had to come to the rescue of his unfortunate colleague and plead the country's dire need of men.

The answer is that there are still many thousands of young men employed in Government offices. These ought to go into the ranks before the old men.

---

*   As director of public recruiting from early 1916, he divided the country into regions and launched a new system of handling recruits, which met with much criticism. After the war, he was British ambassador in Washington. He died in Chichester in 1954.

WEDNESDAY JULY 3

I am very busy these days with my Belgian Workroom where I have to work every morning to replace Mme de Ruysscher, my forewoman. She was taken suddenly ill with appendicitis some days ago. She is so capable that she has all the details of accounts and books at her finger tips. So this morning I have been busy drawing out the week's wages-list, at tariffs varying from 3d, 3½d, 4d, 4½d, 5½d per hour, with certain allowances for bus-fares.

Also I have just started a new scheme, making shirts for the English Government at 9d a shirt, all materials provided by Government and the shirt ready cut. This is a very good price indeed, as the workers can earn good wages when they are quite familiar with the rather complicated shirt. We tried Belgian Government shirts, but these are only paid 6d, and the worker has to provide her own cotton.

I had a few days ago an official letter from the Belgian Minister, Baron Moncheur, informing me that the King of the Belgians has been graciously pleased to confer on me the *Médaille de la Reine Elisabeth* in recognition of the kind help and valuable assistance I have given to the Belgian Refugees and Belgian Soldiers during the war. The Insignia of the Order will be forwarded in due course through the Intermediary of this Legation. So there's an honour!

THURSDAY JULY 4

Independence Day! Celebrated with much flag-waving throughout London today. Drags full of American soldiers driving through the town on pleasure bent, have been widely cheered all day and the fact that one million Americans are now at the Front or in France, lends much significance to the enthusiasm the Americans are everywhere arousing. They look such smart, business-like fellows too!

SATURDAY JULY 6

I saw a few baskets of strawberries today, small ones and evidently bought in the open street markets. We have seen *none* in any of our West End shops this season, although they are released by the Government every Saturday for public consumption. Otherwise they are commandeered by the Government to be turned into jam for the Services. All the soft-fruit crops have failed this year, because of the drought and late frosts.

SUNDAY JULY 7

Daddy and I were walking down the Brompton Road this afternoon when we saw a Royal Carriage coming, drawn by two fast-going horses. There was a tall upright handsome man sitting on the right with curly fair hair and a pince-nez. We recognised King Albert, the most heroic figure of the World War. There were three officers with him. Very few people were about and no one recognised him, but I said to Daddy 'Quick, take off your hat, it is the King of the Belgians'.

He and the Queen have come to London for the Silver Wedding festivities. It is 25 years yesterday, since King George and Queen Mary were married. I saw the wedding procession from a window in the Strand and remember how pretty she was, with a dazzling complexion.

I wish Florence Younghusband and I would be decorated with our Belgian Order now, while the King and Queen are in London. It is so tantalising not being able to wear our bit of ribbon.

TUESDAY JULY 9

When I arrived at my Belgian Workroom this morning as usual, I found a registered packet awaiting me. It was from the Belgian Legation and contained the *Médaille de la Reine Elisabeth*! It is a very artistic bronze, or gilt bronze, medal of irregular outline, showing a charming head of the Queen, finishing above her head in a l aurel wreath. The ribbon is in smoke-grey watered silk, edged with old rose – very pretty. I shall always wear the ribbon during the war, if I can get the ribbon at Spinks. Florence Younghusband has just been to see me and is very excited; hers has not yet arrived, to her sorrow, because she is attending a big Concert at the Albert Hall tomorrow at which the King and Queen of the Belgians are to be present. I offered to lend her mine for the occasion, but she wouldn't take it, for fear of losing it!

WEDNESDAY JULY 10

How do you think the King and Queen of the Belgians came to England? They flew across from Le Havre in two seaplanes!

FRIDAY JULY 12

Muz and I went to Westminster to see the Zouaves Band march from the Cathedral where a Requiem Mass was sung for all the French who have lain down their lives in the War. The Zouaves have come over on a visit to London, a return visit for the one paid to Paris by our Guards' Band. These men were being entertained at the Baltic Exchange to lunch.

These dear Zouaves, so typical of France, were such handsome fellows, bronzed, with fine-cut, aquiline noses and smart upturned mustachios. I shouted 'Vive la France' with quite a catch in my throat. They remind me so much of my childhood.

MONDAY JULY 15

I am so busy every day with my Belgians, as Mme de Ruysscher won't be back for at least a fortnight. I had to use much diplomacy in the workroom in her absence, in settling down the workers to their new conditions of work, which means stiffer work but better pay.

FRIDAY JULY 19

General Foch, the French C in C, has made a brilliant counter offensive with his French troops. The initiative has now passed to the French on that front. It must dishearten the Germans to have the tables turned against them, when the wretched men had been promised Paris without fail, and British Armies driven into the sea.

Also, what will be the effect on the starved and deluded civilians, who have only been keeping quiet because of the promise of victory? The Americans are fighting splendidly with the French and share with them the honours of this show, while our front is quiet so far.

SUNDAY JULY 21

The ex-Tsar Nicholas has been murdered by the Bolsheviks. He, the Tsarina and their four daughters were shot in cold blood on July 16, because of the counter revolution in Siberia by Czech troops, which is gaining so much ground. The Bolsheviks feared that an attempt would be made to release him.

The progress we are making with the developments in the Air Service is so extraordinary, that there are two main objectives in view which may easily be carried out within the next five months, viz: to bomb Berlin, and to cross the Atlantic.

What strides since Blériot first flew the Channel nine years ago, on July 25 1909.

MONDAY JULY 22

I have again parted with you, and sent you on ahead to Wales before the holiday crush. Travelling nowadays is a dreadful ordeal. There are not half enough seats in the reduced trains for the passengers and corridors are filled with people standing. I did manage to get you and Nannie corner seats, but not in the through carriage. The platform was a seething mass of humanity, fighting for the different through-carriages, so I nipped past them and made for the far end of the train which the passengers had not yet stormed.

THURSDAY JULY 25

We are having drenching storms every day. They prayed for rain, and now we've got it! The dearth of fruit, and the horrible price of what there is of it, is a disaster in these times of scarcity. Cherries are 3/6 a pound, 2/6 at cheap shops, plums 2/6, which normally are 6d.

But the bread is improving, and getting much whiter, meat and bacon are more plentiful. Jam is unprocurable and has been for several weeks, because of the failure of the fruit crops. Everyone craves jam now, as all sweet stuff is practically non-existent. Still we do very well on the whole.

SATURDAY JULY 27

There is a very fine and gallant set of American women police in London, come to safeguard the morals of the young women here and, presumably, of the American troops! The Americans are swarming here now; they have to land in England first, before setting off for France.

WEDNESDAY AUGUST 7

Francis Hotel, Bath
I came here suddenly last Sunday, having been summoned by wire on Saturday evening to come to Aunt Edie, seriously ill in a Nursing Home. She had been here for a fortnight alone, taking internal douches for the colitis she has had for nearly a year. Her condition becoming worse instead of better, her Doctor suggested treatment at Bath. So she came alone, poor darling, then suddenly collapsed, with a high temperature.

Uncle Lionel, on military duty at Shirehampton, came at once and moved her into a Nursing Home. Here it was discovered that there was serious internal trouble and the operation took place two days go. She was in a very critical state all Monday, but today she seems to be rallying. I am thankful I was able to come to poor Lionel, who was terribly cut up, and had he been alone in these hours of anxiety, they would have been past bearing. She is still in danger, but so far nothing has gone wrong, so we live in hopes.

THURSDAY AUGUST 8

Darling Edie passed away at 6.15 this evening. I was with her all day, for she had had a very restless night. Poor Lionel returned at 4 o'clock from his military duty and as soon as he came into the room he saw she was very altered. She was conscious and talked a little almost to the very end, when her heart failed. They gave her brandy which she partly swallowed, raising her head to take it, but then her face changed suddenly and she ebbed away. Oxygen was tried, but was of no avail.

Oh! the tragedy for Lionel! He kept referring to the splendid help she had always given him, and asking what is to happen to the children who are left motherless, with him obliged to be away during the rest of the war. I am going back to Gelligemlyn tomorrow, as I can do no more and Lionel returns to Camp, after making arrangements for the funeral. I am so thankful to have been with him through his terrible trial. Now we have to think of what we are going to do for the children.

FRIDAY AUGUST 9

Gelligemlyn
I arrived at 7.15 at Dolgelly after a 10 hour journey from Bath. Found Daddy, Uncle Alex and Aunt Ethel waiting for me on the platform, but Aunt Beatrice had never received our wire telling her that all was over. She has arrived at Bath to find Lionel and me gone, and that the worst has happened. I ought perhaps to have waited at Bath and stayed over for the funeral on Monday – but Lionel's emphatic wish is to have nobody but Henry with him.

I arrived in the midst of the little wedding party – Armorer Nicholson is to be married from here tomorrow and I found the house prepared for the very quiet wedding of our beautiful young widowed cousin. We had dinner, *sans cérémonie*, in the servants' hall, as the dining-room is prepared for early lunch tomorrow. I hate to bring a shadow over the party, and asked Daddy in my wire to keep the news from them till after the wedding, knowing I should be strong enough to control myself, under the ordeal.

Death is now so familiar to us all, that we have learnt to live with it in our midst.

SATURDAY AUGUST 10

The wedding is over. The bride and bridegroom left at 3 o'clock and I have been able, while taking off my 'wedding clothes' to relax a bit and come up to my room and be alone. Oh! the restfulness of this beautiful place, and the lovely feeling in the country air that refreshes one after the crushing atmosphere of Bath!

Charlie Campbell, Major in the Horse Artillery is a distinguished-looking man, who will, I know, make Armorer happy. He has been back three times to the Front, and wears the Mons Medal and the Military Cross. The last time he came back it was after being severely gassed. Armorer looked lovely. She is so natural, simple and unspoilt, with all her charm.

SUNDAY AUGUST 11

I went to spend the day at Glyn with Ethel who is there for a few days. She returns to Cheltenham on Wednesday to her poor husband Baynes who is dying slowly in the Home in Cheltenham. She and I discussed the future of poor little Winnie and Geoffrey. They present a heavy responsibility to us three remaining sisters.

FRIDAY AUGUST 16

All this time of grief and personal anxiety, the tide of war has been running in favour of the Allies. The German invasion has become a retreat.

The battle line is now 16 miles from Amiens, at its nearest point. A service has just been held in the lovely old Cathedral to celebrate its rescue from peril. The shells had only partly damaged it and as all the valuable glass had been removed from the windows to a place of safety the damage is not irreparable. Also, Paris is now out of range of the long-distance guns, nicknamed 'Bertha'.

THURSDAY AUGUST 22

My Birthday! A broiling hot day, spent by Daddy and me travelling back to London, in packed carriages. We arrived three hours late at Paddington. When we got there at 8 o'clock, Daddy had to go out scouring the streets for a taxi, during which I had to stand by our luggage for 25 minutes, persuading a sulky porter not to abandon us. Our only hope of dinner lay in the small bit of meat we had brought up from Dolgelly with our ration books, as one can't buy meat in more than one place without great formalities!

After ten gruelling hours in the train we were tired and exhausted. Only the wonderful harvest scenes we travelled through from Dolgelly to London kept up our spirits. After Ruabon it was one golden sheet of corn. The harvest is a record for our times, even without reckoning the enormous additional areas given over to corn growing. Some time ago there was a panic, first over the prolonged drought, then over the too continuous rains, but since the great religious intercessions on August 4th, everything seems to have gone right with the Harvest and Foch's smashing Victories.

MONDAY AUGUST 26

Villages are falling like packs of cards according to the papers – so good to read such articles, after our experiences in March! The German break-up is in sight, and which of us could have hoped for, or expected, such a state of affairs to happen so soon? We knew it must happen but somehow were resigning ourselves to a longer wait. The Germans are beginning to admit their reverses, but did ever brute beasts more justly deserve retribution?

TUESDAY SEPTEMBER 3

The news is splendid tonight. Our successes are gathering like an avalanche and one leads to another. Today, joy of joys, Lens, the city of the coalfields, has fallen into British hands. All these years France has groaned under the loss of her coalfields, and repeatedly the Germans have arrogantly declared that their retention of the French coalfields must be a *sine qua non* at the declaration of peace. Now they have lost them.

This is our bag since Foch turned the tide of war, from July 18 to August 31:

123,302 prisoners, including 1674 officers
2,069 guns
13,783 machine guns

besides a considerable amount of stores and ammunition.

THURSDAY SEPTEMBER 5

The German retreat continues, and the British, French and Americans are in hot pursuit. There are now 1,600,000 American troops in France.

The Bolsheviks have murdered the British Naval Attaché to the Embassy in Petrograd, Captain Cromie. 18 months ago he distinguished himself conspicuously by his exploits in the Baltic when, in command of his submarine, he destroyed many German ships.

The Bolsheviks have declared that if any more attempts are made on their leaders they will instigate the assassination of Allied Statesmen in their own countries.

This is because of their fury over the half-murder of Lenin, who was shot by a Russian girl (but not killed, worse luck). The British Government has sent a wireless message to the Bolsheviks to the effect that we shall hold as hostage their precious 'Ambassador' Litvinov who, with 50 prominent Russians, was to depart for Russia this week. These men are being detained.

I am busy making warm things for the winter which we are all dreading because of the fuel shortage. All those people who don't provide themselves with warm underwear and stockings and socks will be very cold, for none are being made and the small stocks left are an outrageous price. There are no more woollen goods. I am planning a really warm tea gown for evening, black velvet, with a cosy soft woollen lining (pre-war treasure) and fur trimming. So I shan't dread my nightly changing for dinner.

MONDAY SEPTEMBER 9

While everything is going well on the Western Front, the Russian chaos grows steadily worse. The Bolsheviks are now the declared enemies of the British, French and Americans and are committing outrages on those who remain in Petrograd and Moscow. Very little is known of what is happening, but the Allies left in those cities are in hiding. Civil War is rife.

BOOK XI

SEPTEMBER 12, 1918 – NOVEMBER 11, 1919

THURSDAY SEPTEMBER 12

3 Ovington Gardens
Every time I begin a new book the price of it goes up by leaps and bounds. I suppose this one would have cost about 6d formerly, it is now 1/9. I begin this book with excellent news. The Americans are 'striking' at last on their own account. With the French, they are attacking near Verdun on two fronts.

Meanwhile the Kaiser's frantic appeals to the Germans at home, to keep cool and trust in the German Army are significant. They come a week after Hindenburg's manifesto to the people, enjoining them not to listen to the 'traitors' who are spreading malicious rumours about German reverses. Above all they are asked not to take notice of the million leaflets that are being dropped by the enemy from aircraft as propaganda etc.

Lloyd George made a most cheering speech today at Manchester, where he was given the freedom of the city. He was bidding us not to exaggerate our victory, but not to minimise it. But the 'worst is over', he stated emphatically. He attributed our recent success to Marshal Foch's supreme command, and to the German ignorance of our reserves in March, when we suffered our big reverse.

FRIDAY SEPTEMBER 13

Beatrice has been visiting the shell-shocked officers at Nannau Hospital. The poor fellows get bored to death up there. They suffer so much from insomnia and headache, and have the most terrible nightmares.

There is an Army Chaplain, whose nerve broke down in the end. On top of everything else he buried singlehanded 15 men and officers mangled by a shell, to some of whom he was greatly attached. He always sees the corpses before him. Many of these shell-shock cases won't tell even the nurse what they have on their mind, but they shudder at the recollection. They look all right outwardly, but they stammer at times and make a sort of grimace with their mouth.

Bee deplores the deluges of rain which have ruined the splendid Welsh crops before they could be harvested. It has poured incessantly for a fortnight. What is not standing in stacks is laid flat and has started sprouting! The farmers are furious. Their own lovely crops, which promised to be so heavy, will only be fit for horses and chickens.

SATURDAY SEPTEMBER 14

The Yanks have achieved a splendid victory on the great salient at St Mihiel south east of Verdun. They have advanced 14 miles, flattening the line and taking 13,000 prisoners and 150 guns. It is splendid. They are now only twelve miles from Metz which they can shell with long-range guns, and fourteen from Conflans, the junction of a great network of railways which connects the great iron fields of Briey with all parts of Germany. If and when we recover Briey, which produces 60 per cent of the iron and steel the Germans use for munitions, this will be a mortal blow.

WEDNESDAY SEPTEMBER 18

Such a disappointment! Daddy and I were to have started this morning for our longed-for holiday at Gelligemlyn. But the attack of influenza he started last Saturday is still enough to keep his temperature up. Feeling so much better yesterday after the drastic treatment I had given him, he got up and went to Westminster after lunch, to finish up things left undone. When he came in at six, his temperature was up again to 100! Back he went to bed, and there he is today. So we must wait till Friday. What a nuisance and you are awaiting us so eagerly, and I am so dying to see you!

SATURDAY SEPTEMBER 21

Gelligemlyn
We travelled down yesterday, just avoiding the threatened railway strike, which seemed alarmingly close last night. You were in the porch, as I hoped you would be and there were such shows of excitement!

You have grown out of all your trousers and I must get Williams, the Dolgelly tailor, to work at once! You came to unpack my trunk and look for 'surprises'! This time my imagination had led me no further than a pound of plain chocolate (the one and only sort procurable now, and 1lb the limit), a box of dominoes and a pair of rounded scissors for cutting out pictures.

WEDNESDAY SEPTEMBER 25

Rain, rain, rain every day. General Allenby has had a splendid victory over the Turks in Palestine. Meanwhile, the Bulgarians are getting badly knocked by the Allies in the Balkans. The Allied army has penetrated into Serbia to a depth of 40 miles and its complete recovery is well within the bounds of possibility before long. With the Turks and Bulgarians getting driven back on all sides, the Germans are not very happy.

Our railway strike did start two days ago. When the Finnises left yesterday, their prospects of getting beyond Ruabon were meagre. But Charles, in his Scots Guards' uniform, would perhaps have been able to force a passage in a troop train for himself and his wife!

MONDAY SEPTEMBER 30

There was snow on Cader Idris this morning when we awoke. It has been a fine gleamy day for the first time for weeks. We all went, you and Nannie included, to Penmaenucha, to spend the day with Sybil Wynne-Jones and her dear little son, Andy, 14 months old. Charley W-J, his Father in 17th Lancers, had just returned to the Front the day before.

This evening, Evelyn Haig Brown arrived to stay.* She brought the news of Bulgaria's sudden collapse. For the last few days the Bulgarians have been retreating before the invading Allied Armies, and yesterday they begged for an armistice of 48 hours. We haven't yet heard the terms of the surrender.

On the other fronts we are winning all along the line. There are seven different offensives going on in the West, from Nieuport in Belgium to Verdun, and everywhere the Germans are getting beaten back. The Belgians personally headed by King Albert have gained a fine victory. Further South the British are almost back in Cambrai, while in Palestine, Allenby is pushing towards Damascus.

TUESDAY OCTOBER 1

Bulgaria has surrendered unconditionally. The terms are highly satisfactory to the Allies. The Allies take control of the railways, the Danube front and transport. This enables the Allies to use Bulgaria as their campaigning ground against Austria and Turkey. Austria will now have to recall many troops from the Italian Front.

The news was received in London with extraordinary calm but *intense* interest. The Nation is now strung up to such control of itself that the stupendous news that comes in day after day now is received with perfect composure.

SUNDAY OCTOBER 6

Glaslyn
Daddy and I came to Glaslyn yesterday for a few days salmon fishing. It is three years since I stayed in my old home! It is looking lovely. But the weather is so stormy that the Wye remains in high flood and quite unfishable. The constant rains have lasted over six weeks now. Uncle Henry has cut down a good many trees, opening out the river, which shows nobly now all along the garden front. We all argue very much (Aunt Ethel is here too) over the trees still to be cut down.

MONDAY OCTOBER 7

Uncle Henry burst upon us in our bedrooms this morning with the news that Germany has asked the Allies for an armistice! In a second we were all out on the landing in various attires, tearing the paper out of each other's hands, and all gabbling at once.

---

*   Daughter of William Haig Brown, headmaster of Charterhouse from 1863 to 1895. He
     moved the school from its original site in the City of London to Godalming in Surrey.

'How they have been bluffing!' 'I knew they would collapse suddenly!' 'Baynes said it would be over this autumn!'

On reflection, we gathered that the Germans are tricking us into a discussion of peace terms, only to be able to tell their people that we the Allies won't make peace, are bent on their destruction and therefore they must fight to the end and not surrender.

But how it shows how they quail before internal uprisings. The situation at home seems desperate and it looks as though something must give way, as the strain is getting too great. Things are going badly for them everywhere.

WEDNESDAY OCTOBER 9

The Germans are burning Douai and Cambrai, and devastating the regions they are leaving behind. The unfortunate civilians are given 2 hours notice to evacuate and are only allowed to take about 100lbs of possessions away. The factories and churches are blown up wholesale, even the soil is ruined for cultivation.

The French Government is issuing a solemn warning to the Germans, declaring that the uttermost toll will be exacted. For every French town or village destroyed, a German town or village shall be similarly treated. Punishment will be meted out to every officer or man guilty of these outrages against civilisation.

The French have also informed Austria that for every French airman executed by Austria for dropping propaganda leaflets, the French will execute two Austrian officers. Far from repenting of all they did in Belgium, the Germans are doing even worse things in France out of spite.

It is interesting that the Berlin public was worked up to such a pitch of nervous tension the day Prince Max made his new Peace overture known in the Reichstag. Huge crowds gathered speculating upon the terms the new Chancellor would make to President Wilson. Of course the Allies are laughing at the Armistice proposals, but no official reply has yet come out. Our papers are two days late here.

It has poured consistently during our short visit here, and the Wye has been in flood all the time, hopelessly so for salmon fishing. We return to Gelligemlyn tomorrow.

FRIDAY OCTOBER 11

Gelligemlyn
The British troops under Haig have gained a splendid victory. Cambrai is ours, but alas there is nothing left of it. The Huns blew up most of it. Still our victory is forcing the Germans to retreat on a broad front. President Wilson's reply is contained in two clauses 1) no parley with Germany as long as a German soldier remains on any invaded territory, 2) no parley with any of the German rulers or leaders who brought about the war.

Meanwhile, events move so rapidly that anything is possible. There is open talk now in Germany of the Kaiser abdicating in favour of his grandson, the mere whisper of which, a few weeks ago, would have been enough to place the offender into prison.

Can you imagine the intense excitement of these days, when at any moment the most stupendous changes may take place? General Allenby's splendid campaign and successes in Palestine are of course responsible for the collapse of the Turks.

SATURDAY OCTOBER 12

Even now, when everything is against Germany, their savagery is still all too evident not only in their retreat from France, but also at sea. They have just torpedoed the Irish Mail Boat after leaving Kingstown in the midst of a gale, drowning 500 out of 750 people including numbers of women and children.

The *Leinster* carried mostly Irish people, with an Irish Captain and crew; she sank in a few minutes. The boats had no chance in the angry seas. The Duke of Abercorn's sister is among the drowned. Two torpedoes were fired, the first causing damage which might not have prevented the *Leinster* from reaching Holyhead, but the second was fatal. Can you imagine, after the world-wide hatred the Germans caused by sinking the *Lusitania*, that they could still at this stage, when their game is lost, arouse the terrible feelings of revenge such an act will draw upon them?

MONDAY OCTOBER 14

Yesterday we were all thrilled by a report, emanating from a semi-official telegram that came to the post office at Ganllwyd stating that 'Germany has accepted President Wilson's Fourteen Points as a basis for Peace'. Nannie and you brought back the news in the afternoon after a walk up the valley. You came in to the garden room where tea was going on and said solemnly 'There is Peace'.

I was at Hengwrt at the time and heard it from some of the shell-shocked officers who had come over from Nannau. They explained that, if it was true, it meant Germany's unconditional surrender. We could hardly believe this could be true. However, we awaited the postman's arrival at 10 o'clock this morning in great impatience, and found that it was the same old game: to stop fighting first and let peace terms be discussed on the basis of Woodrow Wilson's proposals!

The President's reply to this fresh overture from Germany is expected to be brief and categorical: no peace till Germany surrenders unconditionally.

WEDNESDAY OCTOBER 16

President Wilson's reply is splendid:
'The armistice asked for by Germany is a question for Marshal Foch to decide. But:

1.   There can be no peace with the Hohenzollerns.
2.   Absolute military guarantees must accompany any armistice (for instance our occupation of such military positions as Metz).
3.   Atrocities on land and sea must cease, before any armistice can be considered.'

The President's reply also contains this passage 'Relaxation now (on the Allies' part), hesitation now, would mean defeat when victory seems to be in sight. It would mean years of war, instead of peace on our terms'. Then an Official (U.S.) statement adds: 'The U.S. Government will continue to send over 250,000 men, with their supplies, every month, and there will be no relaxation of any kind.'

Today there is further excellent news from Flanders: we are within 3 miles of Lille.

FRIDAY OCTOBER 18

3 Ovington Gardens
Daddy and I travelled back to London today, leaving you behind at Gelligemlyn for another week. All the time before we drove off, you didn't leave me for one second, but ran behind me like a little dog, fetching and carrying, running to and fro with messages, carrying down my bags, finding my umbrella and making yourself invaluable in a variety of ways.

Just as the car was being packed up with our luggage, the postman arrived with the papers, giving the splendid news that Sir Roger Keyes (Admiral in Command at Dover) and naval forces have captured Ostend. Meanwhile our troops have taken Lille on the same day, marching into the town with bands playing, amid the indescribable enthusiasm of the remnants of the population who are liberated after four years of slavery. The Germans did not destroy the town before leaving, thanks no doubt to President Wilson's solemn warning against 'atrocities on land and sea', and also to the French and Belgian Governments' threat of reprisals on German towns.

But the systematic theft of everything of value in museum, private houses, looms and machinery, has been going on these four years and this Manchester of France is bereft of all its wealth. All those men and women capable of work have been deported.

The King and Queen of the Belgians landed at Ostend in a British destroyer yesterday and visited the town.

SATURDAY OCTOBER 19

The Germans have today evacuated the Belgian Coast right up to the Dutch frontier. Zeebrugge is ours too. Great joy reigns in Paris over the liberation of Lille and demonstrations have taken place in front of the statue of Lille in the Place de la Concorde.* Lord Derby the British Ambassador deeply touched the Parisians by laying a wreath at the foot of the statue, as a token of the joy felt all through Great Britain.

Another fine gesture, which has thrilled France, was that of General Sir Richard Haking of the 11th Division. He had held the sector before Lille for three years. When his men arrived at the town, they were made to halt to make way for the French *poilus* to enter the town first. The population was immensely touched by this and furthermore

---

*   One of eight giant statues representing provincial capitals, installed by King Louis-Philippe round the periphery of the Place de la Concorde. The statue of Strasbourg had been shrouded in black since 1870, but was triumphantly unveiled at the Armistice.

Sir Richard sent the pennon of the 11th Division, via his Chief of Staff, to the Military Governor of Paris, stating that he would be proud if he would place it on the Lille Statue. On the flagstaff a paper was affixed with these words, 'A tribute of affection and admiration to the French Nation from the Officers, NCO's and men of the 11th Division who entered Lille on the evening of October 17th 1918'.

MONDAY OCTOBER 21

On going to my Belgian Workroom this morning I found a letter from M. Maeterlinck, Vice President of the Belgian Red Cross. He told me that they were sending me a 'badge' as a small token of appreciation of my 'untiring' work on their behalf. But it came as hot coals on my head, this letter, because the Chelsea Committee has decided that it cannot possibly finance the work any longer. Our expenses in wages and materials have reached the sum of £100 per month, as against about £20 at first.

So I have had to write and tell M. Maeterlinck that I am 'desolated' by the forcible closing of this work, the Committee having no funds to meet the expenses. I said that my only consolation is that the Belgian Red Cross will soon be in a position to do without help, but that I should dearly have loved to go on with the work till peace is signed. I was the one to start it and I am glad that I have seen it through.

The workroom will not be closed. On the contrary, we hope to give more Belgians work, but it will be uninteresting shirts for the British Army and for the Belgian Government, paid at 9d and 6d a shirt respectively, the Belgian Army shirts being much less complicated to make. All materials are provided by the Governments and they arrive ready cut, so there is no scope for variety. There is no more correspondence for me in French with the Belgian Red Cross authorities, the Queen's ladies-in-waiting, and even with Queen Elisabeth herself.

WEDNESDAY OCTOBER 23

I have been interviewing three different schoolmistresses today, because I feel that now you are to be five on Monday, you must begin your little discipline in concentrating your mind on things which are not all play. But my chief concern is for you to have the companionship of other children and that you should learn to do things with others.

The first school I went to was Mr Wagner's in Queen's Gate but it is too old a school for you, you would already have to wear uniform and join in the games in the afternoon. The teaching there was on the same lines we were taught, the very opposite to the interesting Montessori method. Mr Wagner, or his wife whom I interviewed, impressed on me that there is no golden road to learning, it must be done by grinding at plain facts. My heart smote me at the thought that my baby will, in a year or so, have to sit down on a hard school bench and assimilate hard dry facts.

The third school I went to is the one to which we shall send you at Christmas if all is well. A delightful one in Glendower Place, where there are in the tiny class about twelve children of your age. I saw them do the physical drill and attended the reading class, where the children were being taught in threes, with a mistress each. I took a hint, and you and I are going to have a little lesson each morning, so as to know something before you join up.

SATURDAY OCTOBER 26

The British 2nd Army under Plumer, the 3rd (Byng) and the 5th (Birdwood) are now moving on through all the German resistance. Ever since the great victory at Cambrai they have gained momentum and now Valenciennes is almost surrounded. Some of the troops are fighting again over the old scenes of the retreat from Mons, thereby taking a glorious revenge for the defeat our little army sustained in 1914.

The most terrible accounts reach us, from Russia, where the Bolsheviks are rapidly killing off all the leisured classes. People are being shot down in the streets for a mere remark betraying a longing for freedom from the terrible tyranny of Lenin and Trotsky.

MONDAY OCTOBER 28

Your fifth birthday, bless you, and the day Austria sued for Peace, without awaiting the result of other negotiations (with Germany and Turkey). The Austrian Emperor Karl is reported to have left Vienna hurriedly, and all the Archdukes have taken refuge in a Castle, Gödöllo, in Hungary. This sounds like revolution, but what possibilities it opens up for the Allies!

Also General Allenby's armoured cars have captured and occupied Aleppo at the head of the Baghdad Railway before it traverses Palestine and Mesopotamia. The German General, Liman von Sanders, at the head of 20,000 troops, retired from Aleppo before our advance, scarcely making any resistance.

THURSDAY OCTOBER 31

Turkey has asked for peace. Events are crowding one on top of the other with such rapidity that we can't take them all in. Everything is crumbling around Germany. She is isolated, her frontiers are open to invasion and she is hemmed in on every side. One of the results of Turkey's surrender will be the opening of the Dardanelles to our Fleet. Above all our prisoners will be released, notably the heroes from Kut, with General Townshend at their head.

FRIDAY NOVEMBER 1

In Austria, the whole Empire is in revolution. In Vienna, a Republic is being formed. The Archduke Joseph who had been sent to Budapest to take the reins of Hungary in his hands has been hastily recalled. The Emperor has fled to Gödöllo Castle, taking 18 wagons full of furniture, food and money, not to mention Crown Jewels! Count Tisza, the former Austro-Hungarian Prime Minister has been assassinated.* He was shot

---

*   On 8 July 1914, Count Tisza had initially warned the Emperor that if Austria attacked Serbia it 'would, in human possibility, provoke the world war'. But he changed his tune a week later. Martin Gilbert, *First World War*, p. 19.

by a soldier while walking with a friend in Budapest, where there is open revolution and bloodshed.

Meanwhile the Austrian Army on the Italian front is in full flight.

MONDAY NOVEMBER 4

The Armistice with Austria is signed and we are to know the terms tomorrow. Meanwhile, there are no signs yet of the surrender of Germany, though Bavaria is beginning to exhibit great uneasiness at the sudden exposure of her frontiers to invasion.

Foch has today begun a fresh offensive, which may prove the last blow that will crumple all German resistance. Yesterday the Americans and French made a splendid advance towards Sedan and Metz, and were only 9 miles from Metz. The Belgians are quite near Ghent; they have closed in on 3 sides.

This evening I attended one of our Committees (Chelsea War Refugees), an emergency one to decide whether to grant our funds (mostly American money collected over there by Mrs Fitzwarren, Mrs Childers' sister) in answer to an appeal for the inhabitants of the liberated regions of France and Belgium, who are left destitute by the retreating Huns.

In Lille alone, thousands of the civilian population have been left only with the clothes they stand up in. The work of succouring all the civilians liberated by our troops is carried on by British funds. We voted a grant of £1000, for clothing, boots and blankets, and this is to be done at once, in view of the winter now beginning. Besides this we are sending out 7000 letters appealing for partly worn clothing to be sent as well.

The Emperor and Empress of Austria are said to be retiring precipitately to Switzerland, which is also the asylum of the ex-King of Greece, Constantine. The whereabouts of ex-King Ferdinand of Bulgaria are unknown and now his son Boris has also suddenly abdicated and retired hastily to Vienna, where he won't be allowed to rest long, I imagine.

TUESDAY NOVEMBER 5

We have just come in, you and Nannie, Muz and I from an exciting sight. Daddy rang us up at 10 this morning from Westminster telling us to go at once to the Mall, to see the placing of captured German guns on both sides of the route from Buckingham Palace to the Admiralty Arch. It was a lovely sunny morning; an Investiture at the Palace had brought a certain number of people, who were charmed of course to find a far greater attraction awaiting their curiosity.

There are some hundreds of guns being placed there, fresh from the battlefield in France, and bearing scars from shell and shot, strangely camouflaged too. What a splendid triumphal alley they will make. There is such a feeling of victory in the air and coming Peace. Calm as we are, we are already adjusting our thoughts and ideas to the coming peace and happier conditions and a great feeling of strain is being relaxed.

THURSDAY NOVEMBER 7

There is a revolution in Germany. The Navy has mutinied at Kiel. The sailors have seized the warships and arrested all the officers, killing some who resisted. All Germany's warships are under the Red Flag, and the 'Soldiers and Workmen's Council' set up in Kiel has ordered the removal of the whole Fleet from Kiel Harbour.

It is to steam to Norwegian or Swedish ports, to be interned. The opinion is prevalent that orders were given to the Fleet by the High Command to steam out and engage the British Fleet, and that the sailors refused to commit suicide. Thus ends the Kaiser's dream of successfully challenging our command of the sea.

On the Western Front, the retreat of the Germans continues. The Allies have notified the enemy Government that, if they want an Armistice, they must send envoys *under the White Flag* to meet Marshal Foch in the field. Thus a truce party composed of three German Generals duly arrived at noon today on the road indicated in the Allies Note, and were convoyed to Marshal Foch's and Admiral Sir Rosslyn Wemyss's Headquarters! Our Admiral has been appointed the Naval Representative of the Allies, empowered to negotiate alongside the Military Representative, Marshal Foch.

The prevailing opinion is that the Germans are bound to accept the terms of the Armistice, however stiff, because their frontiers, especially the southern (left unprotected by the Austrian defection) are exposed to invasion by all the victorious armies. Last but not least, the country is seething with revolution. If the terms of the armistice are refused by the Government the people are threatening to deal with the situation, so *anything* may happen from day to day. What a collapse, what a downfall for Germany and her arrogance!

Today I made up a large box of clothing and took it to Crosby Hall, the collecting place for the French and Belgian civilians' relief. I found two or three ladies in the office feverishly preparing to despatch 7000 appeals for clothing (my parcel is the very first one received!) and rather desperate for want of help. I there and then volunteered to help and sat down to the task. For one and half hours I sorted, folded and placed in envelopes three different leaflets from three piles. It took much longer that I thought – though I was working quickly, my total was only 200.

SATURDAY NOVEMBER 9

Today was the most notable Lord Mayor's Show in history, and it was made a naval, military and aerial pageant of Victory. Such a unique occasion was not to be missed by you, small as you are, just 5, so you went to see it, with Daddy, myself and Nannie. Lunching at 12.30, we took a taxi as far as the Strand, and pushed our way down a side-street to the Embankment to reach Norfolk House.

We had to go through a terrible crush for about 50 yards, although the procession was only due at about 3.30. Finally we reached Norfolk House, where the firm of Williams and James occupies the first floor. The huge bow-windows in all the rooms look out right over the Embankment, so we had a splendid view. The procession itself was 2 miles long; there were contingents from all the services, including the Women's Auxiliary Army Corps, the Women's Royal Naval Corps and the Women's Flying Corps. The women of the Land Army looked splendid, mounted on military horses which they managed skilfully, even those that pranced to the music! The air-women looked smart in their Hungarian blue uniforms, the same colour as the men's.

There were captured German Guns, some of the very heaviest, dragged by the 'caterpillar' traction lorries, and three tanks, male, female and whippet, running on their own power. It was the usual sort of military pageant, but the difference lay in the wonderful elation that thrilled the thousands in the dense throng, the knowledge that victory is ours at last.

I kept reverting to the contrast in Berlin. The panic rush on the banks all over Berlin indicates the state of mind the Germans must be in. I could almost feel sorry for them, richly as they have deserved every humiliation and bitterness.

The marvel of the day, for your fond parents, was the walking all the way home of our little sportsman in the dusk after the show. It took us an hour all the way from the Temple, along the Embankment to Northumberland Avenue, through the crowds, evidently out for the night, along the Mall where the hundreds of German guns looked eerie in the semi-gloom of the shaded arc lights.

The crowd was very busy around the guns, and the little London boys have never had such a time in their lives, playing with these guns, clambering along the barrels and trying to work the machinery, for there are no officious 'don't touches' to restrict the Londoners' curiosity. Think of the Germans' fury if they could see their precious guns exposed to the familiarity of London crowds!

SUNDAY NOVEMBER 10

There is Revolution in Berlin! It is true. The Kaiser and Crown Prince have abdicated, at least the Kaiser has. So there is an end of the Hohenzollerns. Lloyd George announced this at the Lord Mayor's Banquet last night. Probably the Kaiser's decision to abdicate at once instead of waiting for a sort of plebiscite, was prompted by knowledge of the armistice terms. He had gone to Spa, to the Headquarters, placing himself under the protection of the Army.

The meeting of the German Armistice Envoys with Marshal Foch took place on Friday morning, 8th November in the Forest of Compiègne. The German Envoys[*] were not prepared for what they heard. Deeply moved, they listened to the terms in silence, realising the magnitude of Germany's defeat. They made one request, that hostilities might cease at once, until Germany's reply could be received, but Foch replied that this was impossible.

The Envoys then spoke only a few words, representing the difficulties in carrying out some of the secondary conditions. Then a courier was sent with the Terms to the German GHQ. Owing to the heavy German barrage the courier could not get through

---

[*]   Led by Matthias Erzberger.

the lines. So after some delay he was taken up in an aeroplane and taken to Spa. The answer from the German Government is expected to be delivered tonight.

MONDAY NOVEMBER 11

Day of Days in the history of the War! At eleven o'clock this morning the guns boomed the great tidings: the Armistice has been signed. Germany has surrendered unconditionally!

I was at the Belgian Workroom, talking in my sanctum with Mme de Ruysscher, when the guns boomed forth. Everyone flew to the windows, only to see other heads leaning out. We all knew what it meant. I couldn't stay, a demon of unrest seized me, I must go out into the streets to join my family. But I had the presence of mind to go into the workroom to congratulate my poor Belgian women and there they were laughing and crying all at once. Needless to say they were given a holiday for the rest of the day.

As I hurried home, it was curious to see the awakening of London to enthusiasm and excitement. People ran about, flags began to appear at all the windows; women from the aeroplane and munitions factories poured into the streets, standing in big groups, cheering and shouting. In an hour the streets were transformed.

Flags were flying everywhere, everywhere were people, old and young, hurrying by with flags and flag-staffs, hastily bought and not even wrapped up, to hang them out. Meantime I had got home in ten minutes and added my big French tricolour flag (made by me) in our bedroom window to the dear Union Jack I made 18 months ago in anticipation of this great day.

You and Nannie came in at midday from your walk bedizened* with ribbons. You were almost concealed under a tricolour rosette as big as yourself. We lunched and then had hoped to make a little tour in a taxi, round by Buckingham Palace to see the King, perhaps, on his balcony. But the crowds were enormous. Not only was there no chance of getting a taxi, but the streets by this time were a pandemonium of cheering and shouting, lorries full of soldiers and munitioneers waving flags and letting off crackers.

We went down Constitution Hill where motor cars festooned with flags, filled with servicemen and women made a continuous stream towards the Palace, and the crowds all converged there too. Once in front of the Palace we found thousands of people there, the monument in front black with human beings who had climbed on to the heads and behind the wings of the marble figures.

Evidently the King and Queen were expected to drive out, as a lane was kept free through the crowd. While we waited, we noticed with amusement that workmen were scraping off the black coating from the clusters of electric lamps over the gateways in the courtyards of the Palace. This was a welcome sign that the light-shading restrictions are to be abolished.

We waited a long time in the crowds but the rain came on, so we walked home, not having seen the King. Tonight we are dining at the Heads in Pont Street, and are to go

---

*   Decked out gaudily.

in morning dress, to walk in the streets and see the excitements. The most noticeable thing about the crowds, among the older people, is the expression on their faces – the transfiguration – smiles and gladness, shining through the sorrow and unutterable regrets which are the lot of the bereaved.

Florence Younghusband was on the top of a bus when the guns were fired. In front of her were two soldiers one with his face horribly scarred. He looked straight ahead and remained stonily silent; the other just bowed his head in his hand and burst out crying. The omnibus conductress dropped into the vacant seat by Florence, leant her head on her shoulder and cried too. 'I lost my man two months ago, I *can't* be happy today', she murmured.

TUESDAY NOVEMBER 12

London is all beflagged. The streets are calmer today, but there are still plenty of signs of rejoicing. The Heads told us last night that the finest experience they had lived through was the singing of *God Save the King* at the Stock Exchange. Mr Head 'phoned to his wife to come at once and join him as soon as he got down there in the morning.

While we were annoyed at having missed seeing the King and Queen at the Palace yesterday, we went there this morning to see them drive off to St Paul's for the Thanksgiving. The crowds were as huge as yesterday, and during the whole hour that we waited we could measure the loyalty of the people to the throne. No small praise to the King and Queen in these days when, as Lloyd George said on Saturday 'Empires and Thrones, Kings and Crowns are falling like dead leaves before the storm'.

The Kaiser and his staff have fled into Holland in ten motor cars! The Kaiser intended to surrender in person to the British, but was headed off by Revolutionary troops from entering the British lines. The terms of the Armistice are out and they are so stern as to call for a whine from the German Chancellor to President Wilson, begging him to intervene to soften the 'fearful terms'.

WEDNESDAY NOVEMBER 13

The joy in France and Italy is as unbounded as it is here. The change in Alsace-Lorraine is already taking place. The roads are being re-made and the restoration of the beloved provinces to France is taking place rapidly. Everyone is wondering what is going to happen to the Kaiser. It is unthinkable that he can be allowed to remain in Holland, a fountain of intrigues and plots! The German Socialist Government seems to keep the country calm; Bolshevism hasn't yet broken loose, let us devoutly pray it won't.

FRIDAY NOVEMBER 15

Today, just as I was preparing to go to the Belgian workroom, Florence Younghusband ran in rather breathlessly, telling me to be quick and come with her, Muz too, to the Te Deum Service at Westminster Cathedral, for King Albert. It is his Fête day and also the

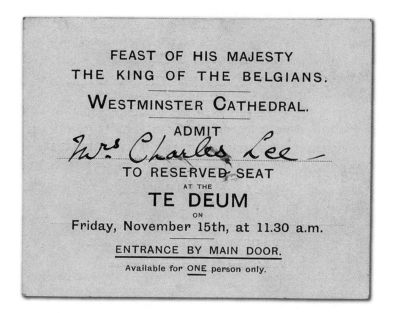

FEAST OF HIS MAJESTY
THE KING OF THE BELGIANS.

WESTMINSTER CATHEDRAL.

ADMIT

Mrs Charles Lee

TO RESERVED SEAT

AT THE
TE DEUM

ON
Friday, November 15th, at 11.30 a.m.

ENTRANCE BY MAIN DOOR.

Available for ONE person only.

Entrance ticket
for the King of
the Belgians'
Festival Service.

day on which he is making his triumphal entry into Brussels. Muz and I flew into our hats and furs and I wore my *Médaille de la Reine Elisabeth*. It was a most impressive service. The great Cathedral was overflowing, mostly with Belgians.

We had very good seats, thanks to our 'reserved' tickets, near the High Altar, and by the aisle up which Cardinal Bourne passed. He officiated in all the splendour of his scarlet robes and was surrounded with ecclesiastics. The King of the Belgians was represented by Princess Clementine, who was accompanied by her husband, Victor Napoleon. It was a most moving moment when the Brabançonne* was played on the grand organ at the end of the service. I noticed the gleam of happiness and triumph steal across the face of a fine, dignified Belgian officer, among the group behind the Princess and realised what this *dénouement* means to him and his compatriots after four years of patient endurance under their country's martyrdom.

I wore my decoration all day in honour of King Albert's day, and when I got home in the evening and took off my cloak, my precious medal was missing! The clasp must have unfastened somehow, and slipped down in the dusk of the street. I am miserable about it.

SATURDAY NOVEMBER 16

I went to the Belgian Legation to declare my loss and see if I can replace my decoration. They were so overrun with work, owing to the restoration of Belgium and the imminent repatriation, that the secretary I saw asked me to write down my request. She gave me the hope that another medal might be sent.

---

*   The Belgian National Anthem.

SUNDAY NOVEMBER 17

Daddy and I went to a wonderful Thanksgiving Service at Mr Gough's, the popular War preacher at Holy Trinity, Brompton. The crowds were so enormous that Daddy withdrew, hating a crowd, and came in for a charming 'overflow' Service held in the churchyard outside, by the flower-decked Shrine, for those fallen in the War. It was frightfully cold and poor Mr Gough looked so perished, clad only for the interior of the Church.

There was such a crowd that Nannie grew alarmed, elbowed her way out and took you to St Paul's, Onslow Square. There you sat through the service, enthralled by a big soldier who sang the psalms, hymns and responses lustily. You could hardly take your eyes off him.

TUESDAY NOVEMBER 19

19 Sion Hill, Clifton

I came down here yesterday to stay a week in Uncle Lionel's house to see little Geoffrey and Winnie whom I haven't yet seen since their mother's death. The children have grown a good deal. Winnie, now ten, is a pretty child, with a lovely satin complexion and beautiful long fair hair, tumbling down her shoulders. She speaks her mind out on every occasion, and asked me at lunch today whether she might suggest a hockey stick for my Christmas present to her. Only it appears she really needs it at once while the hockey season is on! Needless to say she jumped at my offer to her to come with me and choose one for herself.

WEDNESDAY NOVEMBER 20

Lionel took us this afternoon to a wonderful Thanksgiving Service in the Cathedral. There were detachments of all the forces, about 100 clergy, the Lord Mayor, the whole Academic body in their Scarlet robes, and the most beautiful feature of all, six fine young men bearing the six chief allied flags. A stalwart sailor bearing a huge white ensign and on each side of him two soldiers with the Union Jack and American flag. Behind these came the French, Belgian and Italian Flags. You have no idea of the solemnity of these six lovely colours floating up the grand nave, above the heads of the thousands thronging there. When they first appeared, a sudden emotion choked my throat. They are the emblems of so much glory, such heroism and devotion, exultation and final triumph after the agony of four and a quarter years.

THURSDAY NOVEMBER 21

The great Naval Triumph pageant began yesterday when 20 of the finest German U boats surrendered at Harwich to Admiral Tyrwhitt. There are plenty more to come, but this was the first batch.

We are all horrified at the last act of German brutishness over the release of our prisoners. These poor men, reduced already by want and starvation, were turned out of the prisons without a crumb of food and sent off in herds to find their way back to the British lines. Many had sixty miles to go and were in no state to march. Those that have arrived were in a pitiable state of exhaustion, but many have perished from cold and starvation. No doubt the Germans are in want themselves, but they could have given the men three days rations of bread!

FRIDAY NOVEMBER 22

Daddy has forwarded me a letter from the Belgian Minister, Baron Moncheur, informing me that another insignia of my Belgian decoration is being sent to me to replace the one I lost. Isn't it good of him!

We are all delighted at Admiral Wemyss's *mot* to the German Plenipotentiaries. They were whining at the excessive rigour of the terms of the Armistice which included the surrender of most of the German Fleet. 'But surely', they contended, 'it is

24
No. 9109

LÉGATION DE BELGIQUE,

59, SLOANE GARDENS,
S.W.1.

November 18th, 1918.

Dear Madam,

I beg to acknowledge the receipt of your letter of the 16th instant, and am forwarding you herewith a new Medal of Queen Elisabeth to replace the one which you have lost.

If your first medal should be returned to you, I should be pleased if you would send the second one back to the Legation, as, of course, it is only under very exceptional circumstances that we can give a second insignia to a recipient of the Medal.

Believe me,

dear Madam,

Yours truly,

Mrs. Charles Lee,
3, Ovington Gardens,
S.W. 3.

Letter from Belgian Minister.

inadmissible to exact the surrender of a Fleet yet unbeaten?' Fixing his eyeglass in his eye, Wemyss said 'They had only to come out'.

SATURDAY NOVEMBER 23

I returned to 3 Ovington Gardens today, and found you so delighted to see me. Aunt Ethel came yesterday to Sion Hill, to see me and we went to Mr Board's studio to see the portrait he is painting of dear Aunt Edie, from the photo taken just before her last illness. He had just had one interview with her before she fell ill, but of course had to paint the whole picture from the photo. Well, when we went in and stood before the picture, it was so extraordinarily like Edie, and so lifelike, that Ethel, taken unawares, burst into tears.

SUNDAY NOVEMBER 24

The surrender of the German Fleet is proceeding daily. Many of the big battleships are now safely berthed at Scapa Flow.

FRIDAY NOVEMBER 29

I have been helping these last two days to sell at a Belgian Lace Sale held at Mrs John Astor's in Grosvenor Square. It was most interesting. Lady Winifred Elwes who with some of her family is living with Florence Younghusband for a while, is one of the patronesses of the Association of Lace Workers, and she asked me to help her.

Many fashionable people were present, including Lady Diana Manners,* Lady Lavery, Lady Randolph Churchill, Viola Tree, Lilian Braithwaite and various other celebrities from the social and theatrical world.

They were all helping to sell the wonderful lace. This was made in secret during the occupation of Belgium and sent over to be sold in England, to outwit the Germans who did their utmost to capture the lace trade. We did very well, I think. We took in £150 yesterday, besides many orders for lingerie, and I don't know what today's record is. Gervase Elwes, Lady W's husband, the great singer, sang most delightfully yesterday and was a great draw.**

SUNDAY DECEMBER 1

I have had such a thrilling afternoon! I saw Marshal Foch and Clemenceau on their triumphal drive from Charing Cross through London and what an ovation they had! Daddy was unable to come, having a cold, but I went with the Romer Wynns to see the show from his office balcony in Piccadilly. Never have I felt such thrills of joy in me and all around me! I took a big French flag to wave.

---

*	British actress and author, she became Lady Diana Cooper in 1919 on her marriage to Duff Cooper, 1st Viscount Norwich.

**	The leading tenor of his day, Gervase Elwes (1866–1921) died prematurely in an accident in Boston, Massachusetts.

The route was closely lined with troops and from our balcony we could see the whole slope of Piccadilly from the Cavalry Club up to the Ritz. When we sighted the outriders in the distance, the roar of cheers had already been sounding for some time like a roll of thunder far away; thousands of flags and handkerchiefs fluttered. At last the state carriage came bearing the hero of the world, Marshal Foch. He sat, a grave, pale, perfectly calm figure in the French blue uniform, turning now and again to say a word to the Duke of Connaught at his side. We all shouted ourselves hoarse, I shouted *Vive Foch!* I hoped you were doing it too, darling, in your calmer recess in Hyde Park, as I coached you last night!

After a pause came Clemenceau with Lloyd George. Clemenceau was looking very much overcome by the nerve-shattering reception he received. He kept leaning forward making sweeping gestures with his hat; his big, square, bald forehead shining prominently in the dim grey light of the murky weather seemed to tower above his dark eyes.

Lloyd George beamed at his side, his long grey locks hanging over the astrakhan collar of his coat. When just past us, he turned right round in his seat to get a full view of Piccadilly as the carriage retreated towards Hyde Park Corner, and he must have had a glorious sight of the thousands of cheering people kept in bounds by the close-lined troops along the kerb.

I walked back here through the Park, past the French Embassy where I was held up by the vast crowds hoping to see Clemenceau on the balcony. I waited three quarters of an hour, much amused by the efforts of the people to induce him to appear. They yelled in unison 'We want Clemenceau!' 'We want the Tiger!' After a time he *did* appear, but at a window which I didn't command, so I never saw him. When I came home, I found Florence Younghusband talking to Muz, very proud of herself because she had seen Clemenceau at the window! And after a while you and Nannie returned. You had seen the 'three Prime Ministers', you told me, 'the French, the English, and the Italian!'.

Foch, Clemenceau and the Italian Prime Minister* have come over to discuss with our Ministers what is to be done with the Kaiser. There is a general clamour among all the Allies to get the Kaiser handed over to them by Holland, to be put on his trial, for the misery he has brought on the whole world. With him also the Crown Prince and all the chief miscreants who have ordered the atrocities committed by the Germans.

MONDAY DECEMBER 2

A rather nice little story about Clemenceau has just been told to me. While the discussions were going on between the Allied Ministers on the Armistice terms, Clemenceau and Lloyd George both lost their fiery heads and a sharp wordy duel ensued. Lloyd George then bounced out of the room after delivering a burning shaft! Bonar Law turned to Clemenceau, making excuses for his impetuous colleague,

*   Signor Vittorio Orlando.

whereupon the Tiger snapped out 'Mr Lloyd George has been very rude, but I love him and, if you interfere between us, I shall hate you!'

SATURDAY DECEMBER 14

Nearly a fortnight has passed since I wrote, there seems nothing to record, till today. We are all more or less 'flat' as a reaction after the great events. But today one of our 'silent' revolutions has taken place and been consummated with scarcely a comment. I mean the Women's Franchise, which came into effect today for the first time, in this General Election. I don't know how many extra million votes the new measure brings.

How very astute Lloyd George has been in his sudden championing of the Women's Cause a year or two ago, and the passing of the Women's Franchise Bill, so quietly. I am confident that their new prerogative must have come as a sudden surprise to many women, when, a few days ago, they were served with the official intimation, informing them of their registered number and polling station! It almost took *me* unawares! Lloyd George, to do the thing handsomely, has even gone so far as to notify to his own supporters, the Coalition Candidates, to stand aside, and make way for the candidature of several well-known women, such as Christabel Pankhurst!

This has been loyally complied with, and the Coalition Candidate has not only stood aside for her, but has placed his own electioneering organisation at her service. She is sure to be returned, and as her main campaign is against the 'Bolsheviks' by which name she stigmatises her Labour opponents, much to their chagrin, we all wish her the best of luck. Lloyd George has strongly denounced the Labour representatives who are seeking election such as Snowden, Ramsay Macdonald and Henderson as the 'wrong sort'.

Daddy and I went solemnly together to vote. As we each voted for the rival candidates we might have stayed at home! But I was determined to give a vote for the National Independent Party. Daddy never wavered from his allegiance to the Coalition pure and simple, but I want the Coalition and something stronger added to it. No secret party funds, no buying of honours, purity and no bargaining, so I hope my man will win, as he promises to support Lloyd George in the main.

This last week I have been awfully busy getting ready our house in Brunswick Gardens to lend for a while to my poor friend Mrs Aston Talbot whose husband died at Nairobi in two days from Influenza. She is distracted, having had no news beyond the cable announcing the fact. She wanted to come up to London but had nowhere to go.

London is so overcrowded now, with the movements of officers and men always passing through. Everybody has returned to their houses who had left them because of the air-raids and it is impossible to get rooms at hotels or to find empty houses.

THURSDAY DECEMBER 19

Today London gave a rousing reception to Sir Douglas Haig and Generals Plumer, Horne, Byng, Rawlinson and Birdwood of the 'Anzacs' who all arrived today. They drove in open Royal Carriages from Charing Cross down Pall Mall, up St James's

Street, Piccadilly, past Constitution Hill to Buckingham Palace where they were received by the King and Queen and had luncheon there.

Oh, the reception we gave them! Muz and I went and stood on the pavement in Constitution Hill with our back to the Palace and saw them beautifully. Sir Douglas came first, a very handsome upright figure, his hand at the salute all the time, a gleam of gratified triumph in his eye; Plumer was in the next carriage, his little round keen face wreathed in smiles. I shouted Plumer! Plumer! and waved frantically, for he is Uncle Guy's and Uncle Tich's General, and the most successful. They all looked splendid, Birdwood especially, the man who wiped out the defeat of the 5th Army last March.

CHRISTMAS EVE

Muz and I finished our shopping today. Never has there been such a Christmas. Never have the shops been so besieged. It is as though the sudden slackening of the dreadful strain of the last four and a half years has reacted on the strings of the purse! Everyone is buying presents. It is also your first 'conscious' Christmas, where you have made your own little purchases! There is a present for Daddy, a tiny leather eye-glass wiper and a surprise in store for me. Besides presents for Nannie, red velvet bedroom slippers and handkerchiefs for Granny. Tonight before you went to bed, we spread our 'stockings' about the chimney in the sitting room.

CHRISTMAS DAY

A glorious Christmas Day, fine and frosty. We went to early service at 8 am and came back to breakfast to find you wild with impatience to open your 'stocking', – a pillow-case crammed full. There was a lovely big real watch from Uncle Lionel, ticking away from the inside of the pillow-case, a magic-lantern and a score or so of other gifts. You excitement was so amusing to watch, that our own presents were only opened as an afterthought!

After this, we went to Church again, while you and Nannie walked to Piccadilly and St James's to see the preparations for President Wilson's arrival tomorrow, Boxing Day. His visit here was rather suddenly arranged from Paris. Very great expectations are set upon this visit by the Allies, as on the results of the conferences depend the future of the whole world. There is a distinct misgiving on this side as to Wilson's real meaning of 'the freedom of the seas' which is one of his Fourteen Points to the Germans. British opinion is unanimous and very strong on the impossibility of our giving up one iota of our sovereignty of the seas, which in this war has proved our salvation.

THURSDAY DECEMBER 26

This morning Muz and I walked to Piccadilly, down St James's, the Mall, past Buckingham Palace and home by Constitution Hill to see the procession. The weather was glorious, frosty and bright, and never has London looked more beautiful. The decorations are lovely. Venetian masts draped in scarlet, hung with huge flags, British, American, French, Italian and Belgian and festooned with strings of bunting, line the whole route.

Every house is hung with huge flags, laurel wreaths hang from scarlet strands. St James's is hung overhead with flags, and quiet crowds surge by with happy faces, surveying these signs of joy and momentous happenings. As we returned through the Mall, we saw the great semi-circle round the Victoria Group in front of the Palace outlined with Venetian masts hung with huge flags floating, peaceful and graceful, in the quiet frosty air.

Going past Constitution Hill, by the side of the Palace, there was a regular sea of small silk American flags, and these fluttered from the caps of various Corps of American women, and soldiers and sailors, grouped along the pavement. The women were all in uniform, Red Cross, Police, YWCA etc., and they were chanting in soft sweet voices refrains of American catch-songs, led by a man with a megaphone:

> Over there!
> Over there!
> We won't come back
> till it's over, over there!

Many of the sailors and soldiers were dancing in pairs their funny bunny-hug and fox-trot steps.

Muz and I stood there, laughing and enjoying the gaiety of it all hugely. I would have loved to have stayed there and eaten a sandwich on the kerb, waiting till the President passed 3 hours later. Unfortunately we had taken seats for the theatre this afternoon, little knowing that Wilson was coming today.

When we came home at 5.30 from the theatre, I heard your little experiences; you are getting rather too much excitement just now. It shows itself in sudden tears for very little cause. The crowds of today were altogether impossible for you. It was a sea of people, what with Bank Holiday, gorgeous weather and an American President due to drive through the great Arch at Constitution Hill (the first uncrowned head to drive through it). So Nannie took you on the fringe of the crowd at Hyde Park Corner, just inside Hyde Park.

While waiting, there was the sudden crashing salvo of 21 guns from the anti air-craft guns close by. This unexpected rending of the air frightened a little girl, perched by her Nurse on the columns of the archway quite near you, that she wouldn't be pacified till the salute was over. Then the aeroplanes came over and looped the loop, of which you gave me a minute description in bed this evening.

To return to President Wilson, you told me that you couldn't see him because of the crowd in front, but you waved your American flag when the cheering told you he was going by. You will soon get to think that these exciting times through which London is living is the usual state of affairs. A change to the quietness of Wales will do you good. We are going to Penmaenucha to Sybil Wynne-Jones on January 3rd.

SATURDAY DECEMBER 28

Muz and I went to see President Wilson and his wife leave Buckingham Palace on their State drive to the City, where they lunched at the Mansion House. We had a very good view of them from the fringe of the crowds and they had a splendid ovation.

The President is said to be gratified by his wonderful reception. The conference between him and our Ministers is progressing most satisfactorily. Lloyd George is said to be delighted. The President had declared in France just before crossing to England, that 'there is no fundamental difference of opinion' between America and the Allies.

The election results came out this evening. Lloyd George's Coalition Party wins a sweeping victory. Asquith's party is defeated utterly, Asquith himself is turned out of Fife, which he has represented 35 years. All the women candidates are defeated except the one Sinn Feiner, Countess Markiewicz, the firebrand, who is returned for St Patrick's, Dublin. And all the Bolshevik element are defeated, Ramsay MacDonald, Philip Snowden, Henderson etc. etc. So Lloyd George has a clear field.

1919

We begin the New Year with the waters of time still turbid with the storms of four years and a half. They will take long to settle and become clear again.

Edward Heron-Allen*

FRIDAY JANUARY 3

I have been laid up since Monday with a touch of Influenza. Nothing approaching the serious nature of the great influenza epidemic** which has been killing off thousands of people all over the world, but just the same old pains with a temperature. We *were* to start today for Penmaenucha, but as my temperature was not normal, quite, last night, we have put off the long journey till tomorrow.

I heard the New Year come in from my bed, and it was a din! For ten minutes church bells, sirens, hooters, aeroplanes overhead, and, for the last blessed time, the all clear bugles sounded by the Scout boys who used to sound them during the air-raids. All these were going from the moment midnight struck, for about ten minutes. Let us hope the bugles have sounded the right note for this great victory year. But the situation in

---

*   *Journal of the Great War – from Sussex Shore to Flanders Fields*, p. 276.
**   This pandemic dwarfed all the other casualty lists of the war. 'Spanish 'flu' caused a mortality rate of twenty times the norm for influenza. Death often occurred within a few hours. David Payne, 'The Influenza Pandemic of 1918', *Stand To!* No. 67, April 2003.

Russia, and in Germany, where the Bolsheviks seem to be gaining ground, is hardly all clear.

SUNDAY JANUARY 5

Penmaenucha
We got down here safely last night, but I felt rather seedy in the train. It is delightful being with Sybil Wynne-Jones and her dear of a husband, who is only home on Christmas leave and has to go back next week. His regiment is at Liège. He doesn't think the cavalry will get into Germany, because of the lack of fodder.

THURSDAY JANUARY 9

Sybil and Charles left us yesterday in possession of the domain for some days. They have gone up to London for his departure to the Front. She wished us to stay here to cheer her on her return alone. So today we went for the day to Gelligemlyn, and struck the stormiest day of the year. Already we had a gale three nights ago which played havoc with Sybil's mountain bungalow on the slopes of Cader Idris. A farmer came down to tell her that a section of the roof had been lifted off and furniture hurled right away on the mountain side.

THURSDAY JANUARY 16

Our stay here at Penmaenucha has been delightful. We have had very good weather, mild and often very sunny; our only bad day was the one described above. We walked up to Cregennan to see the damage done to the bungalow in the big gale on the night of January 6th. When nearing the bungalow, we saw splintered boards lying about the hill-side, debris of the wing which had been partly carried off in the whirlwind. We had a lovely day up there and ate our lunch under the veranda facing the sea.

We have seen little Winnie and Geoffrey at Glyn, and two days ago we had a children's party there. Daddy and I acted various scenes with Geoffrey, Win and Patience on a little stage prepared by Aunt Ethel. The latter was called away suddenly to Cheltenham on Tuesday to Uncle Baynes whose condition is growing very serious. The end cannot be far off. Ethel had only left him a week ago to return to Glyn to be with Patience for a while. She has to divide her time between the Nursing Home in Cheltenham and Glyn and the perpetual long journeys and anxiety are telling on her health.

SATURDAY JANUARY 18

3 Ovington Gardens
We came back here yesterday and were lucky enough not to be over-crowded on the journey. Travelling is a nightmare. Crowded trains, very limited trains, and transit very much slower. Crowds of soldiers always filling carriages and corridors. Perhaps when Peace is signed, things will improve.

But the world is in a terribly unsettled state. Our miners are clamouring for a 6 hour work day and of course they will get it. This means that all social conditions will be affected. Coal will increase by at least 5/- a ton and all industries will suffer.

In Germany Bolshevism is being brutally repressed. During riots in Berlin, Karl Liebknecht and Rosa Luxemburg* were being carried off to prison by the Government authorities when they were set upon and lynched by the mob. But there seems no doubt that the police escort allowed the murders to be committed.

SUNDAY JANUARY 19

Your little extempore prayer every night is so sweet. You always put in something that is on your dear little mind. Tonight it was 'Please God, don't let me have any bad dreams tonight, and take care of Mummy etc'. You are nervous at night, ever since the alarms and getting up for the air-raids. Were it not for Nannie's firmness, we should have a fuss every night when after tucking you up, she goes to sit in the adjoining room.

How I do long for a little companion to share your nursery with you! It makes me very anxious to find a proper substitute for your Nannie, who is leaving us in a few days to join her husband who is returning from the Front. She has been very kind but firm and she understands how to manage you and yet give you confidence.

Tomorrow is the first important day of your life. You are going to School! Only for two hours or so every morning. I fear you will be very miserable on finding yourself all alone among strangers for the first time in your life. But because you are sensitive and shy of strangers, I have made up my mind to send you among other children.

MONDAY JANUARY 20

Well, you have had your first taste of school and Nannie came home with you quite satisfied. It is true you cried and clung to her and would only be pacified by her sitting close to you during the 1½ hours of your ordeal, a privilege granted you by the kind mistress. But when it came to your being placed with five other children in an alphabet and spelling class, you were the best of the six and had the mark 'excellent' placed against your name! At all events you came home quite prepared to go back again tomorrow.

SATURDAY JANUARY 25

Nannie left today, and Gwen is taking her place until we get back to Brunswick Gardens and start a new Nursery Governess.

MONDAY JANUARY 27

I took you to school today and was allowed to sit in the classroom for 1½ hours of your lessons and was gratified to see you join in everything, though looking subdued.

---

*   They were the leaders of the Spartacists (German Bolsheviks).

But though you were at the far end, I could see you piling up the letters in front of you. The letters are given you when you think of a new word beginning with that letter. Miss Cornwall told me afterwards that you were a clever little boy.

THURSDAY JANUARY 30

Since I took you to school again on Tuesday, you have been unwell with gastric catarrh. After school on Tuesday you were so languid, you wouldn't eat your dinner, nor your tea and were very anxious for bed, a most unusual symptom! All yesterday you were so miserable that I sent for Doctor Beauchamp. His partner Dr Kirkwood (who assisted at your birth) came, as Dr B is in France on official duty. He told me to keep you in bed for two days and you are yourself again this evening, having gone to sleep as happy as a king. This is my first experience of nursing you myself and it has gone off very satisfactorily. It is the first time I have been in sole command and had you all to myself!

TUESDAY FEBRUARY 4

The state of unrest in the country is becoming more and more alarming. Strikes burst out every day. Yesterday the drivers of all electric trains struck, paralysing the Tubes. So now the congestion caused by the awful crowds in the Tubes is transferred from below to overwhelm the omnibuses.

Today the Metropolitan Railway is closed and the streets this morning when I took you to school, were surging with the multitude of workers tramping from west to east. Tomorrow the electric light workers are to strike and, unless a miracle happens, all our world will be plunged into darkness.

MONDAY FEBRUARY 10

The strikes were settled after all, for the present, without too much bad blood and the light was not cut off. My chief concern has been yourself. You have been out of sorts for some days and on top of that you started a bad cold. But the climax came this evening when you fell against the stove in the hall and seared your hands. You yelled for nearly ¾ hour, till I put you to bed, exhausted and you fell asleep at once, after sobbing your prayer. This was it: 'Please God, see that I have no bad dreams and please see that I get nothing worse until I get rid of all this!'

THURSDAY FEBRUARY 13

I had a wire from Aunt Ethel to say that Uncle Baynes died at 4 o'clock this morning after more than a year's illness. The strain for her has been terrible.

SATURDAY JUNE 28

38 Brunswick Gardens
Peace was signed at Versailles today by all the delegates at 3.12 pm. The Germans have at last bowed to the inevitable. After a four month interval, I feel I must record the Day

LONDON, SATURDAY, JUNE 28, 1919. ONE PENNY. London, E.C.2. (Please quote E.S.)

PEACE TREATY SIGNED.

WORLD WAR ENDED

GERMANS SIGN THE PEACE TREATY THIS AFTERNOON.

SCENE AT VERSAILLES.

SALVOES OF JOY IN LONDON AND PARIS.

Versailles, Saturday.

The German Plenipotentiaries signed the Peace Treaty at 3.12 this afternoon.—Reuter.

All the Allies also signed the Treaty, in alphabetical order of the names of States.

Peace was signed by Germany and all the Allies at Versailles this afternoon.

The Great Powers signed first—United States, British Empire, France, Italy, Japan—then the 22 Allies and Associates; Germany last of all.

As soon as the Treaty has been ratified by the German National Assembly and the Parliaments of any three of the Allies the war will be legally over. The Big Five decided yesterday as almost their last act that German prisoners are not to be sent back until ratification by Germany has taken place.

CEREMONY WITHOUT SPEECHES.

GERMANS ENTER UNANNOUNCED.

IMMEDIATELY FOLLOWING ALLIED DELEGATES.

SCENES AT CEREMONY.

NOTIFIED IN PARIS BY FIRING OF SALVOES.

VERSAILLES, Saturday Afternoon.

All the invited guests were seated before 2.30.

The Allied delegates on arrival were conducted to the royal apartments, which were used as assembly rooms, and just before three o'clock entered the Hall of Mirrors in a body announced by an usher.

All present rose to their feet as the delegates entered.

The German delegates left the Hotel des Reservoires at 2.45 and entered the Hall of Mirrors unannounced immediately after the Allied delegates.

When all were seated M. Clemenceau announced that the Treaty and other documents would be signed by the delegates of the various nations in alphabetical order.

REMARKABLE SCENE.

CLEMENCEAU'S JOY AT GREAT TASK FINISHED.

This afternoon's ceremony made a deep impression upon those who saw it, but the atmosphere was free from the tension of the scene some weeks ago, when Brockdorf-Rantzau first received the Allies' terms.

Versailles was ablaze with flags, and crowds in the streets were more dense and excited than this old royal city has witnessed for many a year.

It was at first intended that the proceedings should be without military display, but in the end there were soldiers everywhere.

Germans Arrive Unseen.

Spectators outside saw nothing of the arrival

HOW LONDON HEARD.

SCENES IN STREET, CLUB, AND THEATRE.

DAY OF JOY.

GREAT AUDIENCE'S MESSAGE TO THE KING.

The first intimation of the signing of Peace to thousands of people waiting in the City after offices and businesses had been closed was the appearance of the "Evening Standard" within a few seconds of the receipt of the news.

The newsmen had the utmost difficulty in getting through the crowds, and the papers were snatched out of their hands with frantic eagerness.

Soon the streets resounded with shouts of jubilation, bells were set ringing, and the firing of guns could be heard.

In the Clubs.

In the clubs there was only one drawback to a complete and satisfactory celebration—"Dora" still held sway, and the popping of corks had to be postponed until an hour when it was within legal limits.

Vendors of flags and streamers did a roaring trade along the Strand. Their original supplies were exhausted within a few minutes, but reinforcements came along on trolleys and in wagons, and the situation was saved.

In the West End there was unrestrained joy, passengers on buses cheering and waving at one another as they passed.

The announcement was thrown on the

WAR AND PEACE DATES.

1914.—June 28: Murder of Archduke Francis Ferdinand of Austria (ostensible cause of the war).
Aug. 1: War declared by Germany.

Peace Treaty Signed: Newspaper headline.

of Peace, after weeks and months of anxious and stormy debate at Versailles and impotent fury on the part of the Germans.

Peace was to be signed on several occasions, but the Germans always created delays. One of them was caused by the sinking of their interned Fleet at Scapa Flow by their own Admiral von Reuter on the day he expected peace to be signed! His *beau geste* was not at all admired by the Allies who looked upon it as another proof of German dishonesty.

The French are furious, as they expected to replace some of their naval losses by taking over some German ships. We don't much mind, as our wish had been to take the fleet and sink it in mid-Atlantic.

We all waited for the guns this afternoon, knowing the signing was to be at 3 o'clock. But Daddy and I heard nothing from this house, though our windows were all open and our flags ready to be hoisted on our balcony at the signal. You and Mademoiselle came in at 5, saying the guns had been fired and peace was declared. So up went our flags, and the houses opposite followed our example.

You awoke at 10 pm to the sound of rockets. I wrapped you up to let you see the search-lights and fireworks that went up in all directions and which we could see from your nursery windows. The real celebrations are to take place later.

Letter from Lloyd
George to King
George V.

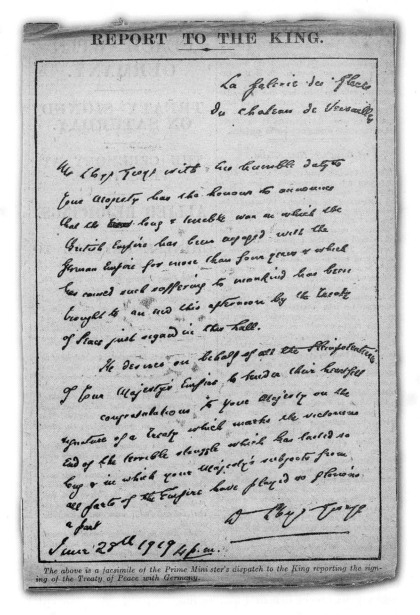

REPORT TO THE KING.

The above is a facsimile of the Prime Minister's dispatch to the King reporting the signing of the Treaty of Peace with Germany.

THURSDAY JULY 17

London is seething with preparations for the Great Peace Celebration on Saturday July 19. Every day I take you to a different place to see the decorations going up, plaster statues, white pillars to be garlanded and hung with flags and Venetian masts.

The route chosen for the march of 18000 British and Allied Troops is a novel one. The men all muster in Hyde Park, as Kensington Gardens is one vast camp of tents large and small. The troops will march out at Albert Gate, go down Sloane Street, Pont Street, Belgrave Square and down Vauxhall Bridge Road, then across the river.

Back over Westminster Bridge, up Whitehall, through the Admiralty Arch and down the Mall to the King and Queen. They will be seated on a dais, with the Royal Family, just in front of the Victoria Memorial and at the end of the Mall. They will thus get a *coup d'oeil* of the victorious armies from the Admiralty Arch straight to their Royal selves.

We are busy with our own decorations, for although we are far from the route, we want to do our bit. Our balcony above the portico will be draped, and we are making great wreaths. Not of laurels, for I can't get them, but wreaths of victory to hang, each with its emblem, for Scotland, Belgium, Wales, England, to represent the four nationalities in this house! Besides this my big Union Jack and French Tricolour will float and in the evening our windows and balcony are to be illuminated with coloured lights. If only it is fine!

SATURDAY JULY 19

PEACE DAY

It *wasn't* fine! (I write this next day.) The rain held off mercifully for the morning procession. Afraid of the crowds, Daddy and I did not attempt to take you to see the whole show. But we saw a great deal by walking down Kensington Road towards Albert Hall, and through the Park railings we saw many contingents moving forward in procession on their way to Albert Gate, out of which the procession filed out at the start. Kensington Gardens have been closed to the public for days and remain one vast camp. In the afternoon the rain began and prevented our visiting Hyde Park. It rained all the evening and ruined our decorations. But we lit our fairy lamps in all the windows.

When it cleared a little towards 9.30, we picked you out of bed, dressed you and walked out with you, Mademoiselle and Daddy towards Albert Hall once more to see the fireworks in the Park. The electricians had downed tools so there were practically no illuminations. Only private houses had fairy lamps and the Gas Light and Coke Company in High Street, Kensington made a jolly good advert for Gas by illuminating the whole of their facade.

The fireworks were fine, in spite of the rain which spoilt some of the set pieces. You gazed in wonder until 11 o'clock when we walked home and had some hot soup and light supper, for the first time in your life.

NOVEMBER 11, 1919

ARMISTICE DAY ANNIVERSARY

On this first Anniversary of Armistice Day, there was a wonderfully impressive celebration of all that this Day meant to us, a year ago. A Two Minutes Silence all over the Empire. During this, every movement was suspended and perfect silence prevailed. At eleven o'clock, the hour at which the Armistice came into force a year ago, all trains stopped, factories ceased working, ships on the sea stayed their course.

I was anxious you should live these two minutes with Daddy and me at the heart of London. We chose the spot in Whitehall where the Cenotaph, or Memorial to the Glorious Dead, has become a national shrine and the symbol of our sacrifice and glory. So we started off early with Mademoiselle and walked from Piccadilly Circus, joining the vast crowds all thronging towards Trafalgar Square.

Whitehall was a dense mass of people. But we struggled through as far as the Horse Guards and we could get no further. People in deep mourning, many carrying floral tributes, threaded their way as far as the Cenotaph. Others like ourselves, not bereaved, naturally made way for them.

So we halted just under the clock of the Horse Guards, where we could see the approach of 11 o'clock. On the stroke of eleven, guns boomed forth, and instantly the ceaseless stream of motors and buses and other traffic, which was being diverted from Whitehall down a side street opposite us, ceased moving.

Heads were instantly bared, officers and men stood to attention. Not a sound broke the stillness fallen on these thousands around us, save here and there a sob, and the muffled sound of motor engines. The Two Minutes seemed like ten. You stood, cap in hand, like a man, and I think you felt something of the solemnity of it all.

BIOGRAPHICAL NOTE

on GEORGINA LYDIA LEE
(NÉE DAVIS)

BORN 22 AUGUST 1869 – DIED 27 NOVEMBER 1965

My grandmother was a remarkable woman. Living in the Victorian age, she was the third of seven children born to Henry William Banks Davis RA and his wife Georgina Harriet (née Lightfoot) at St Etienne au Mont, near Boulogne-sur-Mer. She had two elder brothers, Ernest who died at Rawalpindi aged 26 and Henry who was an eminent ENT surgeon in London, both of whom remained single. Her three younger sisters, Beatrice, Edith and Ethel and a younger brother, Arthur, all married and produced offspring. Her mother died in 1879, when little Arthur was only 2, and as Georgina was the eldest daughter she remained with her father, looking after the family along with her father's two spinster aunts, until all the children had grown up.

Georgina spent most of the first twenty years of her life living with her family at Château de La Barrière Rouge, St Etienne au Mont, in northern France. She was educated at a boarding convent in Boulogne, which she attended along with her sister Beatrice. She knew Boulogne intimately and gives a vivid description of the scene when Sir John French is greeted at the quayside by the Mayor, in August 1914.

Georgina's father, my great-grandfather H.W.B. Davis RA, was a Welshman who grew up in Boulogne. He became a well-established artist, a Royal Academician, and was accepted at the Royal Academy Schools at the age of 16 (one of the youngest), on the strength of a bronze sculpture of a cow. He worked either at his house at St John's Wood, which he had bought from Sir Edwin Landseer, or at the studio at St Etienne. He chose oil landscapes as his favourite medium and many of his finest paintings included cattle or horses in the foreground. One of his first sketches was of the stretch of coastline from Cap Gris Nez to Boulogne, which Napoleon selected as a springboard for the invasion of England. His most famous painting, entitled *Mother and Son*, of a horse and foal, was purchased by the Tate Gallery (along with several others) and it was one of the Medici Gallery's best-known prints in the 1950s and adorned many Sharps Toffee tins, which at school many of my friends used as pencil boxes.

Georgina was fluent in French as a result of her upbringing and education, and wrote it most beautifully. She also spoke German, as she and Beatrice were sent to Düsseldorf to study for two years when she was 14. With her European upbringing it is evident that she felt particularly moved not only by the slaughter in northern France, but also by the wanton destruction of French and Belgian towns, such as Louvain, and of historic buildings, such as Rheims Cathedral.

By the time the youngest child, Arthur, was grown up at the turn of the century, Georgina and her father had left France, after over forty years, and moved into Glaslyn. They set up home together, with Georgina running the house and my great-grandfather painting in his studio. Glaslyn is a wonderful Edwardian house on the banks of the River Wye, near Rhayader in mid-Wales. My great-grandfather Davis died towards the end of 1914, only two months before my other great-grandfather, 'Gran', Charlie's father Harry Wilmot Lee. 'HWB' was laid to rest in a vault in Llanwrthwl churchyard and 'Gran' was buried in Llanelltyd graveyard. Many of HWB's fine later works were painted from his studio that overlooked the River Wye, and some of them depict the great river in full spate.

When Georgina's sister Beatrice, to whom she was very close, moved to India with her husband Alex Dunsmure in 1895, she must have missed her dearly, but carried on with what she felt was her duty, looking after her elderly father. It was during this time that she met Charles Wilfrid Lee, introduced by a good friend of hers who was Charlie's cousin. She was torn between the joy of settling down as a married woman and leaving her father on his own. Later on, Beatrice and Alex Dunsmure lived in the marvellous house, Hengwrt, situated about 2 miles south of Gelligemlyn, part of the Nannau estate belonging to the Vaughan family.

Charles Wilfrid Lee, who was three years younger than Georgina, became the senior partner in his family firm of solicitors, Lee Bolton & Lee. This had been founded by his grandfather John Benjamin (the first Lee in the firm's name), along with Henry Bolton. His father, Harry Wilmot, became the second Lee partner. From 1870 onwards the latter was Legal Secretary to four successive Archbishops of Canterbury. The firm was founded in 1855 and moved into 1 The Sanctuary, Westminster, next door to the Abbey, where it is still flourishing and last year celebrated 150 years of existence. During the First World War, Charlie was Legal Secretary to the popular Bishop of London, Arthur Winnington-Ingram.

So this was to be Georgina's new life, in London, supporting her husband as a strong and adoring wife. They were married on 7 April 1910 and she was already 41 years old. Three years later she gave birth to her only child, on 28 October 1913, by which time she was 44, an extraordinarily late age for a woman to give birth to her first child nearly a century ago. The baby was my father, Harry Illtyd Lee, for whom she wrote these war diaries. It is obvious from reading them how much she adored this one and only child.

As she says in one of the early entries, she decided to write down for her baby son's benefit what she saw happening from the outset of the war. Little did she expect that she would still be writing her wartime diary in 1918. Her descriptive passages are moving and enlightening, and fortunately she frequently included articles cut out from daily newspapers. Her diaries provide a continuous and unique record of life on the Home Front from 1914 until the first anniversary of the Armistice.

Charles Lee was the eldest of four brothers and was followed by Harry Romer CMG DSO, who married Clara Hilger of New York. They had two sons, Charles and Knyvett.

Romer, as he was known, or 'Tich' – who had served in the South African War – was to become a Lieutenant Colonel in XXth Hussars. The third brother, Gerry, married his childhood sweetheart, first cousin Brenda Wason, and they decided not to have any children. Gerry became a member of the Stock Exchange. The youngest of the four brothers was Guy Lee, DSO MC, whom my grandmother adored. He was married first to Ella Sale Hill, who died, sadly, two weeks after the birth of their only daughter Ella. Fifteen years later he found happiness with Maud Hanley, whom he married in 1923. He served in the Buffs (Royal East Kent Regiment) and in December 1914 he became a Chevalier of the Légion d'honneur.

War broke out when baby Harry was 9 months old. Georgina sent him to her father's house Glaslyn, where he was looked after by Nannie, but sorely missed by his parents. One can sense that Georgina felt it only right that she should remain by her husband's side, but I can tell how desperately torn she was between doing her duty and leaving her baby with her father. Her father-in-law Harry Wilmot Lee ('Gran') lived at Gelligemlyn with his wife Minna Constance. This wonderful house outside Dolgelly in the valley of the Eden, where Charles and his three brothers, Harry Romer, Gerry and Guy had grown up, was a special place that I remember visiting as a child. As the reader will have discovered, Georgina was very attached to Minna, her mother-in-law, whom she affectionately called Muz and with whom she shared many wartime experiences.

While their four sons were growing up, Minna and her husband Harry Wilmot Lee had lived partly in the Charterhouse in London, where he was Registrar, and partly at Gelligemlyn, north of Llanelltyd. In March 1941 Georgina and Charlie inherited Gelligemlyn on Minna's death, but by October of that year Charlie was dead, and Georgina carried on there on her own until she was in her eighties. Charlie's brother Harry Romer and wife Clara had a house at Bryn Cemlyn, just below the Tyn-y-Groes Hotel. This is the point at which the Romer-Lee branch of the family is introduced, Clara persuading her husband to include his second Christian name 'Romer' into their surname, as there were 'too many Mrs Lees in the Valley'!

Harry grew up in Wales, spending the earliest part of his life with his grandfathers at Glaslyn and at Gelligemlyn. He was fortunate to have a very close family. Growing up at Gelligemlyn with his three Lee cousins and with visits from his five Davis cousins, in this large rambling house, must have been wonderful because the grounds extended down to the River Mawddach. This river is joined by the Eden, and the Lees had 2 miles or so of fishing rights. Harry grew up to love country pursuits, and in particular fishing and climbing. When he was only 6 he climbed up Snowdon with his parents, and he regularly ascended Cader Idris and the Precipice Walk behind Gelligemlyn.

Harry was sent to St Aubyn's Preparatory School at Rottingdean at the age of 8. He was terribly homesick to begin with, and it must have been a wrench for his mother also. He then went on to Eton and to Trinity College Cambridge, where he obtained a law degree. My father didn't join the family firm, but was recruited into MI5. After he married Judy Spencer-Smith and my brother and I were born, we were posted to Port of

Spain, Trinidad, in 1949, from where my father travelled to others of the Windward Islands. We returned home in time for the Coronation. My father was then offered another posting, I believe in New Zealand, but turned it down, partly on account of his elderly mother.

On my father's return to England he went back to MI5. He had been at Eton with Guy Burgess and also at Cambridge, along with Kim Philby, Donald Maclean and Anthony Blunt and he worked with them all, as did Ian Fleming. My father's superior was Roger Hollis, the Director General of MI5. Graham Mitchell, the Deputy Director General, who was a close friend, was his immediate boss in the unit responsible for counter-espionage. At the height of the Cold War, I recall that he was present at the handover in 1962 of the American U2 spy-plane pilot Gary Powers, on the Glienecker Bridge, Potsdam, in exchange for a Russian spy. Looking through my father's address book, I am amused to see an entry: *MI6 Tel: Waterloo 5600!* When he retired he devoted his time to his garden at Graffham, just as his mother had before him and his daughter does now!

Unfortunately I never met my Lee grandfather, as he died just before I was born. For a while Georgina managed the large Welsh estate with various gardeners, a chauffeur, and the ghillies. Shoots were organised and the family fished some of the best salmon imaginable. She developed a great circle of correspondents and spent almost every teatime writing to her family and friends. She was extremely attached to her three brothers-in-law, in particular Guy, and was devoted to her two sisters Ethel and Beatrice. She also spent a lot of time updating family records and making notes on the reverse of her father's paintings. She compiled a history of both the Davis and Lee families. She was a skilled needlewoman and I still have some of the tapestries she worked. She played the piano and loved to have people singing with her.

Then my father felt that the time had come to sell Gelligemlyn, as it was impossible for him to keep it up. So at 84 my grandmother, who had spent over 40 years in this house, sadly packed up and moved south to live with us in Chiddingfold. Georgina lived in one part of our house with her housekeeper, and played an important part in our family life, living to be 96 years old.

I well remember her coming into our drawing room to play *Land of Hope and Glory*, singing in a fine strong voice, and when I hear it now I am sometimes moved to tears. Each Easter she would organise an Easter egg hunt with wonderful clues, and this has since become a family tradition. She would compile little cryptic rhymes and hide them under various objects in the garden, and they would lead you onwards to another. She lived to see the birth of her first great-grandchild, my firstborn son, Max.

Granny had an inter-communicating door upstairs that came out next to my bedroom and I well remember her coming in and saying, 'Ann, darling, if you don't tidy your bedroom I won't give you your sixpence pocket money!' I used to go and sit with her and we would spend hours talking, and reading her war diaries. I was so enthralled that I vowed that when I had the time I would endeavour to get them published. I believe that my grandmother's diaries provide an invaluable chronicle of life in Britain during the First World War. They also give the reader an authentic and personal insight into the lives of those gallant, unsung womenfolk who kept the home fires burning. Their lives, as Georgina rightly predicted, would never be the same again.

As it is now coming up to Easter I shall be busy creating cryptic clues for the Easter-egg hunt for Georgina's great-grandchildren, who will be staying with me here in Norfolk!

Ann de La Grange Sury
Foulsham, Norfolk, March 2006

SELECT BIBLIOGRAPHY

The place of publication is London, unless otherwise stated.

Bell, D.H., *A Soldier's Diary of the Great War*, ed. Henry Williamson, Faber, 1929

Bilton, David, *The Home Front in the Great War*, Leo Cooper, 2003

Brown, Malcolm, *1914 – The Men who Went to War*, Sidgwick and Jackson, 2004

Clapp, Edwin J., *Economic Aspects of the War, 1915*, Yale University Press, New Haven, 1915

Dagget, Mabel Potter, *Women Wanted*, Hodder and Stoughton, 1918

DeGroot, Gerald J., *British Society in the Era of the Great War*, Addison, Wesley Longman, 1996

Diggle, G.E., *Blighty, a Portrait of Civilian Life in Britain during the First World War*, Venton White House Library, Melksham, 1975

Emden, Richard van, with Steven Humphries, *All Quiet on the Western Front – an Oral History*, Headline Publishing, 2003

Gibson, R.H., *The German Submarine War 1914–1918*, Constable & Co., 1931

Gilbert, Sir Martin, *Winston S. Churchill*, vol. 3, Heinemann, 1971

—— *First World War*, Weidenfeld & Nicholson, 1994

—— *The Routledge Atlas of the First World War*, Routledge, 1994

Grayzel, Susan, *Women and the First World War*, Longman, 2002

Hattersley, Roy, *The Edwardians*, Little, Brown, 2004

Heron-Allen, Edward, *Journal of the Great War – From Sussex Shore to Flanders Fields*, Phillimore, Chichester, 2002

Hickey, Michael, *Gallipoli*, John Murray, 1995

History of Ministry of Munitions (vol. 6), 1922: Pt I – *Manpower and Dilution*

Hocking, Charles, *Dictionary of Disasters at Sea, 1824–1962* (2 vols), Lloyds Register of Shipping, 1969

Jenkins, Roy, *Asquith*, Macmillan, 1991

Jones, H.A., *The War in the Air*, Oxford University Press, 1935

Lawrence, Sapper Dorothy, *The Only English Woman Soldier*, John Lane, 1919

MacDonagh, Malcolm, *In London during the Great War*, Eyre and Spottiswoode, 1935

Marlow, Joyce, *Women in the Great War*, Virago Press, 1998

Marwick, Arthur, *The Deluge-British Society and The First World War*, Bodley Head, 1965

—— *Women at War, 1914–1918*, Fontana, 1977

Minnoch, Jim, 'The Worst Train Wreck in History', *Stand To!* No. 66, January 2003

Montgomery-Massingberd, Hugh and David Watkins, *The London Ritz – a Social and Architectural History*, Aurum Press, 1980

Morris, Joseph, *The German Air Raids on Great Britain, 1914–1918*, Sampson Low, Marston, 1925

Munson, James (ed.), *Echoes of the Great War: the Diary of Andrew Clark*, Oxford University Press, 1985

Nicol, Dorothy, *Memoirs of a VAD (1915–1917)*, Department of Documents, Imperial War Museum

Nicolson, Colin, *The First World War, Europe, 1914–1918*, Longman, 2001

Nicolson, Harold, *George V – His Life and Reign*, Constable, 1952

Payne, David, 'The Influenza Pandemic of 1918', *Stand To!*, No. 67, April, 2003

Peel, C.S., *How We Lived Then, 1914–1918*, Bodley Head, 1929

Playne, Caroline, *Society at War, 1914–1916*, Unwin Brothers, Woking, 1931

—— *Britain Holds On, 1917–1918*, George Allen & Unwin, 1933

Pollock, John, *Kitchener*, Constable, 2001

Reader, W.J., *At Duty's Call – a Study in Obsolete Patriotism*, Manchester University Press, 1988

Robinson, Douglas, *The Zeppelin in Combat*, Camelot Press, 1962

Roynon, Gavin (ed.), *Massacre of the Innocents – The Crofton Diaries, Ypres 1914–1915*, Sutton Publishing, 2004

Salisbury, Frank, *After the Battle*, No.18, Plaistow Press, 1977

Sheppard, E.W., *The Ninth Queen's Royal Lancers, 1715–1936*, Gale and Polden, 1939

Slater, Guy, *My Warrior Sons – The Borton Family Diary*, Peter Davies, 1973

Spears, E.L., *Liaison, 1914*, Heinemann, 1930

Strachan, Hew, *The First World War*, Vol I, *To Arms*, Oxford University Press, 2001

Taylor, A.J.P., *The First World War*, George Rainbird, 1963

Thompson, Julian, *The Imperial War Museum Book of the War at Sea 1914–1918*, Sidgwick & Jackson, 2005

Turner, E.S., *Dear Old Blighty*, Michael Joseph, 1980

Williams, Emily, *A Family at War*, The London Press, 2004

Wilson, A.N., *After the Victorians, 1901–1953*, Hutchinson, 2005

Wilson, Trevor, *The Myriad Faces of War – Britain and the Great War, 1914–1918*, Polity Press, Cambridge, 1986

Winter, J.M., *The Great War and the British People*, Macmillan, 1985

Woodward, Sir Llewellyn, *Great Britain and the War of 1914–1918*, Methuen, 1967

Woolf, Virginia, *Letters, 1912–1922*, Hogarth Press, 1998

Wykeham-Musgrave, W.H. *Letters and Collected Papers*, Department of Documents, Imperial War Museum

INDEX